26/4

HANDBOOK FOR
MODERN LANGUAGE TEACHERS

UNIVERSITY OF LONDON INSTITUTE OF EDUCATION

Handbook for
Modern Language Teachers

EDITOR
ALAN W. HORNSEY
Senior Lecturer, Teaching of Modern Languages
University of London Institute of Education

Methuen Educational Ltd
LONDON · TORONTO · SYDNEY · WELLINGTON

First published 1975
by Methuen Educational Ltd,
11 New Fetter Lane, London E C 4P 4E E
© 1975 University of London Institute of Education

Printed in Great Britain
by Cox & Wyman Ltd, Fakenham, Norfolk

ISBN 0 423 89690 3

Contents

v

ALAN W. HORNSEY (EDITOR)

University of London Institute of Education

Introduction

This handbook is not a guide; it does not purport to tell teachers what to do. It is a compendium of views, arguments and suggestions for debate and discussion. Teachers might like to try out some of the ideas with their classes and then modify or reject them in the light of their experience.

The descriptions of lessons or sequences within a lesson are necessarily incomplete, for in any teaching situation the number of variables is so great that only a charlatan would pretend to be able to allow for them all. Take one of the simplest of exchanges which might occur in a foreign-language lesson:

Teacher. (Picking up a pencil.) *What's this?*
Pupils. (Silence.)
T. *It's a pencil. All together: 'It's a pencil.'*
P. *It's a pencil.*
T. *Giovanni! 'It's a pencil.'*
G. *It's a pencil.*
T. *Good. And what's this?* (Picking up another pencil.)
P. (Silence.)
T. *It's a pencil too.*

Fine. But what if another pupil, Alfredo, who has heard 'pencil' from his Australian girlfriend, blurts out the word in Australian English strongly corrupted by his native Sardinian accent? That first pregnant silence is shattered and we are on the slippery slope of pronunciation difficulties. What if the learners object to saying things in unison? What if Giovanni mispronounces his reply or does not even realize he is being asked to repeat the sentence? What if the unfortunate Giovanni has an embarrassing speech defect? What happens if the second pregnant silence does not occur? Suppose the second pencil happens to be of a shape, length and colour such as to make some pupil search for a different word because his native

ix

language makes a distinction not made in English! And does the teacher always get away with such an easy introduction of 'too'? Is this heard as a 'penciltoo', a parallel to those other nouns *'grande-maison'* and *'loncontoir'* (*long comptoir*) gathered from audio-visual French courses?

Teachers will recognize all these rhetorical questions as a parody of reality, but they will see what is being suggested, for they constantly have to make decisions during their lessons which no outsider can make for them. The adviser, the inspector or the writer of handbooks can only make the most tentative suggestions, and it is literally impossible to prescribe the course of a whole lesson – it would in any case make tedious reading. Nevertheless, contributors to this handbook have tried to give summaries and examples of *possible* dialogues, because the other risk in writing about practical teaching problems is to be too vague. One well-known book which gives advice on teaching foreign-language skills actually begins by justifying a total absence of examples: 'Many of you may wonder why, in the pages of this book, no examples are given in any particular language. There are several reasons. . . .'* In this handbook copious examples are given.

The main concern of all the contributors is to help the learner in his learning task. Variety of content and approach is approved by many, but not at the cost of clarity. The teacher is recommended to select and grade his material carefully in order to restrict the learning load. A considerable accumulation of half-learnt material contributes little to skill in communicating. On the other hand, restriction to the limited possibilities of pictures or *realien* makes a scarcely greater contribution. Some sections of the handbook take us beyond these into textual and non-tangible areas; we are sent on foot or by train through France and introduced to the linguistic potential of the world of sport or adventure. Where appropriate, the shopping basket or the kitchen table sets the scene.

A variety of aids are discussed: the overhead projector, pictures, documents, etc. It is worth noting that these are not grandiosely described as 'methods'. There is no 'overhead projector method' or 'picture method'. All of these things help, but it is the teacher who decides the strategies and procedures which go to make up his style of teaching, his method. An aid will help him to overcome some

* RIVERS, W. M. (1968) *Teaching Foreign-language Skills*, preface p. x. Chicago and London: University of Chicago Press.

problems; it will not tell him how to teach. The purchase of a language laboratory and a set of drills or the latest audio-visual course will make no difference to the task of teaching a foreign language unless the teacher can integrate them into a coherent set of procedures. If he cares that his pupils understand what they are saying, that they should use language authentically and that they acquire real competence in using it, he will adapt the aid and improvise accordingly.

The all-too-common disdain for the written word which sometimes characterizes 'oral' approaches to language teaching is not supported in this handbook. Linguists may talk of the 'primacy of speech' with good reason, but they are not thereby telling teachers to reject the written word. 'Primacy' is surely not to be equated with 'superiority', and there are good reasons, as some contributors suggest, for seeing the written word as a significant part of the language learning process with a useful contribution to make as an aid to memory, as a support for learners who learn less well orally and as a further experience of the language.

What has become clear over the last decade is the inadequacy of the view that language is a habit structure. We cannot experience all of the possibilities of a language and yet somehow we have to acquire the ability to produce and understand a vast range of utterances. At the risk of sounding reactionary, I suggest that the evidence, sparse though it is, points to the need for the language learner to learn rules. G. A. Miller, writing about native language acquisition, makes the point very clearly.* First he quotes the following sentence from what appears to be a textbook with a recognizably behaviourist bias: 'Certain combinations of words and intonations of voice are strengthened through reward and are gradually made to recur in appropriate situations by the process of discrimination learning.' Miller comments:

By a rough, but conservative calculation, there are at least 10^{20} sentences twenty words long, and if a child were to learn only these it would take him something of the order of 1,000 times the estimated age of the earth just to listen to them. Perhaps this is what the word 'gradually' means? In this interpretation he [the writer of the previous quotation] has clearly violated my fifth admonition,

* In OLDFIELD, R. C. and MARSHALL, J. C. (1968) *Language*, pp. 209–10. Harmondsworth, Middx: Penguin.

that there is no limit to the number of sentences to be learned, and so has wandered perilously close to absurdity. Any attempt to account for language acquisition that does not have a generative character will encounter this difficulty.

The simplest survival situations in a foreign country require some ability to 'generate' language, even if only to cope with understanding the foreign person's 'inconsiderate' use of his own language:

Geoffrey (in Germany, trying to survive and stopping 'the German in the street'). *Ik – wollen – tablets – Apotheke.*

The German in the street. *Ach so, ich verstehe, Sie suchen eine Apotheke. Leider bin ich hier unbekannt, aber ich glaube schon irgendwo . . . nein, jetzt hab ich's, neben dem Dingsda, wie heißt's? neben dem Denkmal . . . gehen Sie hier geradeaus . . . nein, fragen Sie lieber die Dame drüben . . . nein, besser nicht. Tut mir leid, ich hab's eilig . . .* (hurries away).

Geoffrey may well have got his message over, but how does he re-constitute the reply, cope with the redundancies (which he cannot recognize as such) and interpret the German's answer? Clearly Geoffrey needs to know the rules, but the question for his teacher is how to help him to acquire them without involving him in out-of-date grammatical analysis, in terminology which is in itself a barrier to learning and in trying to attain a standard of prescribed grammatical excellence which is beyond even the native speaker.

Whatever rules are learnt, the teacher still has to ensure that his pupil knows **when** and **where** as well as **how** to apply them. Language teachers are probably sick of hearing the phrase 'meaningful context', but it cannot be left out of the discussion. The learner must be able to understand what he is saying, to recognize the context and to know the limitations of the piece of language he is learning. *Gehen* must be seen as acceptable for motion on foot but not for motion by car, *cahier* can refer to some 'books' but not others, and *il est jaune* can refer to *crayon* but not to *chemise*. This last sentence expresses truths which are not readily available to the learner if he has not been enabled to acquire an awareness of them through continual practice in a variety of unambiguous contexts. Indeed, this handbook offers the frequent reminder of the need to pay careful attention not only to correctness of form, but also to the appropriateness of the circumstances in which it is used.

PART 1

Grammar

Communication in a language is only possible after one has acquired some of the tools to communicate with. The teacher's job is to ensure that this acquisition takes place and his primary task is to get the learner to see how the language works – in other words, to learn the grammar – for without this he will only be able to reproduce what he has heard before or learnt by heart; he will not be able to generate speech for himself. But what does knowing the grammar mean? Does it simply mean knowing how the language is patterned and structured? Does it mean that one should be able to apply this knowledge in what are commonly called 'meaningful situations'? What are meaningful situations? In what ways can grammar be effectively taught?

In this section a number of writers address themselves to some of the problems of teaching grammar and they lay special emphasis on:

– the need for an adequate number of similar but not identical, clear examples of language patterns;
– contexts which ensure that the language makes sense to the learner;
– selection of 'digestible' amounts of material, as opposed to a multiplicity of rules or paradigms which, although they may corporately be said to constitute, say, the perfect tense, are quite bewildering if presented all at once;
– a thorough grasping of each piece of grammar before progressing to the next;
– an awareness of which structures may conveniently precede others;
– above all, facility of learning.

The reader is left in no doubt about the role of carefully structured question and answer work in the acquisition of grammar; at the same time, there is no suggestion that the exchanges which result are 'normal conversation', or even what is sometimes referred to as 'Gallic chat'.

DAVID A. WILKINS

Department of Linguistic Science, University of Reading

Aspects of oral grammar

Introduction

A concern with spoken language is a characteristic of both modern linguistics and modern-language teaching. The linguist sets out to describe the structural features of the spoken form of language, because the written form is to a large degree derived from it. The language teacher is concerned with speech, because both the aims and the methods of language teaching have, in recent years, been oriented towards spoken language activities. In neither case is the importance of writing denied. The linguist, however, has paid very little attention to it. The language teacher, particularly where his pupils are children rather than adults, has been encouraged to concentrate the early stages of his teaching on speech and to develop a writing ability only when a substantial knowledge of spoken language has been built up.

Although such developments seem strikingly in contrast with an older tradition of language study, they are by no means as radical as they appear. In language teaching the nature of the activities conducted in the classroom may have changed, but the subject-matter remains largely the same. **What** is taught now is much what was taught previously. It is the **how** of language teaching that has altered so markedly. To put it another way, although the principle that is shared by linguistics and language teaching is reflected in the amount of spoken activity in which the pupils engage, it is not adequately reflected in the form of language that they speak and hear. To a large extent, what they now say is what in an earlier generation they would have written, and this in turn is derived from descriptions of language that are based on the written not the spoken form.

This might not be much of a problem if the written language, which is fundamentally a representation of speech, was indeed accurately related to current speech. However, where speech is

2

dynamic and continually changes, writing tends to be static, the more so where normative teaching strengthens uniformity and inhibits change. The results can be a growing discrepancy between the forms of speech and writing. French provides ample evidence of this and, indeed, the difference is so great that in the school teaching of French as a mother-tongue a good deal of attention is given to the prescriptive reinforcement of the forms of written French, which contrast so strikingly with the forms of language that the child has acquired in the home before he or she has any contact with written French. It is important, of course, that the difference between speech and writing should not be exaggerated. There is much in common between the two. However, there are sufficient points of contrast for one to be able to assert that someone who knows written French still has to learn the spoken language and vice versa. It follows that however oral the method, if the language is a sample of the written form of French, the pupil cannot truly be said to have learned spoken French. Indeed, not only will his achievement be less than what was really intended; the process of learning may also be less efficient because it has failed to take into account the characteristics of spoken French.

The lack of fit between speech and writing is a feature of all languages that possess a written form, although there may be considerable differences in the type and quantity of contrast according to the language. There is a far more straightforward relation between orthography and pronunciation in Spanish, for example, than in either French or English. Consequently the learner of Spanish will find spellings a reasonably accurate guide to pronunciation. However, discrepancies of some kind will be found in all languages where there is a well-established written form. Although the discussion here relates entirely to French, the arguments can be applied in the analysis of other languages.

Before looking in some detail at the verbal system in French, it is worth glancing briefly at the different ways in which the type of language that pupils usually encounter in the learning process contrasts with the facts of everyday spoken language.

It is not commonly recognized that the model of French pronunciation that is taught will not necessarily reflect adequately the pronunciation that the pupil can expect to hear in France. Given that French has no less variety of accent than any other language, familiarity with the standard model of pronunciation as taught is not likely to prevent difficulties of comprehension in any real speech situation. Even that model, however, is itself based on norms that are not kept to by many educated French speakers. Often a three-term rather than a four-term system of nasal vowels is operated – /ɛ̃/, /ã/ and /ɔ̃/. The distinction between long and short /a/ and /a/ is often not made and, indeed, open /ɛ/ and closed /e/ are not distinguished as rigidly as prescriptive teaching demands. Some speakers fail to differentiate between /ɸ/ and /œ/. The 'rules' of liaison and elision that are commonly taught are often ignored or irregularly applied by native speakers of French.

At the level of grammar there are differences in morphology and it is to the problems of verb morphology that this chapter is principally devoted. Difficulties with considerable pedagogic implications also arise in relation to the way in which gender is marked in the French adjective system.[1]* In languages with fairly complex systems of inflection it is not uncommon even among educated speakers for inflections to be ignored or 'incorrectly' formed. French speakers do make mistakes of gender and agreement. They do not always make past participles agree with a preceding direct object. (In fact, with the majority of verbs the agreement is not marked in speech anyway.) The syntax of speech tends to be more simple than that of writing, and the foreigner may quite simply use forms that, although permitted, are uncommon in speech. For example, the use of subject-verb inversion in the formation of interrogatives is becoming increasingly rare in French where constructions beginning *est-ce que* ...? or positive declarative sentences with question intonation are preferred.

The language taught in textbooks is usually stylistically neutral and very often without variety. Not only is the learner accustomed to producing sentences that are grammatically 'correct' and complete; he is used to producing them all on the same level, neither very formal nor informal. Yet the speech situations in which he might eventually use the language are characteristically informal. In spite of the amount of spoken activity in which he has been involved, he will find that he can neither express himself in speech as he would wish nor understand fully the usual speech of native speakers. This is partly a matter of such things as the rate of speech, with all the concomitant 'accidents' of speech which occur in the process of utterance. It is partly a matter of knowing how to use the grammatical

* Notes and references normally appear at the end of each chapter.

system in the ways that are appropriate to the purpose and context of utterance. It is also a matter of vocabulary. Many French speakers avoid the use of words that have formal, literary and archaic associations.

The learner who has mastered effectively the contents of his textbook should not be surprised if he is told when he goes to France that he speaks French 'more correctly' than the native speakers. Unfortunately, there is no ground for complacency in this. It means that the Frenchman can see at once that the foreigner is not speaking the language as he speaks it. However, because he has received years of prescriptive teaching himself, he comes to the conclusion that the foreigner speaks better French than he does. If the learner is truly to acquire a mastery of spoken French, he must be led to understand French as it is normally spoken by native speakers and to produce the major features of that speech himself.

The verb in spoken French

The morphological characteristics of verbs in French are one of the major problems that face the learner. One way or another he is presented with a number of regular conjugations as models for the formation of the different tenses and in addition a substantial list of irregular verbs whose different forms cannot be derived from the regular conjugations. The conjugations and irregular verb lists may not be taught in isolation, but even in materials where paradigms as such are avoided the underlying analysis of the system may be the traditional one. As it happens, the usual analysis is based on several different criteria, principally the orthographic forms of the verbs and their manner of forming infinitives and past participles. The purpose of this chapter is to examine the consequences of deciding to teach spoken French without reference to factors arising from the nature of the written language. How adequate is a traditional analysis of the verb system if a course is wholly oral or alternatively makes no use of the written language in its early and intermediate stages?[2]

A number of more or less self-evident observations can immediately be made. To begin with, orthographic considerations are no longer relevant. Further, the past historic and the past subjunctive are to all intents and purposes extinct in the spoken language. We do not need to include either of these sets of forms in a paradigm of the spoken, verbal system, nor do we need to take them into account when making general statements about tense formation in French. We need not concern ourselves either with verbs that are never or scarcely ever used in spoken French. The burden of learning the forms of French irregular verbs has always been an unnecessarily large one, because of the practice of including in the inventory, more or less exhaustively, all the irregular verbs in French as well as unnecessary forms of verbs like *naître* or *bouillir*. They were taught because they were there, not because they were of any great use. Those that are archaic, literary or very formal can be excluded from our consideration, just as they are already excluded from materials which are based on frequency criteria.

It is perhaps necessary to give a warning. The aim in this chapter is to make generalizations about the structure of the French verb which can be embodied in the organization of teaching materials. They must be generalizations which assist the learner in his progressive discovery of the facts of French grammatical structure. It is too much to expect that the rather complex French system can be reduced to a neat and brief analytical statement. Whatever we achieve, there will be a fair amount of untidiness. Unfortunately, it is some of the most frequently used verbs which escape inclusion in the generalizations that we are able to make. This is because, being frequently in use, they are not subject to the analogizing process by which irregular forms become more regular, nor can they be dropped from everyday use by substitution of near-equivalent regular verbs, as has happened with other irregular verbs. Only by retreating into greater abstractions can wider generalizations be made. Unfortunately, such statements become less and less useful to the language learner.[3] The data we are to consider, therefore, are the present, imperfect, future and conditional (indicative), the (present) subjunctive, the three non-finite forms and the imperative.

The most useful way for us to look at the finite verb forms is in terms of **stem** and **inflection**. This in turn leads to what is probably the one most striking characteristic of the spoken system, that is, the regularity and consistency of the system of inflection. Once orthographic considerations are removed, all but a very small number of verbs are seen to operate identical systems of inflection. With the exception of the future, the singular forms of each tense and often, but not always, the third person plural are identical. This applies equally to those verbs that are traditionally regarded as irregular. A number of examples of present tense and imperfect forms will demonstrate this. The verbs *marcher, remplir, recevoir, battre, pouvoir* and *partir* would have the following singular forms in all persons:

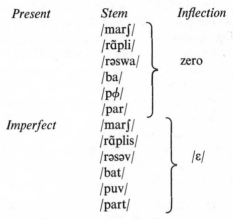

Present	Stem	Inflection
	/marʃ/	
	/rãpli/	
	/rəswa/	zero
	/ba/	
	/pɸ/	
	/par/	
Imperfect	/marʃ/	
	/rãplis/	
	/rəsəv/	/ɛ/
	/bat/	
	/puv/	
	/part/	

A further consistent feature is the recurrence of /ɔ̃/ and /e/ in the first and second persons plural. The complete set of inflections is therefore as follows:

	Sing. 1, 2, 3	Plur. 1,	2,	3
Present indicative	-zero	-ɔ̃,	e,	zero
Present subjunctive	-zero,	-jɔ̃,	je,	zero
Imperfect	-ɛ,	-jɔ̃,	je,	ɛ
Conditional	-rɛ,	-rjɔ̃,	rje,	rɛ
Future	-re, ra,	-rɔ̃,	re,	rɔ̃

These facts are not, of course, absent from the traditional analysis, but they tend to be obscured by the multiplicity of regularities and irregularities.

The learning problem posed by the inflections alone is not great. In this kind of analysis the variability of forms is explained in terms of alternations in the stem, yet even here there is more that is systematic than might at first appear. The most general class of verbs is made up of those that possess a single form for the stem. These are principally the traditional class of *-er* verbs, *marcher, chanter, donner*, /marʃ-, ʃãt-, dɔn-/, and, with reference to their finite forms only, a number of *-ir* verbs, *ouvrir, offrir*, etc., /uvr-, ɔfr-/. The class also includes *rire*, /ri-/. The addition of the future inflection /-re/

commonly requires the insertion of /ə/ with these verbs. In the case of *ouvrir* the vowel may be /i/ rather than /ə/.

The other major class consists of those verbs that have two stems, although the distribution of these stems in the tense system is not identical. In the case of verbs like *finir, écrire* and *lire*, one stem, /fini-, ekri-, li-/, is used for the present indicative singular, the future and the conditional, while another, /finis-, ekriv-, liz-/, is used for the present indicative plural, the imperfect and the subjunctive. Another sub-class has alternations between two stems which are highly regular and come close to being automatic. If they were fully automatic, they would be included in the first major class of verbs. In principle one stem is used with the present indicative singular and third person plural and with the future and conditional. The other stem is used with the first and second persons plural of the present tense and with the imperfect and the subjunctive.

	3rd pers. present and future	1st pers. plur. present
nettoyer	/netwa/	/netwaj-ɔ̃/
	/netwa-ra/	
prier	/pri/	/prij-ɔ̃/
	/pri-ra/	
jeter	/ʒɛt/	/ʒət-ɔ̃/
	/ʒɛt-ra/	

The existence of verbs like *rire*, stem /ri-/, first personal plural form /ri-ɔ̃/, contrasts with *prier* and means that /j/ cannot be interpreted as being required wherever a stem ending in /-i/ combines with /-ɔ̃/ and other vowels. However, it is worth noting that many speakers in fact produce forms like /rij-ɔ̃/ and /rij-e/ so that there is analogical pressure on the use of such verbs. There is similarly analogical pressure on speakers to make verbs of this sub-class conform with the pattern of the previous sub-class (*finir*, etc.) by giving all the plural forms of the present indicative the same stem. This is traditionally accepted with verbs like *balayer*:

il balaie /balɛ/   *ils balaient* /balɛj/

Some speakers, at least, extend this to verbs like *nettoyer*:

il nettoie /netwa/   *ils nettoient* /netwaj/

The remaining group of two-stem verbs consists of those like *partir, répondre, suivre* and *dormir*, where the stem used in the present indicative singular is distinct from that used for all other forms. These are the only verbs among those we have looked at so far where the future is not formed from the present indicative singular stem.

Present tense 3rd pers.		Future
sing.	plur.	
/par/	/part/	/partira/
/repɔ̃/	/repɔ̃d/	/repɔ̃dra/
/sɥi/	/sɥiv/	/sɥivra/

We have now accounted for the most productive aspects of the finite verb system in French. By **productive** we mean both that there are substantial numbers of verbs in each of the classes and sub-classes described and that new verbs in the language are assigned to the single-stem class, e.g. *programmer*. This first sense of 'productive' is important pedagogically, since it is what enables the learner to generalize from a limited number of examples to a much larger number of verbs which he will not in fact learn until much later stages of learning.

We have now established two major facts about the morphology of the French verb. First, it possesses an inflectional system of great regularity and no great complexity. Second, a large proportion of all French verbs possess either one or two stems. We must now consider those verbs which, in one way or another, are not accounted for by these statements. The exceptions to the statement on inflection are very few. There is little practical point in recognizing distinct stem and inflection for the present tense of *être*, *avoir* and *aller*. The five forms of *être*, /sɥi/, /ɛ/, /sɔm/, /ɛt/ and /sɔ̃/, could be regarded as alternant stems followed by zero inflection, but it is not clear that anyone would be helped by such an analysis. The irregularity in the other two verbs is found in the singular forms and in the third person plural, /e/, /a/ and /ɔ̃/ and /vɛ/, /va/, /vɔ̃/. Apart from this, the inflectional system of all three verbs is regular, although a number of different stems have to be recognized:

être	/swa/ + zero	subjunctive
	+ /jɔ̃/, etc.	
	/et/ + /ɛ/, etc.	imperfect
	/sər/ + /e/, etc.	future
avoir	/ɛ/ + zero	subjunctive
	+ /jɔ̃/, etc.	
	/av/ + /ɛ/, etc.	imperfect
	/ɔr/ + /e/, etc.	future

aller	/aj/	+ zero	subjunctive
	/al/	+ /jɔ̃/, etc.	
	/al/	+ /ɛ/, etc.	imperfect
	/ir/	+ /e/, etc.	future

The only other inflectional oddity to be noted is in the second person plural of the present tense of *faire* and *dire*, which occur as /fɛt/ and /dit/ respectively. It is interesting to note that less frequently used derivatives of these verbs (e.g. *contrefaire, contredire*) are less resistant to analogical change and occur with the regular /e/ inflection.

The remaining verbs are inflectionally regular but have a larger number of stems than the major verb classes. The most common of such verbs in spoken French are *faire, pouvoir, vouloir, savoir, venir, tenir, prendre, apprendre, valoir, comprendre, devoir, recevoir, boire, connaître, plaindre, paraître, voir, envoyer* and *s'asseoir*. A thorough treatment of these verbs is not possible here, but a brief indication can be given of the kind of analysis of the spoken forms that would prove pedagogically interesting.

If we look at the forms of the present tense, we can see how far they resemble the major verb classes. They share with them the characteristic of making no contrasts within the singular forms:

je chante			je comprends		
tu chantes	}	/ʃɑ̃t/	tu comprends	}	/kɔ̃prɑ̃/
il chante			il comprend		

je veux		
tu veux	}	/vɸ/
il veut		

The verbs *voir* and *envoyer* resemble the single-term verbs in also having an identical form for the third person plural, *il voit* ~ *ils voient* /vwa/ ~ /vwa/. In general, however, the distribution of stems in the present is closer to that of the two-stem verbs like *finir* and *partir* in that the singular contrasts with the plural:

finir	sing. 1, 2 & 3	/fini/ +zero	*savoir* /sɛ/ +zero
	plur. 1 & 2	/finis/+/ɔ̃, e/	/sav/+ɔ̃, e/
	3	/finis/+zero	/sav/+zero

Valoir, connaître, plaindre and *paraître* also follow this pattern.

The remaining verbs have three stems in the present tense, the third person plural being distinct from the other forms:

pouvoir	/pɸ/	+zero	*venir*	/vjɛ̃/	+zero
cf.	/puv/	+/ɔ̃, e/	cf.	/vən/	+/ɔ̃,e/
vouloir	/pœv/	+zero	*tenir*	/vjɛn/	+zero
prendre	/prɑ̃/	+zero	*devoir*	/dwa/	+zero
cf.	/prən/	+/ɔ̃, e/	cf.	/dəv/	+/ɔ̃, e/
apprendre,	/prɛn/	+zero	*recevoir*	/dwav/	+zero
comprendre					

The reader will be able to see for himself in what way the other finite forms of these verbs would be handled. It is worth noting that if the alternation between nasal consonant and nasal vowel in verbs like *venir, plaindre* and *prendre* was treated as largely predictable (it is a common phenomenon in other areas of French morphology), these verbs would resemble the regular verbs more closely.

Only brief mention can be made of the non-finite verb forms. The present participle is formed on the stem of the first and second persons plural in the present tense. There are few exceptions to this (*ayant, sachant*). With the infinitive and the past participle, no such simple statement is possible. Most of the single-stem verbs belong to the traditional *-er* conjugation. In this case past participle and infinitive alike are formed by the addition of /-e/ to the stem. Verbs like *ouvrir* which have only one stem for the finite verb forms are distinguished by having a distinct stem for the past participle, /uv-/, and a distinct inflection, /-ɛr/. Verbs of the two stem class which have a stem ending in /-i/, e.g. *finir* and *conduire*, add /-r/ to the stem to form the infinitive. With the past participle the situation is more difficult. In the case of *finir* the past participle is identical with the stem, /fini/, but in the case of *conduire* we have to allow for the possibility of a preceding feminine direct object, so that /kɔ̃dɥi/ alternates with /kɔ̃dɥit/. Without going further into the matter it is evident that there are no simple rules for deriving infinitives and past participles from stems and, indeed, that it is not always the same stem that is selected as the base. However, the picture is no more complex than in a traditional analysis where, equally, the finite forms are often unpredictable from the infinitive, which is usually taken as the basis for the inflectional derivations.

The analysis presented here has been able to suggest in only rather summary fashion what a complete analysis of the verbal system would look like. For this reason there would be no point in attempting to look in detail at any pedagogical implications. None the less, there are already some points which are relevant to the way in which the teaching of spoken French might be structured. In the first place, the initial teaching of the verbal system can call upon virtually any verb in the language, *être, avoir* and *aller* apart, without regard to which of the traditional conjugations the verb belongs and including many of the so-called irregular verbs (e.g. *voir, envoyer*). A single invariant form of the verb can be taught and it can be used with *je, tu* or *il/elle* as subject. In consequence part of the subject pronoun system, various kinds of sentence structure and the lexical meaning of a number of verbs can be learnt without the simultaneous complexity of needing to master the inflectional characteristics of the verbs. If the verbs are limited to the single-stem class in the early stages, the subject pronouns can be extended to include the third person plural. The first and second person plural inflections are probably best introduced through the single-stem verbs and only extended later to the two-stem verbs. There is no reason why verbs like *savoir* and *connaître* should not at this stage be included with the *finir*-type of two-stem verbs, provided their inclusion at all is thought desirable at this stage. The three-stem verbs (e.g. *pouvoir, venir, recevoir*) would be established as a third class of verbs at this stage.

The other implications are fairly self evident. It must be assumed that the present tense of *avoir, être* and *aller* would be taught early in any course because of their great utility. The fact that the future tense inflections can be derived from the present tense of *avoir* means that it is logical to teach the future after *avoir*, but this is normal practice anyway. The infinitive as such has no place in the first weeks of teaching. It is superfluous if the present tense forms are not to be derived from it.

The past participle cannot be avoided. It will be needed as soon as the *passé composé* is introduced. Although advantage will be taken of the fact that the majority of single-stem verbs have /-e/ as markers of the past participle and that many two-stem verbs have /-i/, there will be many verbs that fall outside such generalizations and the learning of past participial forms will always require that the learners' attention be drawn to the various smaller classes of verb where the participial form is not predictable from knowledge of the characteristics of the stem or of the inflectional features of the verb.

There is no obvious way in which the learner's burden in acquiring the morphology of the French verb can be eased in these areas.[4]

Notes and references

1. I have discussed the analysis of French adjectives in *Linguistics in Language Teaching* (1972), pp. 10–15 and 89–90, London: Edward Arnold.
2. I have no time to discuss here the view, with which I have some sympathy, that if the written language is to be introduced at all, in the case of French it should be introduced at an early stage. The linguistic organization of teaching materials that would result from such an approach would differ from that suggested by the analysis presented in this chapter.
3. Much greater regularity in the French verb system can be demonstrated if one is prepared to represent the verb forms in a fairly abstract way, i.e. in a way that does not directly indicate the phonetic shape of the forms. Such an approach is adopted by s. a. SCHANE (1968) in *French Phonology and Morphology*, Cambridge, Mass.: MIT Press. The author does not claim any pedagogic significance for this type of analysis and it seems unlikely that it would do anything other than confuse the learner to base a spoken language programme on such an analysis.
4. I have based this chapter principally on DUBOIS, J. (1967) *Grammaire structurale du français: le verbe*, Paris: Larousse, and MARTINET, A. (1958) 'De l'économie des formes du verbe en français parlé', in HATCHER, A. G. and SELLIG, K. L. (eds) *Studia Philologica et Litteraria in Honorem L. Spitzer*, Bern: Francke Verlag.

NORMAN HILL

University of London Institute of Education

Teaching a tense

Linguistics has reminded us that traditional attitudes to grammar have encouraged misconceptions like 'tense in language signals time'.[1] It is clear from the following unexceptional headlines (*Le Figaro*, 4 Nov. 1973, pp. 1 and 2) that the present tense of *affirmer* here tells us of past assertions (the assumption we make about the past time of the statements reported in the headlines is confirmed in the subsequent article); and that perhaps one of the confident statements is more tentative than the other, the conditional perfect tense (*aurait fait*) telling us at least as much about attitude as about time:

> *A Washington on affirme que Mme Golda Meir aurait fait des concessions au président des États-Unis.*
> *Mais en Israël on affirme qu'aucune pression n'a été exercée sur le premier ministre.*

(The second of these headlines, incidentally, also exemplifies the truth that gender does not always signal sex.)

In the quite common present tense statements, (1) *J'arrive demain* and (2) *J'arrive de Londres*, the adverb of time, on the one hand, and, on the other, the adverbial phrase combined with the physical presence of the speaker signal (1) future and (2) past time.

These examples and our experience, in French, of the so-called historic present, or even future (*A partir de 1833, il trouve une consolation dans l'amour tendre et vigilant de Juliette Drouet, qui lui restera fidèle jusqu'à la mort*)[2]; of the conventional *Il y a 50 ans, mourait Barrès*;[3] of the 'tentative' imperfect or future (*Je me demandais si tu pourrais m'aider à . . . | Je vous demanderai de bien vouloir . . .*) warn us that there are descriptive as well as pedagogic problems in this area of language teaching.

Anyone who is teaching in a school has not enough time to study the systems of his foreign language with the 'systematicness' indispensable for an adequate linguistic analysis. While he awaits the publication of a satisfactory, accessible description, the teacher must not ignore the occasional utterances of the student of linguistics, but he must more urgently make decisions, based on his experience of what the native speakers he knows usually say and write, about his classroom procedures – procedures which will permit a co-operative pupil to carry out in the foreign language a proportion (according to ability, intentions, eagerness, time available, etc.) of the following programme:

– to talk about what he does and what happens within his experience (present);
– to describe what he is doing and what is happening (present);
– to relate past events and incidents, and what had preceded them (perfect, pluperfect);
– to describe the circumstances in which they happened (imperfect);
– to give an account of past habits and former activities (imperfect);
– to read, with understanding, narrative accounts (past historic, past anterior);
– to reveal plans for the future (future, 'immediate' future, future perfect);
– to indicate what would happen or would have happened in certain circumstances (conditional, conditional perfect);
– to become aware of the special, if fairly common, cases (1) where a particular time is signalled by a different tense (*Il disait dans sa lettre que j'ai reçue hier qu'il prend sa retraite dans trois ans*) and (2) where a tense signals something other than time (*Il aura manqué le train*).

This represents a considerable programme, even if a glance at all the persons of all the tenses of the 8,000 verbs of *Le nouveau bescherelle: l'art de conjuguer* (Hattier-Harrap) does make us realize what a lot – uncommon verbs and unused parts of common ones – we do not have to teach . . . or learn. (It struck me, when my copy opened at page 89, that in a quarter of a century of domestic co-operation, in which coffee-grinding and French-speaking have been fairly regular, I don't remember ever saying '*Veux-tu que je moule le café?*')

One of the points which the teacher has to consider in his planning is the usefulness or indispensability of the pattern he is thinking of presenting next. Frequency counts may offer some guidance, but their value will depend not only on the needs of the pupils but also on what periodicals the researchers consulted or where they went with their tape-recorders. Discussion within departments, exchange of ideas between schools and systematic, but classroom-oriented research would help in this matter more than the views of the present writer, who may have changed his mind before the date of publication. But, without much reflection or discussion and in spite of what the contents of some course-books may lead us to believe, we can safely neglect *je bous, tu as bouilli, nous bouillions,* etc., and we can be severely selective in our teaching of *naître* and *mourir.* More serious consideration has to be given to other problems like whether to teach the future at all (perhaps not, if we are aiming only at survival skills); if so, which form, in French, shall we teach? (perhaps *aller* + infinitive, both elements being necessary in situations like *Il va à la consigne | pourquoi? | pour reprendre sa valise,* and the pattern being familiar to the English-speaking learner); if for the sake of more complete communication for the more able and willing we decide to teach both, which shall we teach first?

Having decided that it is 'worth while' to teach a particular tense of a particular verb, we must check that we are sure of the form. In this handbook it would be impertinent not to take for granted on the part of the teacher a sound knowledge of and an ability to use fluently the patterns involved in the various tenses of the most used verbs. But since anyone who never makes mistakes is not likely to be a teacher, I would just mention two small problems which seem frequently and perhaps forgivably to have escaped mastery at school or university: (1) the question form of the *passé composé* with a noun subject; one occasionally hears **Où est Robert allé?*[4] (When are questions taught? Do undergraduates often ask them?); (2) quite often the distinction *Elle est descendue | Elle a descendu l'escalier* comes as a surprise to a graduate training to be a teacher.[5]

One of the reasons for grammatical insecurity after the first five years of French may be the rapid but uncertain 'progress' made under the influence of an unfortunate sense of urgency. For those whose bright pupils pick up, remember and apply the rule that 'to form the immediate future, you use the appropriate person of the present tense of *aller* before the infinitive', the suggestion that a lesson should give more thorough coverage to a narrower field may be unwelcome. Observation of and participation in the process, and examination of the consequences, lead me to think that a well-prepared situation in which statements are made and questions are asked about visible individuals who are clearly about to carry out a very restricted number of actions will be more satisfactory than a statement of rules followed by examples and exercises. Each teacher must judge the amount of new content according to the difficulty of the pattern to be learnt and the ability of the learners; but an adequate sense of achievement may result from the oral and written mastery (involving not only careful repetition but also right choice) of, say, *elle va acheter* (*du pain, de la viande, des fleurs*), *il va prendre* (*le bus, le train, l'avion, un taxi*) and, perhaps, *ils vont jouer* (*au tennis, au football, au rugby*), as well as the understanding of *Qu'est-ce qu'il va* (*elle va, ils vont*) *faire?* There are enough examples to demonstrate the 'rule'; the inclusion of *prendre* establishes, even at the oral stage, that *acheter* |aʃte| is an infinitive; there are plenty of opportunities for practice; for a fairly 'good' class, there would not be too many examples for retention. This choice of few verbs and one person (the third[6] singular and possibly plural) may be determined not only by what is useful and already known, but also by what is pictorially presentable and comprehensible as being about to happen; even so, it is important to make an early check[7] of the pupils' understanding of the special significance of a series of drawings, so as to avoid apparently efficient but in fact uncomprehending response to questions.

Having examined the questions **What?, Why?** and **How much?**, the teacher will make his task easier if he considers what his pupils must know in order to understand and to learn to use the new pattern. In the case of the 'immediate' future it is clearly important and likely that they will have become familiar with *aller* (*chez le marchand de fleurs, au stade, à la gare*) and that, if questions have been put about reasons for going to these places, a number of infinitives will have been used with *pour*. It is important, too, that any lexical items involved in the chosen situation (the purchases, the vehicles, the games) should be known.

The selection of the situation in which the new tense pattern is to be presented and practised is important not only because we would like our lessons to be interesting, but also because we want meaning to be clear and we want to convey the importance of context, of the circumstances in which the pattern is used. Our experience of the 'immediate' future in out-of-class situations should tell us that 'immediacy' is not an essential ingredient. Our classroom situation might reveal Madame Fontaine entering what is visibly a butcher's shop and she can be fairly safely assumed to be about to purchase some meat; this will permit a true use of the tense, but it will not be the whole truth. Subsequent situations must not only increase the commentaries we can make on the visible (*Les enfants vont traverser la rue*; *Jeanne va descendre l'escalier*; or *Je vais d'abord peser les œufs*; *ensuite je vais peser tour à tour la même quantité de sucre, de farine et de beurre*), but also extend the use of the tense to, say, consultation of a page of a diary, so that we can see and say what Monsieur Rivière is going to do or what I am / we are, etc., going to do next week or next month.

The first lesson on the *passé composé* may well consist of imperatives, actions and questions and statements about what X, Y or Z has done. But this situation, however well developed, does not convey completely the function of the tense; other experiences of it are necessary: Madame Fontaine could be seen walking **out** of the butcher's shop with her meat; cakes can be seen to have been burnt, a bowl to have been broken; children can be seen to have crossed the road. We can talk about what happened in the story we have just read; or about what happened last Thursday when Monsieur Clair, having forgotten to set the alarm, set off for work half an hour late:

(usual times crossed out)

This last sequence groups situationally a number of verbs which behave alike grammatically in the perfect tense (*partir, arriver, monter, descendre, arriver, entrer, sortir, aller*) and offers the chance to talk with understanding about a normal series of past happenings, provided the habitual programme has been dealt with in the present and provided one insists frequently on the special circumstances of last Thursday.

It is important, as the use of various tenses is acquired, that the opportunity should be created for the use of two or more within the same context, so that our attempt to establish a new tense in the right sort of situation does not create isolated compartments of verbal habits which would make the following situation as risky for the language learner as it often proves to be for the pedestrian:

Careful exploitation of well-chosen texts, pictorial and documentary materials will help pupils to move flexibly and for good reasons from one tense to another.

The choice of specific aids by means of which to establish the teaching/learning situation might be guided by the criteria of normality, clarity, facility and fruitfulness. To have performing musicians in the room, for our present tense lesson on *jouer de*, would be difficult and distracting. A visible illustration of Richard and Marie etc., would help us to identify the people and instruments concerned, and to establish the meaning and form of *Il joue de la guitare*, etc. A controllable recording (*Écoutez Marie maintenant ... elle joue du piano*) provides a similar opportunity, on condition that questions are asked and statements are made while the music continues not too loudly. The regular daily timetable of Richard and Marie suggests, for French, a means of catering for other circumstances in which the present tense is used. (Of course, for English it is the type of situation needed to distinguish 'plays' from 'is playing'.) *Richard joue de la guitare (de 5 à 6 heures du soir)* is

	R	M
17h – 18h		
18h – 19h		

different, not only musically, from *Julian Bream et Django Reinhart jouent de la guitare | Yehudi Menuhin et Stephan Grappelli jouent du violon*, where we are thinking of a profession rather than a pastime; but the thought does remind us of the possibility of using a list of well-known names for at least revision and extension purposes.

The wide range of situations which one can create for the practice of the present tense – pictorial, documentary, symbolic, audial and textual – does not seem to be available for the teaching of the pluperfect, which presents special problems. The major difficulty is that there are few situations where the pluperfect is indispensable or inevitable. 'He had locked the door before he left' or 'He locked the door before he left' both reveal the same facts in the same sequence. If we use a letter, written by Gabrielle in the past tense on 15 August 1971, *Je suis allée au cinéma hier* might suggest the question: *Qu'est-ce que Gabrielle avait fait le 14 août? Elle était allée au cinéma* reflects the form of the question, and it arises naturally but not inevitably from the situation. The first sentence of an invented passage, *Jeanne revenait de la gare, une pile de journaux dans la sacoche de son vélo*, allows us to infer *Elle était allée à la gare; elle (y) avait acheté des journaux; elle y était allée à vélo; elle avait mis les journaux dans la sacoche de son vélo*. But again, if the teacher wants the pluperfect tense in, say, the last of these four answers, he will have to avoid the question, which might come just as easily as the one he needs, *Qu'est-ce que Jeanne a fait avant de remonter à vélo?* Sometimes '*pourquoi*' questions lead normally to pluperfect tense; *Pourquoi est-ce que Georges a téléphoné à ses parents? Parce qu'il avait manqué le dernier train* (a fact revealed in direct speech in the perfect tense).

Recently a student quite successfully introduced this tense by a means which I would not previously have recommended, but now suggest is worth consideration and development. The visual aid consisted of several drawings of separate situations, **all dated in the past**, where it was clear what had happened; e.g. Claudette on her wedding day, August 1972, standing at a table on which were six teapots, receiving a teapot from Simon: *Pourquoi Claudette n'était-elle pas contente?* (The need for the inclusion of *déjà* in the answer reminds us of this frequent association.)

Needless to say, no answer will be forthcoming to this or any other question, if no examples of the pattern required have been given. The statements the teacher makes in relation to his illustrations, documents or recordings are very important. Even in a simple situation like:

	'74	'75	'76	... (assuming that '74 = this year)
Jacques	14			
Colette	16			
Jean	18			
Marie	20			

we shall need statements of present ages and a number of examples such as *Jacques aura 15 ans en 1975*; *Marie aura 22 ans en 1976* to be listened to, and repeated in groups and individually, before we can get answers to questions like *Et l'année prochaine, est-ce que Colette aura vingt ans? Et Colette, quel âge aura-t-elle en 1977?* The statements the teacher makes about his own future activities 'this evening', for which the following might serve as a symbolic reminder:

will help the pupils to establish their own visual programme (different, but containing some of the same verbs: *quitterai, arriverai, prendrai, irai, dînerai, lirai, regarderai, me coucherai*) about which they will be enabled to speak.

When we come to our choice of questions to be asked, we must decide what responses we have a right to expect and how helpful we wish to be. The sentence *André est arrivé à la gare à six heures avec ses parents* offers us evidence for these answers: *André; à la gare; à six heures; avec ses parents; il / André est arrivé à la gare* and, if we insist (justifiably, in my view), *il y est arrivé à six heures* and *il y est arrivé avec ses parents*. However, some teaching and testing still seems to suggest (in my view without justification) that the whole sentence is a correct answer to all the questions: *Qui? Où? Quand? Avec qui? Qu'est-ce que André a fait à six heures? Qu'est-ce qui s'est passé à six heures?*

About Richard and Marie (above, p. 19) when I ask the question *Qui joue du piano?*, the answer I want is *Marie*. In reply to *Quand est-ce que Richard joue de la guitare?*, I expect no more than *Entre cinq et six heures du soir*. In order to elicit *Elle joue du piano*, I must ask *Que fait Marie entre six et sept heures du soir?* The useful question-type *Que font Marie et Robert entre cinq et six heures?* allows us to require a fuller answer: *Marie regarde la télévision et Richard joue de la guitare.*

Questions posed in the first lesson on the perfect tense must be carefully chosen so that the appropriate answer pattern is the one we want to get practised; other questions must be reserved for the time when other patterns (e.g. with pronoun objects) need to be practised. For example (after checking ability to identify relevant objects and furniture), *X, prenez la boîte / Y, prenez la bouteille / Z, prenez la clé*; *A, qu'est-ce que X a fait?*, etc.; *X, mettez la boîte sur la table / Y, mettez la bouteille dans le placard*, etc.; *B, qu'est-ce que Z a fait?* (– *Il a mis la clé sous le paillasson*), etc. (To be avoided at this initial stage: *Qu'est-ce que Y a fait de la bouteille?* and *X, prenez la boîte et mettez-la sur la table. . . .*)

The oral work, organized to produce appropriate answers in sufficient number and concentration to make complete understanding, correct association and reasonably accurate production possible needs to be followed up at each stage by the written form of what can be said. And increasingly there should be opportunity for more sustained spoken and written accounts produced in response to a hint or request like *Dites-moi ce que faisaient ces gens célèbres*: *H. G. Wells, Shakespeare, W. H. Auden, Maurice Chevalier, Pablo Casals*; *Écrivez quelques phrases au sujet de X (dont nous avons parlé) et de la vie qu'il menait avant son déménagement / son service militaire / avant de devenir médecin.*

I propose finally to re-open some of the questions I have raised by offering a few notes on the tense just referred to: the imperfect.

The imperfect tense will be needed:

– if pupils' use of French is to include even simple narration of personal experiences or reading of narrative in novels or newspapers;
– if the learner is ever likely to describe earlier habitual activities;

It can be delayed:

– until a stage at which the pupil has **chosen** to continue his study of French.

Guided by our answers to the questions: How necessary is this use? Is it simple or complex? Can I find or create a suitable situation in which to teach it?, we might establish the following tentative order:

1. *Aujourd'hui c'est le 2 janvier; hier c'était le premier janvier.*	*Quelle était la date dimanche? C'était le 30 décembre. Et samedi dernier?*	Calendar s|29 déc. d|30 73 l|31 m| 1 jan. m| 2 74
2. *Jean a 18 ans (maintenant en 1974); il avait 16 ans (en 1972).*	*Quel âge avait-il en 1970? Il avait 14 ans. Et en 1971? Et les jumeaux, Pierre et Paul? Et vous?*	Table similar to the one on p. 21.
3. *Il était 9h25/Il pleuvait quand on a pris cette photo.*	*Quelle heure était-il / Quel temps faisait-il quand on a pris cette photo? Il était onze heures (du matin) / Il neigeait.*	Photos, slides
4. *Casals jouait du violoncelle / était musicien. Auden écrivait des poèmes / était poète.*	*Que faisait Shakespeare? Quelle était la profession de Maurice Chevalier?*	List of names of the famous dead (problem here of 'general knowledge')
5. *C'était un homme / un oiseau qui chantait / une cloche / un réveil qui sonnait.*	*Écoutez cet enregistrement. . . . Qu'est-ce que c'était? C'était une femme qui chantait / un téléphone qui sonnait.*	Recordings of continuous sounds
6. *Avant son mariage elle habitait (une maison) à Orléans / Avant de devenir plombier il travaillait dans une ferme.*	*Comment Mme Rivers s'appelait-elle avant son mariage? Quel âge avait-elle en 1971? Parlez-moi / Écrivez quelques phrases au sujet de la vie de Mlle Fontaine. (Extend re M. et Mme X – lorsqu'ils habitaient au Maroc. Et vous et votre famille, que faisiez-vous quand vous habitiez à Wigan / au Kenya)? Que faisiez-vous à l'école primaire? Qu'est-ce que je faisais avant de devenir professeur?*	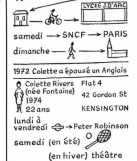

* Based on a lesson given by Mrs L. Humphreys, Henrietta Barnett School, London.

7. *Hélène jouait du piano (quand) le téléphone a sonné | Colette tapait à la machine (quand) on a frappé à la porte.*

Revision of 4 (above):
Qu'est-ce que c'était?
Qn. qui jouait du piano.
Oui, c'était Hélène.
Qu'est-ce qu'elle faisait?
Elle jouait du piano.
Oui et puis elle s'est arrêtée, n'est-ce pas?
Pourquoi? (Parce que) le téléphone a sonné. Bon.
Qu'est-ce qui se passait au début de l'enregistrement? Hélène jouait du piano. Oui. Et puis? Le téléphone a sonné.
(Later: *Parlez-moi de cette série d'enregistrements que vous venez d'écouter.*)

Recordings of identifiable 'imperfect' music, talking, typing, snoring . . . interrupted by 'perfect' phone, knock, alarm, etc.

8. *Il attendait depuis dix minutes.*

Quand est-ce que Yves est arrivé devant le cinéma?
A 7 heures. Oui, et Louise?
Elle y est arrivée à 7h10.
Oui, c'est-à-dire . . .?
Dix minutes plus tard.
Oui; que faisait Yves à 7h10? Il attendait.
Oui, il attendait . . .
depuis combien de temps?
Depuis dix minutes. Bon, il attendait depuis dix minutes.

Text or, for concentration purposes, a number of brief textual situations like: *A 7 heures Yves arriva devant le cinéma. Sa copine, Louise, n'y arriva qu'à 7h10.* Questions + invitation to draw conclusions along lines indicated.

9. *Il disait dans sa lettre qu'il habitait à Sèvres et qu'il travaillait chez Renault.*

Both the special case of *'disait'* and the use of the imperfect in reported speech probably need an introductory statement in English.
Qu'est-ce que Mme Colbert a demandé à son mari?
(*style indirect*)
Elle lui a demandé ce qu'il faisait. Oui, qu'est-ce qu'il faisait? Il se lavait les mains. Oui; pourquoi est-ce qu'il devait se dépêcher? Parce que le dîner était prêt. Oui, et . . . sa femme? Elle avait faim.

Letters, and other texts including dialogue, e.g.
Mme Colbert: Qu'est-ce que tu fais? Dépêche-toi! Le dîner est prêt et j'ai faim!
M. Colbert: Je me lave les mains.

Most of these situations (and others which readers may think of) give rise not only to oral and written question and answer work, but also to the sort of brief continuous writing ('a few sentences about') which I would not call composition. Though it involves more or less spontaneous comment, rehearsed during question and answer work, based on listening, observation and not only repetition but also choice and analogy, it does not involve 'composing'. The integration of the various mastered tenses in an organized, shapely composition is just one of the problems this chapter has not dealt with.

Notes and references

1. One of the hypotheses which David Crystal challenges on pp. 96–7 of *Linguistics* (1971). Harmondsworth, Middx: Penguin.
2. CASTEX, P. and SURER, P. (1950) *Manuel des études littéraires françaises: XIXᵉ siècle*. Paris: Hachette.
3. *Brèves Nouvelles de France*, 10 Nov. 1973.
4. I adopt the convention found in books on linguistics: *preceding a sentence indicates that it is not normally used by native speakers.
5. I am *not* deploring a state of affairs, merely admitting a need for teachers and teachers of teachers to go on learning.
6. My reason for this choice is mentioned elsewhere in the handbook in the teaching of modal verbs (p. 82).
7. Possibly in English: What is Mme X going to do? What is Jean going to do? What have all these people got in common?, etc.

JACK STEVENSON

Isleworth Grammar School, Middlesex

A question and answer series
– grammar through use

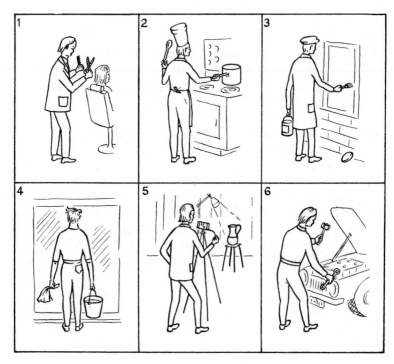

This set of drawings was designed for a class of pupils who, working three periods a week, were roughly half-way through their second year of German. Two of the most important aspects of their lessons hitherto had been first that the German they were learning was presented to them in such a way that they could accurately deduce its meaning and function without needing to be burdened by explanations about its grammar or by translation; secondly, that a consistent attempt was made to give them enough meaningful question and answer practice in handling new material to ensure that eventually they would be able to produce it accurately and spontaneously in any appropriate spoken or written context. Both these aspects were a basic consideration in planning the drawings and in teaching the new material to which they gave the pupils access.

Because they bear on both the reasons for choosing the material contained in the drawings and the way the material was presented to the pupils, it will help to consider the main aspects of the work which the pupil had covered during the earlier parts of the course. These had concentrated mainly on:

1. The establishing of the connections between the indefinite article, and the pronouns, i.e. the *ein – der – er, ein – das – es, eine – die – sie* connections.

2. Verbs in the present tense only.

3. *Wenn*-clauses and *Weil*-clauses.

4. *Müssen, dürfen, wollen* and *können* as used with infinitives.

Other important points had also been dealt with, but as they have less direct bearing on the work done with the drawings, they need only be mentioned briefly. They include the numbers 1–1,000, the time, the days of the week, the months, the date, the names of countries, languages, nationalities, expressions concerning the weather, the parts of the body, the dative of the definite article after *in, auf, vor, hinter, neben* and *unter*, and the dative of the indefinite article after *mit*.

The work on the **connections** between the indefinite article, the definite article, and the pronoun initially involved a limited number of carefully chosen masculine, neuter and feminine nouns. The pupils learnt gradually that the nouns had to be referred to in one context as *ein* or *eine*, in another as *der, das* or *die*, and in yet another as *er, es* or *sie*. In other words, *Was ist das?* produced *Das ist ein Korb / ein Fahrrad / eine Flasche*; *Welcher Gegenstand ist gelb, schwarz, grün?* produced *Der Korb / Das Fahrrad / Die Flasche*; *Welche Farbe hat der Korb / das Fahrrad / die Flasche?* produced *Er ist gelb / Es ist schwarz / Sie ist grün*. Later, pupils were taught to make statements in which the indefinite and definite articles were followed by both an adjective and a noun in the nominative case. In this way they learnt to respond to *Was für ein Korb / ein Fahrrad / eine Flasche ist das?* with *Das ist ein gelber Korb / ein schwarzes Fahrrad / eine grüne Flasche*, and to reply to *Welcher Korb ist voll?*

| Welches Fahrrad ist kaputt? | Welche Flasche ist leer? with *Der gelbe Korb | Das schwarze Fahrrad | Die grüne Flasche*. Once these connections had been introduced, and their functions clarified, by means of a restricted number of familiar nouns, it became an important part of all subsequent work to ensure that the pupils constantly demonstrated their awareness of them in respect of whatever other nouns they met.

The **verbs** taught in the first year included **sein, stehen, sitzen, kriechen, liegen, springen, laufen, fliegen, schwimmen, hängen, heißen, kommen, wohnen, schlafen, sprechen, trinken, lachen, weinen, fallen,** haben, tragen, essen, fressen, lesen, halten, sehen, malen, zeichnen; they were practised in the present tense only. Those in heavy type were taught first because they were fairly easily illustrated and allowed meaningful practice in most forms of the present tense without confronting the pupils with the additional complication of using a noun in the accusative case at the same time. The introduction to the accusative came later by means of the verbs in italic used with the indefinite article. Early practice in it was with statements such as *Er trägt einen Anzug*; *Er frißt einen Knochen*; *Sie liest ein Buch*; *Sie zeichnet eine Katze*. Later practice included answers like *Er trägt einen gestreiften Anzug*; *Er frißt einen großen Knochen*; *Sie liest ein deutsches Buch*; *Sie zeichnet eine weiße Katze*. The verbs *haben* and *tragen* in particular allowed practice in the accusative plural as well, so that pupils were familiar with answers such as *Er hat rote Haare, Sie trägt schwarze Schuhe und weiße Socken, Sie hat blaue Augen*. The verbs in italic had also allowed practice in using the negative forms of the indefinite article in the nominative and accusative and in the singular and plural. Thus, holding up a pencil / book / bottle and asking *Was für ein Kugelschreiber | Heft | eine Dose ist das?* would produce *Das ist kein Kugelschreiber | kein Heft | keine Dose sondern ein Bleistift | ein Buch | eine Flasche*. Asking *Was für einen Hut | ein Hemd | Stiefel trägt sie?* in respect of a drawing of a woman wearing a cap / blouse / shoes would produce *Sie trägt keinen Hut | kein Hemd | keine Stiefel sondern eine Mütze | eine Bluse | Schuhe*. An introduction to the accusative of the definite article was not attempted in the first year.

Simple *wenn*-clauses had been taught to the pupils as soon as they had mastered the accusative of the indefinite article. The following are some of the questions and answers which allowed the early practice in using them:

Wann trägt man einen Regenmantel?	*Wenn es regnet.*
Wann trägt man einen Schlafanzug?	*Wenn man schläft.*
Wann trägt man Fußballschuhe?	*Wenn man Fußball spielt.*
Wann trägt man Tennisschuhe?	*Wenn man Tennis spielt.*
Wann trägt man überhaupt nichts?	*Wenn man badet.*
	Wenn man sich duscht.
Wann trägt eine Frau einen Bikini?	*Wenn sie sich sonnt.*
	Wenn sie schwimmt.
Wann trage ich eine Badehose?	*Wenn Sie schwimmen.*
Wann ißt du?	*Wenn ich Hunger habe.*
Wann trinkst du?	*Wenn ich Durst habe.*
Wann trägt man leichte Kleider?	*Wenn es warm ist.*
Wann trägt man warme Kleider?	*Wenn es kalt ist.*
Wann trägt man eine Brille?	*Wenn man schlechte Augen hat.*
Wann trägt man eine Sonnenbrille?	*Wenn die Sonne stark scheint.*

Weil-clauses were introduced by means of drawings and texts which made possible practice in questions and answers like the following:

Warum lacht das Kind?	*Weil es glücklich ist.*
Warum heult die Frau?	*Weil sie traurig ist.*
Warum sieht er nichts?	*Weil es neblig ist.*
Warum macht sie kein Bild?	*Weil es bewölkt ist.*
Warum fallen die Blätter?	*Weil es windig ist.*
Warum trägt sie einen Regenmantel?	*Weil es regnet.*
Warum ist er so dick?	*Weil er zuviel frißt.*
Warum trage ich keine Brille?	*Weil Sie gute Augen haben.*
Warum trägst du heute keine Jacke?	*Weil es warm ist.*
Warum trägt sie einen dicken Mantel?	*Weil es kalt ist.*
Warum kann ein Wurm nicht sehen?	*Weil er keine Augen hat.*
Warum kann eine Schlange nicht laufen?	*Weil sie keine Beine hat.*

The introduction to *können* was made with reference to animals and pupils in the class, who could obviously do some things but not others. This gave rise to material such as the following:

Kann ein Wurm sehen und kriechen?
  Er kann kriechen, aber nicht sehen.
Kann ein Fisch laufen und schwimmen?
  Er kann schwimmen, aber nicht laufen.

Kann ein Vogel sprechen und singen?
　Er kann singen, aber nicht sprechen.
Kannst du fliegen und laufen?
　Ich kann laufen, aber nicht fliegen.
Kann ich Spanisch und Englisch?
　Sie können Englisch, aber kein Spanisch.

Later, drawings in which people were obviously intending to do certain things, or were not permitted to do certain things, or were obliged to do certain things, gave the opportunity to practise *wollen*, *dürfen*, and *müssen* in the way that the following statements suggest:

Er will schlafen.
Sie will baden.
Er will Fußball spielen.
Er will Briefe tippen.
Man muß halten.
Man muß geradeaus fahren.
Man muß vorsichtig fahren.
Man darf nicht rauchen.
Man darf nicht nach rechts fahren.

When the pupils met the six drawings shown on p. 26 for the first time the teacher verified the assumptions on which he was going to base his introduction of the new material. He also took the opportunity of revising whatever previously taught material the drawings gave access to, even though it was not directly relevant to the new work. The following are some of the questions and answers involved in this first step, with the drawing of a barber as a model:

Was ist das?	*Das ist ein Mann.*
Was ist das?	*Das ist eine Schere.*
Ist das auch eine Schere?	*Nein, das ist ein Kamm.*
Was ist ein Kamm?	*Ein Kamm ist ein Gegenstand.*
Ist ein Mann auch ein Gegenstand?	*Nein, ein Mann ist ein Mensch.*
Bist du auch ein Mensch?	*Ja.*
Bist du auch ein Mann?	*Nein, ich bin ein Junge/Mädchen.*
Wieviele Jungen gibt es auf Bild I?	*Es gibt keine(n) Jungen.*
Wieviele Mädchen gibt es?	*Es gibt keins / kein(e) Mädchen.*
Gibt es keine Gegenstände auf Bild I?	*Doch, es gibt zwei.*
Was hält der Mann?	*Er hält eine Schere und einen Kamm.*

Welche Farbe hat die Schere?	*Sie ist grau.*
Ist der Kamm auch grau?	*Nein, er ist schwarz.*
Was sind Grau und Schwarz?	*Farben.*
Was sind eine Schere und ein Kamm?	*Gegenstände.*
Welcher Gegenstand auf Bild I ist grau?	*Die Schere.*
Welcher Gegenstand auf Bild I ist schwarz?	*Der Kamm.*
Was für eine Schere hält der Mann?	*Er hält eine graue Schere.*
Hält er auch einen grauen Kamm?	*Nein, er hält einen schwarzen Kamm.*
Was für einen Kamm hast du?	*Ich habe einen roten / kurzen / neuen Kamm.*
	Ich habe keinen Kamm.
Was für eine Schere hast du?	*Ich habe eine kleine / alte Schere.*
	Ich habe keine Schere.
Halte ich eine Schere?	*Nein, Sie halten ein Lineal / einen Kugelschreiber.*
Was hältst du?	*Ich halte nichts.*
Woraus ist das Lineal?	*Es ist aus Holz.*
Ist der Kugelschreiber auch aus Holz?	*Nein, er ist aus Kunststoff.*

Similar questions were put in respect of all six drawings. During this revision exercise the new nouns *Lappen, Schraubenschlüssel, Farbtopf* and *Werkzeug(e)* were taught.

Then came the first main new point: the teaching of the names of the trades or professions represented by the people in the drawings. They were introduced by means of the following procedure:

1. The teacher pointed to the drawing of the barber and asked *Was hält er?* On receiving the answer *Er hält eine Schere und einen Kamm*, he said *Ja, er hält eine Schere und einen Kamm – er ist Friseur,* and had the class chorus *Er ist Friseur.*

2. Pointing then to the cook he asked *Was hält er?* Having been given the answer *Er hält einen Topf und einen Löffel*, the teacher repeated it, adding *Er ist Koch*, and had the class chorus his addition.

3. Moving back to the barber he asked *Ist er Friseur von Beruf?* and got the answer *Ja.* He then pointed to the cook and asked *Was ist er von Beruf?* and got the answer *Er ist Koch.*

4. Pointing next to the painter he asked *Was hält er?* and was

given the answer *Er hält einen Pinsel und einen Farbtopf.* Then he asked *Was ist er von Beruf?* In accordance with the procedure established from the beginning whereby pupils not knowing the answer to a particular question put the same question to the teacher in order to get the required answer, he was asked by one pupil, *Was ist er von Beruf?* This question was then chorused by the class before the answer *Er ist Maler* was given and practised.

5. *Er ist Fensterputzer, Er ist Fotograf, Er ist Mechaniker* were taught in the same way.

6. *Bin ich Mechaniker von Beruf?* prompted the answer *Nein* and the question to the teacher *Was sind Sie von Beruf?*, to which he answered *Ich bin Lehrer.* When he then asked *Was bin ich von Beruf?* he got the answer *Sie sind Lehrer*, which was chorused by the class.

7. Later, pupils were taught to respond to the question *Was bist du von Beruf?* with the answer *Ich habe keinen Beruf, sondern ich bin Schüler(in)*, and eventually, moving away from the set of drawings, questions such as *Was ist Harold Wilson / Gerd Müller / Rod Laver / Cliff Richard / Frau X* (the school secretary) / *Frau Y* (the school cook) / *Dan Archer / Dr Finlay / Laurence Olivier / Steve McQueen / von Beruf* allowed them practice with *Politiker / Fußballspieler / Tennisspieler / Sänger / Sekretärin / Köchin / Bauer / Arzt / Schauspieler / Filmschauspieler.*

The next lot of new material was the description of what each of the six people on the drawings did. The class was familiar with only one of the verbs in question, viz. *malen.* Practice with the new verbs went as follows:

Was macht ein Friseur?	*Er schneidet Haare.*
Was macht ein Koch?	*Er kocht.*
Kocht ein Maler?	*Nein, er malt.*
Malt ein Fensterputzer?	*Nein, er putzt Fenster.*
Was macht ein Fotograf?	*Er fotografiert.*
Was macht ein Mechaniker?	*Er repariert Autos.*
Was macht ein Lehrer?	*Er unterrichtet.*
Unterrichtet ein(e) Schüler(in)?	*Nein, er / sie lernt.*
Was macht Harold Wilson?	*Er redet viel*!

Er spielt Fußball / Tennis came from earlier references to *Gerd Müller* and *Rod Laver. Er singt / Sie tippt Briefe / Sie kocht / Er heilt die Kranken* all came from the references to Cliff Richard, the school secretary, the cook, and Dr Finlay.

Er will + infinitive had already been introduced, but the drawings offered the opportunity to increase the number of examples of this structure. As a result work with the following ensued:

Was will der Friseur machen?	*Er will Haare schneiden.*
Was will der Koch machen?	*Er will kochen.*
Will der Maler auch kochen?	*Nein, er will malen.*
Und der Fensterputzer?	*Er will Fenster putzen.*
Was will der Fotograf machen?	*Er will fotografieren.*
Und der Mechaniker?	*Er will ein Auto reparieren.*

Since simple *wenn*-clauses had already been introduced and since the pupils were also familiar with the accusative and the indefinite article, it was obvious that *brauchen* could now be introduced. The statement *Man braucht eine Schere und einen Kamm, wenn man Haare schneiden will* made the meaning of *brauchen* clear, and the following material was then practised:

Was braucht man, wenn man Haare schneiden will?
  Man braucht einen Kamm und eine Schere.
Was braucht man, wenn man malen will?
  Man braucht einen Pinsel und einen Farbtopf.
Braucht man einen Topf und einen Löffel, wenn man Fenster putzen will?
  Nein, man braucht einen Eimer und einen Lappen.
Wann braucht man einen Topf und einen Löffel?
  Wenn man kochen will.
Was braucht man, wenn man ein Auto reparieren will?
  Man braucht Werkzeuge.

Although *mit* + the indefinite article had already been introduced, it had not been used with any of the objects which the people on the drawings were holding. This suggested practice in the following structures:

Womit schneidet man Haare?	*Mit einer Schere.*
Womit malt man?	*Mit einem Pinsel.*
Putzt man Fenster mit einem Topf und einem Löffel?	*Nein, mit einem Lappen.*
Was macht man mit einem Topf?	*Man kocht damit.*
Womit fotografiert man?	*Mit einer Kamera.*
Womit hämmert man?	*Mit einem Hammer.*

Womit kämmt man sich die Haare? Mit einem Kamm.
Womit repariert man Autos?   Mit Werkzeugen.

The same material lent itself to an introduction of the use of *um . . .zu*:

Wozu braucht man eine Schere?	*Um etwas / Haare zu schneiden.*
Wozu braucht man einen Hammer?	*Um zu hämmern.*
Wozu braucht man einen Topf?	*Um zu kochen.*
Wozu braucht man einen Pinsel?	*Um zu malen.*
Wozu braucht man einen Kamm?	*Um sich (die Haare) zu kämmen.*
Wozu braucht man Werkzeuge	
zum Beispiel?	*Um ein Auto zu reparieren.*
Wozu braucht man eine Kamera?	*Um zu fotografieren.*
Wozu braucht man einen Lappen	*Um Fenster zu putzen.*
zum Beispiel?	

Having given the definition of '*ein Friseur*' as *Ein Mann, der Haare schneidet*, that of '*eine Lehrerin*' as *Eine Frau, die unterrichtet*, and '*eine Schülerin*' as *Ein Mädchen, das in der Schule lernt*, it was possible to practise other relative clauses in the following way:

Was ist ein Koch?	*Er ist ein Mann, der kocht.*
Was ist eine Köchin?	*Sie ist eine Frau, die kocht.*
Was ist ein Maler?	*Er ist ein Mann, der malt.*
Ist ein Fensterputzer ein Mann,	*Nein, er ist ein Mann, der*
der Autos repariert?	*Fenster putzt.*
Was ist ein Fotograf?	*Er ist ein Mann, der fotografiert.*
Was ist ein Mechaniker?	*Er ist ein Mann, der Autos*
	repariert.

Further practice was possible by means of reference to the other trades and professions introduced earlier: *Sekretärin, Arzt, Sänger, Tennisspieler*, etc.

Because *in* + the indefinite article + noun had already been taught it was now possible with the following question and answer series to introduce (1) the accusative of the definite article, (2) the accusative pronouns *ihn, sie, es*, (3) *in* + *der* + adjective + noun.

Welchen Gegenstand hält er in der linken Hand?
    Er hält den Kamm.
Welchen Gegenstand hält er in der anderen/rechten Hand?
    Er hält die Schere.

In welcher Hand hält er den Pinsel?
    Er hält ihn in der rechten Hand.
In welcher Hand hält er den Farbtopf?
    Er hält ihn in der anderen/linken Hand.
Ich halte zwei Gegenstände – ein Heft und eine Tasche –.
In welcher Hand halte ich das Heft?
    Sie halten es in der rechten Hand.
Und die Tasche?
    Sie halten sie in der linken Hand.
Welchen Gegenstand halte ich in der rechten Hand?
    Sie halten das Heft in der rechten Hand.
Und der Fensterputzer?
    Er hält den Eimer in der rechten Hand.
Und welchen Gegenstand halte ich in der linken Hand?
    Sie halten die Tasche in der linken Hand.
Und der Fensterputzer?
    Er hält den Lappen in der linken Hand.

Clearly the pattern made up of *in der* followed by an adjective and a noun would need to be practised a great deal more in other contexts, but these had already been prepared and within a short time the pupils would be adding to *in der rechten | linken | anderen Hand* phrases such as *in der weißen | blauen Tasse, in der großen | kleinen Vase, in der linken | rechten Tasche, in der ersten | letzten Stunde, in der ersten | zweiten Pause, in der braunen | schwarzen Mappe, in der fünften | vierten Klasse,* etc. Indeed, from the point at which all the work on the six drawings had been exhausted, care would be taken to extend and revise it in all its aspects whenever appropriate.

ALAN W. HORNSEY

University of London Institute of Education

Introducing a new case

To English children learning German, especially those who have done no Latin, statements like 'this is a new case', 'it is the accusative' or 'it is used for the direct object' are not helpful. They need instead:

– to hear and see a change in a word already known in another form: *ein Tisch – einen Tisch*;

– to practise the change in contexts where they can see what it means, so that they can eventually reach general conclusions about it. These might at first be 'it's what happens after *haben*', 'it's what also happens after *tragen, besitzen, halten, stellen*', then 'it sometimes occurs after *in*', 'it always occurs after *für*'. Eventually it will need to be seen as indicating a direct object, even sometimes occurring **before the verb**: *einen Garten hat er, aber . . .*;

– finally, much later, it might be worth while subsuming examples of the form under the heading 'accusative' when this is the label for a concept **already experienced**.

What seems to be standard practice?

The new case is first introduced in association with a whole range of new verbs. One course (1931) uses *haben, lesen, interessieren, rauchen, besetzen* ('*eine Dame besetztden Stuhl*'!!); another (1967) *haben, bringen, abnehmen, auflegen, essen, sehen, nehmen*. The English-speaking learner has to cope with an unusual noun form and about a dozen new verb forms – surely an unnecessarily steep incline of difficulty.

All possibilities are introduced at once, presumably for the sake of completeness. One course (1954) uses all three genders and the whole range of possible personal pronouns in just a few lines and a more recent one (1968) starts as follows:

Sigrid hat einen Roller. Sie hat auch einen Bruder, Wolfgang. Er ist noch zu jung für einen Roller, aber er findet ihn interessant. Er

36

hat ein Fahrrad; aber das ist natürlich nicht so interessant! Sigrid besucht heute eine Freundin. Sie holt zuerst den Roller für den Bruder.

The new case is introduced via words not met before in the nominative. How, then, can the learner notice the change in form? This is true of the quotation above where *Roller, Bruder, Fahrrad, Freundin* are all new words, as, incidentally, are also *hat, zu, jung, für, besucht, heute, holt, zuerst.*

Abstract terms are used as an introduction, not as a summing-up: 'the accusative = direct object' (1967).

The form is practised without regard to its significance: *Setzen Sie in den Akkusativ!* (1949) where there are no verbs given at all, or it is placed in a drill with scant regard for meaning:

Stimulus. *Das ist das Baby. Was hat die Mutter?*
Response. *Die Mutter hat das Baby.* (1970)

What follows is a possible teaching plan, not a model but a scheme for discussion and adaptation to individual needs. The intention is to limit the material, simplify the learning task and provide a lot of practice.

Stage 1

The aim is to introduce *haben* and *tragen*, in the forms *hat* and *trägt*, concentrating on a few plural nouns but no singular accusatives. It is not suggested that this is the time for a systematic study of the plural, but simply that seven or eight very common plurals be used:

Blackboard. Write up a number of children's names with, opposite each, the number (in figures) of named objects which they possess:

	Bonbons	Bücher	Hefte
Jens	3	4	2
Eva	2	5	3
Peter	7	3	3

The teacher asks questions about these facts and the answers involve revision of numbers and constant use of the target word *hat*:

Teacher. *Wieviele Bonbons hat Jens?*
Pupil. *Er hat drei.*
T. *Hat Eva sechs Bücher?*
P. *Nein, sie hat fünf.*

T. *Was hat Peter?*
P. *Er hat sieben Bonbons, drei Bücher und drei Hefte.*

General. If parts of the body have been previously learnt and one or two names of animals are known, then general questions are possible, again using numbers and practising *hat*:

    T. *Wieviele Arme hat ein Mensch? Beine? Augen?*
        Wieviele Beine hat ein Fisch? ein Insekt? ein Hund?

At this point some teachers might feel that *habe, haben | hast* with the obvious variations could also be practised:

    T. *Wieviele Beine hast du/haben Sie?*
    P. *Ich habe zwei.*
    T. *Und ein Hund?*
    P. *Er hat vier.*

Blackboard. Articles of clothing will probably have been taught with reference to blackboard drawing and pictures:

e.g. **T.** *Was ist das?* (Pointing)
    P. *Das ist ein Hemd.*
    T. *Welche Farbe hat das Hemd?*
    P. *Es ist blau.*
    T. *Welches Kleidungsstück ist rot?*
    P. *Der Rock.*
    T. *Was ist das?*
    P. *Das sind Handschuhe.*

After such exchanges have been thoroughly revised, it is possible, now that the accusative is the target, to turn to the subject of 'wearing' (*tragen*). Here those articles which usually come in pairs afford useful practice:

    T. *Was trägt er | sie?*
    P. *Er | sie trägt Schuhe | Socken | Strümpfe | Handschuhe |*
      Ohrringe.

These articles can be highlighted in colour on otherwise all-white pin-men. As with *haben*, it is again possible to introduce first and second person forms by referring to the learners' own shoes and socks.

    Stage 1 is concerned with mastering the correct form, pronunciation, meaning and function of the two key verbs and thus reducing the learning load in stage 2.

Stage 2

Haben. To introduce the accusative singular the teacher needs pictures or blackboard drawings (pin-men, if his artistic skill is limited). The people in these drawings will be seen with their possessions – not just portable ones, since *haben* must not be taken to mean *halten*:

The objects should be identified: *Was ist das? Es ist ein Hund*, etc., and no learner should be left in doubt as to what they are, what gender they are and how they are pronounced. At first it is probably best to give each figure only one possession and to keep to one gender. Oral work might proceed as follows:

T. *Das ist Max und das ist sein Hund.*
Max hat einen Hund.
Alle zusammen: 'Max hat einen Hund'. (Class repeats.)
Hat Fritz einen Hund?
P. *Nein.*
T. *Wer hat einen Hund?*
P. *Max.*
T. *Gut, also, was hat Max?*
P. *(Er hat) einen Hund.*
T. *Jawohl, Max hat einen Hund. Und was ist das?* (Pointing.)
P. *Ein Regenschirm.*
T. *Ja, ein Regenschirm. Max hat einen Hund, und Fritz hat . . .?*
P. *Einen Regenschirm.*

This is much abbreviated and **P** does not represent the same pupil every time. Once this material is established, the facts could be written on the board and gradually added to, as more pin-men are drawn up with their possessions:

Max hat einen Hund, Fritz hat einen Regenschirm, Paul hat einen Korb.

In later lessons the same procedure will be followed with feminine objects like *Aktentasche, Zeitung* and neuter objects like *Buch, Fahrrad.* The teacher alone will know how often he needs to contrast nominative with accusative forms and when he can mix the genders. Then he can give his people more than one object and progress to exchanges like:

T. *Was wissen wir von Helga?*
P. *Sie hat ein Fahrrad, einen Korb und einen Regenschirm.*

Inevitably the teacher will then want to talk about what he himself has in his pocket and briefcase and what his pupils have on their desks, to ensure adequate practice of first and second person forms.

Further work could then be done by the teacher's putting up on the board a number of family-trees and asking oral and written questions about them:

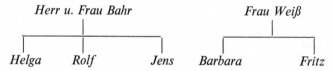

Possible questions. *Wieviele Kinder hat . . .? Hat . . . Söhne und Töchter? Hat . . . Brüder und Schwestern? Hat . . . zwei Brüder?*
Possible answers. *Er hat | sie haben drei. Sie hat einen Sohn und eine Tochter. Er hat einen Bruder und eine Schwester. Nein, nur einen.*

Additionally the names of fictitious housewives could be written on the board and the class could be told that they all have shopping bags. What they have in their bags is indicated by sticking up pictures next to their names: *eine Flasche Wein, ein Brot, eine Zeitung, eine Schallplatte, eine neue Strumpfhose, ein Schreibblock.* Such pictures can be culled from magazines. The appropriate question here will be:

Was hat Frau X in ihrer Einkaufstasche? Einen Schreibblock, etc.

Massive practice is then possible as names are added and the purchases altered. The names of the objects could be written up as a list on one side of the board as an *aide-mémoire* – and since it is the case, and not memory of gender, which is the target of the practice, it might be helpful to follow the practice of using a colour-code in the list: blue for masculine nouns, red for feminine and green for neuter.

Tragen. Pictures and drawings provide the necessary stimulus for statements like:

> *sie trägt eine Bluse, er trägt einen Anzug,* and eventually: *er trägt einen blauen Anzug.*

The final stimulus here might well be not a question but an instruction:

> **T.** *Beschreib' | beschreiben Sie den Mann!*
> **P.** *Er trägt einen blauen Anzug, ein weißes Hemd und einen gestreiften Schlips.*

Such descriptions can then be extended to the learners themselves – describing one another and even having the satisfaction of being able to describe themselves more fully in German than just giving name, address and age. This kind of language use suggests a simple game: one member of the class leaves the room and in his absence the rest choose one of their number as the object of the game. The pupil outside returns and must discover who the chosen person is by asking no more than six simple questions in German, to which the class answers with either *ja* or *nein*:

> *Ist es ein Junge | ein Mädchen?   Trägt er ein graues Hemd?*
> *Hat er rotes Haar?   Trägt er einen blauen Pullover?*
> *Trägt er eine Brille?   Hat er einen gelben Bleistift auf dem Pult?*

Stage 3

Stages 1 and 2 will be recognized as the bread and butter of oral work; each teacher will want to add his own ideas and reject some of the examples given. He will probably extend his pupils' mastery with carefully worded dictations and by asking for written statements of the pupils' own possessions and the clothes they wear, beginning with:

> *Ich habe zu Hause | in meinem Pult. . . .*
> *Gewöhnlich | in der Schule | zu Hause | sonntags trage ich. . . .*

However, even more practice is probably needed and the following drills or exercises are offered as possibilities which seem more meaningful than those which invite pupils to turn words into the accusative for no good reason. It is not suggested that they represent 'natural' language use, but they do try to give a context and the learner is required to do some thinking; responses will not be mindless. The data of the drills can be given:

- in duplicated handouts, as a test in the classroom or for homework;
- on an overhead projector;
- on a sheet to be taken into the language laboratory;
- on a blackboard – providing unlimited variety.

Drill type 1

In the left-hand column are the names of people; at the head of the chart are the names of clothes (*tragen*) or possessions (*haben*):

	Pullover	Bluse	Hemd	Rock	Hose	Schlips
Helga	√	√			√	
Michael	√		√		√	√
Franz			√		√	
Eva		√		√		

Any number of people can be used and the teacher places his ticks to show what each is wearing, making sure that the result would be reasonable. At first 'warm-up' questions can be used in which the learner merely shows comprehension:

T. *Wer trägt eine Bluse und einen Rock?*
P. *Eva.*

Subsequently, the learner has to interpret the data and give the facts:

T. *Was trägt Michael?*
P. *Er trägt einen Pullover, ein Hemd*, etc.
T. *Beschreib' | beschreiben Sie Franz!*
P. *Er trägt ein Hemd und eine Hose.*

	Haus	Wagen	Garage	Garten	Wohnung
Herr A	√		√	√	
Herr B	√	√	√	√	
Frau C		√	√		√
H. u. Fr. D	√	√	√		
H. u. Fr. E	√	√		√	
die Geschwister F		√			√

T. *Was hat Herr A?*
P. *Er hat ein Haus, eine Garage und einen Garten.*
T. *Was haben die Geschwister F?*
P. *Sie haben eine Wohnung und einen Wagen.*

Worded differently, this drill could be used to practise *besitzen*.

Drill type 2

Basically the same as above, but here the teacher agrees with his class that the first-named person has a complete 'set' of possessions or clothes and that a full description of the others will include what they do **not** have or are **not** wearing:

	Garage	Fernseher	Wagen	Haus
Herr A	√	√	√	√
Frau B			√	√
H. u. Fr. C		√	√	√
Geschwister D	√	√		√

T. *Herr A hat ein Haus, eine Garage, einen Wagen und einen Fernseher. Und Frau B?*
P. *Sie hat ein Haus und einen Wagen, aber keine Garage und keinen Fernseher.*

In this drill it is best not to mix the sexes when practising *tragen*; there is little value in sentences like *er trägt ein Hemd, aber er trägt keine Bluse.*

	Mütze	Jacke	Hemd	Schlips	Pullover	Hose
Martin	√	√	√	√	√	√
Franz		√	√		√	√
Heinrich		√	√	√		√

(This drill could be used in other languages, although the target would be different in detail. In French it would be *pas de*:

Marcel porte un pantalon, une chemise et une cravate, mais il ne porte pas de casquette.

or even *ni . . . ni*:

Franz (above) *porte un pullover, une chemise, un pantalon et un veston, mais il ne porte ni casquette ni cravate.*

In Russian it would practise the way of expressing possession, the case of noun and pronoun after y and the genitive after negatives:

у Виктора есть дом, а у него нет машины)

Drill type 3

This drill uses the negative and concentrates on small sets where the response could have the accusative in the sentence before *haben*:

	Bruder	Schwester		Wagen	Garage		Gabel	Messer	Löffel
Fritz	√	√	Hannes	√	√	Rolf	√	√	√
Hans		√	Otto		√	Ruth	√		√
Barbara	√		Helga	√		Franz		√	√

T. *Fritz hat einen Bruder und eine Schwester. Und Barbara auch?*
P. *Nein, einen Bruder hat sie, aber keine Schwester.*
T. *Rolf hat eine Gabel, ein Messer und einen Löffel. Ruth auch?*
P. *Nein, eine Gabel und einen Löffel hat sie, aber kein Messer.*

Other possible pairs: *Radio | Plattenspieler, Sohn | Tochter, Haus | Garten.*

Drill type 4

This drill is entirely verbal and requires the comprehension of a short factual statement. The general idea is to give information in which a noun is in the nominative and then required a restatement of the facts with the noun now in the accusative. The first examples include adjectives, since this helps to distinguish between masculine and neuter nouns:

Model **Facts.** *Ein grüner Wagen steht in Manfreds Garage.*
           Q. *Was hat Manfred in seiner Garage?*
           A. *Einen grünen Wagen.*

In what follows the genders are kept separate. However, greater demands will be made on the learner when the genders are subsequently mixed:

Facts. *Ein brauner Schrank steht in Manfreds Schlafzimmer.*
Ein alter Regenmantel hängt in Manfreds Garderobe.
Ein roter Lehnstuhl steht in Manfreds Wohnzimmer.

Eine große Kuckucksuhr hängt in Manfreds Wohn-
zimmer.
Eine grüne Tischlampe steht neben Manfreds Bett.
Eine moderne Waschmaschine steht in Manfreds
Küche.
Eine sehr alte Eiche steht in Manfreds Garten.

Ein braunes Sofa steht in Manfreds Wohnzimmer.
Ein neues Fahrrad steht in Manfreds Garage.
Ein englisches Wörterbuch liegt auf Manfreds Schreib-
tisch.
Ein schönes Bild hängt in Manfreds Eßzimmer.

Model **Facts.** *Helgas Hut ist rot.*
Q. *Was trägt Helga?*
A. *Einen roten Hut.*

Facts. *Ottos Schlips ist gelb.*
Peters Anzug ist grau.
Hedwigs Pullover ist schwarz.

Manfreds Jacke ist alt.
Ottos Hose ist blau.
Evas Bluse ist weiß.
Magdas Strickjacke ist gelb.

Werners Fußballhemd ist gestreift.
Hildegards Kleid ist kariert.
Brigittes Halstuch ist grün.
Jürgens Sporthemd ist weiß.

When all of this work has been completed, it is obviously still premature to describe the accusative case as 'done' – the definite article and use after prepositions have not yet been taught, for example – but the three stages described serve to indicate the kind of grading of material and opportunities for practice which the writer feels are necessary if more than the very able minority are to make progress in grasping and using the case-structure of a language like German.

MARK GILBERT

Formerly University of London Institute of Education

Grading and selecting

The selection and grading of linguistic material is a fundamental and difficult problem in language teaching. Faulty selection and bad grading can result in an enormous amount of time wasted and they can be the cause of much confusion for the learner. Many aspects of this topic are developed in other chapters; here the chief object is to discuss in more general terms the selection and grading of (1) patterns, (2) exercises including question and answer work, (3) textual material, (4) lexical items, (5) visual material. Assumptions underlying the discussion are that the approach to language teaching is oral, that the main function of language is to convey meaning, and that foreign-language teaching is concerned with the formation of new linguistic habits and the acquisition of new skills.

Selection involves the choice of the most useful patterns, of exercises which justify the time spent on them, of texts suitable for specific purposes and at the correct level of difficulty for the particular class, and of pictures which clearly convey the meaning intended.

Grading implies the simplest progression from step to step, from pattern to pattern.

The teacher should aim at both ease and quality of learning – economy of effort for both teacher and pupil, and the kind of learning which will result in clear understanding, meaningful practice, relatively flexible and fluent reproduction and firm retention: 'No amount of sentence-constructing ingenuity will compensate for the inability to produce "clean-cut" responses. The "clean-cut" response is one of the indispensable conditions of progress in the study of a living language. The student either possesses a given sentence or he does not possess it.'[1] If the teacher requires responses to questions which are obviously beyond the capacity of his pupils, he will not get such a response, therefore the speech material forming the groundwork of the lesson should never be in excess of the pupils' capacity for assimilating it.

An oral approach implies that pupils should learn to say each pattern before they read and write it. It is almost impossible to grade material too simply for oral work. Too much presented at once, too many new words or patterns produce confusion, poor retention, inaccurate reproduction, discouragement because pupils have continually to re-learn what they have never learnt properly. They can only learn orally one or two patterns at a time. They cannot, for instance, assimilate and use orally a whole new paradigm or tense of an irregular verb at once. They will have to learn to use the separate persons one by one, in a certain order. In the traditional coursebook the tense is the unit of learning. The whole tense is presented and learnt in a fixed order. If the pupil is then given a written exercise, he is expected to select the appropriate person, and the outcome depends mainly on his intelligence. In oral work this practice is self defeating, since the pupil has obviously no time to run through the whole tense before selecting the appropriate person. He has a different problem – to produce immediately, according to the context, the relevant oral pattern. One single tense consists of a number of such patterns: sound patterns – for example, *je tiens, tu tiens, il tient* may be considered as one pattern (apart from the pronouns), but the three persons of the plural constitute three different patterns. Any one of these has to be produced at once in response to the relevant stimulus – usually a question. Thus in this example the four relevant stimuli have to be provided one by one until a 'clean-cut' response is received in each case.

The teaching of the perfect tense provides an example of grading within the teaching of a single tense. There are numerous problems and these are seriously underestimated by many writers of coursebooks. It needs to be taught in graded steps:

1. The perfect with *avoir* is relatively easy to acquire, with regular verbs and with no pronoun objects. The introduction of pronouns can be postponed for some time if specific questions are asked which require a noun in the answer – after actions are seen to have been done (*dessiner, fermer, indiquer, montrer, toucher, essuyer*) as follows:

Qu'est-ce qu'il a fait?   *Il a fermé la porte.*

or

Est-ce qu'il a fermé la fenêtre?   *Non, il a fermé la porte.*

2. After step 1 irregular past participles can be gradually introduced (*écrit, pris, ouvert*, etc.), one by one, and thoroughly practised
in different situations. Oral practice of such irregularities is by far
the best way of ensuring better written work and of avoiding the
O-level absurdities like *boiré, prenu, misé*, etc., which abound in
both the oral and written examinations.

3. Perhaps next some of the verbs with *être* may be taught, although
there are linguists who think they should be taught first. This perfect
has its own six patterns, but these are, of course, those of the present
tense of *être*, which should be well known already. The chief difficulty, however, lies in acquiring an awareness of when to use *être*
for the thirteen verbs, and the only way to achieve this is by considerable practice of each verb separately, in a large number of
different contexts, especially narratives, where such common verbs
frequently recur. In time, perhaps two or three years, even weaker
pupils can acquire this awareness, provided that negative forms and
other distractors have not been forced on them too soon. The anti-
thesis of all this, as regards grading, is the giving of a list of the
thirteen verbs to learn, or the use of mnemonics and the chanting of
complete paradigms, in the positive, negative, etc., in the hope that
something will be retained in the memory.

4. The reflexive verb offers six quite different patterns to learn;
each person has therefore to be practised separately in an appropriate context. The remarkable mistakes made in O-level and other
written examinations reveal insufficient practice separately of *je me
suis, il s'est*, etc., until a 'clean-cut' response is obtained.

5. Pronoun objects should be introduced before the negative. Then
there are two oral patterns for each person: *il l'a mangé(e)* and *il les a
mangé(e)s*. Different verb + pronoun clusters are obtained with two
pronoun objects: *il le lui a envoyé, il me l'a envoyé*. However, careful and persistent practice with a number of well-known verbs will
gradually help pupils to make analogies and so produce correct
responses with new verbs.

6. With each of the three types of perfect the negative introduces
new patterns. If the previous steps have been thoroughly learnt with
a limited number of verbs, this step will be simplified.

7. Sentences with both negatives and pronoun objects should perhaps be avoided for a long time, except for comprehension or with
bright pupils.

8. The agreement of the past participle with *avoir* is mainly a

written problem, but some teachers think it is helpful to practise first the few common participles which are sounded in the feminine: *il les a prises, ouvertes, mises.* This may instil some idea of the need for a different written ending in the pupil's mind. The agreement with *être* is best treated as an adjectival problem, and can be introduced much more quickly. With reflexive verbs the form *elle s'est lavée* is sufficient for some time, avoiding *elle s'est lavé les mains.*

Thus there are many problems involved in the teaching of the perfect tense, which is a key tense, whose introduction cannot be limited to three lessons in a course-book. It is also obvious that unless the perfect is thoroughly mastered, the pluperfect will present the same problems and possible confusion.

There is also the general question of the gradation of tenses. It seems that the present tense should be taught first – for continuous activities because pictures are used with effect in the first year, and for habitual activities because of the necessity to relate verbs taught in the third person through pictures to the everyday lives of the pupils when the first and second persons are practised.

Traditionally the future tense has been taught next, but perhaps the 'immediate' future – *je vais chanter demain* – is more frequently used and is simpler. It provides also a useful way of introducing the infinitive.

Next the perfect tense can be introduced very gradually as indicated above. But as soon as stories, related in the past, are used, it seems essential to introduce the imperfect tense in its appropriate place in stories – the three uses presented separately – so that its functions may gradually be recognized. These two tenses will then be used in conjunction and practised through question and answer up to CSE or O level.

The future tense will perhaps come next, in the third year, and then the pluperfect, using the verbs mastered in the perfect, and re-tracing the same learning steps. For some pupils the conditional will be introduced in the fourth year, when the future of many verbs is well known. The past historic tense will be used for reading only. Perhaps the traditional habit of asking questions in this tense – even at O level – has now disappeared.

According to one pre-war investigation in Canada on types of mistakes in the learning of French, about 60–65 per cent of errors are committed in using verb patterns[2]; hence the necessity for such careful gradation in their teaching and the likelihood that it will take four years at least for the majority of pupils to master them. To include them all in book 2 (except the past historic), as happens in so many traditional courses, can hardly be said to constitute simple grading.

Other patterns too have their problems, which mainly result from the traditional habit of teaching a complete category at once – without any attempt at grading – a habit inherited from the 'grammar-translation' method. There seems to have been, and perhaps still is, a delusion that the child will be helped by seeing the whole category (or paradigm) at once. In fact it presents a bewildering array to most pupils. Grammatical categories have to be split up into their component parts and the separate items taught one by one in appropriate meaningful situations, e.g. demonstrative and possessive adjectives and pronouns, the genitive and dative of the definite article, the partitive article. Personal pronoun objects certainly present the most obvious example of the necessity for careful grading. There are two stages: (1) one single pronoun before the verb; (2) two pronouns together in their correct order. Together with *ne – (pas)* they form the various verb 'clusters' which need special attention.

In each group the 'football team', so admired of old, has to be split up into relevant cohesive groups to be taught separately:

1. *le, la, les.* Taught one by one, and then practised by switching from one to the other until fluency is obtained. Pupils cannot really use these until they can slip them into an answer in place of a noun in a question: e.g. *Est-ce qu'elle vend le journal au monsieur ou à la dame? – Elle le vend à la dame.*

2. *lui, leur.* The same comments apply: *Qu'est-ce qu'elle vend à la dame? Elle lui vend un journal.*

3. *me, te, nous, vous. Est-ce qu'il vous (t') a donné un vélo? – Non, il nous (m') a donné une moto.*

4. *y. Il y va à pied.*

5. *en.* Presents many different patterns. *Il y en a, il en a, j'en ai,* etc.

From the oral point of view these have to be acquired separately and, of course, gradually. Once again each step is greatly complicated by the introduction of the negative, which should therefore be postponed until the pronouns are freely used in the affirmative sentence. The same applies to their use with the perfect tense. *Il ne les a pas donnés à sa soeur* constitutes a big step forward from the affirmative. Teachers should be very careful about grading all the steps with the different persons.

The use of these pronouns before the infinitive has to be isolated from the above, and also their use in affirmative and negative commands. At least a year should elapse before any attempt is made to practise the order when two pronouns come together before the verb. An oral examiner at O level is quite pleased to hear single pronouns used correctly. It is often easy and advisable to avoid the use of 'two-pronoun' groups, and it is doubtful whether their active use should be recommended for CSE pupils.

When two pronouns are used in conjunction, they present different groups or 'clusters', which have to be mastered one by one:

1. *le*	*lui*	2. *l'*	*y*	3. *lui*	*en*	4. *m'*	*y*
la	*leur*	*les*		*leur*		*t'*	
les						*nous*	*en*
						vous	

The perfect tense (the first compound tense to be learnt) and the 'category' of personal pronouns present so many complications that they have to be acquired in carefully graded progressive steps over a period of years, and hence are sometimes called 'progressive' patterns, in contrast to some other categories which contain fewer items or separate structures and may therefore be acquired in a much shorter time, and are sometimes called 'static' patterns, e.g. demonstrative and possessive adjectives and pronouns, the partitive article.

But these too must be divided into their various structures, each of which must be taught separately. Some examples are to be found in other chapters. It is doubtful, however, whether there is much to be gained by adopting for classroom purposes the two names mentioned above.

Many teachers are of the opinion that, although each separate structure may be best acquired through usage in meaningful situations, there comes a time when each category or tense should be viewed as a whole. With tenses or paradigms there is some support for this view in the fact that in French many verb endings are silent, and that therefore one should be able to refer to the paradigm only for spelling purposes. Yet there are cases where an analytical view of a complete category may even destroy temporarily what has been carefully built up over the years. This is especially true of interrogative pronouns. Pupils learn one by one the various forms and can use *Qu'est-ce qui? Qu'est-ce que? Avec quoi? Lequel?*, etc., quite happily until one day they are confronted with the whole list, the different forms are 'explained' and the pupils are asked to study the list. After this they make more mistakes than before. Grammatical analysis in this case is best left until the sixth form, and the same is probably true in the case of the relative pronoun.

There is no immutable order of events even in the first year. Traditional course-books have, on the whole, instituted a traditional order for which there is no pedagogical or linguistic justification, e.g. *en* usually appears in the second year, but *il y en a* can be taught efficiently and reasonably in the first few lessons of the first term. What is certainly both possible and practical is to teach what are sometimes called 'horizontal' slices of language rather than the 'vertical' blocks favoured by traditionalists. This simply means, for instance, that the third singular of a few verbs may be taught rather than the whole tense of one verb, whilst at the same time structures are gradually introduced from other categories, e.g. *mon, ma, son, sa*, before introducing *ses*; *du* genitive (or partitive) before or at least separately from *de la* genitive (or partitive), which will be left for a later lesson. This method of teaching simultaneously individual structures from different categories springs naturally from the principle of teaching through situations, at first pictorial and then narrative. It is the opposite of 'grammatical' teaching, through complete tenses or categories.

There is, however, obviously some interdependence between patterns. The essential or helpful word or pattern will have to be taught first, before the dependent pattern is reached, e.g. the perfect tense before the pluperfect, the infinitive before the future tense, the future before the conditional, the indefinite article before the definite. *Avoir* and *être* (present tenses) should be thoroughly mastered before the perfect tense is attempted. It has been found helpful to teach family relationships before the possessive adjectives, e.g. *le frère de Marcel* before *son frère*. These and other essential or helpful steps are not always thoroughly taught.

In this brief chapter it is possible to consider only a few of the many detailed problems involved.

1. Traditional courses almost invariably begin the first lesson with the definite article: *c'est le livre* (although no book has been

mentioned). Logic and normal usage indicates that *c'est* **un** *livre* is the form used first for identification.

2. The link between *un, une, des* and *le, la, les* must later be carefully made, or pupils may be confused, e.g. (through pictures).

Voici une tente et un garçon.
Le garçon est dans la tente.

3. In **oral** French most nouns are invariable in the plural, since the final 's' is silent. Thus whether a noun in French is singular or plural is generally revealed orally by the pronunciation of the preceding word, the 'determinative', e.g. *le livre, les livres* = | lə livr, le livr, mɔ̃ livr, me livr |, etc. These determinative words are very important, yet they are often neglected.

Because there are two oral forms of *le* and *les* (i.e. prevocalic or otherwise), both forms require separate thorough practice, i.e. | lɑ̃fɑ̃, lez ɑ̃fɑ̃ |. Similarly with *aux enfants* = | oz ɑ̃fɑ̃ |, *mes, tes, ses, des, ces*.

4. The use of *il(s)* and *elle(s)* for nouns in answer to questions is a major difficulty, which should, however, be faced immediately. The longer it is avoided the more difficult it becomes.

5. With *du, de la, des*, genitive or partitive, some teachers believe it is best to practise *du* first really thoroughly, since it so often degenerates into *de le*. Experience seems to confirm this view.

6. *Moi, toi, lui, elle*, etc., might well be taught before the conjunctive personal pronoun, since they present far fewer problems of position and sequence, for English-speaking children, e.g. *Donnez-moi un bonbon. Tu viens avec moi? C'est à toi, à lui*, etc.

7. Prepositions are usually introduced before adjectives because they are invariable and fit into easy concrete situations.

8. Which adjectives should be introduced first – *bleu, noir, jaune, rouge, jeune* (same pronunciation masculine and feminine, singular and plural) or *grand, petit, assis, vert, gris, content*, etc. (different pronunciation)? Some teachers believe in teaching the latter first, as pupils seem then to remember more about the changes when writing. Some linguists believe it is advisable to teach the feminine of such adjectives first, since it is easier for a pupil to learn to drop the last sound from the feminine, e.g. | pətit — pəti | than to add it to the masculine. With regard to the position of adjectives, it is considered

better to practise first of all some adjectives which follow the noun in French rather than those which precede the noun as in English (cp. Politzer[3]).

The above examples are only a few amongst many and are included in order to stress the importance of the detailed consideration of grading. Teachers should consider carefully the problems relevant to their own classes. In general, the more the course progresses the more flexibility is possible.

One of the chief difficulties for any language student is caused by the **interference** of patterns of the mother-tongue. English pupils have acquired fixed language habits which are very difficult to overcome. The teacher must, of course, note these and give regular corrective practice. The trouble is worse when sometimes there is a parallel with English and sometimes not, e.g.

1. The perfect tense
   He has eaten, *il a mangé*
   He has gone, *il est parti*
2. Position of adjectives
   Un bon professeur
   Un professeur intelligent
3. *C'est un bon professeur*
   Il est professeur

'It is much easier to teach the contrasting constructions if the parallel ones are not introduced simultaneously, but are presented only after the contrasting constructions have been firmly established'[3] (p. 138). This would indicate, for instance, that the perfect with *être* should be taught first.

English teachers will be aware of many other cases of interference, e.g. position of object pronouns, negatives, *depuis*, expressions with *avoir* and *faire*, question order after a noun, and many verbal constructions, e.g. verbs like *demander*, or *chercher*, or *obéir*, verbs which take *à* + infinitive, etc.

Patterns which are easily confused should be separated in time, e.g. affirmative and negative of present and perfect tenses; *il en a* and *il y en a* and their negatives; *cet, bel, vieil*, etc., and their feminine forms.

All this affects grading to a considerable extent. Practice of such difficulties must be built into a syllabus with repeated revision. This is essential with verbal structures. Fortunately these constructions occur so frequently that this is not difficult. Learning lists of such verbs cannot solve the problem.

Comparison of English and French is not necessarily the best way of overcoming these difficulties, especially in the early stages of the course. It may even confuse the student. For him nothing can replace the drill and meaningful use of the French speech patterns[3] (pp. 153–4).

The selection of the most profitable **exercises**, oral and written, is obviously one of the teacher's most important responsibilities. Perhaps it is relevant to consider first what we expect the pupils to be able to achieve by O or CSE level, from the oral point of view. We hope that they will be able to ask and answer simple questions on useful topics from everyday life, and to make statements about what they have done recently, what they do regularly, and what they will do shortly or in future vacations. Why not use these two kinds of oral activity as the main forms of practice? They can then learn how to write down what they can say.

When pupils answer questions in French they have to:

(a) understand the question,
(b) refer it to its situation,
(c) select the correct answer according to the context,
(d) change patterns, e.g. put pronouns instead of nouns, change the persons and/or tense of verbs.

This is both a practice and a test and very profitable, giving meaningful and flexible learning and reproduction. Some pupils will be able to answer more and more complicated questions and to make longer statements about what they have read or seen, leading to compositions.

It is obvious that questions will have to be carefully graded in order of difficulty, e.g. 'teaching' questions such as *Est-ce qu'il joue bien ou mal?* will precede 'testing' questions such as *Comment est-ce qu'il joue?*; teaching questions such as the specific verb questions *Qu'est-ce qu'il vend, achète, lit, écrit, porte?* should be practised before the general question, *Qu'est-ce qu'il fait?*, is attempted. Questions which require one-word answers or prepositional clauses, e.g. *Qui, quand, où?* should be put before those which demand longer answers, e.g. *Pourquoi?* Examples of such question and answer work will be found in other chapters.

There are, however, some patterns which it is either very difficult or impossible to practise by means of natural questions and answers, e.g. negatives and conditional sentences. Perhaps here it is possible to use 'mechanical' pattern practice, which in general is inferior as an exercise to question and answer, since pupils often complete such exercises correctly without even knowing the meaning and their transfer value is doubtful. The learning of conversations by heart is no solution, since it does not lead necessarily to fluency in language. The pupil can only repeat the language so learnt in a rigid way. 'Pattern drills and dialogue memorization have not led automatically to fluency in varied situations.'[4]

Multiple-choice grammar 'exercises' are of very doubtful value, e.g. *Il (êtes, suis, est) dans le jardin*; *Il peut (chanté, chanter, chantez)*. The pupil is compelled to study two wrong patterns as well as the correct one. Why introduce him needlessly to incorrect forms? These exercises are really a disguised form of 'traditional' exercise.[5]

The two most fruitful exercises are, therefore, in this writer's opinion, question and answer work and varied graded compositions.

Selection also includes the careful choice of **textual material**. In the first year, situations which are capable of pictorial representation should be used and the texts should in general be an exact description of the relevant pictures. They should not be in the form of conversations, since it is impossible to devise pictures which depict accurately what two people are saying to each other. At this early stage, too, conversational material is much more difficult to grade than descriptions of simple pictures. Very brief conversations on everyday activities, **if based on language already learnt**, may however be usefully introduced as an auxiliary practice.

Brief narrative texts should be introduced when the perfect tense is being learnt, linked sometimes with a series of pictures which tell a story. In a picture or narrative passage it is possible to find linguistic elements of different categories which naturally come together in the passage, and so they should quite naturally be practised together, regardless of grammatical categories. In other words, situations should, at this stage, be allowed to produce their own practice, which will then be quite naturally linked with an obvious context. This, of course, implies that a teacher will choose his passage carefully to suit the ability of his class, and that he will make notes of the patterns thus introduced and practised. This is what has been described earlier in this chapter as grading through situations.

Writers of traditional textbooks who introduce a complete new category and perhaps new tenses of three irregular verbs in one lesson find it almost impossible to write a passage which will exemplify all the items in the category. Often they give only one or two examples of the new category or tense; or, in striving to exemplify all the items, they create a stilted, unnatural and overloaded text.

All pictures and most texts introduced, at least in the first three years, should be suitable for intensive oral practice through question and answer. They should usually deal with a narrative situation, a series of incidents with possibilities for contrastive practice, taken from everyday life, and introducing few new words.

In the selection of **lexical items**, there must be a distinction between 'function' words and 'content' words. Function words, which denote relationships and grammatical meanings, belong to syntax – words like pronouns or the negatives in French, whose use depends mainly upon grammatical considerations. They must be learned as part of the whole construction. These, from the points of view of grading, obviously come within the ambit of grammar.

An oral approach will necessarily imply the introduction of very few new 'content' words in each school lesson. Advanced language students who have been exposed to a new language such as Russian, Polish or Welsh have agreed that they can only learn to use five to seven new words in a short oral lesson, and these have to be revised in the next lesson. Thus it is quite wrong to include twenty, thirty, forty or even fifty new words in one textbook lesson for average young children. They cannot even learn to read such material; they can only decipher, transliterate, and little useful oral practice is possible. In the first two or three years most pupils will have difficulty in acquiring the essential structures and they should not be overloaded with lexical items.

Later in the course, in the fourth year of a five-year course (or possibly in the third year for able pupils), there may be a conscious attempt to widen more rapidly the passive vocabulary by:

1. The teaching of (a) cognates (words similar in form and meaning), e.g. actor, *acteur*, joyous, *joyeux*; (b) families of words, based on a word in the text studied, e.g. *mentir* might include the mention of *un mensonge, (un) menteur, long* might bring in *allonger, la longueur*. The extent to which this is used will obviously depend on the ability of the class, and selection and grading are here still essential.

2. Rapid reading of graded readers, for comprehension only. (See

section on 'reading', p. 251ff.). Which words should be selected? Briefly there seem to be two complementary methods: (a) to use the vocabulary of *Le Français fondamental*; (b) to make a list of centres of interest and 'survival situations' suitable for the pupils, drawn from their everyday activities, and from situations which may arise during travel in France or when staying with a French family.

The selection of **visual material** is discussed elsewhere in this book (pp. 193–204), and also earlier in this chapter. However, it is perhaps worth stressing here that pictorial material has only limited possibilities; for instance, as previously mentioned, pictures cannot reasonably be used to give the exact meaning of conversational material. Again, they cannot usually provide the meaning of tenses other than the present, except when used in a series. It is, for instance, much more practical and simple to use **times** to practise the past and future tenses than to use pictures with 'bubbles'.

Other chapters in this book will expand and exemplify in a much more detailed manner some of the topics presented rather summarily in this chapter.

Notes and references

1. PALMER, H. E. and D. (1959) *English through Actions*, pp. 20–1. London: Longman.
2. *American and Canadian Modern Foreign Language Study* (1931), vol. 6, pp. 475–89. Toronto: University of Toronto Press.
3. POLITZER, R. L. (1965) *Teaching French*. Waltham, Mass.: Blaisdell Publishing.
4. RIVERS, W. (1964) *The Psychologist and the Foreign-language Teacher*, p. 73. Chicago and London: University of Chicago Press.
5. Vid. *Modern Languages*, June 1961, 'Some problems of language teaching' for a fuller discussion of such 'traditional' exercises.

PART 2

Limited aims – the single structure

Before he begins to teach any structure or pattern, the foreign-language teacher has to ask himself a number of questions:

1. What is the correct form of what I want to teach?
2. When does the native speaker use it?
3. Which among the acceptable uses will be easiest and clearest to use in introducing the form to a class of schoolchildren.*
4. Are there special problems? An example would be the need to avoid, when teaching possessive adjectives in French, any attempt by English-speaking learners to equate *son* with 'his' and *sa* with 'her'.
5. Are there other pieces of language which ought to be taught first? There are German teachers, for example, who prefer their pupils to be able to cope with expressions like *um zu essen* before they start to teach prepositions like *in* and *an* with the accusative, because they are then able to ask questions like *wohin geht Fritz, um zu essen?* and require answers like *ins Restaurant.*
6. How can I provide my class with sufficient practice of the new pattern?

These questions have already been touched on in relation to the teaching of a new tense or a new case. In this section five examples are given of how teachers have tackled more restricted language forms: the difference between two Spanish verbs which both apparently mean 'to be', verbs of motion in Russian, *an . . . vorbei* in German and the partitive article and modal auxiliaries in French. The writers put forward their suggestions tentatively. It is hoped, however, that the examples will encourage teachers to tackle other areas in a similar manner.

*cp. HORNSEY, A. W. and M. and HARRIS, D. (1970) *On parle français 1, Teachers' Handbook*, pp. 44–6. London: Heinemann.

ANTHONY BENNETT

University of London Institute of Education

The Spanish verbs 'ser' and 'estar'

Traditionally the verbs *ser* and *estar* are regarded as a pair and are believed to constitute a learning problem. For example, in the well-known grammar *A Manual of Modern Spanish*, by L. C. Harmer and F. J. Norton, an entire chapter is devoted to these two verbs. Yet on the face of it they have little in common, since they neither belong to the same conjugation nor have similar functions except in so far as they both occasionally precede the same adjectives.

What, then, causes the problem for so many grammarians and teachers? What makes a similar difficulty of the verbs *tener* and *haber* and the prepositions *para* and *por*? It is, of course, the fact that each of these pairs can be translated into English by one word. The student who is trying to learn by translating an English sentence or word into Spanish is faced with a difficult choice long before he has been able to assimilate the correct forms of the language and develop a feeling for its structure. The ghost of translation haunts us so persistently that it is a great temptation to accept uncritically such statements as 'When the English verb "to be" implies a permanent or inherent quality the verb *ser* is used in Spanish, and when "to be" implies position or transitory state *estar* is used'. The value of this as a guide to the English learner is clearly reduced by the consideration that position is often permanent and inherent qualities can not infrequently be subject to change. If we remember as well that forms of the verbs *haber, quedarse, hallarse, encontrarse* and *ir* can also be translated as 'is' or 'are', the unhelpfulness of this approach becomes even more obvious.

It is difficult to see how one can translate from one language to another unless the specific pieces of language needed for the operation have already been learnt beforehand. Yet traditional grammars and textbooks end each chapter with two-way translation tests and abound with such statements as 'Learn the gerund of *dormir*', 'Study the imperfect subjunctive of *saber*' or 'learn the following

60

vocabulary'. The manner of learning or studying is left entirely to the devices of the pupil, thus leaving a methodological chasm for him to cross. As teachers, however, far from leaving the pupils to learn on their own, we have to concentrate on and concern ourselves with the very processes which the grammars take for granted.

If we are to devise a course in which translation is avoided as a learning exercise, we will want to teach our two verbs logically through the four major skills of understanding, speaking, reading and writing in the belief that oral mastery is the necessary basis for work leading to written fluency and accuracy. The crucial skill is understanding, since without translation meaning must be conveyed by other techniques. If we are to convey the meaning of *ser* and *estar* orally we will need to consider how meaning is conveyed in general.

First, it is conveyed at the elementary, concrete level by the use of a given piece of language in a real-life situation and by the linking of that language to real objects and people. The sentence *María esta sentada entre Carmen y Antonio* has meaning as soon as the teacher mimes and points to the appropriate people. Two or three similar situations with different people, some sitting and some standing, make the meaning even clearer. Second, the narrow restrictions of the real-life situation in the classroom can be widened by the use of visual symbols representing real-life situations and objects. (A mountain cannot be brought into the classroom, but a picture of one can be.) This, of course, constitutes the audio-visual stage of language learning. Finally, the mental images aroused by words themselves and conveyed by their context lead us to the audio-lingual stage and away from the concrete and visual level. At this stage definitions of words, similarities and contrasts between them, as well as their frequency of use all help to convey meaning at the advanced, abstract level.

An example of the development through the three stages is that provided by the problem of teaching the meaning of the simple past tense.

With the aid of a picture of a calendar we can say *Hoy es miércoles*. And pointing to the previous day on the calendar, *Ayer fué martes*. The pointing is mime (stage 1), the picture of the calendar is a visual aid (stage 2), and the contextualized words *hoy* and *ayer* are mental images which provide settings for the contrasted verb forms (stage 3). The meaning will then become even clearer and further defined on the introduction of other verbs used with *ayer* and the subsequent introduction of *mañana* with the future and so on.

If we draw up a list of the most common patterns of our two verbs in such a way that they range from the concrete to the abstract, and from the more frequent to the less, they will reflect the framework of meaning mentioned above and offer us a natural order for teaching them without translation:

Ser

1.	Identification of persons	*Es José.*
2.	Identification of things	*Es una casa.*
3.	Indication of possession	*Es la casa de Maria.*

Estar

4.	Indication of position	*La plaza está a la izquierda.*
5.	Progressive tenses	*Está leyendo una novela.*

Ser

6.	Indication of origins	*Es de Zaragoza.*
7.	Profession or occupation	*Es camarero.*
8.	Description by substance	*Es de madera.*
9.	Adjectives	*Aquel hombre es muy rico.*

Estar

10.	Past participle adjectives	*La puerta está cerrada.*
11.	Adjectives	*Está contento.*

Ser

12.	Adjectives with impersonal verbs	*Es necesario que venga.*
13.	Past participles forming passives	*Su libro fué estudiado por todos.*

We are now in a position to see which of the two verbs has the wider range of structure. It also becomes clear that before any of the structures with *estar* can be introduced a range of nouns will have to be taught with the help of *ser*. Since we are assuming not unreasonably that it is likely to be easier to learn one thing at a time rather than two, we shall have to teach *ser* first and *estar* at later stages.

While there is considerable freedom in arranging the structures in any order we want, the desire to be efficient will cause us to lay great store by such criteria as the relative simplicity and frequency of the patterns and usefulness for leading to further extensions of the language. The structure 1 is simpler in form than 2, since the complications of the gender of the article do not arise in the former. Similarly 3 is plainly more complicated than 2.

At this stage it is possible and desirable for the sake of variety and contrast as well as maximum potential use of what is yet a very limited range to introduce *estar* in the form of 4. Now persons and objects can be related in position to other persons and objects through prepositions. The number of combinations is mathematically high and with the introduction of 5 all nouns so far introduced can be permutated as both subjects and direct objects, the present continuous tense being the natural tense to use with pictures, figurines and other visual aids. The verbal ideas conveyed by the accompanying present participles later provide clues for the meanings of the simple present tense.

Of the remaining structures, 6, 7 and 8 are the most simple and offer further means of increasing vocabulary but in rather isolated areas, in the sense that they do not lead on readily to other useful patterns. All three of them lend themselves to visual presentation, though 7 is most limited in this respect and depends on forms of definition as well as the knowledge of verbs other than those we are concerned with here. 8 offers a way of describing objects to some extent without introducing adjectival agreement but is rather more limited in usefulness for further development than 7. 9 forces us to teach adjectival agreement and tends in many textbooks and courses to be overemphasized unnecessarily early on, particularly since it is a form so unnatural to the English speaker. Once this is done, however, the less frequent structures 10 and 11 can be introduced with *estar*, since they reinforce and make further use of adjectival agreement and both differ from 9 in a similar contextual way. 12 and 13 have been placed in this particular order largely because of their relative infrequency. The passive is a rare phenomenon in Spanish and since it is one of the two structures where both *ser* and *estar* can be followed by the same words, in this case past participles, its rarity tends to diminish any difficulty rather than augment it.

Similarly the use of *ser* with an adjective which is normally preceded by *estar* is also a rare occurrence, applying to only a very small number of adjectives, and is overemphasized by many teachers.

This brief analysis and suggested hierarchy of the structures used with *ser* and *estar* shows plainly that these two verbs have very little in common in their actual function.

How, then, do we get our pupils to comprehend the structures and speak them without confusion? The vital link between the skills of understanding and speaking is, of course, the technique of putting questions and eliciting answers. If the teacher has an understanding of the function of the different types of questions he can ask, the pupils can easily be led to produce language without translating.

There are four main kinds of question which can be asked on any given piece of language, and when arranged in a logical order they bring the student naturally from comprehension to production of the language. They are the 'yes' or 'no' answer type which we can call the comprehension question; the positive alternative question, where a choice is given; the negative alternative where the wrong answer is suggested and the learner is expected to supply the correct answer; and finally, the special or structural question which in Spanish begins with words such as *¿Qué? ¿Cómo? ¿Dónde? ¿Quién?* and so on. In all the four types of question there is an element of practising and an element of testing. Obviously in the first two the practising element is uppermost and in the last two the testing element is most evident.

The following examples based on structures 2, 4 and 5 show what a wide range of question is available to the teacher, even at the simplest level of language work. Each example has more than one item in it in order to produce a choice and show up the pattern involved.

Example 1

Es una casa   Es un molino   Es una montaña
1. *¿Es un molino? ¿Sí o no?*   *Sí/No.*
2. *¿Es una casa o un molino?*   *Es una casa.*
3. *¿Es un molino?*   *No, es una montaña.*
4. *¿Qué es?*   *Es una casa/un molino*, etc.

Example 2

El barco está en la botella. El pájaro está en la jaula.
1. *¿El pájaro está en la botella? ¿Sí o no?*
   Sí | No.
2. *¿El barco está en la jaula o en la botella?*
   (Está) en la botella.
3. *¿El pájaro, está en la botella?*
   No, está en la jaula.
4. *¿Dónde está el barco | el pájaro?*
   Está en la botella | la jaula.

Example 3

María está bailando.   Carlos está cantando.   Felipe está tocando una guitarra.

1.	*¿Carlos está cantando?*	*Sí.*
	¿Está bailando también?	*No.*
2.	*¿María está bailando o cantando?*	*Está bailando.*
	¿María está tocando o bailando?	*Está bailando.*
3.	*¿Felipe está bailando?*	*No, está tocando una guitarra.*
4.	*¿Quién está cantando / bailando, etc.?*	*Carlos, María, Felipe.*
	¿Qué están haciendo María y Carlos?	*Ella está bailando y él está cantando.*
	¿Qué instrumento está tocando Felipe?	*Una guitarra.*

The purpose of this list of questions is to show the range available, but it is not suggested that every one of them has to be asked each time a new piece of language is introduced. For some classes the special or structural questions with perhaps a few of the others will not present too much difficulty and will therefore be the normal technique used for faster learners, but for slower pupils, or where the comprehension of the language is more difficult, the first two kinds of questions can provide a finely graded ladder of success which will enable them eventually to answer the testing questions without the despair of non-comprehension which is experienced by many average and slower learners in oral lessons.

If structures like *ser* and *estar* and, indeed, the rest of the language patterns are approached through a controlled question and answer teaching sequence, the pupils build up a feeling for the language and its structures in a more natural way. The pupil who has often and systematically experienced the question *¿Dónde están ...?* and the pattern of the answer *Están en ...* would never think of translating at a later stage the question 'Where are your books?' or the answer 'They are on the shelf' with any other verb but *estar*. With a translation approach, however, little feeling for the language can possibly be nurtured and developed. It is a matter, then, not so much of separating *ser* from *estar* or *para* from *por*, but rather of providing sufficient controlled oral practice to cause an unbreakable association to occur between the language patterns to be learnt and the context in which they naturally arise.

The same is equally applicable to more advanced levels of language work. If the teacher is convinced that a particular structure is frequent enough to be worth teaching, he has to offer the learner a series of examples sufficiently numerous to make the pattern evident and to devise questions on the examples which promote linguistic experience of the pattern. The student who can answer the question *¿Qué dijo que no era necesario?* with *que su amiga estuviese en casa todo el día* is not likely to experience much difficulty in deciding whether to use *ser* or *estar*, since it is impossible to produce this kind of answer without having first had a great deal of practice and real experience of the language involved.

The result of insisting on a basically oral approach, then, is that our energies are redirected away from artificial problems towards the more rewarding realities of the language as it is spoken and used. If we persist in this, our sense of proportion is improved and we begin to realize what is important to teach and what can be omitted until a later stage. Translation instead of clouding our vision can then be used as an exercise in its own right, in its proper place at the more advanced stages of the language learning process.

G. M. SINCLAIR AND JOHN M. SHARMAN

Ravensbourne School for Girls, Bromley, Kent

The preposition 'an . . . vorbei'

These lessons are intended for pupils who are already familiar with the dative case used after prepositions. They will also have used verbs with separable prefixes in sentences like *Herr Braun steht um sieben Uhr auf.* Particularly in the early stages, the buildings used will also have been taught before. Additional, new buildings could be added later when the new pattern is well established.

The introduction is made without a text but with the aid of drawings (pp. 68–71). Each pupil could have his own copy, but there will be a large master copy drawn or pinned on the board as a focus of attention to which the teacher can refer by pointing. Alternatively an overhead projector could be used.

1. Character and locality are introduced:

Teacher. *Kurt Stempel ist Postarbeiter. Er wohnt in der Königsallee in Kleinstadt. Seine Arbeit beginnt jeden Morgen um halb neun. Er geht zu Fuß dorthin. Er braucht eine halbe Stunde.*

Questions. *Was ist Kurt von Beruf? Wo arbeitet er also? In welcher Stadt wohnt er? In welcher Straße? Wann beginnt seine Arbeit? Wie geht Kurt zur Arbeit? Wie lange braucht er? Wann verläßt er also das Haus?*

2. The details of Kurt's walk to work are now introduced:

Teacher. *Er verläßt sein Haus in der Königsallee um acht Uhr. Er überquert die Straße und biegt in die Kirchstraße ein. In der Kirchstraße sind drei Gebäude: die Peterskirche, die Max Planck Schule, die Bäckerei „Semmel".*

These buildings are pointed to on the drawings and their names and Kurt's actions are thoroughly practised, with the teacher pointing to the blackboard as appropriate:

Wie heißt diese Straße?	*Die Königsallee.*
Wem gehört dieses Haus?	*Es gehört Kurt Stempel.*
Was macht Kurt um acht Uhr?	*Er verläßt sein Haus.*
Was macht er dann?	*Er überquert die Straße.*
Wie heißt das erste Gebäude in der Kirchstraße?	*Die Peterskirche.*
Welches Gebäude steht neben der Kirche?	*Die Max Planck Schule.*
Wie heißt das nächste Gebäude?	*Die Bäckerei ,,Semmel".*
Zwischen welchen zwei Gebäuden steht also die Schule?	*Zwischen der Kirche und der Bäckerei.*
Vor welchem Gebäude spielen Kinder?	*Vor der Schule.*

3. The pattern *an . . . vorbei* is now introduced. A movable cardboard figure is useful here.

Teacher. *Hier ist Kurt. Er verläßt sein Haus, biegt in die Kirchstraße ein und geht an der Kirche und an der Schule vorbei.*

Practice in chorus follows: *an der Schule – vorbei – an der Schule vorbei*, each item being said in unison by the class and then repeated by individual pupils. The phrase is then written on the board and read aloud.

Geht Kurt hier an der Schule vorbei?	*Nein, an der Kirche vorbei.*
Wo steht der Baum?	*Neben der Kirche?*
Was macht Kurt wieder? Geht er in	
die Kirche?	*Nein, an der Kirche vorbei.*

The figure of Kurt is now moved on:

An welchem Gebäude geht er hier	
vorbei?	*An der Schule.*
Was macht Kurt? (to another pupil)	*Er geht an der Schule*
	vorbei.
Wie heißt das dritte Gebäude in der	
Kirchstraße?	*Die Bäckerei ,,Semmel.''*

At this point the routine is deliberately broken. Pupils must learn when **not** to use the structure being practised. The teacher says *Kurt kauft gewöhnlich Brötchen für die Morgenpause*, and the figure is pushed **into** the shop:

Geht Kurt an der Bäckerei vorbei?	*Nein, er geht in die Bäckerei.*

At this point it is probably wise to revise orally and in writing the material learnt so far, contrasting *an . . . vorbei* with *in, neben, vor.*

The teacher now continues Kurt's walk and takes the necessary opportunity to see whether his class will use *an . . . vorbei* with a feminine noun not previously practised:

Teacher. *Um fünf nach acht kommt er aus der Bäckerei und geht weiter.*

Was steht vor der Bäckerei?	*Eine Telefonzelle* (practised if
	new)
Geht Kurt in die Telefonzelle?	*Nein, an der Telefonzelle vorbei.*

If this is correctly produced, Kurt can be allowed to continue his walk.

4. Masculine and neuter words are now introduced.

Teacher. *Kurt biegt um die Ecke in die nächste Straße. Sie heißt die Bahnhofstraße. In der Bahnhofstraße sind das Bahnhofsrestaurant, das Bahnhofshotel und der Südbahnhof.*
Gerda Kurzbein ist Kellnerin und sie geht jeden Morgen in das Bahnhofsrestaurant, wo sie arbeitet.

Ist Kurt Stempel auch Kellner?	*Nein, Postarbeiter.*
Geht er ins Restaurant, um zu arbeiten?	*Nein, auf die Post.*

Teacher. *Kurt geht nicht ins Restaurant; er geht an dem Restaurant vorbei.*

An dem Restaurant – vorbei – an dem Restaurant vorbei: these are now said in unison and individually.

Was macht Kurz hier?   *Er geht an dem Restaurant vorbei.*

The teacher now moves the figure on and *an dem Hotel vorbei* and *an dem Südbahnhof vorbei* are taught in the same way as the feminine buildings in the *Kirchstraße*. The teacher will then wish to revise all the material and, in particular, to ask questions which will make his pupils choose between *an dem* and *an der . . . vorbei*. In writing, they could now be required to describe Kurt's route to work as far as the *Südbahnhof*.

5. The genders are mixed in the area in front of and next to the station:

Teacher. *Vor dem Südbahnhof sind ein Taxistand und ein Zeitungs-kiosk. Neben dem Bahnhof ein Tabakladen und eine Gaststätte.*

After practising saying the names of these places, the teacher then demonstrates Kurt's movements:

Wartet Kurt auf ein Taxi?   *Nein, er geht an dem Taxistand vorbei.*

Kauft er eine Zeitung?   *Nein, er geht an dem Kiosk vorbei.*

Geht er auch an dem Tabakladen vorbei?   *Nein, er geht in den Tabakladen.*

Was macht er wahrscheinlich dort?   *Er kauft Tabak | Zigaretten.*

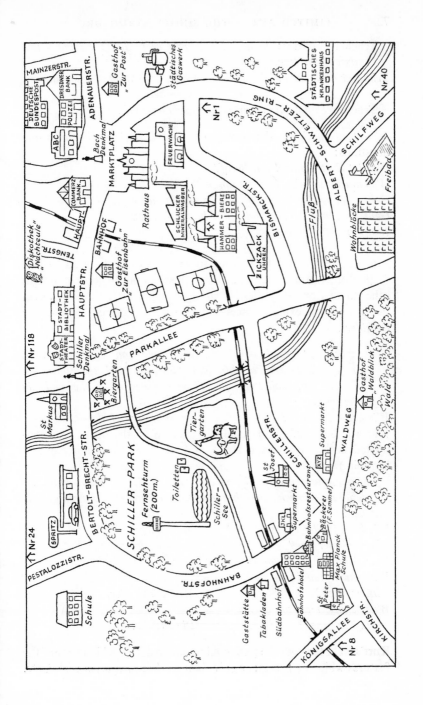

Teacher confirms: *Ja, jeden Tag geht er in den Tabakladen und kauft Zigaretten.*

Trinkt er auch ein Bier?   *Nein, er geht an der Gaststätte vorbei.*

Teacher. *Und dann kommt er zum Schiller-Park.*

A written check on the work so far might include the following questions:
Was ist Kurt Stempel von Beruf?
Was macht er jeden Morgen um acht Uhr?
Geht Kurt gewöhnlich in die Kirche und in die Bäckerei „Semmel"?
Geht Kurt in den Tabakladen und in das Restaurant?
Kauft er eine Zeitung?

6. The rest of Kurt's journey to work can now be used to give further practice of the *an . . . vorbei* construction, to contrast it with other known or new patterns (*entlang*), to present some new lexical items and to exploit street-names for background knowledge (*Schiller*).

Teacher. *Kurt erreicht den Park. Er geht nicht an dem Park vorbei. Er geht durch den Park. In dem Park sind der Fernsehturm, ein kleiner See, Toiletten, ein Tiergarten, eine Brücke und ein Biergarten.*

Wie heißt der Park?   *Er heißt der Schiller-Park.*

Wer war Schiller? (Facts could be put up on the board and contrasted with, say, Victor Hugo and Shakespeare, Churchill and Einstein.)

Language to be used. *Ein Dichter. Ein britischer Staatsmann. Er lebte im sechzehnten Jahrhundert. Er ist vor zehn Jahren gestorben.*

Wie hoch ist der Fernsehturm?   *200 Meter.*

Wie heißt der See?   *Er heißt der Schiller-See.*

Was sieht man in einem Tiergarten? Tiere.

Was macht man in einem Biergarten?   *Man trinkt Bier.*

Was benutzt man, um über den Fluß zu gehen?   *Die Brücke.*

Kurt's walk through the park could then be described in terms of the features which he passes: *er geht dann an dem Tiergarten vorbei,* etc.

7. The buildings in the *Hauptstraße* will need to be identified and, especially if they are new to the class, their names (*Theater, Kino, Bank*, etc.) can be practised by describing their relative positions: *die Bank steht zwischen dem Kino und dem Hauptbahnhof*; at a more sophisticated level they can be re-used in association with questions like *Warum geht man ins Theater, wann geht man in den Gasthof?*, etc. The class can then be asked to describe Kurt's progress to the post office in terms of the buildings he goes past.

8. Once pupils have become familiar with the map, it can be exploited further as the basis for the routes of other people than Kurt Stempel, using all the associated structures, including *an . . . vorbei*:

Fräulein Kreidebleich ist Lehrerin. Sie wohnt in dem Schilfweg (Nr 40) und arbeitet in der Pestalozzistraße. Beschreiben Sie, wie sie zu ihrem Arbeitsplatz kommt!

Herr Dr Krebs ist Arzt. Er wohnt in der Pestalozzistraße (Nr 24) und arbeitet am Krankenhaus. Er fährt mit dem Wagen zum Krankenhaus.

(This would make an opportunity to use *vorbeifahren*. Further practice would arise in using the railway journey between the two stations.)

A car or bus journey could be established, and then the regular times of the journey could be contrasted with an occasion when the journey did not take place as usual:

Herr Braun ist Busfahrer. Er verläßt die Garage um 7.30, fährt die Hauptsraße entlang und fährt um 7.40 an dem Schillerdenkmal vorbei. Gestern aber hatte er wegen des starken Verkehrs zehn Minuten Verspätung. Was ist gestern geschehen?

Thus the perfect tense could be practised. Practice of the conditional is also possible.

Wenn Sie neben Herrn Stempel in der Königsallee wohnten und als Beamte an der Kommerzbank arbeiteten, wie würden Sie zu Ihrem Arbeitsplatz kommen? (wenn Sie es eilig hätten? wenn Sie viel Zeit hätten und das Wetter schön wäre?)

There are also possibilities of using the imperative:

Stellen Sie sich vor, Sie sind Polizist! Ein Ausländer/Fremder fragt Sie am Marktplatz, wie man zum Hauptbahnhof kommt. Was sagen Sie ihm?

Clearly these more advanced applications would be spread over a longer period of time. The map might even be put away, to be brought out again much later.

9. The use of *an . . . vorbei* with a pronoun equivalent would be appropriate in exchanges like the following:

Geht X in die Kirche?	*Nein, er geht daran vorbei.*
Wartet Y am Taxistand?	*Nein, er geht daran vorbei.*

Because of the complexity of the material, it has not been possible to provide details of all possible questions and variations. Nor has it been possible to refer to the associated construction *an . . . entlang*. Because in the experience of most learners the latter usually only occurs with rivers and because there is a danger of confusing *den Fluß entlang* with *am Fluß entlang*, many teachers will not wish to teach it at all. However, it is hoped that the limited suggestions we have given for exploitation of a map will be found useful and that our suggestions will give rise to productive discussion rather than tie teachers to fixed formulas. What is certain is the fact that a construction like *an . . . vorbei* will not be taught simply by including it in a list of prepositions which take the dative and leaving it at that.

NORMAN HILL

University of London Institute of Education

The partitive in French

I had no right to be surprised when one of my students sensibly interrupted me to ask what I meant by the 'partitive article'. Clearly she had not been brought up on the book which tells us **why** *du, de la, de l', des* | dy / də la / də l / de / dez | are known as partitive articles: 'The partitive article is so called because it limits the noun to a part of the whole (**some** sugar only).'

Perhaps this definition does not help – any more than some of the descriptions and prescriptions, which are found even in some quite recent course-books, where all the partitives and *de* / *d'* after a negative or before some adjectives are 'dealt with' in one chapter. This degree of categorization and instant completeness (typified in another book of the 1960s by the example *Le nouvel élève vole dans le vieil avion avec le bel aviateur*) has become unpopular with many teachers. Some producers of audio-visual courses have been so tempted by the importance of moving away from 'formal grammar' and of getting pupils to participate in dialogue, that 'grammatical categories' are made neither explicit nor recognizable; examples of them appear *en vrac*, presumably to be experienced 'globally' and to be reproduced in the scripted dialogue at the appropriate 'ping' as we look at the picture.

The French housewife needs no 'ping' and may not be acquainted with the label 'partitive article'; but she probably produces rapidly and audibly, if asked what she puts in her *vinaigrette*, not only *huile, vinaigre, moutarde, sel, poivre, herbes*, but also the accompanying and appropriately placed *de l', du, de la, du, du* and *des*. Perhaps we can encourage our pupils to react in a similarly practical situation, not to an artificial cue, but to the need for the required form.

The foreign learner, like the native speaker, might be expected, in an out-of-class situation, to mention the ingredients needed for a kitchen, laboratory or workshop process; or, having made **une** *mayonnaise*, to ask: *Voulez-vous de la mayonnaise?* or, having seen

75

the warning *Peinture fraîche* too late, to ask the dry cleaners if they can remove *de la peinture* from his/her trousers. For confident use of the familiar and for correct analogy making in less well-known areas, categories have to be established in the mind of the learner; categories which, in early stages, help us to make conscious decisions, and which we later think less about as we increase our experience of everyday food, drink, cleaning products, fuel, etc.

Attention to native conversation reveals sufficient use of the partitive article to convince us that it is indispensable for communication within fairly modest circumstances. Clearly one asks for *un pot de confiture* or *un sac de charbon*, one adds *une pincée de sel* or *une cuillerée d'huile*; but one might well want to ask if there is any of any one of these commodities in the shop, larder or cellar. I am assuming, therefore, that there is no doubt about the need to teach this particular pattern.

The conclusion about the usefulness of the partitive may precede or follow a need to talk about what the characters in our French lessons buy and consume. Certainly food and drink provide us with the most familiar out-of-class subject, offering many common examples, with which we can create a classroom teaching situation.

A series of lessons on the partitive would have as its objective the ability, on the part of the learner, to produce, say, in answer to the question *Qu'est-ce qu'il y a dans le frigo?*: *Du beurre, de la bière, de l'eau minérale et des oeufs.* This seems a more immediately and usable selection than, say, *du lin, de la laine*; *de la terre, de l'engrais*; *de l'essence, des produits pharmaceutiques*, which might well become important to individual learners later in their foreign-language experience.

What, then, in practical terms are the materials we are going to use in order to present the new language so that its meaning is clear and to get it adequately practised in appropriate circumstances? I have seen a basketful of shopping very successfully exploited; but presentation of the goods by means of illustrations found in magazine advertisements is obviously more convenient.

Our decision about what items to teach may be limited – or even inspired – by what well-illustrated advertisements are available; but other considerations are obviously important. We may know from previous experience that, if we try to teach even only two of the partitive article forms (say, *du* and *de la*), they will be confused; we may have come to the conclusion that it would be preferable to establish *du* + noun **or** *de la* + noun first. But which one? *Du*, because traditionally masculine precedes feminine? *De la*, just to be different? Possibly not *de l'*, since there aren't many familiar examples. And we have already met and used *des* as the plural of *un / une*. If we are guided by the immediate availability of suitable pictures of common items, we shall probably start with *du*, giving ourselves a little more time to find illustrations of *de la bière, de la farine, de la crème, de la moutarde, de la viande, de la margarine*.

Whatever we start with, some temporary wrong conclusions will be drawn by the learner: '*Du* is the word you always find in front of words for food (*du beurre, du pain*), for drink (*du vin, du lait*), for food and drink (*du pain, du thé*), for liquids (*du café, du parfum*), for solids (*du sucre, du charbon*), or for stuff you put or find in or on something. ... Some of these assumptions can be rapidly dispelled and are less troublesome than the confusion which would undoubtedly arise if we tried to eliminate them all in the first lesson; we could certainly include liquids and solids, and perhaps something which never appears on the dining-room table, but we can wait quite some time for *du courage, de la patience, de l'enthousiasme* and *des idées lumineuses*.

Once we have decided which of the set (*du, de la, de l', des*) we are going to start with, and what eatables, drinkables, burnables or smellables we are going to point at or hold up and talk about, we have to decide **how** we are going to talk about them. Will it be ... statement: *Regardez ceci ... C'est du pain*; question: *Qu'est-ce que c'est?*; answer: *C'est du pain?* It could be with some illustrations, though the native reaction might be *un morceau / une tranche de pain* (similarly *un morceau de fromage, un rôti de boeuf*). But when we point to a bottle of milk or a bottle of scent, the answer to *Qu'est-ce que c'est?* is normally (*C'est*) *une bouteille de lait / un flacon de parfum*. To get the answer *du thé, du fromage, du charbon*, we might prefer to ask: *Qu'est-ce qu'il y a dans la tasse, sur la planche, dans le sac?*

In order to reduce the burden of this introductory lesson to the unknown *du vin, du pain, du fromage, du café*, it would clearly be wise to have taught previously, say, (*C'est*) *un verre, une bouteille, une assiette, une planche, une boîte, une tasse, une cafetière*, etc.; there might be a good case for ensuring that a number of these useful containers find a place among the objects one identifies and talks about at the beginning of the course. The question *Qu'est-ce qu'il y a* and the prepositions *dans* and *sur* will also have been used in other contexts. One thing the pupils cannot have used before meeting the partitive article is the noun indicating the commodity; *thé, café*, etc., will almost certainly not have been taught previously. We meet *sucre* in isolation only in shopping lists and on shop-window publicity; we meet it in the more precise *un kilo de sucre* after we have decided to buy *du sucre*, because some is needed in the recipe we are going to follow; *le sucre* is what we ask someone to pass when we need some in our coffee; *un sucre* is the familiar and postponable form of *un morceau de sucre*. So there is no convenient early association of *du* with *un* or *le*, or *de la* with *une* or *la*.

After a clear and repeated statement about the contents of various containers (*Il y a du lait dans la bouteille* | *Il y a du sucre dans le bol*) and some 'pure' repetition of the sounds | dy lɛ | dy sykr |, questions need to be asked; in the early stages perhaps helpful questions like: *Dans la boîte, il y a du sucre ou du fromage?* (*Il y a*) *du fromage. Et dans la tasse, il y a du vin? Non,* (*il y a*) *du thé*; but, as soon as possible, increasingly testing questions like *Qu'est-ce qu'il y a sur l'assiette?* (*Il y a*) *du beurre*; questions requiring 'full-sentence' answers like *Qu'est-ce qu'il y a dans la tasse et le verre? Dans la tasse il y a du café; dans le verre il y a du lait*; and different kinds of stimuli – producing a more spontaneous response – like *Parlez-nous de ce que vous voyez sur la table.* (The timing of this progression cannot be decided by someone writing an article, only by the teacher aware of his particular pupils' mastery and needs.)

There were problems of knowing where to start; there are problems of deciding where to go to next. The follow-up work might include:

1. Further use of the same situation to produce *du* with a few other nouns, confirming the pattern and disturbing any temporary false conclusions about the nature of the stuff we are talking about.

2. The move to *de la* (*bière, viande, laine, peinture, farine*) or to *de l'* (*eau, huile, essence, argent*), with very careful practice of the mixture of the previously and the newly learnt – *Qu'est-ce qu'il y a sur le pain? Du beurre et de la confiture.*

3. *Des*, which, although met as the plural of *un* | *une*, will need to be re-used, especially with *frites, légumes, fruits*, which may not have been met in the singular, and with nouns which reveal |dez| to be different from |de|: *des oranges, des autos.*

4. Dissociation from 'containers': *Quels sont les ingrédients de ce gâteau? Un oeuf, du beurre, de la farine et du sucre*; or *Décrivez les repas que vous prenez à la maison.*

5. Extension to *du sucre en morceaux, du fromage blanc, de la bière hollandaise, de l'eau bouillante.*

6. Use of *de* or *d'* in some negative patterns and before some adjectives.

Throughout the series of lessons organized to enable the learner to make the confident, correct choice of partitive article, the specific and the general questions suggested earlier could be used as both practice and testing stimuli. To supplement these, and to concentrate oral and written effort – in classroom or language laboratory – on this set of patterns, other practical exercises might be used:

– illustrations of shops (with visible goods or signs), allowing us to ask *Qu'est-ce que Monsieur X vend? Qu'est-ce qu'on achète chez . . .?*;

– shopping lists (nouns only) leading to *Qu'est-ce que Madame Z va acheter?* or *Qu'est-ce que Mademoiselle B a acheté?*;

– recipes, with illustrations of ingredients; or illustrations of what is necessary for some other process: *Qu'est-ce qu'il faut pour faire une sauce béarnaise | du feu | des meubles*, etc.

M. C. ELSTON, PAT BROCKMAN, DAVE CROSLAND,
JAN FELL, NORMAN HILL
Hackney Downs School, London, and University of London Institute of Education

Modal verbs in French: 'vouloir', 'pouvoir', 'devoir'

Assistant editor's note

Some teachers are nowadays devoting a lot of time not only to lesson preparation but also to discussion about classroom procedures. This work, for which timetables should cater, makes a more valuable contribution to enjoyable progress in language learning than the publication of 'exciting' new courses or developments in so-called 'educational technology'. I was privileged to join a group of teachers, in a department where communication is regular, and the gist of our discussion constitutes the present chapter. These notes do not reveal all that was said; readers are invited to imagine and discuss what they might have said had they been there – what different assumptions they would have started with, what gaps they would have filled, what experiences they would have brought, what alternative selections, techniques and materials they would have decided to use.

Introduction

Our general aim: to encourage skill in understanding and in oral, then written, use, in appropriate circumstances, of common correct forms of French. During the process as little English is to be used as possible; this allows maximum time for French, minimum interference from mother-tongue sounds and spellings. Though English could be used if vital for complete understanding, we must not allow this possibility to make us less attentive to the careful structuring of sense-revealing situations, which provide opportunities to ask questions and the evidence required to answer them.

In this comprehensive school French is taken by all pupils in years 1, 2 and 3, where boys of mixed ability are taught in groups

80

of about twenty; a large number of them choose to continue learning French in the fourth and fifth years. We expect, in our discussion, to concentrate on some of the problems of introducing selected forms of the three verbs within a five-year course without entirely neglecting some of the work to be undertaken with those who will wish, and have the opportunity, to use French beyond the fifth year.

Selection of patterns

A glance at the range of uses of these verbs in various contexts and tenses leads us to recognize the need for selection and grading. We disagree with the course-book writer who presents to third-year learners examples of and statements and warnings about most of the tenses of the three verbs as part of the grammatical content of one chapter.

If we consider the needs, in this area of language, of those who speak French regularly, we might be able to select the limited, more urgent needs of learners of French; to see which patterns can be postponed until the sixth year or reserved for enthusiastic specialists; which might be dealt with as soon as a need or an opportunity arises, because they are not only 'useful' but comparatively easy to understand and use.

Taking *vouloir*, for example, we note that we might require to express a wish:

Je voudrais un jeton; *je voudrais téléphoner*;****
Nous voulons | voudrions suivre un cours de. . .;****

to make a statement about someone else's wish:

Elle veut prendre le train de neuf heures; *il voudrait sortir*;***
Ils voulaient dîner au restaurant;***

to ask a question:

*Voulez-vous prendre le petit déjeuner dans votre chambre?*****

to make a request:

*Voulez-vous me demander ce numéro, s'il vous plaît.*****
Veuillez agréer, Monsieur, l'expression de. . . ;**

to give an explanation:

Il a voulu vérifier l'heure (reason for going back to look at station clock);***

Il voulait écouter un concert à la radio (reason for staying at home);***
Il voudra manger avant d'arriver à Lyon (reason for taking sandwiches);**
Il aurait voulu gagner un prix (explanation of look of disappointment),* etc.

Provisional ratings:
**** certainly (essential for minimum communication);
 *** probably (likely to be met or needed by most users);
  ** possibly (will increase communication possibilities for the willing and able);
    will be taught.
   * unlikely to be taught (except to those who aim to acquire a fairly complete mastery of the language).

Similar thought about *pouvoir* and *devoir* seems to eliminate from pre-O-level stages patterns like: *Il pouvait avoir 50 ans*; *Il aurait pu y avoir un accident*; *Richelieu mourut en 1642*; *Louis XIII devait mourir un an plus tard*; and for many learners, *Vous pourriez vous faire mal*; *Vous devriez visiter Versailles*; *Il a dû manquer le dernier bus*; *Nous aurions dû réserver une chambre*.

Grading and choice of situations

What shall we start with? And **how**?

We recognize the importance, for users of French at any level, of the forms *je voudrais* and *nous voudrions*, indispensable for reasonably polite requests for something, or to do something, in a French café or in a French lesson.

In spite of our desire for a sense-revealing situation, and in spite of our preference for the introduction of verbal patterns, first of all in the present tense, via the third person (action by someone who is third person for both teacher and taught and can be seen or heard to be doing or to have done something), an early, first-year priority might be *je voudrais*, a first person, not strictly present tense form, whose meaning cannot be totally revealed in any situation we can think of.

Perhaps it can be taught as a formula which precedes, for example, *du pain, s'il vous plaît*; *cent grammes de jambon fumé*; *la clé du placard* as an answer to *Qu'est-ce que vous voulez?* or *Vous désirez quelque chose?*. If you want any of these things – on the menu, shopping list, or classroom table – you say: *Je voudrais.* . . . This statement, or any other, does not relieve us of the responsibility of getting the formula practised with a selection of recognizable, choosable items, within a situation in which they are normally chosen. Later *je voudrais* can be introduced as a genuine 'modal' with infinitives. If learners can use *je voudrais* with noun phrases (or whatever they are called nowadays), and if they can use infinitives with *pour,* in answer to *pourquoi* questions, the combination of the two known elements will be relatively easy. Carefully controlled, the following situation might give rise to *je voudrais, nous voudrions | nous voulons*; *Jean veut, mais moi je voudrais* + infinitive: *Décidez, avec votre voisin, ce que vous voulez manger et boire* (menu); *écouter ou voir* (programmes radio / TV); *faire* (symbolic representations of possibilities – see p. 85).

Apart from the special case of *je voudrais*, which of these verbs stands out as an obvious starter? Pictorially we might be able to present (1) *X, qui a soif*, pointing to a bottle of mineral water (chosen from several visible liquids); a situation which, if multiplied, might justify this sort of conclusion: *Il veut boire de l'eau*, etc., (2) named, or otherwise distinguishable, people (man, woman, boy, girl, police-man) putting a coin into a variety of vending machines (offering drinks, sandwiches, stamps, newspapers, etc.). Possible questions: *Qu'est-ce que c'est? Que fait cette jeune fille? Pourquoi? – Parce*

qu'elle veut acheter une boîte de Coca Cola | boire, (3) people standing at *guichets* (*renseignements, réservations, billets*).

This could lead on to *pouvoir*: *Jean, qui a dix francs, veut aller au cinéma. Il y a deux cinémas*:

Cinévox   prix des places: 15F, 20F.
Roxy   prix des places: 10F, 15F.
Il peut aller au Roxy. Il ne peut pas aller au Cinévox.

The situation of a person, with a limited amount of money and a desire to make a purchase, faced with two different prices, seems to justify *pouvoir*, affirmative and negative; though this will need some investigation into the current costs of minis and maxis, monochrome and colour, cheese and ham sandwiches, etc.

Of course, the introduction of *pouvoir* need not depend on previous acquaintance with *vouloir*; though for various reasons (*peut* is new, infinitives may be new, and we have negative rather than affirmative answers), some of us might prefer to delay the following type of situation: X (member of class) told to cut paper; has no scissors. This would be possible, nevertheless, when the pupils are able to use all the lexical items involved (such as *ciseaux, craie, clé, tire-bouchon, ouvre-boîte*, etc.) and when they can understand and carry out a number of imperatives. There is a problem here about eliciting the desired response: *Il ne peut pas déboucher la bouteille.* Obviously the question *Qu'est-ce qu'il ne peut pas faire?* is, to say the least, not satisfactory. Perhaps *Il n'a pas de tire-bouchon. Donc . . .?* may supply an adequate cue, provided the class is acquainted with this device. *Pour déboucher une bouteille, il faut un tire-bouchon* – with other examples involving *passeport, permis de conduire; brosse à dents, rasoir; oeufs, farine,* etc. – could have been met earlier and would be useful preparation.

Absence of the essential document, tool, utensil, ingredients, etc., leading to the impossibility of carrying out a task makes one of the discussion group think of a transistor without a battery and a car without petrol, and the consequences: *ne marche pas* and *Richard ne peut pas écouter les résultats | Robert ne peut pas reconduire sa tante à la gare.* The topical *coupure de courant* or the permanently possible *panne d'électricité* might mean that *papa ne peut pas regarder la télé; maman ne peut pas passer l'aspirateur; Régine ne peut pas écouter ses disques,* etc.

It will be important to cater also for questions of permission, parental or legal (*jouer au football dans le verger; conduire une voiture, voter*). There is a need here for investigation into ages at which one can, ages before which one can't vote, drive, buy a house, enter a pub, etc., in England and in France. There is a possibility, too, for the future tense: *X a quinze ans; il pourra conduire dans 2 ans.*

Other suggestions: physical inadequacy, involving *trop lourd, trop faible, trop petit, trop haut,* etc.; lack of time, in a situation like *La séance commence à 8 heures; on met 25 minutes pour aller au théâtre;*

il est déjà 7h50: *il ne peut pas arriver à temps*; obstruction: *nous ne pouvons pas avancer*; *la route est barrée*.

The negative seems to be dominating our *pouvoir* examples so far; though a need to teach *pouvoir* (in the affirmative interrogative: *Je peux me laver les mains?*) was felt, when it was observed that French boys visiting Hackney were able to say: 'Can I wash my hands?' Clearly it may be necessary here to explain in English, at the beginning of any dirty-hands, thirst, lack-of-fresh-air situation, that 'we are going to learn how to ask permission to do something'.

Pouvoir in the affirmative is often used when there are several alternatives, e.g. *Pour aller de Paris à Marseille on peut prendre le train ou l'avion*, etc. In order to teach this pattern one might use this type of visual aid:

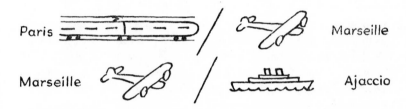

We note the importance of extending the pattern from *on* to specific people (*il | elle | ils | elles*), people for whom, for example, a journey is being planned; to *je* (demonstrated by the teacher himself and elicited by questions put to the pupils about their own transport alternatives); to *vous*; and to *nous* (by means of questions of the type: *Vous et vos parents* (*votre frère | vos amis*), *comment pouvez-vous aller de X à Y?*)

Other ideas: alternative shops (*beurre: crémerie | supermarché*); opportunities for various activities offered by school societies, the local, or imaginary, sports complex;* possible uses (*Avec une feuille*

---

*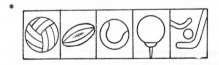

from British Rail Western 'Sports Line' folder, which suggests some of the reasons for travelling from, say, Reading to Wembley, Twickenham, Wimbledon, etc.

de Sopalin, according to the drawings in the advertisement,† *on peut sécher le poisson, égoutter les frites, nettoyer la poêle et la cuisinière, faire les vitres,* etc.); hotel list: hotel names vertically listed, facilities horizontally listed (*piscine, tennis, golf min., salle de danse, TV, change, rest.,* 🚿 , etc.); a visual aid based on the facilities in a station (in SNCF booklet: *Dans les gares vous trouvez tout ce qui vous est utile ou agréable: télégraphe, téléphone, boîte aux lettres, kiosques à journaux, bureaux de tabac,* etc.); or even simpler: *Qu'est-ce qu'on peut faire à la bibliothèque | à la piscine?* or *avec des ciseaux | une allumette?*

Pourrait | pourrions, etc., might well be dealt with, at the appropriate time, in a discussion involving the planning of a visit to a town or of a programme of activities for a proposed youth centre.

A situation involving alternative means of transport or alternative routes could be modified by the now familiar temporary or permanent suspension of all but one of them. This provides us with examples of necessity expressed by *devoir: Normalement, pour aller de A à B, on peut prendre le Métro ou le bus. D'habitude Monsieur X prend le Métro. Mais aujourd'hui les employés du Métro font la grève. Donc . . .? Il ne peut pas prendre le Métro; il doit prendre le bus.*
Or

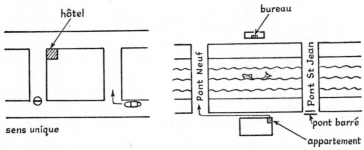

Other examples:

Pour traverser la Manche – bateau | aéroglisseur – mer trop agitée pour l'aéroglisseur; avion | bateau – brouillard trop épais pour l'avion. Pour écouter les résultats sportifs – TV | transistor – panne d'électricité; transistor | journal – piles épuisées.

---

†

Certain things **have to** be done, not simply as a result of bad weather or temporary obstruction, but because of more permanent rules imposed, say, by immigration and customs officials, headmasters, road signs or our desire to arrive or survive. School rules are fortunately no longer supplying us with cap-wearing compulsions, etc.; but before setting off on his holiday *X devra renouveler son passeport | prendre ses billets | réserver une chambre d'hôtel*, etc.; just as *Y*, faced with:

doit continuer tout droit, s'il veut emprunter un livre; and *Z*, driving his car, will recognize the imperative ⟡ ㊵ , etc., just as the pedestrian will know that *ATTENDEZ PIÉTONS* means ... *qu'il doit attendre*. The fact that *PASSEZ PIÉTONS* tells him *qu'il peut passer* reminds us of the importance (in some cases, the inevitability) of bringing these modal verbs together within one situation, so that pupils can learn to use the right one, not merely to use the modal auxiliary we happen to be practising now with one of a series of infinitives.

(In this connection the following present some interesting problems: ⊘ ⊜ which suggest *devoir | il faut*;

⊲ ⊏ 50km *pouvoir*;

⊄ ⊄ ⊄ ⊄ *interdit | défendu | ne pas pouvoir*.

Perhaps the ambiguous function of *il **ne** doit **pas*** can be fulfilled by *il ne peut pas*, on the one hand, and by *il n'est pas obligé de*, on the other.)

Other examples to be looked into:

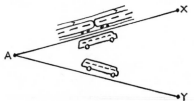

> Si l'on veut aller de A à X,
> on peut prendre le train ou le car.
> Si l'on veut aller de A à Y,
> on doit prendre le car.

In the *Guide Michelin, hôtel sans restaurant* and *nombre de couverts limité* (*prévenir*) might enable us to elicit, at a more advanced stage, when we wish to keep in use what has already been 'taught', *on ne peut pas y prendre les repas, on doit réserver une table.* A text in which Paul, hurrying to finish his homework in order to join his friends, is reminded by his mother that his violin lesson is due to start in fifteen minutes, might give rise to:

Il voulait finir ses devoirs | sortir avec ses copains;
Il ne pouvait pas sortir | rejoindre ses amis;
Il devait rester à la maison | prendre sa leçon de violon.

Supposition (*vous devez être fatigué; il a dû se tromper de train*) can be delayed until learners have a fairly good control over statements of fact and expressions of request and necessity. Those who are going to be involved in conversation with French speakers will need to recognize and understand advice (*vous devriez vérifier l'addition*), whether or not they take or give it. Some, who have made good progress and intend to go on, will be able to understand, practise and become aware of the function of *il aurait dû*, by careful work on a series of two- or three-sentence textual situations, in which lack of forethought and its painful consequences are evident (*Jean a étudié au soleil toute la journée. Maintenant il a mal aux yeux et il a le dos brûlé*).

This discussion, though far from exhaustive, has gone on long enough to throw up many of the problems and a few tentative solutions.

SHEILA ROWELL

Cobham Hall School, Cobham, Kent

Introducing verbs of motion in Russian

The teaching of verbs of motion in Russian is particularly complicated because it involves four uses of language which are unfamiliar
to English speakers:

1. the distinction, as in German, between going on foot or by
some means of transport;
2. the use of different verbs to denote movement in different circumstances (determinate / indeterminate);
3. the perfective and imperfective forms of these verbs;
4. the use of these verbs with prefixes.

I propose to discuss the introduction to this area of language, which
involves points 1 and 2. I shall suggest the steps necessary to lead up
to teaching these points, and ways in which they may be taught and
extended, with particular emphasis upon the gradual structuring of
material, since failure to do this efficiently can lead to a state of confusion which will outlive the Russian course.

I base my teaching upon the following principles: the new structure
is met in a relevant context and practised until its use is mastered
with a limited vocabulary. This use is then extended, by varying the
content of the lesson and using new vocabulary. Finally the student
is asked a variety of questions, only some of which relate to the new
structure, to make sure that it can be produced when, and only
when, it is required, and not merely in answer to a stereotyped
question; in other words, the student should now be concentrating
on the **meaning** of what he is saying rather than on its outward form.

To practise using a verb of motion it is necessary to have a destination, so the first point to be taught is в/на with the accusative.
Progress is more efficiently achieved if only one new structure is
taught at a time; it is therefore assumed that в will have been introduced early in the course with the prepositional (В классе, В школе)
and then contrasted with на заводе, на уроке, emphasis being

89

laid on the correct response to где? The accusative will have been introduced with a verb requiring this case (он носит шапку) and the pupil will be aware that words ending in -a change to -y when used as objects, though he will not necessarily be able to formulate the rule. The phrase в школу does not, therefore, involve any new form of word but a new use of known forms.

But how can the teacher introduce в/на+ accusative without a verb of motion, or vice versa? This is what I suggest: the teacher establishes, by means of a commentary with sketches on the board, that different members of a family work in different institutions:

Папа работает на заводе, мама работает в больнице,
Коля учится в школе, Лена учится в университете.

The phrase каждое утро has already been learnt by giving the English equivalent, which is the most economical way of teaching this particular phrase.

Teacher.
каждое утро Коля ходит в школу, а мама ходит в больницу.
Questions.
Коля ходит в школу или в больницу? — в школу.
А куда ходит мама? — в больницу.

And likewise в институт, на завод, etc., until the question куда? is correctly answered in all cases. In the interests of learning the pattern в+ accusative, I would use ходить with all members of the family, irrespective of their destinations. There is no need for the pupils to use any verb at this stage, however. If the aim is to establish в/на+ accusative, much more practice can be given by restricting answers to the minimum (в кино, в театр) and not demanding full sentences – which here serve no purpose.

When в/на+ accusative has been established, the verb ходить can be taught in an appropriate situation, e.g. with different places to which people go on foot every day. In each case there must be a good reason **why** they go to a place (e.g. because they work there).

Teacher.
Каждый день Маша ходит в библиотеку, Володя
ходит на станцию, Галя ходит в детский сад.
Questions.
Куда ходит Маша? — В библиотеку.
Володя ходит в библиотеку? — нет, он ходит на станцию.

Маша и Галя ходят в детский сад?
нет, Галя ходит в детский сад (туда),
а Маша ходит в библиотеку.
Что делают Иван и Дик? — Они ходят в школу.

Then further questions should be asked to elicit Я хожу and вы ходите. When these have been thoroughly practised, varied questions should be asked:

Куда ходит Маша?
Где работает Галя? etc.

until the question куда? reliably produces the accusative, and где? the prepositional. Varying the destination enables the teacher to practice ходить in a meaningful way.

It is now time to introduce the distinction ходить/ездить. This is easy enough to demonstrate with pictures, but the teacher should beware of using **one** picture for ездить, as the pupil may conclude that the verb means, e.g., 'to cycle'. I would recommend a brief explanation in English of the fact that the Russians distinguish between travel on foot or by other methods of transport (the example of a troika might arouse interest), followed by a variety of examples. Those whose talent with chalk is limited may find it useful to trace a number of small sketches on to a Banda for duplication, or to cut out advertisements of energy-giving products, which often have useful action pictures. Each picture should have under it the names of those depicted, so that the pupils can be asked:

Что делает Иван? Что делают Наташа и Соня?

At this point the adverbial phrases на автобусе, на велосипеде, пешком, etc., should be introduced, as they will enable the teacher to ask a large number of questions to practise ходить / ездить:

Что делает Иван? — он ездит.
Как он ездит? — на велосипеде.
Миша ездит на велосипеде? Нет, он ходит пешком.

Further practice will involve destinations and time questions (в час, etc., will have been learnt with mealtimes):

Что делает Иван в 8ч.?	Он ходит в школу.
А папа?	он ездит на завод.
Вы ходите в школу пешком?	Нет, я езжу сюда на автобусе.

and the addition of бегать for a boy who is always late.

Now we have the following possible sequence of questions, deliberately including some questions which do not involve verbs of motion, but which are relevant to the situation:

В котором часу мама встаёт?	В семь часов.
Что она делает в восемь часов?	Она ездит в больницу.
Почему она ездит туда?	Потому что { она врач. / она там работает. }
Кем она работает?	Она врач.
Папа ездит в больницу?	Нет, он ездит на завод.
Как он ездит туда?	На автобусе.
Куда ходит Коля?	(Он ходит) в школу.
Лена ходит в школу?	Нет, она ходит в институт.
Она работает в институте?	Нет, она там учится.
Где вы учитесь?	В школе.
Как вы ездите сюда?	(я езжу) на велосипеде.
	я не езжу, я хожу пешком.

In this way the new structure is incorporated into the body of learning of the pupil.

At this stage the pupil should be responding correctly to the cues provided by the teacher's questions. In the early stages куда is a useful cue for в школу, but the point cannot be said to have been mastered until the pupil can produce correct language **without** a cue from the teacher, in an appropriate situation: in other words, he may have learnt **how** to say something, but not always **when** to say it. Although it is obviously preferable if the language heard in the classroom is correct, the pupil must be allowed the freedom to make choices, and therefore possibly mistakes, if he is to function successfully without the teacher. The teacher should provide a situation which can be developed into a series; this could be one day's comings and goings in the life of the Russian family familiar to the class, where minimal prompting from the teacher should be sufficient to establish the chain of movements.

If the course allows for four years to O level, I would teach only the indeterminate during the first year. The general impression that Russian is 'difficult' is strengthened by the fact that the pupil has to learn to read and write afresh, and for this reason I think it psychologically advisable to avoid the more complicated points of grammar at this stage when possible (for the same reason I would introduce only three cases – nominative, accusative and prepositional – in the first year). One could, of course, introduce the determinate forms first; however, it is useful from the point of view of vocabulary to start by teaching the everyday actions of pupils and Russian families.

In the second year it is necessary to broaden the content of lessons to include both habitual and specific actions, and it is at this point that the determinate is needed. There are several possible methods of introducing new grammatical structures: one is to give pupils a grammatical rule and let them practise translating selected sentences from and into Russian. Here, however, this method is unlikely to be effective, since он ездит and он едет will both produce either 'he goes' or 'he is going' in English (as will он ходит / он идёт). Structures can also be introduced in a text, but it is difficult to include sufficient examples for absolute clarity without distorting the style of the passage. Pictures are useful, practical and economical aids, despite their limitations in conveying meaning beyond the early stages, but they pose a particular problem here: I consider it perfectly admissible to use pictures to denote habitual actions (illustrations in children's books work on this principle), provided that the pupils are made aware of this by the use of suitable time-phrases; but obviously it is not possible to use the same picture to depict both a determinate *and* an indeterminate action.

It seems to me essential here to explain in English that Russian distinguishes between (a) actions involving movement in more than one direction (which must include habitual action, as the subject has to return to the starting-point), and (b) actions concerned with one particular journey in one direction. To teach this difference it is sufficient to concentrate initially on one pair, e.g. ходить / идти. First, идти must be taught as a verb in its own right, with different persons and destinations. I use a diagram on the board:

понедельник, 8-го марта

школа   больница

дом

библиотека   завод

It is exactly eight o'clock, on a specified day. What is the family actually doing at this moment? And **how** are they moving?

Лене три года	она идет медленно
Иван опаздивает	он идет быстро

When this verb is familiar, it is contrasted with the usual state of affairs (обычно compared with сегодня). During practice the pupils are trained to be guided by key phrases (обычно, каждый день / сегодня, в 8 часов). In the same way the contrast between ездить / ехать will be taught by introducing more people who usually travel instead of walking to work, presidents who fly, and children who run, and whose routine is altered **on a particular day** – through failure to hear an alarm, a change in the weather, illness, etc. Again it is useful to try to establish a chain of events – information is supplied in rough sketches or symbols on the board, showing the normal routine of a particular person or group of people, and a good reason is given for this routine breaking down one day (perhaps the hero ran out of petrol); the pupils then have the opportunity to follow the situation through, supplying their own semantic and syntactical adaptations. For further practice in a realistic situation, two members of the class might conduct a traffic census, the rest being invited to imagine themselves as travellers in the Soviet Union. This could elicit the following questions, asked by the pupils rather than the teacher:

Как вас зовут?
Где вы живете?
Где вы работаете?
Куда вы едете сегодня?
Сколько раз в неделю вы ездите туда?
Вы всегда ездите на машине? etc.

Once the determinate/indeterminate idea is familiar, it is useful to have symbols which remind pupils of the essentials without the teacher having to interrupt the practice for an explanation in English. I use the symbol ↔ to denote the indeterminate, and → to denote the determinate, both on the board and in correcting homework. Obviously, however, the symbol is useless if the pupil has not followed the original lessons. If this is the case, attempts to teach the perfectives and prefixed verbs will merely bring utter confusion.

The same procedure should be followed for the introduction of other pairs of verbs, but this should only include verbs which are likely to be useful at this stage. Бежать, лететь and плыть seem to come into this category, plus нести and везти; I should avoid вести for some time, to prevent immediate confusion with везти, and because it seems less useful than нести and везти anyway. I should certainly not drag in брести, ползти, лезти, etc., simply because they happen to come under the same grammatical description: the criterion for introduction must be the degree of present usefulness to the pupil.

It is difficult to believe that the use of verbs of motion can ever come 'naturally' to an English child, for the mother-tongue is a constant distracter. For this reason, their use cannot be learnt once and for all at a certain stage in a course, as one can learn, for example, that nouns ending in a constant are masculine. Throughout the course, the pupil must have frequent opportunities for meaningful practice, so that he can learn to make the necessary choices rapidly enough to speak the language fluently.

PART 3

Exploiting a text

> The single paramount fact about language learning is that it concerns, not problem solving, but the formation and performance of habits.*

> From experiences of particular utterances and their referents a child learns to produce new responses which have not been specifically practised but which **conform to the rules** of the language. He interiorizes a system for generating appropriate behaviour rather than a list of rote responses.†

Between the poles represented by these two quotations the teacher has to find some working compromise. The danger has been to associate oral work with the former, with habit formation and memorizing, and to associate the latter with traditional grammar. The two chapters in this section serve to indicate that 'oral exploitation' involves procedures which, although largely oral, are not based on 'habit-forming' drills and do not involve memorization as a basis for learning and yet which are so organized and rigorous that the generative rules are learnt. The learner has to retrieve, reorganize and reformulate language in consistently meaningful ways and he is given enough practice to be able to internalize those rules (which could subsequently be explicitly stated) which will permit him to go on using the language even when the specific circumstances are altered. The examples are not learnt by heart; instead they help the learner to generate new pieces of language.

It must be stressed that neither writer is proposing a series of lesson plans for all teachers to follow. Both are indicating the kinds of avenues which could be explored, the examples of language which can emerge from the passage and which deserve treatment. No teacher will wish to follow exactly the same route; many will want to

---

* BROOKS, N. (1964) *Language and Language Learning*, 2nd edn, p. 49. New York: Harcourt Brace Jovanovich.
† BROWN, R. (1958) *Words and Things*, p. 182. Glencoe, Ill.: Free Press.

teach the same language but will use, for example, several different texts to give greater variety and perhaps to reduce or avoid boredom. Within the constraints set by the handbook, the two writers could only treat one passage each and they have tried to get as much out of it as possible so as to provide a richness of example from which each teacher will make his own selection.

ROY DUNNING

School of Education, University of Leicester

French

Introduction

In this contribution I want to suggest some ways in which a stretch of continuous French might give rise to various kinds of oral and written work. Some teachers may prefer to use the material for work in the fifth, others in the lower sixth years. I shall attempt to set out possible ways of proceeding at the same time as I offer some of the reasoning behind the procedures. Although I shall make specific suggestions, I must stress at the outset that I am proposing a model of a possible process and not a set of recipes for a series of lessons. Any interested teacher will have to take what interests him and adapt it to his own needs and teaching style.

By text I mean a stretch of language chosen for the specific purpose of teaching French. The French I wish to teach is the language of the text and the language which can be derived from it or led into it, by changing the focus of language use.

The text I have chosen is narrative. Learning from it will therefore include learning how to tell and write the story. As the story relates an incident in France, learning will also mean learning something specifically French. Since it deals with people, learning can also include learning about how they look, what they wear and also how they communicate with each other.

Using a text implies the acquisition and use of vocabulary and structure in their appropriate contexts. This has three aspects which I shall call structural, cultural and imaginative.

The text is taken from *Faits Divers*, ed. N. Hill, published by Harrap:

AGGRESSION

Un facteur, M. Paul Castel, âgé de 39 ans, venait de commencer sa tournée et était entré dans l'immeuble au n° 110 de la rue La Boétie pour payer un mandat.

Il se trouvait dans la loge du concierge lorsqu'un individu armé d'un pistolet entra dans la pièce. Le malfaiteur s'empara de la sacoche du facteur qui contenait 1.800 NF, puis, ayant demandé au concierge la clé de la loge, ferma la porte à double tour et s'enfuit.

Ce n'est que quelques minutes plus tard, après avoir brisé la porte, que M. Castel et le concierge purent alerter la police. Le voleur avait disparu en direction des Champs-Elysées.

Il s'agissait d'un homme de 30 ans environ, de haute taille, vêtu d'une gabardine beige et d'un chapeau foncé. Le commissaire de police du quartier des Champs-Elysées et les inspecteurs de la 2ᵉ brigade territoriale ont été chargés de l'enquête.

1. *Quel était le métier de M. Castel?*
2. *Quel âge avait-il lors de cet incident?*
3. *Quel est le rôle d'un concierge?*
4. *Où se trouve d'habitude la loge d'un concierge?*
5. *Qu'est-ce que le facteur était allé faire dans l'immeuble?*
6. *Pourquoi le facteur avait-il tant d'argent sur lui?*
7. *Où le gardait-il?*
8. *Pourquoi le voleur a-t-il demandé la clé?*
9. *Pourquoi voulait-il fermer la porte à clé?*
10. *Qu'a-t-il fait ensuite?*
11. *Pendant combien de temps le facteur et le concierge sont-ils restés enfermés?*
12. *Qu'est-ce qu'il leur a fallu faire pour sortir de la loge?*
13. *Croyez-vous qu'il y avait le téléphone dans la loge?*
14. *Selon le signalement donné par la police, quel âge avait le voleur? Que portait-il?*
15. *Dans quel quartier de Paris se trouve la rue La Boétie?*

It will be immediately obvious that the narrative contains features specific to written French: the *passé simple* is the main tense; the sentence structure is regular and often complex; the vocabulary chosen shows items of low oral frequency, etc.

The point here is that the language used in the written narrative is not suitable for its presentation and recovery in an oral form. An example will make this clear. The text reads:

Le malfaiteur s'empara de la sacoche du facteur, etc. No question can recover that piece of language because the question convention requires the use of the *passé composé*. The question *Qu'est-ce qui s'est passé?* might elicit as an answer *Le malfaiteur s'est emparé de la sacoche du facteur*, etc. – which is, of course, a different text. Equally the word *malfaiteur* is unlikely to be the first word to come to mind in the oral telling of the story.

A text presented orally to a class should therefore contain specifically oral features: the use of the *passé composé* as the main narrative tense; shorter, simpler sentences; vocabulary of (relatively) high frequency. Being spoken rather than read, it is more likely to contain redundancies (e.g. repetition of linguistic information) than the printed version.

I am proposing that the work on the printed version might be usefully preceded by work on an oral text containing the features mentioned above. Such a text as:

M. Paul Castel est facteur. Il distribue le courrier dans le quartier des Champs-Elysées.

Au commencement de sa tournée dans la rue La Boétie, il est entré dans l'immeuble au 110 pour payer un mandat.

Quelques instants plus tard il se trouvait dans la loge du concierge. Tout à coup la porte s'est ouverte et un homme est entré dans la loge.

L'homme avait dans les 30 ans, portait un chapeau (gris) foncé et une gabardine beige. Il a pris un revolver dans sa poche et a menacé le facteur et le concierge.

Le bandit a saisi la sacoche du facteur (qui contenait 1.800 NF), puis il a demandé la clé de la loge. Il est sorti, a fermé la porte à clé et s'est sauvé en direction des Champs-Elysées.

Les deux hommes ont mis quelque temps à briser la porte et à sortir de la loge. Ils ont immédiatement alerté la police.

The above text is, of course, only one of several possible oral versions of the printed narrative. Each teacher would do best to construct his own, knowing the level of ability of his class, and knowing in what direction their language work needs to go. The principle should, however, be clear: the construction of an oral text which will map on to the printed version and be immediately recoverable without modification.

As the oral text is a preparation for the later acquisition of the printed version, it can anticipate lexical or structural difficulties. Thus I have used *saisir* instead of *s'emparer de*. This presents in context the sense of *s'emparer de*, which the class will not meet until the printed text is read. *Saisir* should therefore be available to the class at the appropriate time as an alternative expression having the same meaning.

The specification of *un chapeau* (*gris*) *foncé* rather than just *un chapeau foncé* facilitates the teaching of *clair* / *foncé* as colour modifiers if the teacher wishes to do so. The construction of an oral text allows the teacher to skew the data in the direction he wishes the class to go. Knowing the level of his class, he tailors the oral version to their specific requirements.

Throughout this chapter I shall suggest various kinds of oral work without at each point making specific reference to written work. Writing has a special function in language learning since it enables pupils to fix for themselves the language they are learning, gives them some measure of appreciating their own achievements, and provides the teacher with information about that learning which can and should affect his teaching.

Following the principle that only that will be learned which can be, and is, used, I would expect the teacher to work out in advance what writing he wishes his pupils to do; and to see to it that his teaching includes the written forms that they will need. This will mean that the language forms accumulated during the preparation period should be made available to the class both orally and in writing. That is, when the class is learning how to answer a series of questions using the *passé composé*, they will learn both forms by being required to answer first in speech and later in writing such questions as *Qu'est-ce que le facteur a fait? Il est entré dans l'immeuble.* Similarly, when they are learning to compose dialogues, they will also be required to learn the appropriate written forms for what they have been learning to say. This will require the teacher to forecast the writing problems, and to solve them before the class meets them by putting the written forms on the board before the class is required to write them in answers to questions, etc.

I want now to deal with the structural, cultural and imaginative aspects of the work.

If the teacher is to use to the full the potential of the text, he must have thoroughly prepared it beforehand with his class. His preparation will in turn depend on how he proposes to work with the class, on what demands he will make of his pupils. Consequently the work preceding the presentation of the oral text should consist of the isolation and teaching of the structures and vocabulary composing it. The preparation should also include structures and vocabulary not used in the text but required for its exploitation. (Some of this work can be left until after the oral presentation of the narrative.)

Preparation will vary from class to class. I can only hint at some of the possible kinds of work which need to be done in using the text. The class will be asking and answering questions in speech and in writing; playing roles; and talking to the teacher and each other. The preparation must therefore include the language appropriate to these activities. That is to say, since the pupils will be asked to play the role of the concierge, they must have the appropriate verb forms in the first person; since they are going to be asked to construct a dialogue, they must be able to handle the necessary question and answer forms. If this is not done, it is unlikely that they will have the language available for use in a face-to-face situation.

As far as the lexical content of the preparation is concerned, there are many items in the texts (both oral and printed) which will need to be taught or revised if they are to become available as the situation requires. Some of the items will not occur in the texts at all but will have to be taught or revised because they are needed in the exploitation. I shall assume that among the list of lexical and structural items not available to the class are the following: *sacoche, tournée, loge*; *prendre* + preposition, *demander à*. I shall further assume that the class will need to be able to use the construction '*il lui a fallu* + infinitive', although this does not occur in the texts.

The work on the text will therefore take the following form:

1. Preparation of the items composing the texts and of those needed for their exploitation.
2. Presentation and structural exploitation of the oral text.
3. Imaginative exploitation of the oral text.
4. Presentation and exploitation of the printed text.

The cultural aspects offered by the texts can be dealt with in various ways. The reference to *la rue La Boétie* suggests work on the street plan of the relevant arrondissement. The roles of facteur and concierge can be dealt with, at least partially, in the structural preparation. It is, however, likely that some discussion in English will be necessary if the difference between the two and their English counterparts is to be grasped.

Before introducing the structural preparation, I propose to introduce the street plan of the Champs-Elysées (p. 104) and to suggest some work on it.

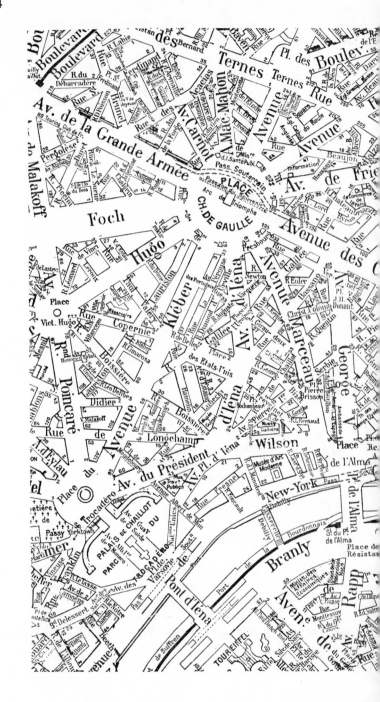

The possibilities presented by the linguistic exploitation of the plan are considerable. They should, however, be limited to subserve precise aims, relating to the later use of the texts. The framework for deciding what to put in and what to leave out can most economically be constructed by asking the question: If the class learns/revises this now, how will they use it now and later?

I would suggest that one of the later role-playing activities would be one in which journalists or television reporters, strangers to the area, ask for directions from different points of the arrondissement to *la rue La Boétie*.

A set of simple reversible procedures might include the following:

Teacher. *Vous êtes dans l'avenue Winston Churchill. La Seine est derrière vous. Vous allez tout droit. A quel bâtiment arrivez-vous sur votre gauche?*
Pupil. *Au Grand-Palais.*

Once the class have heard a reasonable number of times the appropriate *vous*-forms of the verb used to give directions, the roles can be reversed, thus:

T. *Je suis dans les Champs-Elysées. L'Arc de Triomphe est derrière moi. Qu'est-ce que je fais pour trouver la rue d'Artois?*
P. *Vous allez tout droit jusqu'à la rue La Boétie, vous tournez à gauche, vous descendez la rue, vous prenez la deuxième à gauche. C'est la rue d'Artois.*
T. *Je suis devant l'avenue Winston Churchill. La Seine est derrière moi. Qu'est-ce que je fais pour arriver au Grand-Palais?*
P. *Vous montez l'avenue Winston Churchill. Le Grand-Palais est sur votre gauche.*

Not only do the orientation procedures give practice in listening to, understanding and giving directions, they can also be tailored to fit grammatical processes as the teacher thinks fit. Thus, questions of the first type require nouns preceded by the definite article. They therefore help to fix gender. Questions of the second type require genders to be known in their grammatical function when preceded by the preposition *à*. Thus, the question *A quelle rue arrivez-vous?* might lead according to context to **either** *Au boulevard Haussmann* **or** to *A la rue La Boétie*.

Once the pupils are familiar with the plan and the procedures they can be required to give directions to each other, as required by the teacher. As the *vous*-form will be needed later, it should be used in this practice. The teacher/class dialogue can give way to pupils operating in pairs. Whilst they are asking for, and giving, directions the teacher walks round listening and offering help and correction as required. The pupils might refer to data set out as follows on the blackboard or on a worksheet:

Point de départ	*Point d'arrivée*
Champs-Elysées/rue de Berri	*Grand-Palais*

This might then produce the following exchange:

Pour aller au Grand-Palais, s'il vous plaît?
  Allez tout droit jusqu'à l'avenue Winston Churchill, tournez à droite, descendez la rue. Le Grand-Palais est sur votre droite.

Note that the conversational formulas *pour aller à* and *s'il vous plaît* have not been included in the previous practice, but would need to be taught or revised for this purpose.

The structural preparation of the texts will set out to present vocabulary and structure in context. Once the teacher has decided which lexical items need teaching or revising, he has to find suitable means to present them to his class. As far as *loge* is concerned he is likely to want a picture and/or a drawing showing a block of flats and the position of the *loge* itself. The item could be readily related to the school in a series of questions such as:

Où se trouve le bureau du directeur?	*au premier étage,*
Où se trouve la loge du concierge?	*au rez-de-chaussée*, etc.

For a class whose knowledge of French is fairly advanced, the dialogue between the author and the postman of Vigeois (*Vigeois*, Courtney, Longman) would be very suitable, particularly since it contains excellent photographs of the postman on his round carrying his *sacoche*. The plan of the village printed in the book could also be used to establish the notion of *tournée*.

Alternatively, a large wall-picture of the type *Au Bureau de Poste* (Editions Rossignol) could be used to introduce the following:

Voici un facteur. Il porte une sacoche. Voici sa sacoche. Elle contient le courrier qu'il va distribuer. Le courrier – c'est les lettres, cartes postales, paquets, etc., qu'il va distribuer. Il distribue le courrier pendant sa tournée. Sa tournée – c'est le chemin qu'il fait tous les jours pour distribuer le courrier. Le facteur va de maison en maison et donne aux gens leurs lettres et leurs paquets. Il paie aussi les mandats. La sacoche contient l'argent pour payer les mandats. Le facteur fait sa tournée à pied ou à vélo. A la fin de sa tournée il rentre au bureau de poste.

If such a text is the spoken commentary on the wall-picture and on (say) a sketch map showing the postman's round, the meaning of the vocabulary items can be made clear in French. It is, however, likely that whereas *distribuer le courrier* can be related to the items composing the *courrier* and to its semantic equivalent *donner aux gens leurs lettres et leurs paquets*, some explanation in English would be necessary to establish the sense of *mandat*.

It is assumed that '*prendre* + preposition' has to be taught or revised. As the use required in the work on the text is of the *passé composé*, it is essential that the teaching or revision encompass that form.

An appropriate procedure might involve the teacher giving certain instructions to his pupils and summarizing the results, thus:

Prenez ce stylo, mettez-le sur la table.
Prenez cette règle, mettez-la dans le tiroir.
Prenez ce cahier, mettez-le sous la chaise, etc.

Summarizing, he could introduce the appropriate forms thus:

Jacques a pris le stylo, Jean a pris la règle, Marie a pris le cahier.
Jacques a mis le stylo sur la table, Jean a mis la règle dans le tiroir, Marie a mis le cahier sous la chaise.

Instructions to other pupils to pick up the objects could be followed by a summary of what they have done:

Pierre a pris le stylo sur la table.
Chantal a pris la règle dans le tiroir.
Maxime a pris le cahier sous la chaise, etc.

If the teacher feels it necessary to emphasize the preposition used, he could precede the instructions by asking questions locating the objects:

Où est le stylo?	*sur la table.*
Où est la règle?	*dans le tiroir,* etc.

Alternatively, he could ask, after the instructions had been carried out:

> *Où est-ce que Pierre a pris le stylo?*   *sur la table.*
> *Où est-ce que Chantal a pris la règle?*   *dans le tiroir.*
> *Où est-ce que Maxime a pris le cahier?*   *sous la chaise.*

Questions requiring the total structure might then be put thus:

> *Qu'est-ce qui s'est passé d'abord?*
>   *Pierre a pris le stylo sur la table.*
> *Et après?*
>   *Chantal a pris la règle dans le tiroir.*
> *Et après ça?*
>   *Maxime a pris la cahier sous la chaise.*

So far only the third person singular has been presented with three different prepositions. The practice should be extended with different prepositions before going on to the *je/vous* forms.

For this the teacher can proceed in exactly the same way, giving instructions to the pupils to pick up objects from various parts of the room. He would use the *vous*-form in the summary:

> *Vous avez pris le cahier dans l'armoire.*
> *Vous avez pris la règle sous la chaise,* etc.

He would then follow this himself, carrying out the same sequence of events, summarizing thus:

> *J'ai pris le cahier dans l'armoire.*
> *J'ai pris la règle sous la chaise,* etc.

Once both the *je/vous*-forms have been presented, they can be recovered by changing the context of use:

(a) Teacher having taken a book from the cupboard:

> *Qu'est-ce que j'ai fait?*   *Vous avez pris un livre dans l'armoire.*

(b) Pupil having been told to take a pen from his pocket:

> *Qu'est-ce que vous avez fait?*   *J'ai pris un stylo dans ma poche,* etc.

Demander à will also be required in the perfect tense. It can therefore be practised together with the question and answer forms which will be needed later on in the dialogues.

The practice in class of the following questions: *Quelle heure est-il?*

Quel jour sommes-nous aujourd'hui? Où habitez-vous? Quel âge avez-vous? Comment vous appelez-vous? can be linked with the appropriate nouns, *heure/date/adresse/âge/nom,* such that the question form can result from an instruction to a pupil, thus:

Jean, demandez l'heure à Marie.   Quelle heure est-il?
Pierre, demandez à Marie son adresse.   Où habitez-vous? etc.

(In class the questions would, of course, be replied to. If the normal form of address among the pupils was *tu,* then appropriate changes would have to be made, the *vous*-form being required of the teacher.)

As in the previous piece of language practice the teacher would comment on the results of each instruction:

Jean a demandé l'heure à Marie.
Pierre a demandé à Marie son adresse, etc.

The summary of the replies would yield:

Elle a répondu qu'il était 3 heures.
Elle a répondu qu'elle habitait 50 rue du Pont, etc.

Once the verb forms are fixed (i.e. being used by the class as required without mistake), the indirect object pronouns can be added:

Jean a demandé à Marie quelle heure il était. C'est-à-dire, il lui a demandé l'heure.
Pierre a demandé à Marie où elle habitait. C'est-à-dire, il lui a demandé son adresse, etc.

The forms can be recovered from the class by mixing the two:

Maxime, demandez à Jean où il habite.
* Jean, où habitez-vous?*
* J'habite 32 rue de la Poste.*
Qu'est-ce que Maxime a demandé à Jean?
* Il lui a demandé son adresse,* etc.

So far the structures dealt with have been contained in the texts being used. Let us now consider the practice of *il lui a fallu* + infinitive, which will be necessary during the work on the texts. Assuming that the sense of the construction is clear in the present tense, we need to find a series of contexts in which action is constrained in a particular way. For example, a certain operation is to be carried out, requiring the use of a particular object which happens to be missing.

Either the object then has to be borrowed, or the operation has to be abandoned or carried out a different way. All the contexts should have in common an element of constraint.

In the texts presenting the situation there is no urgent need for the target structure to appear:

> *M. Maurice Duval allait passer une quinzaine de jours chez sa nièce à Londres. En arrivant à Orly il s'est rendu compte qu'il avait oublié son passeport à la maison. Il est rentré donc à toute vitesse chez lui.*

This text is based on the simple proposition *il faut avoir | on a besoin d' | un passeport pour passer la frontière*. It implies a series of texts based on similar propositions: *il faut avoir une clé pour ouvrir une porte fermée à clé, il faut avoir de l'argent pour acheter quelque chose*, etc.

The work on such a simple text, after the details had been recovered, would lead to the formulation involving the target structure:

> *Est-ce que M. Duval aurait pu passer la frontière sans passeport?*

The inevitable reply leads into the reformulation by the teacher:

> *Il lui a fallu rentrer à la maison.*
> *Il lui a fallu chercher son passeport.*

The situation is then reversible if the question is put:

> *Qu'est-ce qui se serait passé, s'il n'avait pas eu son passeport?*
> *Il n'aurait pas pu passer la frontière.*

The implication for the work on the structure should then be clear: we have to deal with not one but two structures '*il lui a fallu* + infinitive' and '*il aurait pu* + infinitive'. The decision is not a grammatical one: it arises out of the potential of the situation presented.

By the time the class is ready to start work on the oral text, they should have at their productive command the vocabulary and structures composing it, as well as those that they will need for its exploitation.

Presentation and structural exploitation of the oral text

The story should be told to the class. As the text is a simply constructed oral version of the printed narrative, there is no need for the class to be provided with a copy. It is the teacher's responsibility – by the thoroughness of his preparation and the quality of his presentation – to create a dramatic narrative which can be understood.

Once the story has been told the work on it can proceed. Before detailed recovery of the text can be achieved, the pupils need to become familiar with the material. To this purpose it is useful to construct a series of oral questions whose form is designed to assist with the recapitulation of the story. Such questions will therefore make the minimum demands on the pupils' powers of production, as for example:

1. *Que fait M. Castel dans la vie?*
   Il est facteur.
2. *Dans quelle ville est-ce que cet incident a eu lieu?*
   A Paris.
3. *Dans quelle rue se trouve l'immeuble en question?*
   Dans la rue La Boétie.
4. *Où était M. Castel au moment où le bandit est entré?*
   Dans la loge (du concierge).
5. *Avec qui était M. Castel à ce moment-là?*
   Avec le concierge.
6. *Avec quoi est-ce que le bandit a menacé le concierge et le facteur?*
   Avec un revolver.
7. *Qu'est-ce que le bandit a pris au facteur?*
   La sacoche.
8. *Qu'est-ce qu'il y avait dans la sacoche?*
   De l'argent | des lettres, etc.
9. *Qu'est-ce que le bandit a pris au concierge?*
   La clé de la loge.
10. *Qu'est-ce que le bandit a fait avec la clé?*
    Il a fermé la porte à clé.
11. *Et après?*
    Il s'est sauvé.
12. *Après être sortis, qu'est-ce que les deux hommes ont fait?*
    Ils ont alerté la police.

It will be noticed that the questions taken together with the answers effectively summarize the story. Questions put in this way help to rehearse the details and the language that the pupils need.

After the familiarization of the class with the story it can be retold in sections or as a whole and its component parts recovered by means of detailed questions. The object of this stage of the work is to pose questions such that the structural composition of the story is put within the productive capacity of the class. The questions then have to focus on different aspects of the text, accumulating data for the complete reconstruction of the whole.

A question series of the following type might be tried:

Quel est le métier de M. Castel?
  Il est facteur.
Que distribue un facteur?
  Le courrier.
Que fait un facteur?
  Il distribue le courrier.
Qu'est-ce que c'est que le courrier?
  C'est les lettres, les paquets qu'il distribue.
Dans quoi est-ce que le facteur porte le courrier?
  Dans une sacoche.
Qu'est-ce qu'il porte aussi dans la sacoche?
  De l'argent.
Pourquoi est-ce qu'il porte de l'argent?
  Pour payer les mandats.
Quand M. Castel est allé voir le concierge, est-ce qu'il commençait ou terminait sa tournée?
  Il la commençait.
Que faisait M. Castel alors au commencement de l'histoire?
  Il commençait sa tournée.
Qu'est-ce qu'il allait faire pendant sa tournée?
  Il allait distribuer le courrier.
C'est-à-dire?
  Il allait distribuer les lettres et les paquets.
Où est-ce qu'il a fait la première visite de la tournée?
  Dans un immeuble.
Où se trouvait l'immeuble?
  Dans la rue La Boétie.
Qu'est-ce que M. Castel a fait au commencement de sa tournée?
  Il est entré dans un immeuble de la rue La Boétie.
Qu'est-ce qu'il allait faire dans l'immeuble?
  Il allait payer un mandat.
Où est-ce qu'il est allé d'abord dans l'immeuble?
  Il est allé à la loge du concierge.

Est-ce qu'il lui a fallu monter l'escalier pour trouver la loge?
    Non.
Comment savez-vous cela?
    Parce que la loge se trouvait au rez-de-chaussée.
*Qu'est-ce qui s'est passé quand le facteur était avec le concierge dans
la loge?*
    Un bandit est entré.

When the story has been worked through in this way with the
teacher weaving in the structures that have previously been taught
during the preparation and checking that they are in fact available
when required, he can proceed to the recapitulation of the story. This
can be done in the form of an oral chain in which various pupils (if
necessary prompted by the teacher) string together sentences telling
the whole story. The answers to the questions detailed above might
give rise to a summary beginning thus:

> *M. Castel commençait sa tournée dans la rue La Boétie. Il est entré
> dans un immeuble pour payer un mandat,* etc.

Such a collective oral chain enables the teacher to hear what
language forms can in fact be produced without the stimulus of a
question. It therefore provides him with a feedback about the extent
and the direction of the learning of the class. As far as remedial
action is concerned, if, in reply to the question, *Qu'est-ce que le
facteur a fait?* the answer comes back as *Il a entré dans la loge,* then
the immediate correction by the teacher or another pupil will not
ensure that the correct form and the principle underlying its construction have in fact been learned. For this to happen the teacher
has to present that pupil at a later date with other opportunities to
make similar mistakes to make a correct response in the appropriate situation. Only then does it become clear what sort of generalizations about the composition of the *passé composé* are being acted
on by the pupil.

Imaginative exploitation of the oral text

When the teacher is reasonably sure that the previous work has
been mastered, and that the pupils can produce in accurate French
the elements of the story (in answer to questions) and the story
itself, he can develop the story imaginatively.

The principal purpose of the imaginative development is to involve the pupils in a fiction as active participants and observers. As far as their language work is concerned, this will mean that the work will focus on the first person instead of on the third.

The text refers to the postman, caretaker and the thief. Each of these can be required to tell the story as he was involved in it. The police are informed of the incident, so that a policeman can be imagined receiving or reporting the incident. The story is written in a newspaper so that a journalist can be required to report the story. Apart from the role potential of the story, there are points where speech is implicit or explicit between the participants: the postman and the caretaker; the thief and the two men; the caretaker and the police. Of these speech situations only that involving the thief is constrained by the text.

The teacher can then set out to develop speech situations involving the postman and the caretaker on the one hand, and the caretaker and the police on the other. The preparation for the conversations can take the following form. The class is invited to imagine that it is (say) the caretaker. The teacher can then put questions of the following type:

Où étiez-vous avant l'arrivée du facteur?
    Dans ma loge.
Que faisiez-vous au moment où le facteur est arrivé?
    J'écoutais la radio | je lisais le journal.
Pourquoi est-ce que le facteur est entré chez vous?
    Il avait un mandat à payer.
Que faisiez-vous, vous et le facteur, quand le bandit est arrivé?
    Nous bavardions, etc.

Once the outline has been developed, the class members can re-tell the story from the point of view of the caretaker:

J'étais dans ma loge. J'écoutais la radio quand le facteur est arrivé. Il avait un mandat à payer, etc.

When the roles of caretaker and postman have both been played and each has recounted his version of the story, the teacher can use the data viewed from the participants' point of view as data for the conversation between them. This can be structured in the following way (some of the class reply to the questions as the postman; others as the caretaker):

Qu'est-ce qu'on dit quand on rencontre quelqu'un?
> *On lui dit bonjour.*

Qu'est-ce qu'on lui demande en même temps?
> *On lui demande comment ça va.*

Qu'est-ce qu'on fait en même temps?
> *On lui donne la main.*

Facteur, qu'est-ce que vous dites et qu'est-ce que vous faites en voyant le concierge?
> *Je lui dis bonjour, je lui demande comment ça va, je lui donne la main.*

Facteur, qu'est-ce que vous avez pour les habitants de l'immeuble?
> *J'ai un mandat à payer.*

Est-ce que le mandat est pour le concierge?
> *Non.*

Pour qui est le mandat?
> *Pour un des locataires.*

Quel est le montant du mandat? (Il est de combien le mandat?)
> *Il est de 1.800 NF.*

The teacher might then say:

> *Dans la conversation vous allez vous donner la main, vous allez vous dire bonjour, etc. Concierge, vous allez demander au facteur ce qu'il a pour les habitants de l'immeuble. Facteur, vous allez répondre que vous avez un mandat à payer. Concierge, vous allez demander si le mandat est pour vous. Facteur, vous allez lui dire que le mandat est pour un des locataires. Concierge, vous allez demander de combien est le mandat. Facteur, vous allez dire que le mandat est de 1.800 NF.*

This information written in outline on the board might then lead to the following exchange:

Bonjour, facteur, comment ça va?	*Bonjour, merci, ça va.*
Qu'est-ce que vous avez ce matin?	*J'ai un mandat à payer.*
Il est pour moi?	*Non, il est pour un des locataires.*
De combien?	*De 1.800 NF.*

In the course of the preparation, the teacher could introduce a number of non-structurable items – *tant pis / ça alors*, etc. – for inclusion in the conversations.

The telephone conversation between the caretaker and the police-

man can equally be structured. For this preparation the process can
be modified, thus:

1. *A qui le concierge a-t-il téléphoné?*
   A la police.
   A quel bâtiment a-t-il téléphoné?
   Au commissariat.
   Dans quel quartier se trouvait le commissariat?
   Dans le quartier des Champs-Elysées.
   C'était quel commissariat?
   C'était le commissariat des Champs-Elysées.
   Vous êtes l'agent de service du commissariat du quartier des
   Champs-Elysées. Comment est-ce que vous vous présentez au
   téléphone?
   Ici le commissariat du quartier des Champs-Elysées.
   Où habitait le concierge?
   Dans la rue La Boétie.
   Quelle était son adresse?
   100 rue La Boétie.
   De quel immeuble était-il le concierge?
   Il était concierge du 110 rue La Boétie.
   Vous êtes le concierge du 110 rue La Boétie. Comment est-ce que
   vous vous présentez au téléphone?
   Ici le concierge du 110 rue La Boétie.

2. *Combien d'argent le bandit a-t-il volé?*
   1.800 NF.
   Qu'est-ce que le concierge voulait signaler?
   Le vol des 1.800 NF.
   Pourquoi le concierge a-t-il téléphoné à la police?
   Parce qu'il voulait signaler le vol des 1.800 NF.
   Vous êtes le concierge. Dites à l'agent de service que vous voulez
   signaler un vol.
   Je veux signaler un vol.

3. *Quand est-ce que le vol a eu lieu?*
   Avant le coup de téléphone.
   Donnez d'autres expressions!
   Il y a quelques minutes | tout à l'heure, etc.
   Marie, vous êtes l'agent. Vous voulez savoir quand le vol a eu lieu.
   Françoise, vous êtes le concierge, à vous de répondre!
   Quand est-ce que le vol a eu lieu?
   Il y a quelques minutes.

4. *Où est-ce que le vol a eu lieu?*
    Dans la loge du concierge.
Jean, vous êtes l'agent. Vous voulez savoir où le vol a eu lieu.
Jacques, vous êtes le concierge, à vous de répondre!
    Où est-ce que le vol a eu lieu?
    Dans ma loge.
5. *Qu'est ce qui a été volé?*
    1.800 NF.
Georges, vous êtes l'agent. Vous voulez savoir ce qui a été volé.
Pierre, vous êtes le concierge, à vous de répondre!
    Qu'est-ce qui a été volé?
    1.800 NF.

The incident has already been described but the teacher can have it repeated here if he thinks necessary, in answer to the question:

Qu'est-ce qui s'est passé?
6. *De quelle taille était le bandit?*
    Il était grand.
Pierre, vous êtes l'agent. Vous voulez savoir la taille du bandit.
Frédéric, à vous de répondre!
    De quelle taille était le bandit?
    Il était grand.
Quel âge avait le bandit à peu près?
    Il avait dans les 30 ans.
Dominique, vous êtes l'agent. Vous voulez savoir l'âge approximatif du bandit.
Marie, à vous de répondre!
    Quel âge avait le bandit à peu près?
    Il avait dans les 30 ans.
Comment est-ce que le bandit était habillé?
    Il portait une gabardine beige et un chapeau gris foncé.
Jean, vous êtes l'agent. Vous voulez savoir comment le bandit était habillé.
Marie, à vous de répondre!
    Comment est-ce que le bandit était habillé?
    Il portait une gabardine beige et un chapeau gris foncé.
Le bandit comment était-il? Est-ce que le journaliste a décrit son visage?
    Non.

Bon. On ne sait rien au sujet du visage du bandit. Inventez des raisons pour expliquer ça.

> *Il faisait trop noir | le bandit portait un masque | le concierge n'a pas vu son visage,* etc.

Jacques, vous êtes l'agent. Vous voulez savoir si le concierge avait vu le visage du bandit.

Jeanne, à vous de répondre!

> *Vous avez vu le visage du bandit | son visage?*
>
> *Il faisait trop noir. Je n'ai pas vu son visage.*

The reference points for the conversation might be tabulated on the blackboard, thus (the numbers indicate the order of speaking):

Agent	Concierge
1. *Identification*	2. *Identification. Motif.*
3. *L'heure du vol?*	4. *récente*
5. *Lieu du vol?*	6. *loge*
7. *Montant?*	8. *1.800 NF.*
9. *Récit?*	10. *Récit*
11. *Récapitulation du récit*	
12. *Description – taille?*	13. *grand*
14. *Age?*	15. *30*
16. *Vêtements?*	17. *gabardine/chapeau*
18. *Visage?*	19. *Zéro*
20. *Action*	
21. *Fin*	22. *Fin*

The ensuing conversation might run along these lines:

Agent	Concierge
Ici le commissariat du quartier des Champs-Elysées	*Ici le concierge du 110 rue La Boétie. Je veux signaler un vol.*
Quand est-ce que le vol a eu lieu?	*Il y a quelques minutes.*
Où est-ce que le vol a eu lieu?	*Dans ma loge.*
Qu'est-ce qui a été volé?	*1.800 NF.*
Qu'est-ce qui s'est passé?	*J'étais dans ma loge avec le facteur quand,* etc.
Vous étiez dans votre loge avec le facteur quand, etc.	
De quelle taille était le bandit?	*Il était grand.*
Quel âge avait-il à peu près?	*Il avait dans les 30 ans.*

Comment était-il habillé?   *Il portait une gabardine beige*
                                             et un chapeau gris foncé.
Vous avez vu son visage?   *Non, il faisait trop noir. Je*
                                             n'ai pas vu son visage.
Bon. Nous chercherons le bandit.
Au revoir, monsieur.   *Au revoir, monsieur.*

The successful construction of dialogues depends on the ability of the teacher to be content with small beginnings and to get the class used to operating in the ways suggested. As far as the blackboard help is concerned, as a general rule younger pupils need more specific help than older ones. For the younger pupils it would be advisable to allow the dialogues to arise out of written questions rather than abstract concepts.

Presentation and exploitation of the printed text

The preparation of the printed version of the story will have been accomplished before it is met as a text. The story will have been experienced in various forms; the vocabulary and structure will be within the comprehension of the class; most of the language will be within their productive range.

The text should be distributed and read to the class. It should be explained in English that the form of the story in the newspaper is different from the oral version. If the class is familiar with the *passé simple* they will readily note this as a characteristic.

If the teacher feels so inclined, he can test the availability of some of the language he has been teaching by inviting the class to suggest alternative ways of expressing the contents of the story in the spoken form. The activity might produce a table of equivalents as follows:

*un facteur **âgé de 39 ans***	*un facteur qui avait 39 ans*
un individu armé d'un pistolet	*une personne qui portait un revolver*
*Un homme **vêtu d'une gabardine***	*un homme qui portait un impérméable / une gabardine*
*le **malfaiteur s'empara de la** sacoche*	*le bandit a saisi la sacoche*
*il **s'enfuit***	*il s'est sauvé*

Once this has been done the class can tackle the printed questions, which can be answered orally first if the teacher thinks it necessary.

Throughout this chapter the primacy of well-disciplined oral work has been asserted, not as an activity separate from and inferior or superior to writing, but as the essential form of the learning process in modern-language teaching. All the writing which has been suggested grows organically out of the oral work which alone makes it possible. If all the oral work is fixed in written form during the preparation and exploitation of the texts, the learning process can be consolidated in a number of different ways and directions:

1. If the pupils answer in writing the questions suggested for the printed text, they can show to what extent they have mastered the appropriate vocabulary and structures.

2. If they write an account of the incident from the point of view of the participants, they can show to what extent they are in control of the necessary data and can write a dramatic narrative in the first person.

3. If they are asked to write up a conversation in scenario form, they can show how far they can handle in writing the forms of direct speech.

4. If they write up a report of a conversation, they can show to what degree they can handle the appropriate forms of indirect speech.

To sum up: teaching from a text is an invitation to both teacher and pupils to focus on a variety of language use within a very economical framework.

PETER L. WILLIG

School of Education, University of Birmingham

German

Introduction

It is perhaps advisable to start this article by looking at the main criticisms frequently made against 'traditional' texts and their treatment. The two principal sources of textual material have been the text in the course-book and the general reader. It is often alleged that the stated aim of the former, namely to illustrate in textual form the new structures and lexis introduced in the chapter, is not fulfilled. Inadequate illustration of the new items occurs in the texts; far too many unknowns of varying complexity tend to be introduced simultaneously; the text is not graded with sufficient care and is often too long and shapeless; the content is of little interest to the learners for whom it is intended. The general reader is used perhaps once a week and is seen in theory as an adjunct to the main course. However, there is often little attempt to make it so, and therefore it does not and cannot form an integral part in the systematic assimilation of new language elements. Its length, format and subject-matter have also attracted much criticism.

The traditional treatment of such texts – translation, grammatical analysis and dissection – presents a familiar picture. Statements are made **about** the target language in English and constant comparison is made with the mother-tongue. The foreign language does not exist independently as a possible way of interpreting and representing the reality the learner knows. As a concession to modern trends some questions may be put orally to the class in the foreign language, but the sequencing of the questions and their function are often superficially conceived. At the end of this process one can reasonably expect pupils to be competent in making statements about the foreign language, to be able to translate certain items from one language into another and to compare the linguistic phenomena of the second language with those of their mother-tongue. They cannot, however, be expected to **use** the foreign language, even within the limited confines of their knowledge. An awareness of the linguistic system of the target language, seen in an ability to use the structures they have learnt to meet the requirements of specific or new situations, cannot logically be expected of them. They will be unable to produce unique utterances from known constituent elements which the stimulus of the teacher's graded questions would demand. They should be able to create a new piece of language conforming to conventions of syntax and morphology,[1] but they usually cannot.

The 'traditional' approach to textual material has been predominantly descriptive, analytical and passive. The active skills, particularly the oral ones, have been underemployed and the complexity of the task of learning them greatly underestimated.

There is general agreement about the ultimate aim of active foreign-language learning: the learner should be able to understand, speak, read and write the target language in situations appropriate to his experience and at levels appropriate to the course he has followed. The realization of this aim is, however, subject to considerable divergence of emphasis and opinion, and more research needs to be conducted into the many influences and variables affecting pupils' performance and proficiency in acquiring a second language in a first language environment as well as into the nature of language itself. If, however, one assumes that the inclusion of an active-oral element in the process and an internalization of the linguistic system of the target language are central to a proficient and active acquisition of that language, then the treatment and exploitation of textual material will follow a different model from the 'traditional' one described above and will stem from different premises.

In the initial stages of the language learning process the text has a clear and specific aim in the structure of the course. Its main function is to reinforce and consolidate the structures and vocabulary previously acquired by the learning group. Linguistic elements with which the learners are fully conversant can be presented textually in a new sequence, in different or modified situations. The text therefore offers an opportunity for a rearrangement of the elements acquired and practised before in isolation, and, at a very restricted and elementary level, provides opportunities for pupils to combine and manipulate these elements to form new statements within the sphere of language learnt. The foundations for later work are systematically laid. This is a slow, complex process, requiring from teachers variety and ingenuity in content, presentation and exploitation. The text at this stage contains no new material as such. It does not increase the pupils' repertoire of discrete linguistic elements. By providing an opportunity for continued and varied practice of items already absorbed, the text furthers their awareness of the linguistic system of the language they are learning. Central to the effectiveness of this process is the question and answer technique employed, and this will be discussed in detail later with specific reference to middle school work.

Particularly at middle school level, however, many teachers express the opinion that there is a dearth of suitable textual material in German available to schools, although there are indications that the situation is beginning to improve. This leaves teachers little alternative but to devise their own material or to adapt existing texts with their own individual needs in mind, courses of action which are very time-consuming.

What should these texts be? The subject-matter is very important. The content must be at the right linguistic level, yet also reflect some of the learners' level of sophistication. The contemporary fifteen-year-old will reject texts reminiscent of the atmosphere of *Children's Hour* in the early 1950s and show a distinct preference for topics dealing with human and social problems and day-to-day preoccupations with which he can identify (cp. Buckby's chapter, p. 252 ff.). This point has been reinforced in a recent N F E R report about even younger children.[2] Biographies of well-known people, the worlds of sport, television, journalism, pop, medicine can all provide varied and interesting settings to which the level of language can be tailored. Humour is often difficult to achieve at this level if it is not to appear too childish or condescending, and should therefore be treated with some caution. The length of the text should be limited, and the number of unknowns strictly controlled and graded. Although individual needs will vary considerably, it is advisable to limit most texts at middle school level to under 500 words. In general the length of texts will increase in direct proportion to the corpus of language already acquired.

The points made about the function of textual material in the initial stages of the learning process will continue to operate at middle school level. The text continues to provide the teacher with opportunities to consolidate, practise and manipulate the language, but as the pupils' knowledge of structures, patterns and lexical items grows and the 'creative' permutations at their disposal increase, the process will by definition become more complex. One essential difference will also emerge: it will become increasingly possible and practicable to introduce new items by means of the text. If, for example, the concept of gender has been carefully and systematically acquired during the early stages and practised thoroughly subsequently, it is possible for learners to encounter a new noun in the text, which, once its meaning has been grasped, can be manipulated according to its function. Thus, if *den Stempel* appears in the text, the pupils should be able to produce *er / ihn / dem Stempel / der Stempel* as required. Similarly with adjectival inflections. There is also justification for introducing new structures, as well as isolated lexical items by means of the text. It is clear, however, that such structures should be of only moderate difficulty and not subsume a detailed, graded development. Items such as the pluperfect passive, subjunctives, past tenses of modal verbs are in themselves too complex and comprehensive for introduction via the text. Such topics are best dealt with separately in meaningful situations in a series of lessons carefully graded to illustrate usage and application of the point under discussion. Only then can they be integrated, as known language, into the corpus of textual material where further opportunities for reinforcement and extension are available. The teacher should therefore edit items of such complexity out of the text. Other structures are suitable: the use of *gelingen, gefallen*, verbal constructions like *bitten um, bestehen aus, folgen* + dative. Such items are of sufficient importance to justify extra time spent on them. The teacher will not worry about deviating from the text to convey their meaning, to enable their uses to be demonstrated in other situations and to allow sufficient active practice and application. Grasping the meaning is only the first step in the process. The construction needs to be intensively applied before being fused back into the text.

There also exists the possibility of introducing new items which do not themselves appear in the text but which are prompted by other items which do. Thus *den Zug erreichen* in a text might prompt the teaching of *verpassen*.

Meaning

If it is accepted that the text at this level contains a restricted and carefully evaluated number of new linguistic elements, the first task facing the teacher is to ensure that the meaning of new elements is effectively and unambiguously conveyed to the class. This aspect and its problems tend to be underestimated by many teachers and course-book writers. In most instances the nature of the item itself will determine the mode of conveying meaning and will precede the treatment of the text or emerge from it, depending on the comparative difficulty of the item. What modes are useful?

1. For concrete phenomena some form of visual representation is frequently most appropriate to convey meaning. The object must be clearly depicted to eliminate any possible ambiguity or misinterpretation and if included in a larger picture or photograph should be isolated or highlighted in a suitable manner. The clear, uncluttered picture essential to convey meaning effectively is found all too rarely in course-books. If practicable, the objects themselves can be brought into the classroom.

2. It is difficult to convey the meaning of abstract words by pictures or picture series, as misinterpretations can easily result. For some abstractions, basic subsumptions and prerequisites which are themselves of a concrete nature can be instrumental in transmitting meaning. If *es ist Frühling* is taught by means of a picture of a bird sitting on a tree singing, misinterpretations are sure to arise. It could mean *es ist schön, es ist eine Drossel, es ist Herbst* or even *wie schön ist die Natur*! It does not unambiguously convey the notion of 'spring'. To make this clear, verbal knowledge which has resulted from past learning is also necessary: names of days, months, etc. Only with this additional information can the picture have any value.

3. Certain items can be clarified by reference to an example of the word within the general experience of the pupil – with additional pictures if necessary. To convey the meaning of *Fluggesellschaft* reference can be made to several well-known airlines: *Sabena ist eine Fluggesellschaft, Lufthansa ist auch eine Fluggesellschaft*. It is essential to give enough examples to eliminate misinterpretation because vital criteria are missing. If for *Londoner Sehenswürdigkeit* St Paul's is the only example given, the pupils could quite logically infer that 'cathedral' was meant. Several generic terms can be effectively illustrated by supplying a number of examples of the genre: *Gebäude, Tiere, Verkehr*.

4. At middle school level, it will become increasingly possible to explain new elements exclusively in the terms of the language already

possessed, either as a description in the foreign language of the phenomenon, or as a paraphrase or synonym of the new item: *ein Stummer ist ein Mann, der nicht sprechen kann*; *ein Besitzer ist ein Mann, dem etwas gehört*; *'er heißt Peter' bedeutet 'sein Name ist Peter'*; *'täglich' bedeutet 'jeden Tag'*; *ein Witwer ist ein Mann, dessen Frau tot ist.* Teachers can also employ *ein anderes Wort für* or *das Gegenteil von* in the same way: *'fleißig' ist das Gegenteil von 'faul'*, *'Frieden' ist das Gegenteil von 'Krieg'*, *'anfangen' ist ein anderes Wort für 'beginnen'.* In certain instances the negative can be given as an appropriate illustration: *'falsch' heißt 'nicht richtig'.*

5. Modern German has in the past two decades absorbed many international words into its vocabulary, usually of Latin origin. These are often identical with the English form and can be useful in conveying the meaning of the equivalent words of Germanic origin. This should be done with great care because many of the words have an esoteric or restricted meaning in modern German usage: *eventuell, kontrollieren, organisieren.* Others like *Interpretation, Information, Kommission* do correspond and can be employed to indicate the meaning of *Deutung, Auskunft, Ausschuß.*

6. Finally some observations concerning the role of the mother-tongue in illustrating meaning. Certain items, particularly abstract words and nuances of usage, cannot be satisfactorily explained in the modes described above, and for these reference to the mother-tongue offers the most expedient solution. *Enttäuschung, sich verhalten, es kommt darauf an* are cases in point. To convey meaning effectively either visually or within the terms of the foreign language, even if this is possible, requires far too much time to be spent on one item in proportion to its usefulness and the amount of active language it can promote. The mother-tongue can also be used with discretion to verify that meaning has been correctly transmitted in instances where, for any reason, the teacher may harbour any doubts.

Once the new items have been understood, the text can then be used as a basis for question and answer work designed to promote the active use of the language. Such work divides into three distinct areas:

1. questions on the factual content of the text and the manipulation of structures which actually occur in it;
2. questions on the 'secondary' layer of inferred content;
3. use of structures, patterns and lexical items that are suggested

by elements in the original text, which do not advance the narrative *per se*, but which provide an opportunity for the practice, revision and perhaps extension of language learnt but which would possibly be lost if not frequently re-used.

Work on the simple sentence *Gestern fuhr Maria in die Stadt, um ein Paar Schuhe zu kaufen* will exemplify these three areas in practical terms.

1. The first step is to establish the facts. Questions like:

Wann fuhr Maria in die Stadt?
Wer fuhr in die Stadt?
Wohin fuhr Maria?
Um was zu kaufen?

will elicit from the pupils the appropriate word or phrase from the original sentence. The process is essentially one of comprehension and selection, and does not require anything in the original to be modified in any way. Only the appropriate response should be required. The answer to the first question above would be simply *gestern*. A full sentence would not only be unnatural but it would not supply the teacher with evidence that the force of the question had been fully understood.[3] If a full sentence is required, and there is surely nothing sacrosanct about full sentences, then a question should be put which legitimately demands it. *Was machte Maria gestern?* would produce and require the full sentence *sie fuhr in die Stadt*. Another question form in this area can be termed 'negative prod' – a question which demands a negative response followed by a positive statement, with or without an intervening stimulus:

Fuhr Maria aufs Dorf?   *Nein.*
Wohin denn?   *(Sie fuhr) in die Stadt.*

2. After establishing the factual information, we can then put questions which require some manipulation of the material in the original text. For example, *wo war das Schuhgeschäft?* produces *in der Stadt*. Pupils must show that they understand the difference in significance between *in die Stadt* in the original and *in der Stadt* required by the question *wo?* or *was machte Maria in der Stadt?* requires the pupil to show ability to produce the appropriate form of *kaufen*: *sie kaufte (ein Paar) Schuhe*.

3. At this juncture the arena for question and answer work opens

up considerably as questions are put to which the answers must be deduced from or suggested by the facts already established. *Wie fuhr Maria in die Stadt?* would allow for speculation about various modes of transport. This could then be extended to the ways pupils, their friends and their families travel to various locations. Other areas could be explored: *was wollte sie in der Stadt tun?* (shopping), *wohin ging sie in der Stadt?* (shops and buildings), *was machte sie, bevor sie das Geschäft verließ?, wem gab sie das Geld?* (financial transactions, datives). Obviously different areas will be explored according to individual circumstances, but a wealth of possibilities suggests itself – even as far as asking 'Imagine you are Maria; what did you tell your best friend that you had been doing yesterday?' It is, however, important in this third area not to digress too far and too often from the text and lose sight of it altogether. If every time *gestern* appears in the text, the opportunity is used to revise *vorgestern, morgen, heute, übermorgen* and if every time the *um . . . zu* construction appears, we start asking why one goes to the butcher's, the baker's and the candlestick-maker's, then the work can degenerate into a tiresome rigmarole. But it is well for the teacher to be alert to the fact that such possibilities are worth exploiting **from time to time.**

Thus from simple question and answer work the teacher can gradually bring his pupils to the point where they can begin to create acceptable pieces of language. Each question in the process has its defined, specific function and follows a logical progression. In the middle school our pupils will continue to assimilate an increasing number of constituent linguistic elements, and textual material will play a central role in enabling them not only to add to these elements but to integrate them into an ever wider context. The process pivots on an awareness of the linguistic system of the target language. This can only be achieved and internalized by constant and varied practice, and by provision of opportunities for making analogies and extending the range of use of known language. The treatment of textual material described above and in what follows can help provide such practice. By definition the whole process is complex and cumulative, demanding much ingenuity and resourcefulness from the teacher, but in the long term it is both rewarding and demonstrably attainable if the teacher remains constantly aware of the intricacy of the task.

Detailed treatment of a specific text

The time spent on the text will depend on the needs of the class, but about eight forty-minute lessons will be needed by an average class following an O-level course. The text has been divided into three sections. The items assumed as unknown are indicated. The more complex structures appearing for the first time in the text are dealt with before embarking upon the question and answer work based on it. Other items can be taught and extended when encountered in the narrative. Some new words are introduced, which although not actually occurring in the text prove useful when dealing with items of the second category described above. A case in point is *impfen / eine Spritze geben.* The possibilities of conveying the meaning of each new item are discussed in detail, but lack of space precludes a developmental analysis of the procedures involved in moving from introduction to active use. Some suggestions are given of content areas which relate to the items in questions. As stressed above, comprehension is only the first step in the process leading to active mastery. Once meaning is established, teachers should devise and structure a question and answer series to allow the item to be **used** as well as comprehended. The first reading of the sections should be done by the teacher himself – pupils can hardly be expected to read aloud fluently or accurately material with which they are not familiar.

THE TEXT[4]

(a) *„Der nächste" rief der Mann im weißen Arztmantel. Der letzte Patient trat in die Hütte ein. Der Mann nahm eine neue Spritze. Als er aber die Nadel an das magere, braune Ärmchen des Jungen setzen wollte, lief dieser in die Ecke.*

„Nanu. Hast du auf einmal Angst?" fragte der Arzt. „Wie heißt du denn?"

(b) *„Ruki!" war die Antwort. Die großen dunklen Augen des kleinen Afrikaners sahen voll Angst auf die Spritze. Durch das zerrissene Hemd konnte man deutlich sehen, daß sein Körper fast nur aus Haut und Knochen bestand.*

„Komm Ruki. Es tut wirklich nicht weh!" sagte der Doktor. „Deine Freunde hatten doch keine Angst. Oder willst du nicht gesund werden?"

Ruki nickte heftig.

„*Na, siehst du,*" *sagte der Arzt.* „*Das geht aber nur mit dieser kleinen Spritze. Danach bekommst du von uns auch Milch.*"

(c) *Ruki überlegte. Er wußte, daß der Doktor von der U N I C E F ein guter Mann war, der den bösen Ausschlag wegzaubern konnte. Zögernd kam Ruki näher.*

„*Na, also,*" *lachte der Arzt. Dann ging alles schnell. Ein leichter Stich am Arm – Ruki spürte ihn kaum – dann war die Spritze wieder draußen.*

„*Nun, war es schlimm?*" *fragte der Arzt, während er die Stichstelle reinigte. Ruki schüttelte den Kopf und lächelte.*

„*Dann hol' deine Milch, mein Junge!*" *sagte der Arzt, während Ruki aus der Tür hinauslief.*

ITEMS TO BE TAUGHT BEFORE TREATING TEXT

(a) *Angst haben.* Situations suggested: *Angst haben vor der Dunkelheit, vor Spinnen, Hunden, Flugzeugen, Gespenstern, Schlangen, Feuer, Wasser, dem Schulleiter.*

(b) *Bestehen aus.* Described in association with various articles and collections: *ein Reifen besteht aus Gummi, ein Buch besteht aus Papier, eine Kerze besteht aus Wachs, ein Quartett besteht aus vier Personen, eine Fußballmannschaft aus elf.*

(c) *Während.* As a conjunction. Essential to stress simultaneous nature of the two actions: *Hans schnarcht, während er schläft; Peter raucht, während er liest.* Gradually lengthen the subordinate clause: *während er die Zeitung liest, während er die Zeitung im Wohnzimmer liest.* Employ other tenses: *Maximilian hörte Musik im Radio, während er nach Hause fuhr; die Politiker tranken Wein, während sie das Problem debattierten; ich sehe fern, während ich meine Schulaufgaben mache.*

Wehtun. Exemplify: *mein Arm tut mir weh; ich bin hingefallen, ich habe mir den Fuß verrenkt, er tut mir weh.*

ITEMS TREATED WHEN ENCOUNTERED IN TEXT

Spritze. Photograph, diagram or picture. Teach also *Nadel* and *impfen | eine Spritze geben.* Extend examples: *Der Arzt impfte den Mann gegen Cholera.*

Patient. No problem of meaning but practice needed in handling oblique cases: *man besucht einen Patienten im Krankenhaus; man schenkt dem Patienten Blumen; die Patienten warten auf den Arzt.*

Mager. Explained in terms of known language: *dünn, nicht fett, das Gegenteil von 'dick'.*

Ärmchen. Explanation: *das bedeutet ein kleiner Arm.* Gives examples of other diminutives: *Häuschen, Mäuschen, Kätzchen, Mädchen.*

Auf einmal. Ein anderes Wort für 'plötzlich'.

Dunkel. Ohne Licht, das Gegenteil von 'hell'. Employ with colours: *dunkelblau, hellblau.*

Zerrissen. A torn envelope might be useful as a visual aid, or even a torn rugby shirt. *Nähen, reparieren, flicken, stopfen* might well be introduced or revised here.

Deutlich. Klar. Translate to verify that meaning is grasped.

Körper. Translate. It is probably advisable not to introduce other equivalents of English 'body' (*Leiche, Leichnam*), as this could lead to confusion.

Haut | Knochen. Demonstrate and practise. Useful to revise *fressen: Hunde fressen Knochen.*

Den Kopf schütteln, (*mit dem Kopf*) *nicken.* Introduce together. Demonstrate action and develop: *was macht er? er schüttelt den Kopf, usw.* Once structure is practised, questions could be asked about the actual significance of the actions: *Erika schüttelt den Kopf. Was will sie damit sagen? Helga will etwas bejahen, ohne zu sprechen. Was tut sie?* Other gestures could also be referred to: *gähnen, mit der Hand winken, den Daumen drücken.*

Heftig. Translate.

Überlegen. Über etwas (*nach*) *denken, bevor man handelt.* Meaning checked by translation. Mention of common phrase: *das muß ich mir überlegen.*

Ausschlag. Translate.

Böse. Schlecht, nicht gut.

Zögern. By demonstration. Possible situations: *Peter zögert, bevor er die Straße überquert; die Frau zögert, bevor sie das Kleid kauft; der Bankdirektor zögert, bevor er das Paket aufmacht.* The teacher will try to elicit paraphrases or alternatives in describing these situations: *er überquert die Straße nicht sofort, er wartet einen Augenblick, der Bankdirektor ist unsicher.*

Stich | spüren | reinigen. Link in sequence. Demonstrate action of doctor and check sequence. Check English for *spüren.*

Kaum. Fast nicht.

QUESTION AND ANSWER SEQUENCE ON THE TEXT

A detailed question and answer sequence for the whole text is given below. For section A only, attention is drawn to the function and point of the questions and possible areas for exploitation and extension. As emphasized earlier, any divergence from the text should not be too protracted. The suggested outline is meant as a guide and not as a fixed programme, and teachers will find alternative areas for exploitation and other sequences more appropriate to their own needs.

Section A

1. *Was war der Mann von Beruf? Er war Arzt.*
Pupils must select response from information contained in text and show ability to produce pattern with verb 'to be' and profession. Other professions can be referred to: *Pilot, Student, Lehrer, Sekretär.* A further possibility is to use these to revise relative clauses: *Was ist ein Lehrer? Ein Mann, der in der Schule unterrichtet.*
2. *Was trug er?*   *Einen weißen Mantel.*
Requires the dative in the text to be reformed into accusative. Possible alternatives: *Beschreiben Sie seinen Mantel! Er war weiß; welche Farbe hatte sein Mantel? Er war weiß.* Ability to use uninflected adjective is checked here.
3. *Was rief der Mann?*   *„Der nächste!"*
Comprehension tested only – to advance the narrative.
4. *Zu wem?*   *Zu dem nächsten Jungen/Patienten*
5. *War dieser Patient schon   Nein.*
    in der Hütte?
Patient is being constantly used – in the previous answer in the inflected form. Here the question is a 'negative prod'. The purpose here is to clarify events to make way for the next area of questioning.
6. *Wo war er also?*   *Er war draußen.*
Answer must be deduced from text. Revision of possibly dormant word: *draußen.*
7. *Wo genau?*   *Draußen vor der Hütte.*
Could have been given as previous answer. Question here forces the more specific response.
8. *Warum mußte der Arzt*
    eigentlich rufen?   *Weil der Junge nicht in der Hütte war.*
                                Weil der Junge draußen vor der Hütte
                                war / stand.

Required information implied in text. Word order in subordinate clauses tested by this kind of question. Answers suggested are within possible range of pupils at this stage and as such are acceptable. More complex structures, such as *um gehört zu werden*, would hardly be expected in this context. Even within the limits set by the question, there is still room for different individual responses.

9. *Wann trat der Patient ein?   Als er den Arzt hörte; als der Arzt rief.*
Correct use of *als* and word order being tested. Information implied in text. Again other answers (using *nachdem*, for instance) could be given or encouraged. But, of course, *nachdem* would only be required if the pluperfect is already known.

10. *Warum kam der Junge*
     zum Arzt?   *Weil er krank war.*
Word order checked and given information rearranged.

11. *Was machte der Arzt dann?*
                      Er nahm eine Spritze.
Question to advance narrative.

12. *Was für eine?*   *Eine neue.*

13. *Warum eine neue?*   *Weil jeder Patient eine neue haben muß.*
Sub-questions might be needed before this answer comes in this form: *was für eine Spritze muß jeder Patient haben?*

14. *Was wollte der Arzt eigentlich tun?*
                Er wollte den Jungen impfen / dem
                Jungen eine Spritze geben.
Impfen / eine Spritze geben taught earlier. Here practice of construction with *wollen*.

15. *Womit?*   *Mit einer Spritze.*
Manipulation of elements in the text: dative after *mit*.

16. *Mit was für einer?*   *Mit einer neuen.*
Adjectival agreement with above form.

17. *Warum impfte der Arzt den Jungen?*
                Weil er krank war.
Ausschlag (*weil er einen Ausschlag hatte*) could be offered by teacher here as well as introduction or revision of *Grippe, Erkältung, Masern*.

18. *War der Junge der erste Patient an dem Tag?*
                Nein, (der letzte).

19. *Wo waren die beiden?*   *In der Hütte.*
Change to *in der*, compared with *in die* in the text.

20. *Was setzte der Arzt ans Ärmchen*
     des Jungen?   *Die Nadel.*

Question simply to advance narrative and check comprehension.

21. *Warum?*　　　　　　*Weil er den Jungen impfen wollte.*

Pattern of question 14 now re-used with subordinate word order.

22. *Was ist ein Ärmchen?*　　*Ein kleiner Arm.*

23. *Was für Arme hatte der Junge?*

　　　　　　　　　　Magere (kleine) Arme.

Checking adjective agreement.

24. *Wie sah der Junge aus? Groß*
　　und dick?　　　　　*Nein, klein und mager.*

Uninflected adjectives. Teacher could introduce *unterernährt* here.

25. *Aß der Junge viel?*　　*Nein.*

Preparing ground for next area of questions.

26. *Wieviel aß er?*　　　*Wenig.*

27. *Warum aß er nicht genug? Weil er arm war.*

28. *Was sind arme Leute?*　　*Leute, die wenig Geld haben.*

Using *wenig* again and checking relative clause pattern.

29. *Was ist das Gegenteil von 'arm'?*

　　　　　　　　　　Reich.

Testing knowledge of vocabulary.

30. *Und was sind reiche Leute? Leute, die viel Geld haben.*

Re-use of relative construction.

31. *War der Junge im Text reich?*

　　　　　　　　　　Nein, er war arm.

Question to return to text.

32. *Woher wissen wir das?*　　*Er war mager, er aß zu wenig, er war*
　　　　　　　　　　dünn.

Consolidating facts of text.

33. *Was machte der Junge plötzlich?*

　　　　　　　　　　Er lief in die Ecke.

Advancement of narrative.

34. *Wie fühlte sich der Junge? Er hatte Angst.*

Revision of structure practised before embarking on the text.

35. *Wovor?*　　　　　*Vor der Spritze.*

36. *Vor wem hatte er Angst?*　*Vor dem Arzt.*

Distinguishing between *wovor* and *vor wem* as question forms.

37. *Wann lief der Junge in die Ecke?*

　　　　　　　　　Als er die Spritze sah / als der Arzt
　　　　　　　　　　ihn spritzen wollte / als der Arzt die
　　　　　　　　　　Nadel an seinen Arm setzen wollte.

Further use of '*als*' clauses. Variety of responses possible.

38. *Warum lief er in die Ecke? Weil er Angst hatte.*
Question 34 revised but in a subordinate clause.
39. *Wo war der Junge, als der Arzt*
   dann wieder mit ihm sprach?
                              In der Ecke.
Dative from accusative in text and previous answers.
40. *Was konnte der Arzt dann nicht*
   mehr tun?   *Den Jungen impfen | dem Jungen eine*
                        Spritze geben.
Revision of *können* with associated verb construction.
41. *Warum nicht?*   *Weil der Junge Angst hatte | in der*
                        Ecke stand.
Established facts now in subordinate clauses. Perhaps (*vor Angst*)
   zittern could be revised or introduced here.
42. *Was fragte der Arzt den Jungen?*
                        „*Hast du auf einmal Angst?*"
Advancement of narrative.
43. *Was noch?*   „*Wie heißt du?*"
44. *Wie sagt man anders 'auf einmal'?*
                        Plötzlich.
45. *Wie sagt man anders 'ich heiße Paul'?*
                        Mein Name ist Paul.
Revision of alternative possibilities to those in text.
46. *Was wollte der Arzt wissen?*
                        Den Namen des Jungen.
                        Wie der Junge hieß.
                        Ob der Junge Angst hatte.
Revision of constructions with *wissen*.

Section B

From this point the sequence of question and answer work is
suggested without further comment.
1. *Was antwortete der Junge? Ruki.*
2. *Wer war eigentlich Ruki?   Ein kleiner Junge | Patient.*
3. *War er Deutscher?   Nein.*
4. *Was hatte er für eine Nationalität?*
                        Er war Afrikaner.
5. *Aus welchem Land kam er also?*
                        Aus Afrika, aus einem Land in Afrika.

6. *Aus welchem Land kommt ein*
   Engländer, Deutscher, Franzose usw?
           Aus England, Deutschland, Frankreich.

7. *Was für Augen hatte Ruki? Große, schwarze.*

8. *Und was für Haare? Schwarze, dunkle.*

9. *Was für Augen | Haare habe(n)*
   ich | Sie? Ich | Sie habe(n). . . .

10. *Und X? Er | sie hat. . . .*

11. *Wohin sah Ruki? Auf die Spritze.*

12. *Wie wußte der Arzt, daß Ruki*
    Angst hatte? Weil er in die Ecke lief, als er die
            Spritze sah.

13. *Warum sprach Ruki nicht? Weil er Angst hatte.*

14. *Was für ein Hemd trug er? Ein zerrissenes.*

15. *Warum, glauben Sie, trug Ruki*
    ein zerrissenes Hemd? Weil er arm war; weil er nicht
            genug Geld hatte, sich ein neues zu
            kaufen.

16. *Was konnte er also nicht tun?*
            Sich ein neues Hemd kaufen.

17. *Was sah man durch das Hemd?*
            Rukis Körper.

18. *Warum konnte man seinen Körper*
    so deutlich sehen? Weil das Hemd zerrissen war.

19. *Wie war das Hemd wohl auch?*
            Dünn | alt | billig.

20. *Beschreiben Sie, wie Ruki aussah!*
            Sein Körper bestand nur aus Haut und
            Knochen. Er war mager | unterer-
            nährt.

21. *Woraus besteht . . .? Er | sie | es besteht aus. . . .*

22. *Was bedeutet 'sein Körper bestand*
    nur aus Haut und Knochen?'
            Daß er mager war; daß er zu wenig aß;
            daß er unterernährt war.

23. *Wie sprach der Arzt mit Ruki?*
            Leise, freundlich.

24. *Was wollte er dadurch erreichen?*
            Ruki beruhigen.

25. *Warum wollte er ihn beruhigen?*
        Weil er ihm eine Spritze geben wollte |
        ihn impfen wollte.
26. *Was sagte er eigentlich, um Ruki*
    zu beruhigen?   „*Es tut nicht weh.*"
27. *Peter nimmt Aspirin? Warum?*
        Weil er Kopfweh hat.
28. *Das heißt?*   *Sein Kopf tut ihm weh.*
29. *Liefen die anderen Kinder wie Ruki*
    in die Ecke?   *Nein.*
30. *Warum nicht?*   *Weil sie keine Angst hatten.*
31. *Wovor? Vor wem?*   *Der Spritze. Dem Arzt.*
32. *Was fragte Ruki dann der Arzt?*
        „*Willst du nicht gesund werden?*"
33. *Was sagte Ruki dazu?*   *Nichts.*
34. *Was tat er aber?*   *Er nickte mit dem Kopf.*
35. *Was wollte er damit sagen?*
        Doch. Daß er doch gesund werden
        wolle.
36. *Was heißt das gewöhnlich, wenn*
    ein Mensch mit dem Kopf nickt?
        Ja.
37. *Und wenn man den Kopf schüttelt?*
        Nein.
38. *Was tut man, wenn man ja | nein sagen*
    will, ohne zu sprechen?   *Man nickt mit dem Kopf | man schüt-*
        telt den Kopf.

Here class can be asked to do certain conventional actions.

39. *Was tut er | sie?*   *Er schüttelt den Kopf, er winkt mit der*
        Hand, usw.
40. *Warum nickte Ruki heftig? Weil er gesund werden wollte.*
41. *Wann nickte er?*   *Als der Arzt ihn fragte, ob er gesund*
        werden wollte?
42. *Was sollte ihn wieder gesund machen?*
        Die Spritze.
43. *Was mußte der Arzt tun, um ihn*
    wieder gesund zu machen?
        Er mußte ihn impfen, ihm eine Spritze
        geben.

44. *Was bekam Ruki nach der Spritze?*
     Milch.
45. *Was versprach ihm der Arzt?*
         Ihm Milch zu geben.
46. *Aber was mußte zuerst geschehen,*
     bevor Ruki die Milch bekam?
             Der Arzt mußte ihn impfen.
47. *Und dann?*   *Dann bekam Ruki die Milch.*
48. *Von wem?*   • *Vom Arzt.*

Section C

1. *Was machte Ruki, als er das Wort*
    'Milch' hörte?   *Er überlegte.*
2. *Glauben Sie, daß er die Milch*
    haben wollte?   *Ja.*
3. *Warum überlegte er?*   *Weil er Milch haben wollte.*
4. *Und?*   *Angst hatte.*
5. *Was wußte Ruki von dem Arzt?*
           Daß er ein guter Mann war; daß er
           von der UNICEF kam.
6. *In was für Ländern arbeitet*
    diese Organisation?   *In armen Ländern; wo arme Leute*
            leben; in Entwicklungsländern.
7. *Warum arbeitete der Arzt in diesem*
    afrikanischen Land?   *Weil die Leute dort krank waren.*
8. *Auf welche Weise half er den Leuten?*
            Er impfte Kinder.
9. *Warum?*   *Weil sie krank waren, einen Ausschlag*
            hatten.
10. *Was war mit Ruki los?* *Er hatte einen Ausschlag.*
11. *Warum gab ihm der Arzt eine Spritze?*
            Um ihn wieder gesund zu machen.
12. *Warum dachte Ruki an das Wort*
     'Zauber'?   *Weil er dachte, daß Medizin Zauber*
            ist.
13. *Kam er schnell zum Arzt?* *Nein, er zögerte.*
14. *Warum?*   *Weil er noch unsicher war | Angst*
            hatte.
15. *Er blieb also in der Ecke stehen,*
     nicht wahr?   *Nein, er trat näher.*

16. *Wie?*   *Zögernd.*

17. *Hatte Ruki noch so große Angst wie*
    früher?   *Nein, nicht so große.*

18. *Warum?*   *Weil der Arzt ihn beruhigte, ihm*
                     Milch versprach.

19. *Was zeigte dem Arzt, daß der Junge*
    immer noch ein bißchen Angst hatte?
                     Er zögerte noch; er kam nur zögernd
                     näher.

20. *Wann zögert man?*   *Wenn man unsicher ist. Wenn man*
                     nicht genau weiß, was man tun
                     soll.

21. *Was tat der Arzt, als er sah, daß*
    Ruki doch näher kam?   *Er lachte.*

22. *Zögerte dann auch der Arzt?*
                     Nein, alles ging schnell.

23. *Was machte der Arzt schnell?*
                     Er gab Ruki eine Spritze.

24. *Was für einen Stich machte er?*
                     Einen leichten.

25. *Wo genau?*   *In Rukis Arm.*

26. *Tat es Ruki weh?*   *Nein, er spürte ihn kaum.*

27. *Warum?*   *Weil der Stich so leicht war.*

28. *Woher wissen wir, daß es Ruki nicht*
    wehtat?   *Er lief nicht weg | in die Ecke.*

29. *Wie sagt man anders 'kaum'?*
                     Fast nicht.

30. *Was fragte der Arzt Ruki noch?*
                     „*War es schlimm?*"

31. *Was antwortete Ruki darauf?*
                     Er schüttelte den Kopf.

32. *Was bedeutete das hier?*   *Daß es nicht schlimm war.*

33. *Was tat der Arzt, während er sprach?*
                     Er reinigte die Stichstelle.

34. *War Ruki noch traurig?*   *Nein.*

35. *Woher wissen Sie das?*   *Er lächelte.*

36. *Was durfte Ruki dann tun? Die Milch holen.*

37. *Warum bekam er die Milch?*
                     Weil er so brav | mutig war.

38. *Verließ er auch zögernd die Hütte?*
                          Nein, er lief hinaus.
39. *Warum?*   *Um die Milch zu holen.*

All the new material covered should be collated in some written form at the end of each lesson, either on the blackboard or in duplicated notes. Questions on the work covered in class can be duplicated or dictated for further work. Multiple-choice questions could be given to test comprehension. Guided essay work could emerge from the text – either the collection of simple factual answers to questions put by the teacher to help less able pupils, or as a '*Nacherzählung*', or the incident could be reported by the boy to his friends or his mother or it could even (as an exercise for the very able child) be described in a letter written by the doctor to his parents in Germany. The writing will emerge from the oral work and both support and supplement it and even the learner whose style of learning is more visual than aural will have plenty of opportunity to learn.

Notes and references

1. Cp. HORNSEY, A. W. (1973) 'A foreign language for all: the questions to be answered'. *Modern Languages in Scotland*, **1**.
2. BURSTALL, C. (1970) *French in the Primary School: attitudes and achievement.* Slough: National Foundation for Educational Research.
3. Cp. HORNSEY, A. W. (1972) 'Mr Best's ladder: question and answer work in foreign-language teaching.' *English Language Teaching*, **26**, no. 2.
4. Adapted from MAHLER, G. and SCHMITT, R. (1961) *Wir lernen Deutsch.* Frankfurt: Moritz Diesterweg.

PART 4

Using documentary data

'Documentary data' is used as a convenient term for the sources of information which we consult in daily life and which we can use as teaching aids in the classroom. They are mainly visual, often involving pictorial, symbolic, numerical and abbreviated-language elements, which, as David Swain says in his chapter on timetables, contain 'a lot of language trying to get out'.

The first contribution attempts to discuss the need for documentary data and to hint at the range of such materials. The reader is then invited to join two teachers on a summer journey to Marseilles and in their September classrooms; to explore the important language-using potential of initially unpromising lists of towns, times, teams and points; to move usefully round a shopping area and a railway station; and to investigate the contribution of cooking to the language class.

NORMAN HILL

University of London Institute of Education

Practical suggestions

It is important, when we use language, to understand what we say
or write; and to say or write forms which are appropriate, that is
'correct' and suitable in the circumstances. Our teaching / learning
situations might be expected therefore (1) to assist the comprehension
of language patterns and (2) to provide opportunities for the recognition and active practice of them. Objects, pictorial materials and
texts, carefully chosen, clearly presented, skilfully exploited, often
meet these requirements. Without offering, in so many words, the
language to be learnt, they provide evidence about which initially
the teacher, subsequently the learner, can talk and write.

A drawing may give us ample opportunity to make clear and get
used, among other things, a number of terms about spatial relations.
A series of pictures may enable us to tell and to get pupils to tell a
story, or to give an account of a process. A text, reporting **what
happened**, may provide the facts which will permit us and our learners
to conclude, and say or write, **what had happened** or **what ought to
have been done**. But occasionally, for certain specific tasks, we discover that none of these types of aid is adequate from the point of
view of clarification or practice. For the presentation and use of
expressions such as *at ten o'clock, from nine to five, for $10\frac{1}{2}$ hours, it's
closed on Mondays*, etc., a more satisfactory point of departure might
be provided by a list of shop, library, museum and pub opening
hours. A 'collage' of tickets, timetable extracts, sketch maps and a
'diary page' of suitably arranged symbols might more fruitfully
stimulate questions and answers or, at a later stage, spontaneous or
non-responsive statements about a particular journey or about
travel in general.

If we listen to the comments of a group of people consulting an
Underground map, the *Guide Michelin* or the entertainments page
of the *Observer*, we realize that these 'documents' reveal, in diagrammatic, symbolic or abbreviated verbal form, evidence which we

interpret using language patterns which do not appear on the page and which, in a learning situation, can be intelligently repeated with modified information content:

Sèvres 92 Hauts-de-Seine. **J 5 - G.Paris** – 20 228 h. alt. 95 – Ind. ☏ 1.
Voir : Manufacture Nationale de Sèvres** – Musée de céramique**.
Paris 12 – Boulogne-Billancourt 2,5 – Longjumeau 21 – St-Germain-en-Laye 17 – Versailles 8.

XX **Lapin Frit,** 36 av. Gambetta ☏ 027.02.18 – ❷
fermé août et lundi – R carte 25 à 55 ☖ 5.

CITROEN-AUTOBIANCHI Ets Colboc, 5 Gde-Rue ☏ 027.01.93

PEUGEOT Digue, 7 r. V.-Hugo ☏ 027.00.84
RENAULT Lapeyre, 19 Gde-Rue ☏ 027.04.27

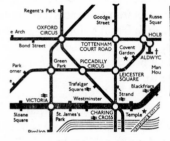

GARRICK. 836 4601. Evgs. 8.0. Sat. 5.30, 8.30, (Mat Wed 2.45 red. price).
SLEUTH
NOW IN ITS FOURTH YEAR
" The Best Thriller Ever " NY Times

GREENWICH 858 7755. Mon.-Fri. 8.0. Sat. 5.0 & 8.0. Tim Barrett, Penelope Keith, Colin Campbell, Sue Lloyd in Alan Ayckbourn's Smash Hit Comedy **HOW THE OTHER HALF LOVES.**

To get from Victoria to Tottenham Court Road you take the Victoria line, north, to Oxford Circus; there you take the Central line, east, to Tottenham Court Road.

Sèvres est à douze kilomètres de Paris, à vingt et un kilomètres de Longjumeau, à huit kilomètres de Versailles. . . .

At the Greenwich Theatre there's a performance at 8 p.m. every day from Monday to Friday, and two on Saturdays, at 5 p.m. and 8 p.m.

The normal out-of-class use made of some of these 'documents' involves inquiry and statement, and they can be used in the class-room to provoke question and answer as well as the other activities – of looking up, checking, calculating, estimating and choosing – which arise in planning a journey, organizing a visit, discussing a day's programme, etc.

Out-of-class familiarity with the form of these aids to living may help the learner to accept and understand them as teaching aids; for some pupils, whose classroom familiarity with pictures or texts may have bred something approaching contempt, the appearance on the desk, blackboard or screen of a railway timetable, a recipe and a shopping list, a page of a diary or the 'local information' section of a regional newspaper, etc., may prove refreshing.

Clearly a team of busy teachers, however sensitive to pupil

reaction, requires a greater justification than mere novelty for engaging in the time-consuming activity of searching for or creating, and discovering how to use, documentary materials. But perhaps such means of talk-provoking fact presentation have a special contribution to make.

Among the teacher's short-term objectives, two seem to be particularly important: (1) to present and to enable his pupils to master a language pattern they have not used hitherto (or have forgotten); (2) to create situations in which are possible revision of, combination of, flexible movement between several patterns already met. In the teacher's planning there seem to be two different points of departure: (a) the occurrence of the problem, followed by the search for a situation; (b) the chance discovery of a promising situation, followed by a study of what it might give rise to.

The occurrence of the problem (a): the time has come to learn this new pattern (1) or to revise this group of patterns (2); what is the most fruitful situation, what are the most effective aids we can find?

We wish to teach the expression: *A est à x kilomètres de B*; we remember, or discover, that the SNCF has published a free map on which are shown the distances between towns; and that, in the *Guide Michelin*, for each town or village, three or four distances from other towns are given. Both these documents provide the information represented in our model sentence by A, x and B; the teacher's statements provide the *à* and his questions encourage its appropriate use.

We wish to teach the prepositional phrases indicating ways of getting from A to B; we can take advantage of the learners' acquaintance with generally accepted symbols and, with their co-operation, can create others as they are necessary, to provide journeys like:

* From HILL, N. (1971) *Life in a London Suburb*. London: Hachette. Reproduced by permission of the publisher.

We wish to revise and encourage correct and flexible use of the French partitive article and *de* with expressions of quantity; we might consider the possibility of using a recipe (e.g. *une omelette*; *de la vinaigrette*; *un gâteau quatre-quarts*), clear abbreviations and drawings or photographs allowing us to avoid the undesirable visual help of full statements.

We wish to organize a controlled discussion on the subject of television (choice of programmes, reasons for watching); a few pages of programme titles and descriptions (*Radio Times* or equivalent) might be our point of departure, so that our pupils have at their disposal at least the basic vocabulary and structures involved in the choice and the expression of their preferences.

The discovery of a situation (b) (in the present case: a document) which looks promising; what can it help us to do?

This torn envelope encourages us to say quite a lot, including: *il y en a quatre | trois grands à un franc, un petit à 5 centimes (timbres)*; *ils représentent un tableau de Georges de la Tour | Raoul Dufy | les armes de la ville d'Auch*; *l'adresse de l'expéditeur | du destinataire, etc.*; but it seems quite exceptionally useful for: *elle a été déchirée | tapée à la machine | imprimée | collée (à gauche | de travers) | pesée | mise à la poste (à Paris, avant 16h15, le 10 février 1970)*; *il a été écrit (au crayon) | collé (à l'envers)*; *ils ont été collés (à droite) | oblitérés, etc.*

This postcard, railway seat reservation, on the other hand, might stimulate a wide-ranging, one-thing-leading-to-another teaching dialogue including the questions: *Combien de places le client a-t-il demandées? Dans quel train? De quelle gare devait-il partir? Pour aller à quelle ville? Où sont Bâle et Libramont?* etc., and including the answers: *le nombre de voyageurs, le numéro du train* and *en chiffres romains.*

The reservation is a ready-made visual aid, needing no modification of content; simply a little retouching for easy duplication and distribution, or for transfer to transparency and overhead projection. But occasionally it may be necessary:

1. to eliminate distracting, for the time being irrelevant information in, say, official documents or television programmes, or to reduce, say, the number of towns on the SNCF distance map;

2. to simplify some of the stages of a recipe or to omit from the symbolically presented list of London telephone information services (speaking clock, dial-a-disc, weather, motoring conditions, recipe of the day, etc.) those items which some of us would find difficult to exploit or even explain in any language – the test match scores and the *Financial Times* Share Index and news service;

3. to bring together a careful selection of, say, small ads on one topic, so that practice in interpretation can lead to concentrated practice in expression: *Que faut-il faire pour se renseigner au sujet de cet appartement? | ce studio? | cette chambre? | Il faut téléphoner au propriétaire | écrire à l'adresse indiquée | se présenter sur place;*

postmark slogans can be similarly collected, selected and arranged according to our needs: (a) to get a pattern practised: *Qu'est-ce que ces flammes nous invitent à faire? – A devenir infirmière | à donner du sang | à visiter les Floralies d'Orléans | à garder notre ville propre*; (b) as a point of departure for a discussion about the desirable features of a holiday resort;

4. to **create** a documentary aid (a) by setting out, using symbols and possibly abbreviated language, a process, a programme, a journey, etc., or (b) by bringing together a number of individual documents providing evidence for the procedures, topic, event, etc., to be discussed (see K. and L. Money's chapter, p. 154 ff.).

Clearly the use of some of the documents I suggest creates problems of preparation and presentation for the teacher. There are also, some have objected, serious problems of understanding for the learner. Since I find unsatisfactory some of the conventions of some published audio-visual courses, on the grounds that the pictorial element does not reveal the sense of the accompanying language, I need to justify my present recommendations.

Symbolic and abbreviated presentation of information, like the use of initials, is becoming increasingly common. One of the most interesting things I picked up at a recent weekend educational conference was a rectangle of absorbent paper, about 14×9 cm, on which one could read the verbal message 'Please don't use the towel'. A supply of these was provided in the room of each visitor. Since, on arrival at breakfast, lunch and dinner, we all appeared not only washed and rinsed, but dried, one can assume that the symbols supplementing the request, a razor blade in one corner, a pair of very red lips in another, had conveyed the rest of the message.

Even more optimistically, when the slide-projector manufacturer has his wares packed in cartons bearing the following message:

Y ⌐T↑ , he hopes that packers, porters, storemen, salesmen

and customers, will not throw the parcel into a pool of water with the arrow pointing downwards. These symbols, in this combination, in this context, are accepted by the world outside the classroom.

(Perhaps I should make it clear that I would not expect ⌐T to con-

vey, in **different** circumstances, 'Don't allow the contents to become damp'; though, in the company of other identifiable objects and accompanied by the appropriate question, it might provoke: 'It's an umbrella'; held by Iris of the weather forecast in today's *Daily Express*, it might well tell readers of that newspaper: 'It's going to rain.')

Iris says:

"Watch out"

It seems reasonable to assume that, if a symbol, even if not a self-evident one, is currently used to convey a message, we either know it or we ought to make its acquaintance; if known or learnable symbols are presented in class by a helpful teacher, the visible evidence and the spoken and subsequently written questions are likely, in favourable circumstances, to lead to intensive (concentration on one or a few patterns within a category) or extensive (flexible movement among situationally relevant patterns) use of the language.

The lesson we catch a glimpse of in 'The journey' (pp. 154–64) gives some idea of the sort of work possible with a combination of both collected and invented documentary evidence. Once the learners are familiar with the materials and the message they convey, questions are asked which elicit answers of varying length and complexity, answers which tell the teacher what has been mastered, what needs to be revised, what has still to be taught. Brief phrases like *en voiture | chez vos parents | pour aller au Havre* are rightly sought and welcomed; the teacher accepts the responsibility of finding the kind of question or stimulus which needs a 'complete sentence' response: *Quelle est la différence entre une autoroute et une route normale? | Donnez-moi quelques détails au sujet de notre départ. | Maintenant racontez-moi tout ce que nous avons fait le samedi 21*, etc. Errors lead to a raised eyebrow, a reminding hint or a few minutes of re-teaching: *Chez . . .? | Bien, mais ça, c'est au présent*; *au passé maintenant . . .? | Est-ce que c'est dans le nord de l'Angleterre? | [à le] Havre – Le Touquet → au Touquet – Le Havre → au Havre* (see p. 159).

Having loosely defined documentary data and hinted at the contribution work with such aids can make to the achievement of some of our objectives, I propose to offer an obviously incomplete list of documentary materials, which have been or might be found useful.

Timetables (daily, weekly, annual): transport; studies; gardening or
farming; radio and TV

suggesting questions like:

When will he arrive in Montreal? do you have physics? did he
plant his tomatoes? does BBC 2 close down?

How long does it / will it / did it take / last?

Where? Where from? Where to?

What kind of programme? / train? / crop?

Which plane would you take? / subject do you prefer? / programmes do you listen to? / vegetables are most profitable?

Why does the 8.40 train arrive before the 8.13? / did he spray
his rose bushes last month?

Page of real / imaginary diary to present future business trip or
past hiking tour, etc.

suggesting answers like:

*Il ira à Bordeaux; il sera accompagné de sa secrétaire; ils pren-
dront le train; ils voyageront en première classe; ils partiront à
9 heures et demie; ils arriveront trois heures plus tard; ils passeront
deux jours à Bordeaux.*

Posters, notices, announcements, programmes

providing detailed information about times of concerts, matches,
competitions, films, meetings, rehearsals, etc.; about participants and the nature of their participation; providing also a
basis for the supposition, the conclusion drawing necessary in
the later stages:

What sort of films do you think these are?

What do you think will happen to the proceeds of this jumble
sale?

Why do they mention the telephone number of the *centre de
secours* on this notice (*Baignades autorisées aux risques et
périls des baigneurs*)?

Extracts from the *Guide Michelin*, telephone directory, post office
guide

the extract on Sèvres (p. 145) invites us to ask between twenty
and thirty questions; telephone numbers are important, if not
inspiring; reasons for dialling a selection of them suggest more
interesting language work.

Recipes, shopping lists and bills

the contribution of recipes is considered on p. 186 ff.; but the ingredients have to be bought, whether usually, next Tuesday or last Thursday, If we look at Mme Pichard's Thursday morning shopping list, based on the evening menu: *omelette au jambon*; *tarte aux pommes*, certain types of questions suggest themselves:

Qu'est-ce que Mme Pichard a acheté à la crémerie et chez le marchand de légumes?
Où a-t-elle acheté la farine?
Où a-t-elle acheté le jambon et les pommes?
Combien de beurre a-t-elle acheté?
Combien d'oeufs et de jambon a-t-elle achetés?
Combien a-t-elle payé la salade et les pommes?

But it is clear from the difficulties involved that it is vital and not easy for the teacher to choose questions according to his pupils' ability to answer and according to his need to practise the partitive article or the pattern – *elle en a acheté un demi-kilo*, etc., or to see how fluently his learners can move from *chez l'épicier* via *elle a acheté le jambon chez le charcutier et les pommes chez le marchand de fruits and elle en a acheté un kilo* to *elle a payé la salade x francs.*

Instructions for processes other than cooking

how to keep the bath clean, or the greenfly off the roses

Lists other than shopping lists

things that have to be done before we go away on holiday

Advertisements and 'messages' on containers

What is this product supposed to do?
What are the various uses of these household gloves?
What will you do first when you make that (packet of) soup?
What can you tell me about the apples that arrived in that cardboard box?
What's the difference between these two pots of yoghurt (flavour, size, price, quantity, fat content)?

Small ads and SOS

like *Urgt.ch.fme.de mén. parlant franç., aimant les enf., pr.trav. 7h.par jour. MED 66–92* or *Rivière Jean (Volvo grise 5678H34 se dirigeant vers Hambourg) rentrer à Marseille d'urgence ou téléphoner 60.51.42. Belle-mère hospitalisée.*

Weather forecasts like

Envelopes, with stamps and postmark slogans; reservations, tickets, maps, plans, etc.

KEN AND LOULI MONEY

Shenfield Comprehensive School, Essex, and Abbs Cross Comprehensive School, Hornchurch, Essex

The journey: London to Marseilles, July 1973

We had already used invented journeys to stimulate structured dialogue about third person activities in the present, past and future tenses. The documents we collected during a real journey in July (p. 155) and the one we subsequently made (p. 156) gave us an opportunity to get our pupils using a number of common, brief patterns and also some full-sentence, second person examples of the *passé composé*. *Vous êtes allé(e)(s) à Southampton* may be less 'frequent' than the third and first persons, but it is necessary, in anything but very superficial communication, both in the question: *Est-ce que vous êtes allé(e)(s) à S.?* or *Vous êtes allé(e)(s) à S.?*, and in the 'résumé' situation found not only in the classroom: *Donc, vous êtes allé(e)(s) à S., et puis . . .?*

Using these materials with both fourth- and sixth-year learners, we found both from the correct answers and from the hesitations and errors that (a) it does not take pupils long to get used to understanding this type of visual aid; (b) this kind of question and answer activity needs to be practised from the initial stages of language learning; and (c) even 'elementary' language patterns need to be revised at all levels.

The initial oral presentation of the journey gave the pupils an opportunity to become familiar with the documentary visual aids. The following transcript offers a selection of the questions asked and answers received as well as an occasional opportunity for less restricted response. It does not reveal all the mistakes, the names, the 'euh's, the essential encouraging comments and appropriate repetitions of the teacher. The whole truth on paper would be far more boring than what happened in class, and might make readers doubt the virtue of honesty.

juillet 1973

vendredi	20	Londres → 🚗 → M4 → Windsor Ascot → M3 → Eastleigh (dép.19h10) (arr. 22h15) 🛏 chez parents de Monsieur M.
samedi	21	☎️ → Normandy Ferries *"pas de places avant mercredi"* 🚗 → Southampton (Thoresen Ferries) *"2 places (Le Havre)"* 21h30 🚗 père de M. → docks (Southampton) 23h 🚢 — (✗ 🛏 dans le bar du bateau)
dimanche	22	→ Le Havre (arr. 07h00) → bar ☎️ oncle (Rouen) *"Je pars en vacances au Brésil"* 70.00.86 (2,50F) ✋ → Rouen centre (arr. 15h00) ROUEN Hôtels → Hôtel de Nice ☎️ < 1 renseignements (1,00F) 2 parents de Madame M. (Marseille 76.18.61 en PCV) 🛏
lundi	23	→ banque (pour changer de l'argent) note (hôtel) 09h30 🚌 n°6 (2,40F) → gare 10h00 🚆 (debout) → Paris-Gare St-Lazare (arr. 11h10) Ⓜ St-Lazare — Concorde → Gare de Lyon (1,30F ×2) (consigne automatique 🧳 🧳 2,00F) 🚶 → bar "Lyon-Tabac", rue de Lyon ☕☕ (2,50F) 14h45 🚆 → Marseille – Gare St-Charles (arr. 22h50) ☎️ taxiphone à la gare (0,40F) → parents de Madame 🚗 père de Mme → gare → chez parents de Mme 🛏

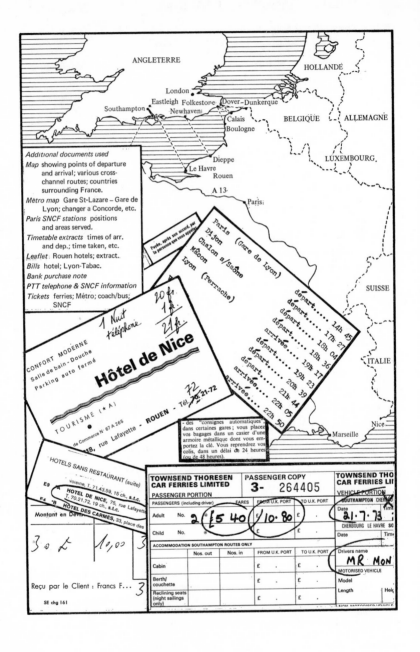

ANGLETERRE

HOLLANDE

London

Eastleigh Folkestone Dover—Dunkerque
Southampton   Newhaven

Calais   BELGIQUE   ALLEMAGNE
Boulogne

Dieppe   LUXEMBOURG
Le Havre
Rouen

A 13·

Paris

SUISSE

ITALIE

Nice

Marseille

Additional documents used

Map showing points of departure
   and arrival; various cross-
   channel routes; countries
   surrounding France.

Métro map Gare St-Lazare – Gare de
   Lyon; changer a Concorde, etc.

Paris SNCF stations positions
   and areas served.

Timetable extracts times of arr.
   and dep.; time taken, etc.

Leaflet: Rouen hotels; extract.

Bills hotel; Lyon-Tabac.

Bank purchase note

PTT telephone & SNCF information

Tickets ferries; Métro; coach/bus;
   SNCF

20 fr.
1 fr.
21 fr.

1 Nuit
téléphone

CONFORT MODERNE
Salle de bain - Douche
Parking auto fermé

Hôtel de Nice

72
Tél. 70.21.72

TOURISME (★A)

de Commerce N° 67 A 265   18, rue Lafayette - ROUEN

Paris (Gare de Lyon)
Dijon
Chalon s/Saône
Mâcon
Lyon (Perrache)

départ..... 14h 45
départ..... 17h 27
départ..... 18h 04
arrivée..... 18h 36
départ..... 19h 17
départ..... 19h 23
départ..... 20h 39
arrivée..... 21h 44
arrivée..... 22h 05
arrivée..... 22h 50

- des "consignes automatiques"
dans certaines gares ; vous placez
vos bagages dans un casier d'une
armoire métallique dont vous em-
portez la clé. Vous reprendrez vos
colis, dans un délai de 24 heures
(ou de 48 heures).

HOTELS SANS RESTAURANT (suite)

E9   voisine, T. 71.43.59, 15 ch., s.t.c.
        HOTEL DE NICE, 75, rue Lafayette
F4 *B   T. 70.21.72, 19 ch., s.t.c.
Montant en Devis HÔTEL DES CARMES, 33, place des

30 £   10,00   3

Reçu par le Client : Francs F... 3

SE chg 161

TOWNSEND THORESEN CAR FERRIES LIMITED	PASSENGER COPY 3- 264405		TOWNSEND THO CAR FERRIES LII
PASSENGER PORTION			VEHICLE PORTION
PASSENGERS (including driver)	FARES	FROM U.K. PORT	TO U.K. PORT
Adult No. 2	£ 5 40	£ 10·80	£ .

SOUTHAMPTON CHERB
Date 21·7·73

CHERBOURG LE HAVRE SO
Date

Child No.	£ .	£ .	£ .
ACCOMMODATION SOUTHAMPTON ROUTES ONLY	Nos. out	Nos. in	FROM U.K. PORT	TO U.K. PORT
Cabin			£ .	£ .
Berth/ couchette			£ .	£ .
Reclining seats (night sailings only)			£ .	£ .

Drivers name
MR MON
MOTORISED VEHICLE
Model
Length   Hei

Quand est-ce que nous sommes partis?	*Le vingt juillet.*
A quelle heure avons-nous quitté Londres?	*[19 h moins 10; à 19 h et 10]**
	A sept heures dix . . . du soir.
Comment est-ce que nous sommes allés à Eastleigh?	
	. . .
En autobus?	*Non, en voiture* (right first time in 4th form; *par auto* in 6th).
Par quels autres moyens de transport peut-on aller de Londres à Eastleigh?	*En car; par le train; en stop.*
Bon; nous avons quitté Londres à 7h10 . . . en voiture. Quelle route avons-nous prise?	*[Nous avons pris . . . le M4.]*
Nous?	*Vous avez pris . . ./* interrupted.
Très bien; maintenant écoutez: La M4 est une route. Quelle route avons-nous prise pour aller jusqu'à Windsor?	*Vous avez pris la M4.*
Oui. Et pour aller de Ascot à Eastleigh?	*Vous avez pris la M3.*
Qu'est-ce que c'est la M3?	*C'est une grande route.*
Oui, c'est une grande route, ou bien . . .?	*Une autoroute.*
Bien. Quelle est la différence entre une autoroute et une route ordinaire, comme, par exemple, la A4?	*Une autoroute est plus grande; une autoroute est plus large . . . plus directe.*
X, écrivez cette phrase au tableau (here and elsewhere).	
Oui, très bien. Et encore? *Parlez-moi de la vitesse des voitures . . .*	*Les voitures vont plus vite sur une autoroute* (in the 6th this answer was immediate and preceded *plus grande*; in the 4th it arrived via *les voitures [allaient]* . . .)

* Incorrect first attempts are in square brackets.

*Bon, donnez-moi quelques détails,
    maintenant, au sujet de notre
    départ: la date, l'heure, le
    moyen de transport, la route
    que nous avons prise.*

*Très bien. Et à quelle heure
    est-ce que nous y sommes
    arrivés?*

*Arrivés à Eastleigh, est-ce que
    nous avons dormi à l'hôtel?*

Chez . . .?

*Savez-vous où se trouve
    Eastleigh? Regardez la carte.
    . . . Est-ce que c'est dans le
    nord de l'Angleterre?*

Et Newcastle?, etc.

*Eastleigh est près de quelle ville
    importante?*

C'est près de quelle ville?

*Oui, très bien. Vous voyez que
    le samedi 21 j'ai téléphoné
    (mon mari a téléphoné) aux
    Normandy Ferries. . . . Pourquoi?*

*Oui, et qu'est-ce qu'ils ont
    répondu?*

*Bien, mais ça c'est au présent;
    au passé maintenant . . .*

*Qu'est-ce que nous avons fait
    ensuite? Nous sommes restés à
    la maison?*

Oui; comment?

*Et vous, X, Y, Z, comment
    êtes-vous venus à l'école ce
    matin?*

*Arrivés à S., nous sommes allés
    à une autre compagnie de Car
    Ferries. . . .Pourquoi?*

(a) *Vous êtes partis le 20 juillet
    à 7h10 du soir.* (b) *Vous êtes
    partis en voiture.* (c) *Vous
    avez pris la M4 et la M3 pour
    aller à Eastleigh.*

[*A 22 heures et quart /
    à 10 heures et quart ce soir*]
A dix heures et quart du soir.

Non, vous avez dormi chez [*ses*]
    parents.

Chez vos parents.

*Non, c'est dans le sud . . . sur
    la côte.*

*C'est dans le nord de
    l'Angleterre.*

[*Il est . . .*]
C'est près de Southampton.

*Pour réserver des places / parce
    que vous vouliez des places
    dans le ferry.*

Qu'ils [*n'ont*] *pas de places
    avant mercredi.*

*Ils n'avaient pas de places avant
    mercredi.*

. . .

*Non, vous êtes allés à
    Southampton.*

En voiture.

X. Moi, je suis venu en voiture.

Y. Moi je suis venu à pied, etc.

*Pour réserver des places / pour
    prendre des billets.*

Oui; pour aller où?	*[Le Havre].*
???	*Pour aller [à Le Havre].*
Brief aside re British Caledonian Gatwick – Le Touquet line → on atterrit au Touquet	
Donc on prend l'avion à Gatwick pour aller . . .?	*Pour aller au Touquet.*
Et nous avons pris des billets pourquoi?	*Pour aller au Havre.*
Bien. Où se trouve Le Havre?	*Dans le nord [de France].*
Southampton se trouve dans le sud de l'Angleterre; Anvers dans le nord de la Belgique. Où se trouve Le Havre?	*Dans le nord de la France.*
Et où est Nice?	*Dans le sud	dans le midi de la France.*
Comment s'appelle le bras de mer qui se trouve entre l'Angleterre et la France?	*La Manche.*
*Nous avons donc traversé la Manche, ma femme	mon mari et moi. . . . Comment?*	*En bateau.*
Comment peut-on traverser la Manche?	*En avion	en bateau	en hovercraft	[à nager].*
Non, on dit: à la nage; répétez . . . (Look out for opportunity to re-use *à la nage.*)	*A la nage.*
Regardez le billet maintenant, le billet de T. Ferries. C'est un billet pour combien de personnes?	*Pour deux personnes.*
Oui. Est-ce que c'est un aller simple, ou un aller-retour?	*C'est un aller simple.*
Oui; c'est-à-dire qu'on peut l'utiliser pour . . .?	*Pour aller en France.*
Et non pas pour . . .?	*Pour revenir en Angleterre.*

Combien coûte (ou plutot coûtait, car les prix ont sûrement augmenté). . . . Combien coûtait le trajet simple, par personne?

Cinq livres quarante.

Et combien avons-nous payé, puisque nous étions deux?

Dix livres quatre-vingts.

Oui, d'accord. Quelle était la date de notre départ?

Le [22] juillet.

Non; c'est indiqué sur le billet . . .

Ah non, le 21 juillet.

C'est ça. Le 22, c'est la date de notre arrivée en France; et 23 heures . . .?

C'est l'heure de votre départ.

Dites-moi maintenant quels sont les renseignements que l'on donne sur le billet. Qu'est-ce qu'on y voit?

On y voit votre nom | le nom de votre mari; la date et l'heure de votre départ; le prix du billet. . . .

A quelle heure avons-nous quitté la maison le samedi soir? Regardez la feuille verte (= p. 156).

A neuf heures et demie.

Et comment sommes-nous allés aux docks?

En voiture.

Qui a conduit la voiture? Ma femme? | Mon mari?

Non, votre père | Non, votre beau-père.

X, qu'est-ce qu'il a fait, mon père | beau-père?

Il a conduit la voiture.

Est-ce que le bateau est parti à minuit?

Non, il est parti à 11 heures.

Oui, c'est ça. Est-ce que nous avons dormi dans une cabine?

Non, vous avez dormi dans le bar du bateau.

Dans un lit? . . . Par terre? . . .

Non, sur une banquette.

Très bien. Bon, maintenant racontez-moi tout ce que nous avons fait le samedi 21 . . . et comment nous avons passé la nuit du 21 au 22?

Vous avez téléphoné, . . . etc.

Bon. Alors où sommes-nous arrivés le 22?

Au Havre.

A quelle heure?	*A sept heures.*
Et la traversée a duré combien de temps?	*Huit heures.*
Oui, depuis 11 heures du soir jusqu'à . . .?	*Jusqu'à sept heures du matin.*
Une fois descendus du bateau, avons-nous commencé tout de suite à faire du stop?	*Non, vous [allez] au bar.*
. . .? au passé?	*Vous êtes allés au bar.*
Pourquoi?	*. . .*
Nous avions passé la nuit dans le bar du bateau; mais nous n'avions pas bu, nous n'avions pas mangé . . .	*Parce que vous aviez faim.*
Oui, parce que nous avions faim et . . .?	*Et soif.*
Donc, nous y sommes allés pour . . .?	*Pour boire et manger.*
Donc, qu'est-ce que nous avons fait au bar?	*Vous avez mangé	Vous avez bu.*
Oui, et ensuite?	*Vous avez téléphoné [ ] votre oncle.*
Ce n'est pas tout à fait juste . . . X?	*Vous avez téléphoné [ ] votre oncle à Rouen.*
Y . . .?	*. . .*
Écoutez; le 21, à Southampton nous avons téléphoné aux Normandy Ferries; alors, qu'est-ce que nous avons fait le 22 au bar? . . . Est-ce que nous avons téléphoné à notre cousin?	*Non, vous avez téléphoné à votre oncle.*
Très bien. Qu'est-ce que nous avons fait, X?	*Vous avez téléphoné à votre oncle.*
Bien. Et qu'est-ce qu'il a dit?	*Il a dit: Je pars en vacances.*
Oui. Qu'est-ce qu'il allait faire, A?	*A. Il allait [parter] en vacances.*
Il allait . . .?	*B. Il allait partir en vacances.*
Bien. Qu'est-ce qu'il allait faire, A?	*A. Il allait partir en vacances.*

Bien. Où allait-il passer ses vacances?	*Au Brésil.*
Où est-ce qu'on peut téléphoner en France? Dans un bar . . .	*Dans un café.*
Oui; c'est à peu près la même chose . . .	*Dans une cabine téléphonique / A la poste.*
Oui, et cela coûte moins cher à la poste. Si ça coûte moins cher à la poste, pourquoi est-ce que nous avons téléphoné dans un bar?	*Parce qu'[il est] [la seule place] possible.*
Non, on ne dit pas 'place' . . . Parce que c'était . . . ? Vous connaissez le mot: 'endroit'? On dit 'un endroit'.	*Ah oui.*
Alors . . . parce que . . .	*C'était le seul endroit possible.*
Oui; pourquoi?	*Parce qu'il . . .*
C'était quel jour?	*C'était un dimanche.*
Oui . . . donc . . .? la poste . . .?	*La poste était fermée.*
C'est ça; la poste était fermée. Combien avons-nous payé la communication?	*Deux francs [et demi].*
Bon, mais on dit plutôt . . .?	*Deux francs cinquante.*
Très bien. Comment sommes-nous allés à Rouen?	*Vous avez fait du stop.*
Qui fait du stop, en général?	*. . .*
Les directeurs de banque?	*Non, les étudiants.*
Pourquoi?	*Parce qu'ils n'ont pas beaucoup d'argent.*
Et pourquoi avons-nous fait du stop ce jour-là?	*Parce que vous n'[avez] pas beaucoup d'argent.*
Ce jour-là . . . le 22 juillet . . . au passé . . .	*Parce que vous n'aviez pas beaucoup d'argent.*
C'est ça. Nous avons eu de la chance; on nous a conduits jusqu'au centre de Rouen. A quelle heure y sommes-nous arrivés?	*A trois heures de l'après-midi.*

Qu'est ce que nous avons fait quand nous sommes arrivés au centre de Rouen?	*Vous avez cherché un hôtel.*
Oui; et nous en avons trouvé un . . . qui s'appelait . . .?	*L'Hôtel de Nice.*
Selon l'extrait du dépliant ('Hôtels sans restaurant'), combien de chambres y a-t-il à cet hôtel?	*Il y en a dix-neuf.*
Que veut dire: Hôtels sans restaurant?	*Cela veut dire qu'il n'y a pas de restaurant . . . dans ces hôtels.*
Oui; c'est-à-dire . . .?	*On ne peut pas [ ] manger.*
Qu'on ne peut pas y manger. (To revise this point, see details about hotel on card – *On ne peut pas y manger . . . mais qu'est-ce qu'on peut y faire? Dormir, prendre un bain / une douche, garer sa voiture.*)	
Que représente le numéro 70 21 72?	*C'est un numéro de téléphone.*
Lequel?	*[De l'hôtel.]*
Celui de l'hôtel . . . Répétez . . . (Further practice with *celui de l'école / de l'hôpital / de la bibliothèque / du médecin*, etc.)	*Celui de l'hôtel.*
Et le numéro 70 21 72?	*Celui de l'hôtel.*
Oui, selon le dépliant; mais regardez maintenant la carte . . . la note que nous avons reçue le 23 au matin.	*Ah oui, le numéro a changé.*
Oui, on a barré le 70 et on l'a remplacé par . . .?	*Soixante-douze.*
Et – encore une fois selon le dépliant – quel était le prix de la chambre?	*Quinze francs.*
Oui, ou plutôt entre 15 francs et . . .?	*Et dix-huit francs cinquante.*

Oui, d'accord. Et selon la note de l'hôtel, combien avons-nous payé la chambre?	*Vingt [et un] francs.*
Non, ça c'est le total, qui comprend un franc pour un coup de téléphone. Combien avons-nous payé la chambre?	*Vingt francs.*
Les prix des chambres ont donc augmenté.	
(Next week, use this week's and next week's shopping list to give plenty of practice in the use of this new verb.)	

etc.

G. E. BULL

Colfe's Grammar School, London SE12

A football league table

I first made up a football league table as a change from the more routine work of textual exploitation and at the same time to explore the possibilities of using documentary data in German. My original table was longer than the one in this chapter, but I found that the material can become rather repetitive and that the records of the three teams at the bottom and top of the table were quite sufficient for my task.

The idea may not seem particularly exciting to teachers of girls, but with boys it can be interesting, entertaining and useful – from it one can teach both new items of vocabulary (even though most are connected with football and will not appear in an A-level paper) and also certain new structures and verb uses. I have used this table with a lower sixth group, but it may well be suitable for a good O-level group.

For reasons that will be clear later, the table shows the position at the end of the season with one vital match still to be played:

		zu Hause				auswärts				
		gew.	u.	v.	Tore	gew.	u.	v.	Tore	Punkte
1. Bayern München	34	15	2	0	51–7	12	3	2	39–8	59:9
2. Mönchengladbach	34	17	0	0	42–6	9	7	1	24–16	59:9
3. FC Köln	33	14	2	0	39–11	12	4	1	30–12	58:8
und in Abstiegsgefahr:										
16. Hertha Berlin	34	5	4	8	17–29	2	5	10	14–22	23:45
17. Hamburger SV	33	7	3	7	20–32	2	4	10	13–34	23:43
18. Eintracht Frank- furt	34	0	2	15	6–52	0	0	17	5–58	2:66

Still to play: *Samstag, den 24 Juni, FC Köln – Hamburger SV*
Disregarding separate home and away records the table would read thus:

		gew.	u.	v.	Tore	Punkte
1. Bayern München	34	27	5	2	90–15	59:9
2. Mönchengladbach	34	26	7	1	66–22	59:9
3. FC Köln	33	26	6	1	69–23	58:8
16. Hertha Berlin	34	7	9	18	31–51	23:45
17. Hamburger SV	33	9	7	17	33–66	23:43
18. Eintracht Frankfurt	34	0	2	32	11–110	2:66

It is not essential to use both tables, but the first gives more detail, while the second is a clearer representation of over-all record and goal averages.

Given the above tables, where does one start? There is such a wealth of information that there are many possible ways of tackling it, but I have found the following sequence both logical and successful:

1. Simple questions to acquaint the pupils with the names of the teams, their location within Germany, and perhaps even the names of some of their best-known players:

Wieviele Mannschaften spielen in der Bundesliga?	*Achtzehn.*
Welche ist jetzt an der Spitze?	*Bayern München.*
Wo ist München?	*In Süddeutschland.*
Und Hamburg?	*In Norddeutschland.*
Und wie heißt die Mannschaft in Hamburg?	*Der Hamburger Sportverein.*
Welche Münchener Spieler kennen Sie?	*Beckenbauer, Müller, usw.*

This procedure would be used for all six teams until the facts are well established. With the use of a map one could then ask further questions:

Wie weit ist es von München nach Hamburg?   (Use of *Entfernung, entfernt, Fahrt.*)

Warum spielt der HSV nicht gern in München?

The other teams, including some not in the tables, could be found on the map, distances compared, local derbies identified and some regional names used (*Ruhrgebiet*, etc.).

2. The records of the clubs could now be discussed, with the

teacher gradually producing the necessary terminology. FC Köln is used as an example (bold type indicates items which are likely to be new):

Wieviele Spiele hat der FC Köln gespielt?
*Wieviele zu Hause und wieviele **auswärts**?*
*Wieviele hat er **gewonnen**? Zu Hause? Auswärts? **Insgesamt**?*
*Wieviele hat er **unentschieden** gespielt?*
*Wieviele hat er **verloren**?*
*Wieviele **Tore** hat er **geschossen**? Wieviele **Gegentore**?*
*Wieviele **Punkte** hat er gewonnen? verloren?*
*Wie ist das **Torverhältnis** vom FC Köln? (69 durch 23 = 3)*
Wieviele Punkte/Spiele hat er verloren und wieviele gewonnen? (Such
   questions reasonably require full-sentence answers.)
Beschreiben Sie jetzt den Stand des FC Köln!

This procedure could be followed for all six teams (unless it becomes too repetitive), thus giving ample practice of items like *auswärts, unentschieden, Tore geschossen, Gegentore, Torverhältnis, insgesamt* and at the same time providing ample practice in handling numbers.

3. Having gone over the basic facts and figures, there are many possibilities for further work. The league championship and relegation issue could be discussed and words such as *Meister, absteigen* introduced. As there are several complex structures that can be introduced and practised here (vid. section 4), I suggest that it may be best to leave this discussion to the end and to concentrate here on getting one's pupils (a) to compare and contrast the records of the teams and (b) to make certain deductions from and comments on the information given.

(a) Here are some examples of the questions that could be asked:

*Welche Mannschaft hat **die meisten Spiele** zu Hause / auswärts ge-wonnen / verloren?*
*Welche Mannschaft hat **die meisten Tore** zu Hause / auswärts / ins-gesamt geschossen?*
*Welche Mannschaft hat **die meisten Gegentore**?*
Welche Mannschaft hat das beste / schlechteste Torverhältnis?
*Welche Mannschaft hat die beste **Abwehr** in der Liga? Woher weiß man das?*

Welche Mannschaft hat die besten Stürmer in der Liga? Woher weiß man das?
Welche Mannschaft hat am besten | am schlechtesten zu Hause | auswärts gespielt?
Hat Frankfurt mehr Tore geschossen als München?
Hat Hertha bessere Stürmer als Köln?
Hat der HSV so viele Gegentore wie Frankfurt?
Was können Sie mir jetzt von Bayern München sagen? (Er hat die besten Stürmer, usw)
Vergleichen Sie den Hamburger SV und Eintracht Frankfurt!

(b) The questions above are still basically factual, requiring the giving of information easily retrieved from the data. Now the pupil can be asked not only for information and manipulation of *weil, mehr als, nicht so gut wie,* etc., but also to make deductions from the information:

Mönchengladbach hat 59 Punkte. Warum ist er nicht an erster Stelle?
  Weil München ein besseres Torverhältnis hat.
Warum ist der HSV an vorletzter Stelle?
  Weil er ein schlechteres Torverhältnis als Hertha hat.
Hat Bayern in Mönchengladbach gewonnen?
  Nein, verloren.
Woher wissen Sie das?
  Weil Mönchengladbach kein einziges Spiel zu Hause verloren hat.
Hat Frankfurt in Berlin gewonnen?
  Nein, weil er kein einziges Spiel auswärts gewonnen hat.
Warum hat Mönchengladbach so viel besser zu Hause gespielt?
  Weil die Zuschauer die Mannschaft ermutigen.

Thus in this section the following structures and patterns could be practised: clauses with *weil, besser als, schlechter als, mehr | weniger Punkte als, nicht so gut wie, eben so viele Punkte wie, nicht so viele Punkte wie, kein einziges Spiel,* etc.

4. As can be seen from the table, there is a match between FC Köln and HSV still to be played, a match which by chance is rather important, for both the championship and the relegation issue depend on its outcome. Speculation about this result leads to scope for much more sophisticated use of language, involving conditionals and modal verbs:

Welche Mannschaft ist der neue **Meister**?
  Man weiß es noch nicht.
Wovon hängt es ab?
  Vom letzten Spiel.
Also warum weiß man noch nicht?
  Weil es vom letzten Spiel abhängt.
Wer könnte Meister werden?
  Entweder Bayern München oder der FC Köln.
Was wird | würde passieren, wenn Köln gewinnt?
  Er wird | würde Meister werden.
Und wenn Köln verliert?
  Bayern wird | würde Meister werden.
Unter welchen Umständen *wird also Bayern Meister?*
  Wenn der HSV das letzte Spiel gewinnt.
Und wenn das Spiel unentschieden **ausgeht?**
  Dann wird | würde Bayern Meister sein.
Warum?
  Weil er ein viel besseres Torverhältnis hat.

Speculation on the championship issue can go even further:

Was muß Köln tun, um Meister zu werden?
  Das entscheidende Spiel *gewinnen.*
Was hoffen die Spieler von Bayern?
  Daß Köln verlieren wird.
Welches Ergebnis ist wahrscheinlich?
  Daß Köln gewinnen wird.
Warum?
  Weil Köln kein einziges Spiel zu Hause verloren hat.

The relegation issue gives rise to similar work:

Wer steigt **bestimmt** *ab?*
  Frankfurt.
Und wer auch?
  Hertha oder der Hamburger SV.
Wovon hängt es ab?
  Vom Ergebnis des letzten Spiels.
Was wird | würde passieren, wenn Köln gewinnt | gewinnen sollte?
  Der HSV wird absteigen (müssen).

Warum?
Weil er das schlechtere Torverhältnis hat.
Und wenn der HSV gewinnt?
Hertha wird absteigen (müssen).
Warum?
Weil er weniger Punkte hat.
Was hoffen die Spieler von Hertha?
Daß der HSV verlieren wird.

5. Having discussed all the possible consequences, the teacher could then make up a result: *FC Köln gegen HSV 1:2.* This then leads to a further series of questions, more deductions and some quite complicated verb forms:

Ist Köln Meister geworden?
   Nein, Bayern.
Warum nicht Köln?
   Weil er das entscheidende Spiel nicht gewonnen hat.
Was hätte also geschehen sollen?
   Köln hätte das Spiel gewinnen sollen.
Warum ist das Ergebnis überraschend?
   Weil Köln bis zu diesem Spiel kein einziges Spiel zu Hause verloren hat.
Warum sind die Spieler von Hertha enttäuscht?
   Weil sie absteigen müssen.
Warum sind die Spieler vom HSV überglücklich?
   Weil sie nicht absteigen müssen.

These are possibilities that one may or may not wish to explore. But one tense is an obvious one either to introduce or revise here, namely the conditional perfect:

Was wäre passiert, wenn Köln doch gewonnen hätte?
   Er hätte in der Bundesliga gewonnen, er wäre Meister geworden, Bayern wäre zweiter gewesen, der HSV wäre abgestiegen, der HSV hätte absteigen müssen, Hertha wäre in der Bundesliga geblieben, Hertha hätte nicht absteigen müssen.
Was wäre passiert, wenn Mönchengladbach in Köln nicht verloren hätte?
   Er hätte zwei Punkte mehr gewonnen, er wäre Meister geworden / gewesen.

One can also practise the *wenn*-clauses:

Unter welchen Umständen wäre Hertha nicht abgestiegen?
Wenn der HSV verloren hätte, wenn Köln gewonnen hätte, wenn
Hertha mehr Punkte gewonnen hätte, etc.

Several other questions about other teams would require similar
answers. The teacher could even change the conditions: *Stellen Sie*
sich vor, Köln hätte das letzte Spiel nicht verloren, sondern 3:1 gewon-
nen, was wäre dann passiert?

6. When all of this material has been exploited and if interest is
still sufficient, the teacher could now widen the range of football talk
by going into positions, tactics, some technical terms, rules, using
words like *Einwurf, Elfmeter, abseits, Strafraum, Freistoß, Ersatz-*
spieler, des Feldes verweisen, Schiedsrichter. This could be supplemented with photocopies of reports from newspapers and pupils
could be asked to imagine themselves as a player in that final match,
to describe the game, their elation or disappointment or even to
imagine what the respective managers said before or after the game.
Some preliminary questions would help:

Was würden Sie tun, wenn Sie Spielleiter / Mannschaftskapitän von
Frankfurt wären?
Ich würde Selbstmord begehen, ich würde mir eine neue Stellung
suchen, ich würde dem Trainer raten, einen neuen Torwart zu
kaufen, ich würde das Fußballspielen aufgeben.

What then, in summary, are the possibilities of a football league
table as data? First, geography (*im Norden, nicht weit von, entfernt,*
etc.), second, useful phrases to describe teams' records (*auswärts,*
verlieren, Tore schießen, unentschieden, Torverhältnis), third, useful
practice of structures (*besser als, nicht so gut wie, weil*-clauses),
fourth, there is the chance to revise or introduce more complex
structures (future: *Köln wird Meister werden, wenn . . .*; conditional:
Köln würde Meister werden, wenn . .; conditional perfect: *Köln*
wäre Meister geworden, wenn . . .; constructions with modals: *der*
HSV wird absteigen müssen, Köln hätte Meister werden können.),
fifth, for those interested, there is ample practice of sport and football vocabulary which, although not immediately useful for A level,
can help to arouse pupils' interest and encourage them to speak
German, providing at the same time a worth-while exercise and a
pleasant change from the more usual work of the sixth form course.

DAVID SHOTTER

Furze Platt Comprehensive School, Maidenhead

A plan

Pictures can be a valuable aid to the foreign-language teacher. However, any picture is limited in its ability to convey meaning by the extent to which it permits difference of interpretation. What in fact does the **visual** representation of a man tying his tie mean in **verbal** terms? Can it adequately represent 'he is getting dressed', or, for that matter, can it adequately distinguish between 'tying' and 'untying'?

It is always possible to avoid ambiguity by conveying the meaning through the mother-tongue. This can, of course, cause further confusion since 'table' is not always going to be a label for the same thing as *Tisch*. Another possibility is to portray things in the form of a plan. This greatly reduces the range of interpretations possible and can provide a clear statement about facts which can be talked about: a house, a school, shops, a supermarket, a store-guide, a station, an airport, a zoo, a park, a town, the arrangement of furniture in a room, a seating-plan for a meal are all possible plans.

Provided that some use of English is accepted in the initial presentation, abbreviations in the foreign language will be a sufficient guide to the vocabulary being used. Abbreviations are likely to be more useful to the teacher than complete words, since the latter restrict the effectiveness of testing questions. They also help to keep the plan uncluttered – which is, after all, one of its significant advantages over a picture.

I should like to illustrate work with plans by concentrating on the layout of a square in a German village and seeing what language emerges:

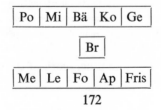

172

1. First it will be necessary to introduce the shops and practise pronouncing them, using the correct gender and writing them in unabbreviated form:

> *Das ist ein Plan eines Dorfplatzes. Das ist das Postamt | die Milchbar | die Bäckerei | die Konditorei | der Gemüseladen.*

These will be introduced one by one and lead to questions like:

> *Ist das das Postamt oder die Milchbar?*
> *Ist das der Gemüseladen? Ja | nein, das ist. . . .*
> *Was ist das?*

The other vocabulary will be introduced and practised similarly:

> *Der Brunnen | die Metzgerei | das Lebensmittelgeschäft | das Fotogeschäft | die Apotheke | der Friseursalon.*

Eventually pupils should be able to identify any of the places pointed to on the plan.

2. If questions are now asked about what can be seen on the plan (employing *sehen*), the accusative forms can be practised. This is the kind of modification to form which English-speaking learners of German need to be constantly asked to make:

> *Was (welchen Laden) siehst du hier?*
> *Was (welchen Laden) siehst du neben der Metzgerei?*

3. There is ample scope for practice of prepositions, particularly *neben, zwischen* and *gegenüber*:

> *Die Milchbar ist neben dem Postamt und der Bäckerei.*
> *Die Milchbar steht zwischen dem Postamt und der Bäckerei.*
> *Die Milchbar ist gegenüber dem Lebensmittelgeschäft*, etc.

In such exchanges as:

> *Ist die Milchbar gegenüber der Apotheke? Nein, sie ist gegenüber dem Lebensmittelgeschäft,*

it is essential to insist on correct use of pronouns, otherwise the work will be constantly hindered by failure to note gender.

4. Supplementary material may now be added to help specify spatial relations: *auf der linken Seite, an der Ecke, rechts von*, etc. Pupils should be encouraged to play the role of a stranger to the village and to put questions to other pupils – *wo befindet sich | ist das*

Postamt, bitte? Eventually answers as full as the following should be possible: *Es ist dort drüben auf der linken Seite des Dorfplatzes an der Ecke neben der Milchbar und gegenüber der Metzgerei.* Questions like *wie komme ich (am besten) zum . . .?* will act as a useful way of practising finding one's way in a German situation.

5. The shopkeepers can now be introduced in terms of:

Wer abeitet in der Metzgerei? etc.
Wo arbeitet der Bäcker? etc.

The contrast between *wer?* and *wo?* is always worth making.

Was macht der Bäcker? Er verkauft Brot, Brötchen, Kuchen, etc.
Was verkauft der Bäcker?
Wer verkauft Brot, Brötchen, Kuchen?

At this point the teacher might move on to generalized definitions of these various tradesmen:

Was ist ein Bäcker? Ein Mann, der in der Bäckerei arbeitet | Brot verkauft.

6. Once each shop has been fully established in terms of who works there and what can be bought there, a shopping expedition may be organized. At first Frau Schmidt (or some other German housewife) could be seen in very basic shopping events – perhaps three per shop:

Frau Schmidt geht ins Postamt. Sie kauft Briefmarken. Sie kommt aus dem Postamt.

With ten shops, this leads to confident use of thirty such statements.

7. Soon Frau Schmidt can be seen in a sequence of such events. Once each is completed and is past, a change of tense becomes necessary:

Was hat Frau Schmidt im Postamt gemacht?

This could lead to:

Wann trinkt sie einen Milchshake? Nachdem sie Briefmarken gekauft hat, nachdem sie aus dem Postamt gekommen ist, etc.

8. Potentially the material still contains a wealth of possibilities which the teacher will choose to exploit as he thinks fit. *Die Bäckerei*

is taken here as an example which could be applied to all the other shops:

In welchen Laden geht Frau Schmidt,	
um Brot zu kaufen?	*In die Bäckerei.*
Wohin geht sie . . .?	*Zum Bäcker.*
In welchem Laden kauft sie . . .?	*In der Bäckerei.*
Bei wem kauft sie . . .?	*Beim Bäcker.*
Wer kauft die Brötchen?	
Wer verkauft sie?	
Was kauft Frau Schmidt beim Bäcker?	
Was verkauft der Bäcker?	
Was ist ein Bäcker?	
Warum / wozu geht Frau Schmidt in die	*Um Brot zu kaufen, weil sie*
Bäckerei?	*Brot kaufen will.*
Wann geht sie in die Bäckerei?	*Wenn sie Brot kaufen will.*
Wann ist sie in die Bäckerei gegangen?	*Nachdem sie . . ., etc.*

It is hoped that some of the structures quoted above will have been introduced previously in other contexts. If they were all to be taught on the occasion when the village-plan is used, confusion would certainly arise. It is, however, a fact that once pupils have become familiar with the way in which a situation may be exploited, similar structures may be practised in a different context.

In conclusion I am presenting a plan of a railway station with its key. The reader is invited to imagine what language could emerge from it if it is exploited in the way I have suggested above.

DER HAUPTBAHNHOF

Ein Hauptbahnhof ist heutzutage wie eine kleine Stadt. Dort findet man alles nötige – außer den Zügen findet man z.B. Geschäfte, Büros, eine Bank, ein Postamt, Automaten und manchmal sogar ein Kino.
 Hier ist ein Plan des Hauptbahnhofs einer großen Stadt:

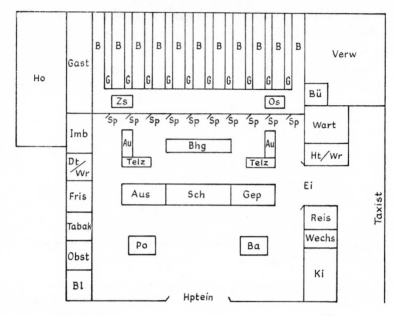

Wortschatz

B	– der Bahnsteig (–e)	Tabak	– die Tabakhandlung (–en)
G	– das Gleis (–e)	Obst	– das Obstgeschäft (–e)
Zs	– der Zeitungsstand (⸚e)	Bl	– die Blumenhandlung (–en)
Os	– der Obststand (⸚e)	Wart	– der Wartesaal (–säle)
Sp	– die Sperre (–n)	Ei	– der Eingang (⸚e)
Gast	– die Gaststätte (–n)	Reis	– das Reisebüro (–s)
Ho	– das Bahnhofshotel (–s)	Wechs	– die Wechselstube (–n)
Imb	– die Imbißstube (–n)	Ki	– das Kino (–s)
Au	– der Automat (–en)	Taxist	– der Taxistand (⸚e)
Bhg	– die Buchhandlung (–en)	Aus	– die Auskunft (⸚e)
Verw	– das Verwaltungsgebäude (–)	Sch	– der Schalter (–)
Bü	– das Büro des Bahnhofs-vorstehers	Gep	– die Gepäckaufbewahrung (–en)
Dt/Ht	– die Damen–/Herrentoi-lette (–n)	Po	– das Postamt (⸚er)
		Ba	– die Bank (–en)
Wr	– der Waschraum (⸚e)	Hptein	– der Haupteingang (⸚e)
Fris	– der Friseursalon (–s)	Telz	– die Telefonzelle (–n)

DAVID SWAIN

University of London Goldsmiths' College

A railway timetable

Inside every railway timetable, with its orderly rows of towns and times and symbols, there is a lot of language trying to get out. I shall argue that provided we work out what its linguistic potential is, we can tap a timetable systematically, at various levels in the school, to put new language across to the children. To begin with an unsophisticated example from first or second year, consider this extract from the current SNCF Paris–Strasbourg timetable.

km		Tr.1601
–	PARIS (Est)	dép 6h 53
	Epernay	arr 8h 14
142		dép 8h 16
	Châlons-sur-Marne	arr 8h 33
172		dép 8h 37
	Vitry-le-François	arr 9h 01
205		dép 9h 04
	Bar-le-Duc	arr 9h 35
254		dép 9h 45
353	NANCY (Ville)	arr 10h 45

The first phase in exploiting this involves a large map, with markers to pick out the towns, a picture of a suitable electric train and a large, clear version of the timetable on the board. Having established *C'est un train, C'est un train français, C'est le train 1601,* the teacher may move over to the map and state: *Le train 1601 va de Paris à Nancy. En route, il s'arrête à Epernay, à Châlons, à Vitry, à Bar-le-Duc.* As each town is mentioned, its marker is placed on the map. To reinforce the place-names, questions can be put to the class of the type:

Q. *Epernay, qu'est-ce que c'est?*
A. *C'est une ville.*
Q. *Vitry et Châlons qu'est-ce que c'est?*
A. *Ce sont des villes.*
Q. *Où le train 1601 s'arrête-t-il d'abord?*
A. *A Epernay.*

177

This in turn can be consolidated by reading from the board, or by choral repetition.

A second phase might focus on the towns, their situation and the distance between them. Phrases such as *à l'est de Paris* and *dans l'est de la France* could be taught, the towns in the timetable being contrasted with towns on the map which are clearly in the north or the west. Again, using the figures in the left-hand column, much practice could be done on the phrase *à – kilomètres de*, or on that useful but neglected expression: *Combien y a-t-il de – à – ?*[1] By the end of this second phase, then, one would expect such question–answer sequences as:

Q. *Où se trouve Vitry?*
A. *A 205 km de Paris.*
Q. *Combien y a-t-il de Nancy à Paris?*
A. *[Il y a] 353 km.*

to be working well.

A third phase could focus on time. Apart from the obvious work on *A quelle heure* one could teach *durer* in such sentences as *Le voyage dure une heure*, or more usefully, *il faut* in the sense of 'it takes':

Q. *Combien de temps faut-il pour aller d'Epernay à Châlons?*
A. *[Il faut] 17 minutes.*

Finally one could turn to events and people, and find ample scope for practising the present tense forms of verbs such as *partir, arriver, rester, descendre, monter*. This is where the predictability of the timetable is so valuable:

Q. *Qu'est-ce qui se passe à la gare de l'Est à 6h 53?*
A. *Le train de Nancy part.*
Q. *A quelle heure arrive-t-il à Bar-le-Duc?*
A. *[Il y arrive] à 9h 35.*

This kind of work can be extended to describe what goes on before the train leaves, during the journey, and at stations. Pictures of people buying tickets, getting on the train, dealing with luggage, showing tickets, eating, dozing and so on will help to flesh out the timetable's bare bones, and will lead from the analytic business of forming patterns and practising verb forms to the synthesizing of what has been learnt in a guided composition on such topics as:

1. *Monsieur Alloncle habite à Paris mais va tous les vendredis à Nancy pour affaires. Décrivez son voyage.*

2. *Vous habitez à Paris mais votre bureau est à Epernay. Racontez votre voyage quotidien de l'apartement au bureau.*

The 'phases' in this scheme are in no sense meant to imply that things should be done in a fixed order: they are meant simply to separate out some of the possible areas of language that can be got at through the Paris–Nancy extract, assuming that the present tense only is known.

At a later stage in the French course a timetable can be useful in presenting a new tense, perhaps because it is in itself temporally neutral. With an adverbial tense marker (*demain, hier, l'année passée*) the transition is quickly made to what will, what did, what used to happen on a particular line. For example, a class familiar with the Paris–Nancy run of train 1601 and with *demain* can be introduced to the future tense with the timetable and the statement:

Le train 1601 part tous les jours à 6h 53. Alors demain, vendredi treize, il partira à la même heure.

Numerous statements can then be made on the lines of:

Il arrivera à Epernay à 8h 14.
Il repartira à 8h 16.
Il arrivera à Châlons 17 minutes plus tard.
Il y restera 4 minutes.

A wider range of verbs can easily be introduced by referring to Monsieur Alloncle and his Friday jaunt:

Il achètera son billet (première classe) au guichet.
Il montera dans le train.
Il s'installera dans un compartiment non-fumeurs.
Il travaillera un peu.
Il s'assoupira.

Essentially the teacher is exploiting a familiar situation, a predictable routine, to get across the meaning and the form of the new tense. His varied statements give listening experience, and enough instances to make a pattern begin to stand out. Further listening, and active answers not involving the new tense, can be developed through what Mark Gilbert calls 'discriminatory questions', e.g.:

Q. *A quelle heure est-ce que le train arrivera à Epernay?*
A. *A 8h 14.*
Q. *Où est-ce que Monsieur Alloncle achètera son billet?*
A. *Au guichet (à Paris Est).*

Finally more testing, 'goal' questions will move the lesson into the phase where the children reproduce the new forms:

Q. *Que fera Monsieur Alloncle ou guichet?*
A. *Il achètera son billet.*
Q. *Que fera-t-il pendant le voyage?*
A. *Il travaillera | s'assoupira | prendra du café.*
Q. *Qu'est-ce qui se passera à 9h 45?*
A. *Le train partira de Bar-le-Duc.*

At this point written consolidation of the heard and spoken forms will reinforce the perception of the pattern. Follow-up work can be done on the *je* forms[2] by a text relating M. Alloncle's journey in the first person, or by a straightforward transition to the world of the teacher and child, in which they discuss (held on a tight linguistic rein) their own train journeys to school:

Q. *Comment viendrez-vous à l'école demain?*
A. *Par le train.*
Q. *Que ferez-vous quand le train entrera en gare?*
A. *J'y monterai | Je monterai dans un compartiment de 2ᵉ classe.*
Q. *Où descendrez-vous?*
     Que ferez-vous ensuite?
     Que ferez-vous pendant le voyage?, etc.

By simply juxtaposing two timetables for the same route, one for 1974 and one for 1950, and adding a short text, a useful situation can be devised for teaching the 'habitual' aspect of the imperfect tense. This one has worked well in several schools:

	1974 Train 1003	1950 Train 1011*
Paris (Est)	dép 8.50	dép 8.50
Epernay	arr 10.04	arr 10.17
Châlons	arr 10.24	arr 10.38
Vitry	arr 10.45	arr 10.59
Bar-le-Duc	arr 11.14	arr 11.31
Nancy	arr 12.19	arr 12.46
Sarrebourg	arr 13.18	arr 13.55
Strasbourg	arr 14.06	arr 14.58

* 1974 times accurate; 1950 times made up.

Text: *Depuis 1951, la plupart des lignes principales de la SNCF sont électrifiées. Les trains dépassent souvent les 140 km/h. Les voyages sont ainsi plus rapides qu'à l'époque des locomotives à vapeur.*

The idea is to exploit the many contrasts between then and now. (In 1950 the train left at the same time as now, but it arrived at Epernay thirteen minutes later. It used to take six hours eight minutes to get to Strasbourg; now it takes five hours sixteen minutes (less on a really fast *rapide*). Passengers for Châlons used to get off the train at 10.38; now they get there at 10.24 . . ., etc.) Again, there are sufficient contrasts available to highlight the pattern of the new tense; but a wider range of verbs and of persons is needed if the imperfect aspect and forms are to be fully grasped. A simple device is to introduce pictures of two or three characters as they are now and as they were in 1950. In those days, surprisingly enough, they all used to travel quite often on the Paris–Strasbourg run, on train 1011. The way is then clear to question sequences such as:

> *Quand Madame X arrivait-elle à la gare de l'Est?*
> *Quel train prenait-elle?*
> *Où arrivait-elle à 10.17?*
> *Que faisait-elle pendant le voyage?*
> *Où montaient Monsieur A et Monsieur B?*
> *Que faisaient-ils pendant le voyage?*
> *Quand arrivaient-ils à Vitry?*
> *Que faisaient-ils en descendant du train?*

A situation of this kind, closely tied to the timetable, extends its interest and scope considerably. Two types of follow-up material have proved particularly valuable in establishing the imperfect tense through this railway context. One is a guided composition, transposing the situation into a first person narrative beginning: *Quand j'étais petit, je faisais souvent avec mon père le trajet Paris–Strasbourg.* . . . The second is a text, based on an article in *La Vie du Rail*.[3] In summary the story is this:

> *Etienne Pasquier – cheminot depuis 1943 – ancien chauffeur à la vapeur – ligne électrifiée en 1951 – maintenant mécanicien – conduit des trains prestigieux sur la ligne Paris–Strasbourg – comment il gagnait sa vie avant 1951 – comment il le fait maintenant . . .*

This is effective as linguistic consolidation; but it is also authentic, and gives a brief glimpse into the social history of the SNCF.

At a more sophisticated level an interesting exercise is to compare different trains which do the same run, and to give details about them through the conventional symbols. The example given below features

four trains: Which stop at all stations? Which stop at Bar-le-Duc?
Which only stops at Nancy and Strasbourg? Which trains don't have
dining cars? Which have a bar? Which is first class only? Which
doesn't run on Sunday? How long does each train take to Strasbourg?
The number of potential contrasts is enormous.

		Train 1601	Train 101	Train 100	Train 63	(1ère classe)
			✗	⊗ 🍷	ⓉⒺⒺ Ⓡ	
					✗ Ⓐ	
Paris (Est)	dép	6h 53	7h 45	8h 50	11h 00	
	arr	8h 14		10h 04		
Epernay	dép	8h 16		10h 06		
	arr	8h 33		10h 24		
Châlons-sur-Marne	dép	8h 37		10h 27		
	arr	9h 01		10h 45		
Vitry-le-François	dép	9h 04		10h 47		
	arr	9h 35	9h 41	11h 14		
Bar-le-Duc	dép	9h 45	9h 42	11h 17		
	arr	10h 45	10h 30	12h 19	13h 40	
Nancy (Ville)	dép		10h 32	12h 29	13h 41	
	arr			12h 49		
Lunéville	dép			12h 53		
	arr			13h 18		
Sarrebourg	dép			13h 20		
	arr			13h 37		
Saverne	dép			13h 39		
Strasbourg	arr		11h 44	14h 06	14h 52	

(column between Nancy and Strasbourg for Train 63 labelled vertically: STANISLAS)

✗ wagon restaurant		ⓉⒺⒺ	Trans-Europ Express
⊗ voiture-bar / gril-express		Ⓡ	places réservées
🍷 vente de consommations		Ⓐ	sauf dimanches et jours fériés

Apart from the information content of a timetable of this kind, which
is considerable (what is a T E E? when do the French take their
jours fériés and how many are there, etc.), it has some interesting
language to offer. On the symbols, for example:

Q. *Que veut dire* Ⓡ ?

A. *Qu'il faut réserver les places à l'avance.*

Q. *Que veut dire 'un jour férié'?*

A. *Un jour de repos, une fête civile ou religieuse où on ne travaille pas.*

Or, developing the idea of **choice** of trains, the structure *si* + imperfect with conditional in the main clause:

Si on prenait le train de 6.53, on serait à Epernay à 8.14.
Si on prenait le train suivant, on y serait à 10.04.
Si je voulais être à Nancy à 10.30, je prendrais le train 101.
Si on prenait le train 101, on ne pourrait pas descendre à Châlons.
Si je voyageais le dimanche, je ne pourrais pas prendre le TEE.
Si nous allions en TEE, nous devrions payer un supplément, etc.

Finally there is a good deal of mileage to be got from the stationary train, at least in the language classroom. Strikes, go-slows, frozen points, crashes, derailments, Acts of God lead inevitably to cancelled trains and delays or disruptions in the timetable. A brief newspaper report, backed up by a timetable extract, produces a situation of some interest through which useful work can be done on structures such as *aurait dû* and the infinitive, or conditional perfects of a more straightforward kind. For example, this *fait divers* item:

Pendant la nuit du 30 au 31 octobre, une locomotive a déraillé à 40 km de Rennes, bloquant pendant plusieurs heures la ligne Paris–Rennes. Personne n'est mort, mais le mécanicien a été grièvement blessé. L'accident va disloquer l'horaire des trains pendant la matinée. On a dû annuler les trains de 6h 45 et de 8h 15 pour Rennes, mais on espère que la ligne sera dégagée avant midi

. . . supported by the timetable:

	Normal	Train 3601 le 31 octobre	Retard
Paris (Montparnasse)	9.05	9.05	
Le Mans	10.52	11.11	19 minutes
Laval	11.41	11.59	18 minutes
Rennes	12.20	12.56	36 minutes

can lead a good class into statements such as:

Le premier train aurait dû partir à 6h 45.
Le train 3601 aurait dû arriver à Laval à 11h 41.
J'aurais dû être à Rennes à 12h 20.

Or, focusing on what would have happened if the derailment had not occurred, it can produce sentences such as:

(Si la locomotive n'avait pas déraillé . . .)
Jacques aurait pris le train de 6h 45.
le train de 8h 15 serait parti.
nous serions arrivés au Mans à l'heure.
je ne serais pas arrivé en retard à Rennes.

I have been suggesting, in the course of this chapter, that with a few twists given to the basic idea, railway timetables can supply useful frameworks for teaching or consolidating a range of language, from adverbial phrases of time and place to new tenses, '*si*' clauses and aspects of *devoir*. There are, I think, two basic reasons why timetables are both useful and flexible aids in language teaching. The first is that they compress much information, both explicit and implicit, into a visual and non-linguistic form, leaving the teacher free to decide what information can be most usefully extracted and put into words for a particular class. The second is that the sheer number of towns and times make it possible to provide in some profusion what F. L. Billows[4] calls the 'variations of the non-essentials on the essential theme'.

Notes and references

1. Clearly this presupposes a good command of numbers; otherwise it will fall flat.
2. I am assuming that the full paradigm is built up gradually, person by person, over a number of teaching periods.
3. Original article published in ANDERSON, J. E. (1966) *La France vers l'an 2000*, pp. 35–7. London: Cassell.
4. BILLOWS, F. L. (1961) *The Techniques of Language Teaching*, p. 2. London: Longman.

Sources of material

1. The best source of up-to-date French timetables is obviously the SNCF (French Railways House, 179 Piccadilly, London W1V OBA). Europe as a whole is covered by Cook's Continental Timetable, which appears monthly and back numbers of which are often available free from public libraries.
2. Valuable background material is available from various sources, including: (a) the French Railways Film Library (Room 1107,

Melbury House, Melbury Terrace, London NW1 6LP) – this has a stock of excellent short films with English commentary, which can be borrowed free of charge by educational organizations; and (b) *La Vie du rail*, published weekly by Editions N.M. Paris (11 rue de Milan, Paris 9ᵉ). The English distributors are Continental Publishers and Distributors Limited (101 Southwark St, London SE1 OJF).

JENNIFER M. FORD

Avery Hill College of Education, Eltham

A recipe

Teachers and children alike often tire of the sameness arising from the presentation of an audio-visual or book-based course. The familiar pattern of warm-up, revision, presentation of structures or situational vocabulary, followed by the necessary recapitulation and language activity to conclude the lesson or unit, sometimes palls even with the most imaginative and highly motivated class. Teachers often seem reluctant to depart from the norm and to seek language teaching materials outside the limits of the published course. Documentary data, carefully exploited, can revitalize language learning at all levels, from the primary range to college of education standard.

One piece of documentary data might be a recipe. Sources of material are plentiful, e.g. the well-known *fiches de cuisine* published weekly in *Elle*; Michel Oliver's amusing book *La Cuisine est un Jeu d'Enfants* (Collins, 1965); or one might adapt a simple favourite recipe. In all cases the stylistic register of the original recipe requires careful attention, and much linguistic adaptation is often necessary according to the level of ability of the pupils.

Recipes can readily be adapted for many purposes. If one's aim is to discuss with a class the culinary aspects of French festivals, then the *fiches de cuisine* are particularly convenient with their illustrated seasonal recipes like *la bûche de Noël, la galette des rois* for Twelfth Night, *les oeufs à la neige* for Easter. The cards can be cut out and after the lesson can be presented in a wall montage, with wrappers from French butter and sugar papers, egg boxes and other materials to make an attractive display which the children will look at and discuss. They are always more stimulated by a display they have helped to make with the teacher than by a commercially produced visual aid.

If Christmas is being presented 'situationally' through question and answer on the religious and secular aspects, followed by pupils' illustrations, carols, the making of Christmas cards, the acting of a short Nativity play, a practical lesson where the children all help to make the Yule Log is a pleasant way of ending the topic. It is unrealistic to follow the advice of one primary French course, which suggests bringing in a Butagaz stove for actual cooking. Clearly such highly impractical ideas have not been tried out in congested classrooms with forty children milling around!

After question and answer on the ingredients and utensils to be used, instructions are written on the board and the children prepare their *bûche* in pairs.

Il faut: *un gâteau de Savoie au chocolat* (a Swiss roll will do)
   2 cuillerées à soupe de cacao
   200 grammes de sucre glacé
   50 grammes de margarine
   une cuillerée à café d'eau froide
Mélangez le sucre, le cacao et la margarine. Ajoutez l'eau. Etalez le mélange sur le gâteau. Avec une fourchette imitez l'écorce d'une bûche. Saupoudrez le gâteau avec un peu de sucre glacé pour faire de la neige. Mettez un rouge-gorge sur la bûche.

During the preparation of the log in a primary school lesson, the children may be questioned about the ingredients (identification, colour, quantities) and on what is being done – or what is done – at each stage of the process.

At a later stage, in the secondary school, the use of and reaction to the imperative (*mélangez, saupoudrez, ajoutez*) and the meaning and function of the present participle (*Faites un roux en mélangeant sur le feu 30 grammes à 40 grammes de margarine . . .*) can be meaningfully presented and practised. *Laissez mijoter, faites dorer les échalottes, faites bouillir la sauce,* etc. will help in the teaching of infinitive constructions. The use of *y* with the imperative and the omission of the article in a 'running' list of nouns are well illustrated in *Ajoutez-y vin, tomate concentrée, sel et poivre.*

Clearly the above indications apply only to recipes which might be discussed and dictated in class, and not actually made at school. Simple French recipes for middle school secondary pupils to make at home might well include:

Les croque-monsieur
Il faut: 50 grammes de margarine
   50 grammes de fromage
   8 tranches de pain
   2 minces tranches de jambon

Couvrez une tranche de pain d'une lamelle de fromage, d'une lamelle de viande, à nouveau d'une lamelle de fromage; puis d'une deuxième tranche de pain. Pressez le tout ensemble pour former un sandwich. Procédez de la même manière pour les trois autres croque-monsieur. Faites chauffer la margarine. Mettez-y les croque-monsieur. Quand ils sont dorés d'un côté, retournez-les. Servez chaud.

A picture of a tin of *pâté de foie gras* could be a useful starting-point for a fourth-year lesson, leading to the special *pâté de foie d'oie truffé* of the Dordogne and thence to a quick survey of other regional dishes: *Sauerkraut* from Alsace, *bouillabaisse* from Marseilles, *cassoulet* from Toulouse and *crêpes* from Brittany. Brief notes could be dictated in French, or a cyclostyled sheet of information in English could be provided for those who will be faced with the civilization element of the CSE examination. Thus a recipe for making *pâté de foie gras* might be used not only for its language content but also to arouse the interest of English children in French dishes which they might otherwise simply dismiss as 'peculiar'. At sixth form level the origins of and reverence for a certain dish in a region might provide the content of a short composition in French. At college level students may incorporate a recipe in a regional study and may subsequently be invited to rewrite it in a different style: imagining how it sounds when a French housewife tells a friend how she interpreted the recipe.

Probably the most successful recipe I have found for exploiting linguistically and gastronomically at all levels from primary school to college of education is the stand-by of all Gallic housewives, *carottes râpées*. More than all the other recipes I have mentioned this has the great advantages of facility of preparation in class, extremely economical ingredients and, most of all, it seems to be served at many French tables once a week, so it will appeal to pupils as being genuinely what the French actually eat.

The ingredients and utensils are presented and identified and questions asked about them: *Est-ce qu'on met de la farine dans une vinaigrette? Non, on y met du vinaigre, de l'huile, du sel, du poivre et de l'ail. Dans quoi allons-nous mélanger l'huile et le vinaigre? Dans un bol.* During the process one can usefully revise the structure *avoir besoin de* and the higher numerals (*Combien de grammes y a-t-il dans un kilo? dans un demi-kilo?*). The difference between *cuillère* and *cuillerée* and between *une cuillère à soupe* and *une cuillère de soupe* can easily be established by demonstration.

Carottes râpées
Il faut: *1 kilo de carottes*
  6 cuillerées à soupe d'huile
  2 ou 3 cuillerées à soupe de vinaigre
  du sel, du poivre
  une gousse d'ail
Épluchez les carottes. Lavez-les et râpez-les. Faites une vinaigrette en mélangeant l'huile avec le vinaigre. Mettez une pincée de sel et de poivre dans la vinaigrette. Ajoutez l'ail haché. Goûtez et rectifiez l'assaisonnement. Mélangez les carottes et la vinaigrette.

While some of the pupils are deputed to prepare the dish, the others watch and are asked questions about the process. The vocabulary and structures may be written on the board. *Est-ce que Marie épluche des carottes ou des pommes de terre? Des carottes. Qu'est-ce que Suzanne fait? Elle râpe les carottes. Combien de cuillerées d'huile faut-il? (Il en faut) six. Qu'est-ce que Colette fait du vinaigre? Elle l'ajoute à l'huile | le verse dans le bol.*

After the preparation an able class might write a dictation based on what has been accomplished: *Après avoir râpé les carottes on les a mises dans un bol. On y a ajouté de la vinaigrette et le tout a été mélangé.* Some pupils will be able to write up the whole procedure in the first person singular as a connected composition. The concluding ten minutes of the lesson will obviously be *la dégustation des carottes râpées.*

Recipes to exploit in other languages might be *paella* in Spanish (strictly a recipe to be made at home, together with *tortilla española*); *gazpacho* can be concocted in the classroom with cucumbers and peppers in season; in German, *Lebkuchen* (at Christmas) or one of the better-known kinds of *Torte* (*Schwarzwälder Kirschtorte* or *Sachertorte*); in Italian, *spaghetti bolognese*.

It is clear that recipes have widely varying uses as non-pictorial data. They are an excellent medium for the revision of basic structures, which are often not consolidated as thoroughly as one would wish. They are a painless way of re-using language patterns some time after they have been introduced. Moreover, not only do they stimulate and sustain interest in French, but they are also a way of introducing the English child to the customs of the country whose language he is attempting to master.

PART 5

Visuals

Pictures are a useful aid in foreign-language teaching. They can represent objects or spatial relations, show colour, shape and size, indicate actions and set a scene. They also have limitations. Often a tense other than the present can only be indicated through non-verbal symbols (arrows, etc.), but such symbols will not be available to the learner when using the language in real life. They cannot convey the content of a dialogue. They are often ambiguous. Is the man writing, studying or working? Or all three? How do we know the chair is 'comfortable'? Is that car 'new' or 'modern', is the other 'old' or 'dilapidated'? These limitations need not be problems provided the picture is used as **a cue to language already known or partially known**, but they can spell disaster for the unwary teacher who expects it to convey meaning.

Pictures in books have the added limitations that they cannot be pointed to and they are under the control of the learner. The wall-chart is an improvement. It is controlled by the teacher, he can show it or remove it as he chooses and he can ensure, by pointing, that the object referred to is clear to all his class. But it is bulky and its 'plasticity' is limited. People on it cannot be seen to come and go and the picture cannot easily be revealed part by part. The flannel-graph is an improvement and the overhead projector even more so. Materials for it are relatively small and can be carried about in a briefcase. It is a piece of equipment which, like the filmstrip projector, is a useful addition to the teacher's means of creating a visual impact.

The ultimate in pictorial representation is the audio-visual or television course. There is no doubt that such courses are valuable **aids**. But teachers need to ask themselves whether such courses are **methods**, whether they **alone** can achieve the results sometimes attributed to them and whether the traditional order of presentation is necessarily the best. If, for example, a teacher is unhappy about making children listen to a recording they cannot understand and then, even worse, repeat the words parrot fashion, he need feel no qualms about changing the order of presentation to one more in line with his regard for children and his understanding of what foreign-language learning is about.

G. RICHARDSON

Department of Educational Studies, University of Hull

Criteria for good teaching pictures

It is impossible to separate an assessment of the effectiveness and value of any tool from a consideration of the purpose for which it is used and the aim of the user. So a sledge-hammer might be a good tool for demolishing a wall, but a bad one for driving a panel-pin; and if the user's aim were simply to enter a building as easily as possible (and there was a door available) the sledge-hammer would be a bad tool to use for effecting an entry, though still a good instrument for demolishing a wall.

Our first question, therefore, should be not '**Which** pictures are we to use in our language teaching?', nor '**When**?', nor '**How**?', but simply '**Why** should we use pictures in the teaching of a language at all?' The criteria for good pictures will vary with the expected uses and functions of the pictures we have in mind, and it has to be admitted at the outset that those uses and functions are of severely limited applicability.

The limitations are basic, and twofold. In the first place, 'a language is not primarily or even substantially visual', and in the second, 'even within this small body of any language which it would be possible to portray visually, there is a great deal which it is inadvisable to present in this way'.[1] So in the first instance, whilst we may welcome pictures which help us to teach concrete vocabulary more effectively, and perhaps see a use for flash-cards in the teaching of the dimensions, or the comparative and the superlative, we must recognize the fact that the greater part of the language will not lend itself to pictorial presentation or explanation, and we shall search in vain for visuals to explain abstract concepts like *immerhin, pourtant, niemals* or *quelquefois*. The second limitation implies that teachers should be wary of using pictures or charts simply because these exist, or are easy to produce; it is, of course, possible (some would say fatally easy) to produce visual aids for the teaching of certain aspects of a language;[2] these may none the less be much better taught by other methods. For instance, the 'football team' or 'hockey team' for teaching the word-order of the French direct and indirect object pronouns; German word-order; verb paradigms, case endings, or adjective inflections – all these and many more are still frequently presented visually. Yet there is little doubt that what the pupil needs in the learning of all these is not the **visual** memory of what the correct structure looked like on the blackboard or the wall-chart, but the **oral** and **aural** memory of what the correct version sounded like in his ear and felt like on his tongue and lips, and teachers who think along these lines will prefer to teach via the oral and aural imagery rather than spend their time preparing visual aids of doubtful value. Once upon a time there were films and filmstrips for the teaching of the sounds of French, as though a picture of *une scie* helped the class to produce a purer /i/, and hand mirrors were once issued so that classes could see themselves whilst saying *une plume* and thus (the theory ran) acquire the correct lip position for the French /y/. These were perhaps less common in boys' schools than in girls', where behaviour was less anti-social, or where there was less sunlight on the back row, but what the teachers who used them – whether male or female – failed to realize was that the 'correct' lip-position for /y/ varies from individual to individual; that as reflected in a mirror it is reversed left to right anyhow; and that, in any case, the visual image is far less important than the kinaesthetic one – the feel of the oral set-up in the organs of speech – and the aural one – the sound of a correct /y/ through the bones of the pupil's skull. In a very real sense a good /y/ can only be acquired from within.

It is thus possible for the use of visual aids to be misplaced, and we cannot decide whether any given aid is good or bad without knowing what its role is – what it is intended to do. We must therefore examine the role of the visual element in the various aspects of language teaching to which pictures are often applied; what, for instance, is thought to be the function of the pictures in an audio-visual course?

Are they intended to make clear the meaning of the new structures or symbols being learned? It seems that this is the view of some of the experts in the field, for at least some of the time. Thus, for instance, P. Guberina,[3] the co-author of CREDIF's *Voix et Images*, and of very much else besides: '... this problem [of understanding] is solved by means of pictures' (p. 4) and 'language is always a reaction to something that has a meaning that can be represented by a picture' (p. 5). As we have seen, it is only rarely true that the meaning of an utterance can be represented by means of a picture: we might use a picture to explain *Das ist ein Mann* or *Il est sept heures*, but the visual representation of the meaning of Guberina's own 'The "Audio-Visual global and structural method" is a global and structural system using audio-visual devices for hearing and seeing, as well as reproduction in speech', would tax the ingenuity of the most resourceful of artists. Nor does this view coincide with that of other experts in the field: Kamenew,[4] for instance, defines the role of the pictures in the TAVOR course differently: '*L'image permet donc d'enseigner le vocabulaire concret*' (p. ii), '*Le rôle de l'image ne se borne cependant pas à présenter des objets concrets. La vogue des dessins humoristiques dits "sans paroles" démontre amplement qu'une image ou une série d'images peuvent communiquer des idées parfois assez complexes, indépendamment de la langue dans laquelle ces idées s'expriment. Il suffit que la culture de celui qui interprète l'image soit assez voisine de celle du dessinateur pour que l'humour ne se perde pas*' (p. iii). This is beyond dispute: few would deny that cartoons, without words of any kind, can raise a laugh, *peuvent communiquer des idées*. But the point is completely irrelevant to our argument: what we are concerned with is not the ability of pictures without words to convey ideas, but the inability of pictures **with** words to convey accurately the **meaning** of those words to a beginner in the language. For instance, if we think the idea of a wealthy German in a Mercedes running out of petrol and having to walk four kilometres in the hot sun is funny, the chances are that we shall find the picture of a bloated Englishman in a Rolls breaking down and having to walk two miles equally amusing. Our cultures are *assez voisines* to make this likely. But the pictures afford little or no guidance as to what the man in the cartoon is **saying**, when we attach speech to the story-without-words. We cannot guess, even in our mother-tongue, which register or mode he is using, nor even, with any accuracy, which aspect of the situation he may be discussing. He may be saying 'That's the third time this week', or 'Here we go again', or 'I'll sack Jeeves when I get home', or indeed almost anything. If, then, he speaks not in the mother-tongue but in a language to which we are newcomers, how much more difficult it will be for us to understand accurately the meaning of what he is saying. Indeed, if the pictures are the only guide we have to the meaning, we shall **not** understand, and it would appear that Kamenew in his heart of hearts is aware of the fact (p. iii): '*En résumé, on peut comparer l'image à un mime. Comme le mime, elle présente des objets ou des scènes et laisse au spectateur le soin de deviner* (my underlining) *les mots, phrases, ou dialogues qui sont censés* (my underlining) *les accompagner.' Et si l'élève devine mal?* There are teachers to whom this kind of guess-work is just not good enough, and it did not need the detailed and scholarly researches of a Malandain or a Mialaret[5] to reveal to the the almost infinite permutations possible in the divergent interpretations children put on a cartoon story. S. Pit Corder[6] sums it up thus: 'If our knowledge were more developed, we should be able to give a visual presentation of a context from which the learner could predict the language which belonged to it with a high degree of certainty. The experiments conducted by the Centre Audio-Visuel de L'ENS de Saint-Cloud have shown that we are far from being able to do this' (pp. 46–7). My own view is that as our knowledge in this field becomes more developed we shall find that those who would predict the language belonging to a given situational context are attempting the impossible, but – given a great deal more research – we shall perhaps see.

The converse of Pit Corder's observation (above) is equally true, of course. As he points out in his next paragraph (perhaps not fully aware that he is stating the converse of his previous remark): 'It is true that we are capable of writing the dialogues for short speech episodes which a native speaker will accept as being "realistic", that is, which he can imagine happening. But to go on from there to predict what the features, visual or otherwise, of the situational context will be for any particular utterance is still far beyond our knowledge.' This, too, it seems to me, will always be impossible: we shall never be able accurately to predict the features of the 'situational context' for 'any particular utterance', because so many 'particular utterances' may be used in an almost infinite variety of situational contexts.

Perhaps the most surprising element in the *apologiae* of the audio-visual specialists for their brainchild is their contradictory and self-contradictory statements about the role of the visual element.

Thus Kamenew[4] admits that the pictures are not always capable of explaining accurately the meaning of the new structures and symbols, and says (p.xxxix): '*On explique dans LA LANGUE MATER-NELLE de l'élève la signification des DESSINS d'une histoire en images*' – a statement which some find difficult to reconcile with his previous '*elles* [*les images*] *sont assez explicites par elles-mêmes pour pouvoir se passer du texte* ... *le sens général se devine sans peine grâce à l'image qui se substitue à la traduction et la rend inutile*' (p. iii) (my underlining again).

Guberina too[3] (p. 5) attaches an unwarranted importance to the role of the picture, and denies even the need to explain the pictures in the mother-tongue: 'Thus the picture has a three-fold value: (1) it enables the understanding of a conventional language symbol' so that (ibid., p. 3) 'In all three parts, only the foreign language is used from the very beginning'. In other words, the pictures alone are adequate to make obvious the meaning of the new language structure or vocabulary, and explanations in the mother-tongue or translations are not given at any stage.

This seems hardly possible, and other experts disagree. As J. A. Jerman[7] puts it (p. 72), 'In an audio-visual course we do not have pictures to illustrate the dialogue, but sounds to illustrate the picture!' Elsewhere (ibid., p. 67) the same authority says there is 'no objection to the use of English, the main thing being to make sure the pupils understand each picture', and C R E D I F in their instructions to the newer *Bonjour Line* insist, under *Déroulement de la leçon*, that '*Le professeur projette deux fois la leçon seule et pose des questions dans la langue maternelle des enfants afin de vérifier la compréhension de l'histoire, puis la compréhension de chaque image*'. As has been shown, verifying the understanding of each frame and of the whole story is quite different from explaining the meanings of the accompanying dialogues, but that is a separate problem, which each teacher using an audio-visual course must solve for himself. There appears to be a difference, in the minds of the specialists, between explaining the meaning of the dialogue in the mother-tongue, and translating into the mother-tongue – if so, there is a nuance here which I am not sufficiently sensitive as a linguist to catch, but which I am sure the Direct Method pioneers would have appreciated – and rejected as strongly as they rejected translation.

It would seem, then, that the role and importance of the visual element in an audio-visual course is relatively small; the pictures do not and indeed cannot provide an explanation of the structure being learned, and act simply as cues, to which the learner responds by repeating the correct utterance. Their only other role is to provide a visual representation of one situational context in which such an utterance might be used, such a dialogue take place. If we accept this, the criteria we should apply to such pictures are relatively simple also; most of them would apply to any pictures we use in a classroom.

They must be big enough and bright enough to be seen by all members of the class; they must be displayed long enough and frequently enough for all the class to interpret them, and in a position where they are visible to all the pupils. They must be planned and produced with the technical excellence of the media which pupils nowadays have come to take for granted: they will not seize the interest nor hold the attention of the pupils of the 1970s, if they are less professional in their draughtmanship or their photography than television or the cinema. They must, obviously, be as up to date in their topics and fashions and appeals to the interest of present-day pupils as their ageing authors can manage to make them: it is perhaps significant that the media (in the shape of the BBC Audience Research at least) list one as 'middle-aged' after 30, and 'elderly' at 50. Teachers beware! In addition to possessing these general characteristics, the pictures in an audio-visual course will also have to supply the situational context for the language, referred to above. If this is done by extensive use of symbols, as in TAVOR, the symbolism must be clear and its use consistent.

Teachers have always, and rightly, insisted on authenticity of the cultural background in the illustrations they use; if we are using pictures of an aspect of the outside world to teach French, then the pictures might just as well portray a French scene, rather than an English one. So the situational context should have as high a degree of authenticity as possible in its portrayal of the French (or German, or Spanish, or Russian, etc.) scene, with only one reservation: 'It is possible to lay so much stress on the authenticity of the foreign background that the English learner does not recognize the picture of the object for what it is'[1] (p. 152); 'Cultural background can affect recognition'[6] (p. 50).

There might be confusion, for instance, between the uniforms of a postman, an AA patrol man and a public works employee. If the national or social environment of the pupil was such that he had never seen the 'pop-up' plug of a continental wash-basin, and the portion of language being taught hinged on the instant and unfailing recognition of this feature, then our picture might have to be the recognizable plug on its familiar chain, and the teaching of the cultural background – which is, after all, a different thing from the teaching of the language – might have to await another opportunity, and perhaps be made the subject of two different pictures – *un lavabo anglais* and *un lavabo français*.

The other two aspects of language teaching which make use of pictures – the teaching of concrete vocabulary and of free composition – are much less controversial. It has long been accepted that pictures are a very effective means of teaching the foreign vocabulary for object names[8] and teachers have made extensive use of picture–word association as being the next best thing to direct method object–word association; it is fairly obviously the logical step onwards from a purely direct method when the vocabulary possibilities of the immediate classroom environment have been exhausted. '*Supposons que le professeur ait à expliquer ce qu'est un moteur. Il peut évidemment traduire le mot, mais s'il préfère la méthode directe et désire frapper l'imagination des élèves, il lui faudra montrer l'objet. Amener un moteur en classe n'est guère faisable. . . . La solution idéale est de montrer une image du moteur*'[4] (p. ii). Pictures for the teaching of such vocabulary would be subject to the general criteria outlined above, and to one or two others relating, again, to their specific purpose. If the intention is to teach new vocabulary as it occurs, and by means of a picture, then it would seem advisable to have the closest possible connection between the two. So if the new words are being presented via a printed page, the pictures portraying the relevant objects ought to appear in the margin at the end of the line in which the new word first occurs. This is the thinking behind the readers produced by S. H. Miller and C. Jacob for Edward Arnold since 1960, and the *Salut!* series of French books written by G. Richardson and M. M. Lord for the same publishers.

There is theoretically no reason why such pictures for the teaching of vocabulary should be incorporated in the book, of course; they could well be made into a filmstrip, and much more research along the lines of the inquiries of Mialaret and Malandain, into the most effective means of presentation, is needed. For the foreseeable future, however, teachers are likely to find the choice made for them, and dictated by purely economic factors. As one of our leading filmstrip and film manufacturers put it, 'It is much easier to convince oneself of the educational value of the type of material proposed than of its economic potentialities'.

Such illustrations, however they are presented, must be completely unambiguous, and the significance of the new word must be at once obvious to the learner. They should teach one concept at a time and be free from superfluous detail. The picture must be capable of carrying the full interpretation of the meaning on its own: if the meaning of the new word only becomes clear when a caption is read, then the picture is not the real method of explanation. Many words cannot, therefore, be represented adequately by visual means, and it is futile to try; others again will need not one illustration but two or three before their meaning is clear and precise enough for teaching purposes. And finally, it should be borne in mind that visual aids are aids, not methods: such pictures are a means of presenting new vocabulary, nothing more. If the vocabulary is to be learned, it will still be incumbent upon the teacher to make sure that the words are brought into use in the classroom and repeated, by question and answer and in conversation, until they have been consolidated to the point at which they may be said to have been learned. They 'are not taught simply by being made the subject of a picture, or a filmstrip frame'[1] (p. 153). 'The teacher cannot assume that school children will readily understand what she teaches them simply because she shows them pictures.'[9]

The final use of pictures to be considered is the least controversial of all. The use of a picture series to set the scene for a free composition has been common in the O-level examination papers of most GCE boards since the late 1940s: since 1951 there has been a flood of useful books, by a wide variety of authors, making use of the approach in schools; teachers in general approve of the technique and of the teaching philosophy underlying it. Since 1973 it has been incorporated even in the Common Entrance Examination: it must be admitted to have 'arrived'!

The criteria for the pictures for free composition are no less closely related to the aims of the teacher than were those considered in connection with audio-visual courses and vocabulary teaching; unlike the other two aspects of language learning, however, free composition is concerned not with learning new material but with practising what is already known, and the role of the pictures in free composition will therefore be completely different. A restatement of the aim of the teacher of free composition may therefore be appropriate.

Free composition is often taught as a separate skill, an examination question which lends itself to coaching in ways of gaining marks easily, of beating the examiner at his own game, of scoring high marks without really trying. It is all these things, of course, but it is at the same time something so basic to the acquisition of a language and the practising of the linguist's trade that it would be a pity if it received less than full credit for what it is.

Free composition, whether written (as in its final, examination, form) or oral (as in any classroom where the pupils are capable of answering questions in the language, or of stringing together a Gouin series describing what they are going to do, or are doing) is the use of whatever the pupil knows to be good French (or German, or Russian, etc.) to deal with the situation in which he finds himself. It is the re-telling of a story in his own words; his personal description of a scene, an action, or a problem, in which he makes use of what he knows and takes good care to omit everything he is unsure of. Now this is something very much more important than picking up marks in an examination. This is precisely what we all do in our mother-tongue all the time in our homeland, and this is what we do even if we are completely bilingual as soon as we set foot in France. We use the words and structures we know to be good French; the ones we have heard before receiving social approval in the circles in which we are moving now, and we do not attempt to think up an elusive word which escapes us for the moment – the notorious [vuleivu reipeitei la kwestion sivuplei] and the [jei ubli le mou fronsei pu 'half-time'] stop at the (exit) door of the O-level orals room. The process is unconscious, or almost always completely so: it is that our very thoughts come couched in words we already know (how, indeed, could they do otherwise?) and if the words are not there to express a thought as a native speaker might perhaps phrase it, we automatically use other words, we express the same thought or need or desire in a different way, we use circumlocutions or definitions instead of precise and concise technical terms. We are guilty perhaps of imprecision, almost certainly of using the wrong register or mode quite often, but we 'get by' – we cope with the situation and the environment, and that is the basic, essential thing.

We may not know how to ask for a half-inch high-tensile steel bolt complete with locking washers and nut in our mother-tongue, still less in French, but we do not allow ourselves to be immobilized for long for the lack of one, whilst we can muster *machin*, *truc* and *chose*.

This ability to 'get by' in the language is 'a fundamental trick of the linguist's trade, and as such should be developed and encouraged'.[10] The pupil's conviction that he can exercise this skill satisfactorily, and the resultant confidence in his ability to use the tool of language adequately and with pride and satisfaction, is the most valuable gift any teacher of languages can pass on to his classes, and this is why free composition, properly understood, is the most important aspect of language teaching.

What, then, of the pictures in a free composition series? They are not meant to teach vocabulary, still less to examine it. 'What is needed is not an immense vocabulary, the greater part of which is passive, but the ability to manipulate a small active vocabulary freely and confidently so that it covers almost any situation. . . .'[11] They are intended to set the scene, to tell the story without ambiguity, and to leave the pupil to re-tell the story or describe the scene in his own way. They do no more than provide the situational context; what the pupil says about it is up to him. The rubric accompanying this question at O level usually runs something like 'Tell in your own words the story *suggested by* (my italics) the pictures overleaf'. The candidate is not required to describe every picture in detail, nor to use the vocabulary the Chief Examiners thought of as being 'essential' to the telling of the story. There has been a tendency in recent years for some Chief Examiners' reports[12] to contain criticisms like 'Candidates who chose the picture composition were frequently hampered by lack of knowledge of the essential vocabulary' – the implication being that the candidates could not describe, for instance, the arrival of soldiers to deal with an unexploded bomb if they did not know the words for 'dig', 'soldier', 'hole' in French. Such a philosophy is completely alien to the spirit of free composition as defined above: to require a candidate to know any specific items of vocabulary is to re-test him in a prose-translation-type skill, and in the free composition question he should be left completely free to choose his own words. If he does not know 'soldier', 'hole' and 'dig', then the soldiers will have to become *Le capitaine Leclerc et ses hommes*, and they will have to forget digging and try to *travailler dur* instead; and, what is more important, if the candidate's characters do just that without any mistakes in their or his French, **he must be given full credit for his version of the tale**.

It will be obvious by now what kind of pictures we need for the teaching of this skill. They should set the scene clearly and authentically, the significant details should be clear and not masked by any irrelevancies; the draughtmanship and sophistication of the drawings must be up to the standard of those in the everyday viewing and reading of the candidates, and they should not include any captions or printed vocabulary items. These are a hindrance, not a help, to the pupil, in that they direct his thought into channels he might prefer to avoid. Similarly with the questions included in the Common Entrance Examination Paper for 1973:

4. *Comment est-ce que*
   l'accident arrive?
   Comment est-ce qu'
   Elisabeth se blesse?

5. *Qu'est-ce qu'un*
   fermier fait
   pour Elisabeth?

It is much more difficult to answer questions like these than it is to find a simple sentence from within oneself to cover the situation shown in the picture – yet this latter skill is all that should be asked of the pupil. The object of the exercise is not to keep him doing his homework until he can ask in faultless French for a doctor to come and attend to Elisabeth who has broken her tibia in three places on falling from her Shetland pony, but to give him the confidence and the willingness to get a doctor, and to do it now.

Notes and references

1. RICHARDSON, G. (1964) 'The use of visual aids in the teaching of modern languages.' In LIBBISH, B. (ed.) *Advances in the Teaching of Modern Languages.* Oxford: Pergamon.
2. See SUMNER, W. L. (1950) *Visual Methods in Education.* Oxford: Blackwell.
3. GUBERINA, P. (1964) 'The audio-visual global and structural method.' In LIBBISH, B. (ed.), op. cit. in 1.
4. KAMENEW, V. (1962) *Cours audio-visuel de Français (Préliminaire)*

Première Série, Livre du Professeur. TAVOR Aids. London: EFVA.

5. MALANDAIN, C. (1966) *Utilisation des films fixes pour l'enseignement des langues vivantes aux enfants*. Paris: Didier. MIALARET, G. and MALANDAIN, C. (1962) *La Perception du film fixe chez l'enfant*. Paris: Didier. Also CREDIF (1961) *Recherche sur la compréhension du filme fixe*. Ministère de l'éducation nationale.

6. CORDER, S. P. (1966) *The Visual Element in Language Teaching*. London: Longman.

7. JERMAN, J. A. (1965) 'Audio-visual methods in modern language teaching.' In DUTTON, B. (ed.) *Guide to Modern Language Teaching Methods*. AVLA Publication 1. London: Cassell.

8. See, for instance, the following: COMENIUS, J. A. *Orbis Sensualium Pictus* – the first edition was 1658. KOPSTEIN, F. F. and ROSHAL, S. M. (1954) *Method of Presenting Word Pairs as a Factor in Foreign Vocabulary Learning*. Training Aids Research Laboratory, AFPTRC, and text of a paper presented to the American Psychological Association on 5 Sept. 1954. HOVLAND, C. I., LUMSDAINE, A. A. and SHEFFIELD, F. D. (1949) *Studies in Social Psychology in World War II*, vol. 3, *Experiments on Mass Communication*. Princeton, New Jersey: Princeton University Press. RICHARDSON, G. (1956) *An Investigation into the Use of Visual Aids in the Teaching of French*. Unpublished M.A. thesis, University of Sheffield.

9. VERNON, M. D. (1962) *The Psychology of Perception*. Harmondsworth, Middx: Penguin.

10. RICHARDSON, G. (1957) 'Visual aids and language teaching.' *Modern Languages*, **38**, no. 3, 102–6.

11. RICHARDSON, G. and FLETCHER, W. (1951) Introduction to *Histoires illustrées*. London: Edward Arnold.

12. For instance, Chief Examiners' Reports for O-level French, Joint Matriculation Board, Manchester, 1965, 1967, 1968.

EVA PANETH

University of London Goldsmiths' College

Techniques of using an overhead projector

INTRODUCTION

The overhead projector is an aid. There is no 'overhead projector method'. Its role is to support the teacher without changing his style of teaching. In practical terms, the machine can be used without the teacher's having to turn his back on the class to write on a blackboard, or without there being any need to black out the room. The drawings or symbols appearing on the screen behind him will underline his points:

any or all of these could support what he is saying while he is saying it, the amount of symbolic underlining depending on the degree of understanding which he reads in his pupils' eyes.

INVIOLABILITY AND INSTANT REFERENCE

Material can be masked and new items superimposed. Words in a text can be pointed to, covered over or removed (if they are written on a superimposed sheet) and re-shown – to emphasize features of spelling, for instance. Such additions and subtractions can be made, and yet it is still possible to return to an unspoilt original, which could not be done on any but the most sophisticated blackboard arrangements.

205

CHANGING RELATIONS

The relation between various pieces of data can be altered; lists can be moved up and down the screen, adding to the variety of combinations possible:

1	2	3
John	aunt	Saturday
Patricia	cinema	Monday
Stephen	youth club	Wednesday

If the lists are made on separate, movable sheets, they can be slid up and down to give the data not only for 'John goes to his aunt's on Saturdays', etc., but also for such variations as 'Patricia goes to the youth club [by sliding list 2 up the screen] on Saturdays' [by lowering list 3]. The equivalent blackboard substitution table requires a much more sophisticated learner to recognize such variants when the data is fixed:

John		aunt		Saturday
Patricia	goes to	cinema		Monday
Stephen		youth club		Wednesday

In any sequence of events, for example, it is possible to say 'something happened **after** something else happened' or 'something happened **before** something else happened':

1	2	3	4	5
après avoir	*il a*	*nagé*	*il s'est frotté*	*avant de se frotter*
après avoir	*il a*	*préparé le repas*	*il l'a mangé*	*avant de le manger*
après avoir	*il a*	*mangé*	*il a fumé*	*avant de fumer*

A shield slid over this material would have slits so arranged that the third column is always visible, that either columns 1 and 4 or columns 2 and 5 appear together. The learner then sees clearly that, although the formulation has changed, the meaning has stayed the same.

LINGUISTIC AND VISUAL ASSOCIATION

Visuals can be masked, too. The teacher can temporarily cover what is not relevant to the matter in hand or highlight what is. A sketch of a bird can be built up – teaching *tête, bec, patte* – adding the words themselves on transparent foil and then removing them for testing purposes. It is, of course, simple too to subtract parts of an animal, a vehicle, etc., to practise such forms as *il n'a pas de* . . ., *il n'y a pas de* . . . or *es fehlt*. . . .

ISOLATION OF FEATURES

We would expect this particular aspect to be developed much more widely as tins can be taken from the shop counter, houses built up, suitcases packed, with the added or discarded objects always easily identified and replaced, presented with and without their labels, while the blackboard has lost for good what has once been wiped out. Pointers and shields help further to isolate the item under discussion, such as the one fruit out of many that can be singled out with an arrow or by being the only one not masked by a dark shield. Alternatively, gradual revelation of the features of a picture – for instance, what first appears to be a well-rounded apple eventually turns out to be a pig – can be an amusing diversion as well as a useful language exercise in identification in which the learner has to do a lot of the questioning: *Est-ce que c'est* . . .? *Non, c'est* . . . *Vraiment? C'est bien un(e)*. . . .

STORY TELLING

It is easier to use textbook illustrations and posters when they can be projected on to a large screen and pointed to. What is more, overlays can then be used to bring about a change in the weather, to indicate changed events (the arrival of a new person or vehicle) or even to alter characters. The man in the chapter on *an* . . . *vorbei* can be seen on the various stages of his walk to work.

The possibility of accumulating detail can lead on to the telling of a sequential narrative: all the learners can follow the course of a car which has just come through the customs at a French port, which keeps to the right at first but promptly enters a roundabout on the accustomed, now wrong, side and crashes into a vehicle driven by one of the natives, without their having to be able to follow all the linguistic features of the story. Such a story could be enjoyed even if little of the language were known, and the teacher would be helped in keeping the attention of, for example, a mixed-ability class. What is important is the value of the visual impact in setting the verbal content in a clear context.

SITUATION AND COMPREHENSION

More detailed comprehension exercises can be presented through both static and mobile data. The superimposition of maps of a town at different stages of its development or the gradual accumulation of furniture in a room in a new house allow unambiguous discussion of what was, what is and what has changed. The movement across a town-plan of arrows, footsteps or figurines can help in teaching how to give and follow directions. Gradually the names of streets and buildings can be removed or not mentioned and the pupils made to follow a route on their individual maps. The progression can be further clarified through the use of shields which allow only the route used (or the relevant parts of it) to be seen.

CONCEPTUALIZATION

From the concrete we move in the direction of concept learning when movement, such as that demanding the use of the accusative after prepositions in German, is shown by moving a figurine **into** a park and *der Park* becomes *den Park*. Even concepts of time can become 'visual' if, for example, a number of victuals on the restaurant table are gradually removed (in the direction of a diner's stomach!) – an image which should support the use of the appropriate tense: what has he eaten? what has he done? what has happened?

AIDE-MÉMOIRE

So that the learner's oral response is not handicapped by his inability to remember facts, we can re-project the clue to the answer, extracting it from the wider context. A street scene may help to establish *der Schupo regelt den Verkehr* or that he does not see what is going on elsewhere *weil er den Verkehr regelt*. Any question about this put later will be answered more readily if the policeman or a symbolic representation of him is projected when the answer involving him is required.

IMPLICIT LINGUISTICS AND SYSTEMATIZATION

The visual presentation may save us not only from the need to use the mother-tongue in concrete situations but may help to avoid too early explicit explanation of more abstract phonetic and grammatical points. Above all, the visual impact is most clearly beneficial when it brings out the scheme underlying oral work. As *elle prend la valise* is

'Underpicture'

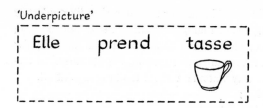

Elle   prend   tasse

Transparent movable strip

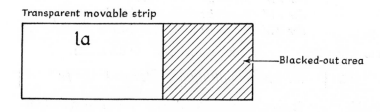

la

Blacked-out area

Strip in first position

Elle   prend la tasse

Strip in second position

Elle la prend

transformed into *elle la prend* in answer to a question like *qu'est-ce qu'elle fait de la valise?*, the changing position of the *la* pulled along on a transparent strip to blot out the noun obviates all necessity for an explicit statement of its change of function, for grammatical terminology or indeed for any statement **about** the language at all.

A strip like the following:

a blotting-out patch

weil		/////////////		ist

can transform a series of statements like

der VW	ist	billig
der VW	ist	praktisch
der VW	ist	modern

into subordinate clauses as it passes down over the sheet:

weil	der VW	/////////////	billig	ist

By this means it should become obvious to the more visually inclined (i.e. the vast majority) of our pupils how the language operates, without the teacher's having to use any metalanguage to explain it.

More important still, when a scheme in direct conflict with the mother-tongue has to be imposed in the foreign language, such a visual impact will more likely carry over into the written work than an exclusively acoustic effect. It was observed after an excellent lesson, in which the learners used *son* and *sa* most competently, that in writing a great many of them assigned *son* to all the boy's possessions and *sa* to all the girl's. If, as well as ensuring that boy and girl possess both masculine and feminine objects, we label the projected figures with the appropriate *son* and *sa*, the point that these forms are not determined by the gender of the possessor can be driven home visually. What matters is that we should imprint on the learner's mind a scheme which by the forceful impact of the visual should override his past mental set of possessives and which will have been seen **and** heard so that both in oral work and in writing the right form is selected. We try to show our students in training that the impact of the pattern, of the functioning of the language can be enhanced by an appeal to the eye as well as the ear, and that this not only helps the slower learners but can contribute to brighter pupils' attempts at systematization. In fact, such systematization, which makes use of visual impact in close association with words of the target language, might well prove to be an effective means of acquiring that kind of language competence which modern theorists have called 'rule governed'.

GENUINE BACKGROUND

It is easy to trace the outlines of pictures on to foils. These can then be projected and the projection used to make a permanent poster. This could mean that even the essential vocabulary of the face could be taught early in the course using a French face, in other words using a real and recognizable face like that of the late President Pompidou:

The teacher with an eye for essentials can pick out the minimum number of lines needed to convey the action from photographs and thus produce posters of rearing horses, running athletes, crashing cars, as his texts require (see p. 212).

INTERPRETING

The overhead projector can render a service which has both didactic and professional applications. The gist of a speech in a foreign language can be translated on it into English by a student, who thus enables the audience to follow its main data. At international conferences it is easier for a delegate to master this technique than for an interpreter to acquire the necessary expertise in the subject; in the classroom it provides excellent practice in extracting essentials from

Ces images

vous parlent . . .

Une histoire de cow-boys
et de Peaux-Rouges.
Reconstituez les
événements et donnez
un dénouement à
l'histoire.

quite simple reports (on where a fellow-pupil has travelled, at what time, etc.).

CONCLUSION

The overhead projector is easy to use, the teacher faces his class while operating it, it allows considerable flexibility in adding to and subtracting from material while in no way spoiling the original. Perhaps the time will come when silently cooled overhead projectors will be sunk into the teacher's desks as a matter of course to provide him with a useful and unobtrusive aid, which has the added charm of having no methodology of its own. If this is a weakness, it is also its strongest recommendation for those who do not want a rigidly programmed aid and who prefer apparatus which can be used in a variety of different ways.*

Bibliography

ALLENDORF, O. and WIESE, J. G. (1972) *Taschenbuch der Overhead Projektion.* Cologne: Interorga.

MILAN, W. (1972) *Arbeiten mit dem Tageslichtprojektor.* Munich: Bayrischer Schulbuch Verlag.

SCHULTZ, M. J. (1965) *The Teacher and Overhead Projection.* Hemel Hempstead: Prentice-Hall.

TOPLING, A. (1970) *Educational Materials for Teachers of French.* GAF(GB), Stourton House, Dacre St, London SW1.

VERNON, P. (1972) 'It's all a question ... of pens and scrolls.' *Times educ. Suppl.,* 1 and 15 Sept.

VINCENT, A. (1965) *The Overhead Projector.* London: National Committee for Audio-Visual Aids in Education.

* As in the case of so much of our most enjoyable work, the development of visual techniques is a co-operative effort and has benefited over the years from contributions from all the members of our changing team under the permanent guidance of Mrs J. Prigmore. Assistants and research fellows have added voices, scripts or ideas; there is no aspect, including drawings, to which the pioneer demonstrator, Miss E. Kismarjay, has not contributed. A video-tape of the material described and further projects can be borrowed from Goldsmiths' College (Methods of Modern Language Teaching Department), New Cross, London SE14 6NW.

PAT BROCKMAN, DAVE CROSSLAND, M. C. ELSTON,
JAN FELL

Hackney Downs School, London

Some work with an overhead projector

Having rejected English as the principal means of revealing the meaning of the foreign language and 'explaining' its syntax and structures, we felt the increasing need in the classroom for visual material which would give rise to the language we intended to teach. The overhead projector seemed to us the most convenient apparatus for presenting many of the visual situations we used.

After solving the initial practical problems, we now feel that overhead projection transparencies have the following **advantages**:

(a) The size of the visual material can be varied to suit the size of the class, so that details are visible from the back of the room.

(b) The stimulus is teacher controlled, in that the focus of attention is the teacher, plus the material he has chosen to use.

(c) There are no distractors, such as other pages of a textbook, loose sheets, next week's lesson (see j).

(d) A transparency can be devised to cater exactly for one's needs, taking into account lesson length and language already mastered by the pupils.

(e) Transparencies can easily be framed, carried, stored, filed into topic / language / year areas (see conclusions).

(f) Visual material in a lesson can easily be changed; there are no pins to extract or adhesives to detach.

(g) Transparencies can be prepared very simply away from school (see production notes).

(h) Black and white, but more especially coloured pictures are more easily produced in transparency form than on paper; it takes more time and space to produce and shade a large enough drawing on paper.

(i) Transparencies can be added to by the use of overlays (see production notes).

(j) Irrelevant parts of the transparency can be covered by masking-flaps until required.

(k) Pupils can easily help in the production of material to be used in class.

(l) The projector is simple to use and has a very low noise level (see production notes).

(m) Black-out is not necessary, nor is a screen, provided one has a sufficiently white patch of wall or a plain sheet of white paper.

Problems:

(a) Each teacher needs his own overhead projector or, at the very least, one within easy reach.

(b) Bulbs, which break if not cooled properly, are costly.

The following list, by no means exhaustive, will give some idea of the kinds of visual stimuli which transparencies can provide.

(a) Pictures of objects not to be found in the classroom.

(b) Pictures of people – in a family, in a job, with possessions, etc.

(c) Pictures of activities about which the present tense can be used appropriately: *il fume, il regarde, il écoute, il lit, il joue, elle mange, elle boit, elle offre, elle court, il coupe, il descend,* etc.

(d) Situations which can offer practice of a specific grammatical point: *à la, au, aux; du, de la, des; elle est verte, il est vert; il va à la gare (pour prendre le train); il y va pour . . ., il essaie de . . ., il apprend à . . .,* etc.

(e) Diary-style pictorial notes to represent activities in sequence (see p. 217).

(f) Presentation of a text for discussion, especially in the early stages.

(g) Presentation of a picture story to be retold in the past tense; or illustration of a text which is to follow.

(h) Maps showing countries, rivers, mountains, seas, lakes, towns, borders, routes, distances, industries, produce, tourism, etc. (Overlays on a basic map are very useful here.)

Hints on the production of transparencies

Two methods exist: direct and transfer. Transparencies are made from acetate or cellofilm, which as surfaces are non-porous, and receptive only to certain kinds of ink. Ballpoint, pencil and water-based ink do not take, the latter being prone to blobbing. Thick mapping ink or Rotring ink is good, as also are spirit-based inks. Mapping pens, especially for detail, are most useful, although even with the best implements acetate is not the easiest surface on which to draw. Care is needed to prevent the pen from slipping. Where 100 per cent accuracy is not essential, quick effective results can be obtained by using spirit-ink felt pens.

Most of our transparencies have been produced by transfer. Several firms produce colour-impregnated acetate sheets which are sensitive to heat reflected from a carbon drawing. When the sheet is passed through a thermal copier, the carbon drawing is reproduced on the acetate sheet. Several different colour combinations exist: black image on clear background, coloured on clear, black on coloured, and frosted. The latter throws a black image on to a screen, but the image itself can be coloured. A test on frosted acetate can thereby have certain words picked out in colour, leaving the rest black.

Whichever acetate is chosen (we use black on clear most often), the technique is the same. A drawing is prepared on plain paper, outlined in heavy pencil or with a mapping pen for greater clarity, and passed through the thermal copier together with the acetate sheet. The copying process only takes a minute, so most of the work can be done at home. Colouring is done, after heat-copying, with a spirit-based ink. Although not essential, framing the transparency has several advantages (frames are produced commercially). It enables the transparency to be stored vertically, and therefore filed with ease. It allows the fitting of masking tape to make the hinges. Finally, whether in use or in storage, the transparency is protected from contact with other sheets and with the OHP by the thickness of the frame, which also serves to keep it flat when in use.

CONCLUSIONS

The great value of overhead transparencies lies not in the fact that they offer a glamorous piece of gadgetry to enliven a dull lesson, nor in that they can be produced in a most sophisticated form. It lies in their function as a teaching aid. Transparencies show what you want them to show. They can be made in a matter of minutes to fit the very special needs of one particular class, given that group's existing vocabulary and the language problems which need solving. They enable the teacher to take direct responsibility for the content of the course he is teaching, a course which by nature will be non-static, dictated by his evaluation of what his class needs to do next.

Transparencies in our department have formed the basis of a 'syllabus', the content of which is continually being revised, added to and improved. The syllabus is changeable (unlike a published course, and personal, yet makes for cohesion within a department of individuals functioning on similar lines.

Diary-style transparency

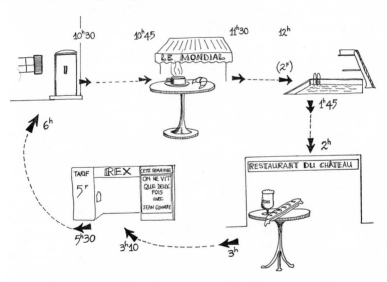

The transparency depicts the events that took place one day when a young man, Jean-Pierre, did not go to work. After some information about his normal working day has been given in the present tense, this visual aid enables us to introduce a number of verbs in the *passé composé*. After identifying the places and items on the transparency, we can use *il a quitté la maison, il est arrivé au café, il a*

quitté le café, il est arrivé à la piscine. Subsequently we can deal with the activities at the stopping places, using a series of decreasingly helpful questions:

A 10h30, il a quitté la piscine, ou il a quitté la maison?
A 10h45, il est arrivé au café, ou il est arrivé au restaurant?
A 11h30, il a quitté la maison?
A midi, il est arrivé au cinéma?
Qu'est-ce qu'il a fait à 10h30?

Further possibilities are: *il a bu, il a mangé / au café, au restaurant*; *il a payé / au cinéma, à la piscine,* etc.; *parce qu'il voulait manger / boire / voir le film de James Bond,* etc.

Eventually the pupils could be asked to retell the story of the day, each person contributing a phrase or sentence. Written work could consist initially of questions and answers, similar to earlier oral questions; later the task might be to rewrite the whole 'mini-text', starting with a description of Jean-Pierre's usual daily work, finishing with an account of his day off.

NADINE K. CAMMISH

Department of Educational Studies, University of Hull

Using A/V materials

Audio-visual courses are sometimes mishandled because habit formation through repetition and pattern drill, based on a stimulus–response format, is thought to be the be-all and end-all of the modern approach to language teaching. When the results are disappointing, audio-visual fanatics refuse to see that anything is wrong, whilst the faint-hearted blame the course itself, push filmstrips and tapes to the back of their cupboards and if there is a pupil's book issued with the audio-visual course, proceed to use it as though it were a traditional textbook.

Modern principles of language teaching are often described in this sort of way: '*Qu'est-ce que c'est qu'assimiler une langue vivante? C'est acquérir avant tout un ensemble d'habitudes, un certain nombre de réflexes, qui permettront de communiquer, c'est-à-dire comprendre et se faire comprendre.*'[1] The misunderstanding stems from too much importance being attached to the first part of this type of statement with its stress on '*un ensemble d'habitudes*' and '*un certain nombre de réflexes*'. This obscures the implication of the second half of the statement – **communication**. As a result some language teachers do not seem to go beyond simple habit formation in limited situations ... or is it that they do not know how to go further? ... or do they think it would be beyond the capabilities of their pupils?

'Language communication involves a relationship between individuals and not merely the memorization and repetition of phrases and the practising of structures'[2] (p. 163); once something has been mastered initially by repetition and pattern practice, it must be cultivated quite deliberately towards creative use; otherwise our pupils will be like those in America described by A. S. Hayes,[3] who after being taught with audio-lingual materials, could juggle with patterns but lacked fluency. It is a misunderstanding of the concept of 'habit formation' to think that it is enough to teach a specific verbal response to a specific pictorial or verbal cue. Moreover, the intellect and emotions of the learner must not be ignored. His 'thoughts, feelings and imaginings'[4] (p. 90) should be involved in the learning process; otherwise the result is 'learning without growth' (ibid., p. 89). Repetition and pattern practice are only steps on the way to self-expression in the foreign language, not goals in themselves. Our pupils must go on to achieve creative, personal expression in the foreign language with each new grammatical or lexical point (see [5]).

When using audio-visual materials, therefore, the teacher should complete every stage of the work and not stop short after pattern practice, or worse, after the repetition section! He must also use **meaningful** language activities in all phases of the development, including the pattern-drill stage. The normal phases of audio-visual work are: presentation, *explication*, repetition, reproduction, pattern practice, question and answer work on the pictures, and finally transposition to creative use of the new vocabulary and structures. Each stage is essential but it is the transposition phase, the final phase, which is all-important and which must have time and attention.[6]

A successful transposition phase requires careful preparation in the earlier ones. The first crucial stage is that of *explication*, since the language must be presented meaningfully from the very beginning. Admittedly the pictures in an audio-visual course provide a context of situation, but it has been proved that except in the case of concrete vocabulary, they **cannot** 'represent' language closely enough to ensure that the learner understands what he hears.[7] Indeed, pictures do not always convey general concepts, and far less so, particular ones expressed in particular linguistic forms: 'beyond a certain limit schematization does not lead to uniformity of reception and perception, but either to incomprehension or to the stimulation of a wide variety of mental processes . . .'[8] (p. 53). The validity of the visual element for expressing dialogue and abstract notions is most dubious for children up to about twelve years of age, but the dangers still applied even to a group of postgraduate students with whom the Guénot tests (see Guénot *et al.*[7]) were repeated by the writer and where very similar results were obtained.

A single error in interpretation is serious: once made, it influences the understanding of subsequent frames. An important element drawn too small, a sentence broken up over several frames, or unexpected dialogue, can all lead to misinterpretation, as can cultural differences or unfamiliar contexts such as middle class suburban life. The meanings of symbols and 'balloons' is not always as obvious as one might think (see Malandain[7]). Moreover, the younger child often interprets a picture subjectively or perceives only the details; he may also fail to follow the story sequence of some audio-visual filmstrips. Paradoxically the pictures which are most useful for general oral work at a later stage are the most frustrating in the *explication* phase because they lack **specific** reference to the dialogue. Finally there are the completely ambiguous pictures: for instance, pupils tested with multiple-choice alternatives decided almost unanimously that 'It's very bare with no furniture, isn't it?' was the most suitable dialogue for a new picture supposedly illustrating 'Have you seen my flat before?,' and another picture, in a widely used course, amuses many English pupils because to them the man ordering two steaks in a restaurant appears to be making an obscene gesture!

Admittedly Guénot's experiments (op. cit.) show that a pupil can be taught to 'read' the symbolism well, as long as the structures do not become too complex. One must also admit that some of the examples above are in fact extreme cases and that the problem of meaning is not so acute later in the course when the learner has already met many of the words in the dialogue. However, most audio-visual courses do suffer to some extent from this problem of comprehension, even though the pictures are useful for other reasons.[9]

Since the learner **must** understand clearly but the visual element does not guarantee that he can, a good teacher must intervene and promote understanding. Before presenting the new dialogue he can perhaps prepare each picture, establishing the context by question and answer work, using known vocabulary and structures. Any necessary new vocabulary item appearing in the picture can then be taught. Only after this will he present the taped dialogue and here he will bring out the linguistic significance of each picture by questions, pointing, gesture, other (limited) examples and reference to existing knowledge. He will achieve his goal faster than in the past when he used the same techniques to elucidate a written passage, even though the dialogue of audio-visual courses is more difficult to tackle than the language of standard textbook passages. Unfortunately we are not all gifted teachers of this type.

C. J. Dodson, who considers that these techniques in any case take up far too much time, suggests using his bilingual approach in the presentation–*explication* phase with an 'interpretation' exercise (Dodson,[7] ch. 4). Some audio-visual courses such as *TAVOR Aids*, *Bonjour Line* and *French through Action* suggests the use of the mother-tongue.[10] Many teachers will feel, however, that the intrusion of so much English into the foreign-language lesson is to be deprecated. Many others will feel that an *explication* in the foreign language, with the aid of the pictures, demands too much time and too much energy from the teacher. But somehow the meaning of what he is to repeat and then manipulate **must** be made perfectly clear to the pupil. He is, after all, a being who uses language to communicate and not a parrot, and only if he has absorbed the meaning of the words and patterns will he want, and indeed be able, to use them himself later to express his own thoughts.

The next phase of audio-visual work which is crucial for meaningful communication later on is that of pattern practice. Some form of practice of the new structure is essential and yet the mechanical responses in drills do not transfer easily to natural conversation later (see [11]). Pattern drills can become meaningless, boring verbalization, learnt parrot fashion. Even in a mechanical process of habit formation, language must be related to experience, or, as Harding puts it[12] (pp. 46–7), the structuralist view of language teaching must be complemented by contextualization.

The basic idea behind contextualized drills[13] is that, instead of replying automatically and without necessarily understanding what he is saying, as in a purely mechanical drill, the pupil 'must choose a response which is appropriate to the stimulus . . . a response on the basis of his own experience or general knowledge' (Buckby[13], 1967, pp. 168–9). Others argue that despite contextualization, a drill remains a drill because it is still tied to the structure being practised, and others that mechanical drilling has its place at an early stage in structure acquisition anyway. Even if this last point is valid, contextualized drills are a further necessary step on the way to creative use of language because they force the pupil to choose a response according to a context, even if at this stage he is not yet choosing what he himself wishes to say.

Meaningful drills include semi-contextual ones such as 'directed dialogue' where the pupil is asked to give instructions, to contradict (mildly, emphatically or perhaps angrily), or to play a particular part. For example, he may be asked to express disappointment all the time:

S. *The cinema isn't open tonight.*   **R.** *Oh! I'd like to have gone.*
S. *I've lost that book I mentioned.*   **R.** *Oh! I'd like to have read it.*
                                        Etc.

The link between stimulus and response is one of meaning: the pupil has to reply appropriately as well as manipulate the structure. Fully contextual drills usually present a problem which the pupil must solve by using his general knowledge, his common sense or his

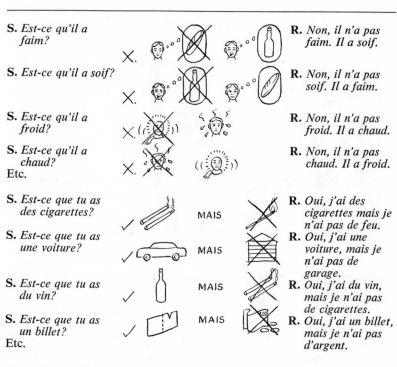

S. *Est-ce qu'il a faim?*   **R.** *Non, il n'a pas faim. Il a soif.*

S. *Est-ce qu'il a soif?*   **R.** *Non, il n'a pas soif. Il a faim.*

S. *Est-ce qu'il a froid?*   **R.** *Non, il n'a pas froid. Il a chaud.*

S. *Est-ce qu'il a chaud?*
Etc.   **R.** *Non, il n'a pas chaud. Il a froid.*

S. *Est-ce que tu as des cigarettes?*   MAIS   **R.** *Oui, j'ai des cigarettes mais je n'ai pas de feu.*

S. *Est-ce que tu as une voiture?*   MAIS   **R.** *Oui, j'ai une voiture, mais je n'ai pas de garage.*

S. *Est-ce que tu as du vin?*   MAIS   **R.** *Oui, j'ai du vin, mais je n'ai pas de cigarettes.*

S. *Est-ce que tu as un billet?*   MAIS   **R.** *Oui, j'ai un billet, mais je n'ai pas d'argent.*
Etc.

Figure 1

logic. Information may be provided during the drill in the form of pictures (see fig. 1 and Buckby, [13] 1970–1 or sound-effects:

S. (sound) *Qu'est-ce que vous entendez?* **R.** *J'entends chanter une femme.*

S. (sound) *Qu'est-ce que vous entendez?* **R.** *J'entends sonner une cloche.* Etc.[14]

The pupil is concerned with meaning: he has to concentrate on the message and answer **appropriately** rather than automatically as in a purely mechanical drill, and when he does this, he is a step nearer to real communication.

The problem of drills is less acute if the practising is done in the classroom rather than in a language laboratory: in the classroom situation the drill is less formal, as it can be integrated into the flow of question and answer work about the filmstrip pictures (see fig. 2) and about individuals in the class. Most of all, classroom drills can be **open-ended** – the teacher can react to a wide variety of answers,

Figure 2
(*Bonjour Line, part 2, Lesson 12*, frame 3)

Question and answer work based on one frame of the filmstrip: 'Dans la nuit, on voit briller les lumières des maisons.'

Où sommes-nous?	*Nous sommes à la campagne.*
Et est-ce qu'il fait jour?	*Non, il fait nuit.*
De quelle couleur est le ciel?	*Il est noir.*
Qu'est-ce qu'il y a dans le ciel?	*Il y a des étoiles.*
Oui, et que font les étoiles?	*Elles brillent.*
Qu'est-ce qu'on voit sur l'image?	*On voit des arbres.*
	On voit la route.
	On voit les maisons.
Et qu'est-ce qu'on voit briller ici?	*On voit briller les lumières des maisons.*
Et ici?	*On voit briller les étoiles.*
Et quand il fait jour?	*On voit briller le soleil.*
Et dans la salle de classe, qu'est-ce qu'on voit?	*On voit le téléviseur.*
	On voit la table.
	On voit le plafond.
	On vous voit.

(This particular class had met '*on*' for the first time in the previous lesson.)

unlike the language laboratory tape, which has to be designed to approve only one 'correct' answer. In the classroom the teacher controls the structure but the pupils can use lexical items at will, expressing their own personal desires and opinions: 'If I were hungry, I would eat a banana', '... a fried egg sandwich', '... chips with salad cream', etc. A lot of the pattern practice is, however, normally done in the language laboratory because of the economy of time and effort, and because there all pupils can practise simultaneously. In the language laboratory, therefore, one must make sure that drills are not merely mechanical and that the structures are exploited by follow-up work in the classroom, or even during short breaks in the laboratory period (see [15]). The pupil then needs the opportunity to choose what he himself wants to say, in detail and unpredictably, and this is the aim of the next phase – transposition.

In this stage the pupil must learn to use the new vocabulary and structures in a creative way, to express his own reactions and to use the new material in a wider range of contexts. It is relatively easy to suggest that this phase should start with general question and answer work on the filmstrip pictures, including extended oral composition on ones which are suitable, and that the class should re-enact the dialogue, with variations. One can then certainly say that the filmstrip and tapes should have served their purpose by this point and should be put aside, and that this creative phase should have time and attention and not just five minutes' work at the end of a lesson. Unfortunately, however, one cannot lay down specific schematic guide-lines for the form that further oral exploitation of the material should take, as it will vary enormously according to the content of each lesson unit.

At this stage, too, one normally introduces the reading and the writing of the new material, moving from simple imitative work (prepared reading, copying, perhaps two-line dictations) to the manipulative level (written drills, programmed work-sheets, work-cards) and the more advanced oral work still to be done tends to be forgotten. By the time the written exercises in the pupils' book have been completed, one is tempted to think that the work on that particular lesson unit is finished. This may, in fact, be as far as some of our pupils can go and they may have indeed done well to get so far, especially where the writing is concerned, but both oral and written work are still not much beyond the merely manipulative level and the average and above average child needs to go further.

The theme with its new vocabulary and structures has still to be related to each pupil's own experience and re-used from the personal angle, or re-used imaginatively so that new stories and dialogues are developed by the class. Individual picture-cards can be used to draw out personal reactions. Plays, maps, wall-pictures, diagrams, songs, poems and other sources of activity, based on the original theme or structures, can be used to provide opportunities for self-expression: the pupil must be put in the situation where he actually wants and/or needs to say things. Great imagination and effort are demanded of the teacher to provide materials and ideas to spark off autonomous use of the foreign language because most audio-visual courses do not supply enough of them and some – none at all.

As Scarborough says[13] (p. 87): 'What is needed is a greater stock of techniques for stimulating the spontaneous production of language from the students . . . our students must be given the opportunity to engage in real language behaviour'.

Inciting one's pupils to speak, to use the foreign language to communicate meaningfully, is a very difficult task but it must be done. Without this final stage our teaching of modern languages fails. Mere repetition and juggling with structures lead nowhere – 'a fruitless activity unless care is taken to see that the skill gained by such training is further extended until the student is capable of autonomous expression'[16] (p. 109). For our best pupils this 'autonomous expression' will be in writing as well as speech. Whatever their abilities, however, learners must be taken beyond the repetition and mechanical drill stage. Pupils who are nothing but parrots are no better than their speechless predecessors of the grammar-grind era.

Notes and references

1. Quoted from GAUTIER, A. *Langues modernes,* May 1962, by JERMAN, J. A. (1965) 'Audio-visual methods in modern language teaching' in DUTTON, B. (ed.) *A Guide to Modern Language Teaching Methods,* p. 41. London: Cassell.
2. RIVERS, W. M. (1964) *The Psychologist and the Foreign-language Teacher.* Chicago and London: University of Chicago Press.
3. HAYES, A. S. (1965) 'New directions in foreign-language teaching.' *MLJ,* **49,** no. 5, 282–93.
4. KELLERMAN, M. (1967) 'French in the primary school: of rats and children.' *Aspects of Educ.,* **6,** 75–91.

5. CLARK, J. (1969) 'Competence and performance: the missing links.' *AVLJ*, **7**, no. 1, 31–6.

6. For good descriptions of the sequence in audio-visual work and ways of exploiting material in this transposition phase see MARROW, G. D. (1970) 'Teaching with *Voix et Images de France*', and SLADE, D. (1970) 'Teaching with TAVOR'. Both *AVLJ*, **8**, no. 2, resp. 75–83 and 71–4.

7. The work of the following has shown the gravity of the problem: DODSON, C. J. (1967) *Language Teaching and the Bilingual Method*. London: Pitman; GUENOT, J. (1964) *Pédagogie audio-visuelle des débuts de l'anglais*. Paris: SABRI; GUENOT, J. et al. (1962) 'Etudes sur l'évolution de l'aptitude des sujets à lire les vues fixes et introduction à une étude sur la lisibilité des vues fixes.' *Études de linguistique appliquée*, 1. Paris: Didier; MALANDAIN, C. (1966) *Utilisation des films fixes pour l'enseigne-ment des langues vivantes aux enfants*. Paris: Didier; MIALARET, G. (1961) 'Les aspects psychologiques: l'enfant et les aides audio-visuelles.' *Cahier de pédagogie moderne sur les techniques audio-visuelles au service de l'enseignement*, 42–56; MIALARET, G. and MALANDAIN, C. (1962) 'La perception du film fixe chez l'enfant.' *Etudes de linguistique appliquée*, 1, 95 ff., and 'Etude de la re-constitution d'un récit chez l'enfant à partir d'un film fixe.' *Enfance*, **15**, 169ff.

8. MIALARET, G. (1966) *The Psychology of the Use of Audio-visual Aids in Primary Education*. Paris: UNESCO.

9. A useful discussion of this point is provided by COLE, L. R. (1968) 'The psychology of language learning and audio-visual techniques.' *Modern Languages*, **49**, no. 4, p. 166.

10. *TAVOR Aids* provides an LI version of each *leçon* to precede the French one; this should, however, become increasingly un-necessary, says Kamenew. With *Bonjour Line* questions in the mother-tongue can follow the initial presentation to elucidate matters, although '... *aussitôt que possible il* [*le maître*] *essaie de poser ces questions en français et n'a recours à la langue maternelle qu'en cas de nécessité*' (*Préface, Bonjour Line*, 1963, p. 10). Similarly in *French through Action* (SYMONDS, P. (1967), London: Oxford University Press), it is suggested that the story be told and discussed in the mother-tongue first, but – once again – without direct translation.

11. OLLER, J. W. and OBRECHT, D. H. (1968) 'Pattern drill and com-

municative activity: a psycholinguistic experiment.' *IRAL*, **6**, no. 2, 165ff.

12. HARDING, D. H. (1967) *New Pattern of Language Teaching.* Education Today. London: Longman.

13. This question of making drills meaningful has aroused enormous interest and discussion: the arguments, counter-arguments and ramifications of the great contextualization controversy, can be followed in the *Audio-visual Language Journal, Modern Languages* and the *International Review of Applied Linguistics* over the period 1967–72. See particularly: BEILE, W. and A. (1971) 'Assessing specific language laboratory drills,' pts 1 and 2. *Modern Languages*, **52**, no. 2, 54–63, no. 3, 104–12; BUCKBY, M. (1967) 'Contextualization of language drills.' *Modern Languages*, **48**, no. 4, 165ff.; BUCKBY, M. (1970–1) 'Another look at drills.' *AVLJ*, **8**, no. 3, 111–17; COLE, L. R. (1969) 'The structured dialogue: an attempt to integrate structural and situational approaches to language teaching.' *IRAL*, **7**, no. 2, 125ff; COOK, V. J. (1970) 'The creative use of language.' *AVLJ*, **8**, no. 1, 5–8; EDENER, W. (1972) 'The development of oral and written skills by free expression.' *Modern Languages*, **53**, no. 1, 18–22; NEWMARK, L. and RIEBEL, D. A. (1968) 'Necessity and sufficiency in language learning.' *IRAL*, **6**, no. 2, 145ff.; OLLER, J. W. and OBRECHT, D. M. (1968) op. cit. in 9: SAGER, J. C. (1969) 'The language laboratory and contextual teaching methods.' *IRAL*, **7**, no. 3, 217–29; SCARBOROUGH, D. R. (1968–9) 'The contextualized drill fallacy.' *AVLJ*, **6**, nos 2–3, 85–8; SMITH, D. G. (1969–70) 'Contextualization: towards a more precise definition.' *AVLJ*, **7**, no. 3, 147–52; SWALLOW, T. (1971) 'Why drills?' *AVLJ*, **9**, no. 2, 97–9.

14. Based on an idea of Miss D. Forrester.

15. ROSS, L. (1970) 'Improving the effectiveness of language laboratory work.' *AVLJ*, **8**, no. 1, 25–35.

16. RIVERS, W. M. (1968) *Teaching Foreign-language Skills.* Chicago and London: University of Chicago Press.

D. HARRIS

University of London Institute of Education

Pictures and recorded speech in A/V courses

Few events during the last fifteen years have made a stronger impact on modern-language teaching in Britain than the advent of the 'audio-visual' course. The result of a number of developments arising out of the needs of wartime, the work of theoreticians and the refinements of technology, the original idea has led to a variety of courses differing not only in the type of pupil (e.g. adult, primary school child, etc.) for which each may be specifically designed, but also in the emphases placed on the various aids. Since 'audio-visual' means different things to different people, it is as well to say at the outset that in this chapter the term will be used to denote any course in which simultaneous presentation of recorded speech and visual materials (e.g. a filmstrip) plays an essential part.

In view of the history of audio-visual courses, it is salutary to remember that we are primarily concerned with their use in British classrooms, for children of average motivation and intelligence, who probably have no pre-established grammatical awareness in the traditional sense and little or no experience of French out of classroom hours. The course (i.e. the materials and what the teacher does with them) must be self-sufficient in that it has to provide the total foreign-language experience of the pupil. The latter is not normally in a position to alternate spells in the classroom with real-life foreign-language experience outside it. Moreover, since the course materials are merely teaching aids and cannot become a teaching **process** at the turn of a switch, they can only be effective if the teacher relates their use to some clear aim. I will indicate three aims that are likely to be on any teacher's list.

First (not chronologically, of course), the pupil must learn how the language works, how the parts interrelate, what is acceptable French and what is not; he must see those patterns without a knowledge of which he will be reduced to repeating verbatim what he has already heard; he must, in other words, learn the grammar, even

229

though this need not involve extensive talking **about** the language. Second, he must know to what contexts a given piece of language is applicable; in other words, he must learn the meaning. To repeat what he does not understand, or to manipulate language forms regardless of sense, does not help him to acquire a knowledge of meaning. Third, he must learn how the skills of listening and speaking link up with the reading and writing skills. A further point that needs stressing is that language lessons in schools cannot normally aim to become language 'baths' in which the learning somehow, but inevitably, 'washes off'. In no sense is a school language lesson a substitute for learning in the foreign country, and learning a foreign language is **not** a repetition of mother-tongue learning.[1] This last point underlines the need to ensure that the grammar is suitably graded.

What part is played by pictures and recorded speech in the furtherance of these aims? Usually the pictures are said to indicate the meaning of the speech which is learnt by repetition and subsequently by extension to different situations. The teacher has a certain role in helping to interpret this meaning. But difficulties can arise if the pictures attempt to illustrate speech which may have no visual counterpart. Areas of potential difficulty include certain tenses other than the present, abstract ideas and dialogue. For example, *Il mange une banane* can be unambiguously illustrated; *Il avait mangé une banane* cannot; abstractions such as *Il est intelligent* cannot be made visual except by recourse to symbols; and dialogue is doubly problematic in that, in addition to the difficulty of illustration, it poses a problem of grading.

Recognition of some of these difficulties has led to the use of symbols, such as question and exclamation marks, arrows and crosses. These in turn have created problems, since each is made to cover a range of meanings, and sometimes the resultant picture has only a tenuous link with the language heard. Inconsistency is inevitable. For example, one course uses question marks which in one unit mean *Où est . . .?* and, in the next unit *Est-ce qu'il y a . . .?* In both cases all the visual features, except the noun, are identical. Elsewhere arrows are used to represent both present and future tenses within the same unit and, in the very same set of frames, pictures **without** arrows represent both present and future actions! Crosses may represent *Non*; *Mais non*; or even *Non, je ne – pas*; *Non, je ne – jamais*; *Je n'aime pas* + infinitive (without *non*) – the last three all in the same unit.

Use of certain types of adverbial phrase, conjunctions, exclamations and other verbal fragments in complete independence of the visuals underlines the divorce of pictures from recorded speech. Inevitably this is particularly true where dialogues predominate. Great ingenuity is exercised in order to bridge the gap; but all too often, as someone once put it, the Gallic shrug is used to mean almost anything. Since, in any case, dialogues do not conveniently lend themselves to grading of grammatical items, it is difficult to see how, if the presentation of pictures and dialogue is the **first experience** of the new items, the latter can possibly be presented one at a time and in sufficient doses for each of them to be learnt.

Grading of material implies that new items should be presented one at a time. Several examples of each one need to be provided if any kind of pattern is to be perceived and the material learnt. The tendency of some audio-visual courses to give insufficient examples merely increases the chances of misunderstanding when the pictures and recording are first presented. One course, for example, in introducing the third persons of one of the commonest irregular verbs gives only one example of each. Granted, pattern drills can vary the contexts at a later stage, but this begs the question of whether the drills are meaningful or merely verbal gymnastics and does nothing to facilitate understanding at the first stage.

Treatment of tenses in audio-visual courses is really a subject for a thesis. The difficulty of visual treatment has been noted. To ignore the difficulty is no solution. When one sees a picture corresponding to eight different utterances, two of which describe the same object in terms of *Il va* + infinitive and *Il vient de* + the **same** infinitive, one can only wonder what the pupils make of it all. It is only too clear that the attempt to marry picture and recorded speech has been abandoned. Arguments about whether the pictures are intended to illustrate or merely to 'set the scene' for the language reflect the confusion in which the whole subject is bathed. For indeed, if the 'scene' is 'set' in such a way that only those **who already know** the language can cope with it at a level above that of the parrot house, the novice can expect to find himself in difficulties.

A recognition of the pitfalls can lead to a different approach, especially if one does not lose sight of the immediate goal, i.e. acquisition of the grammar and, as far as possible, the vocabulary of the unit in question. It is useful to ask what the essentials of this are. If, for example, by the end of the unit we want the pupils to 'know' the third person singular of the verb *avoir*, the first thing we might do is to look at the pictures and see whether they provide enough unambiguous examples. About four would be a good number for an introductory lesson because, if we exclude translation, the meaning of *J'ai* or *Il a* can only be conveyed by several examples, all slightly different but having one common factor. Should the course materials prove inadequate, blackboard pin-drawings can easily convey the ideas corresponding to *Il a un chapeau* (man **wearing** hat), *Il a un ballon* (boy **kicking** football), *Il a une voiture* (man **driving** car) and *Il a une banane* (boy **eating** banana). Four examples, as opposed to one or two, serve not only to ensure a better understanding of the language when it is first heard, but also help to realize two of our declared aims: to see a clear pattern and to learn its applicability to different contexts. The achievement of both these aims will be strengthened as soon as we extend the use of *Il a* to the context of ages, family relationships (e.g. *Il a deux frères et une soeur*), etc. The first person form, which can be practised in similar contexts, would be taught **afterwards**, because the third person, with its common point of reference, affords an easier initiation into a new verb.

The same considerations would apply, all things being equal, to other new grammar items, including tenses. The perfect tense, for instance, could be introduced by reference to classroom activities where three or four specific people are seen to have carried out three or four distinct actions, and subsequently extended to include the real or imaginary activities of a particular person at some time in the past (e.g. *hier, ce matin, la semaine dernière* or whenever).

The distinction between *Il va* + infinitive and *Il vient de* + infinitive, which was not clearly brought out in the picture referred to earlier, could be illustrated in the first place by observed actions which produce statements such as *Il va ouvrir la porte, Il va s'asseoir* contrasted with *Il vient d'ouvrir la porte*, etc. After a number of such examples had been produced in response to questions (e.g. *Qu'est-ce qu'il va faire?*) pupils could be required to make statements about imminent or recently carried out actions without the stimulus of a question. First and second person forms could be practised on a similar basis. Otherwise the third person contrast could be elicited by easily produced pictures of, e.g., person X clearly seen walking towards a kiosk marked *Journaux* and person Y clearly walking away from it, reading or holding a paper. Similarly other persons could be shown entering or departing from buildings marked *Fleurs, Gare, Boulangerie, Piscine, Livres, Coiffeur* and, where appropriate, carrying flowers, suitcases or bread.

The oral work as outlined above would normally be accompanied by the appropriate written forms, so that the four language skills would be taught in relation to the new grammar.

Once the new grammar had been introduced, presentation of the filmstrip **without** the tape-recording would enable the teacher to teach some of the new vocabulary, convey the gist of the 'story' of the unit and present some of the newly acquired grammar in contexts which would now have a greater chance of making sense. At the same time the teacher could take whatever opportunities the pictures might offer for revision or extension of previously learned material. With the tape-recorder safely out of the way, and with the emphasis on what was visible in the pictures, the teacher could operate relatively freely in accordance with his own priorities and his pupils' needs.

During this stage the equivalent written forms could conveniently be taught or revised. Provided that the pupils are allowed to produce the right sounds first, there is no reason why written work should be delayed. Indeed, there are good reasons why it should not be: beyond a certain point, sounds and spelling reinforce each other, and for many pupils fifteen to twenty minutes' oral work is as much as they can take at a time.

Any supplementary course materials could now be exploited in so far as they were compatible with the teacher's aims. Such would include extra pictorial material or texts which developed the grammar and vocabulary forming the nucleus of the unit. Texts could be exploited along lines discussed elsewhere in this book.

Finally, with the filmstrip once again in evidence, the taped recording could be played to the pupils who, as a result of all the work already done, should be in a much better position to understand it than they would have been had the recording constituted the **initial** experience of the language. The pleasure of hearing an authentic French voice uttering **recognizable** speech can only have a positive effect on motivation; whereas listening to **new** language, which may at best be ambiguous, in circumstances which may and usually do preclude a high standard of acoustics, can be confusing and motivationally damaging.

A reading of the teacher's handbook to the new edition of *Voix et images de France* (*première partie*)[2] will show that what the authors call *les grandes phases d'une leçon* are substantially covered by the procedures I have just outlined, but that their order has been changed. Simultaneous *présentation* of filmstrip and tape came at the end, instead of at the beginning. *Explication* took the form of demonstrating use of the essential grammar in unambiguous situations of the teacher's own devising, and teaching of new vocabulary by a real live speaker using the pictures. *Répétition* was an inevitable part of the oral exchanges, but not aiming at 100 per cent recall of the original text. *Exploitation* included questions and answers on the pictures, revision of earlier work and exploitation of supplementary materials such as printed texts. The exception was *mémorisation*. Since what is above all in question is not the learning by rote and the regurgitation of large chunks of language, which may not in any case be clearly understood, but the ability to handle the component grammar and lexis in a flexible way, there is no obvious reason why memorization should be other than incidental.

No commercial course can assume the teacher's responsibility, namely to define and then to achieve certain aims. The role of pictures and recorded speech in an audio-visual course must be geared to the pursuit of these aims. To be aware of sources of potential difficulty in course materials is essential if the aims are ultimately to be realized.

Notes and references

1. Some of these fallacies have been described as examples of the theory of 'learning by osmosis'.
2. CREDIF (1971) *Voix et images de France* (*première partie*) – *Livre du maître*, pp. 14–16. Edition internationale. Paris: Didier.

PART 6

Pronunciation

Some points for discussion:

1. Tolerably correct pronunciation will not be achieved simply by spending several lessons at the beginning of the course practising sounds in isolation or even mouthing whole sentences which one does not understand. First, it requires vigilant monitoring by the teacher throughout the course to ensure that bad habits are not established: the first *i* in *finir* will quickly regress to its English equivalent. Second, sounds do not occur in isolation, they can appear in awkward combinations:

> *plus lourd* (even disregarding the consonants, the two vowels in this combination require considerable attention).
> *je m'appelle* (the French /a/ in isolation is not difficult, but in *m'appelle* it frequently becomes /ə/ when spoken by English children).
> *à six heures* (the habit of learning numerals through counting, even if correctly pronounced, does not prepare the learner for what happens to them in sentences: /si/ /sis/ /siz/).

Third, if the learner practises sentences he does not understand, how can he hope to acquire the right stress or intonation pattern?

2. Nevertheless, deliberate practice in the early lessons can help: short spells (three to four minutes) of precise repetition of familiar words and phrases, or simply listening to and recognizing sounds produced by the teacher. In the early stages it is possible to make acceptable pronunciation the aim of the class; in the middle school embarrassment or disinclination can make it too late then to **start** requiring acceptance of foreign-language sounds as the norm.

3. If the learner is to become self-critical, to monitor his own performance in a language laboratory for instance, then he needs help (as Dr Baird writes in his chapter) in distinguishing between close sounds (*dont / dans*) and in hearing the difference between words

which to him might otherwise sound the same in his mother-tongue and the foreign language, or in one familiar foreign language and a new one:

Eng.	*fair*	Fr.	*faire*		
Eng.	*mayor*	Fr.	*maire*		
Eng.	*television*	Fr.	*télévision*	Sp.	*televisión*
Eng.	*Spanish*	Ger.	*Spanisch*		
Eng.	*England*	Ger.	*England*		
Fr.	*bagages*	Russ.	багаж		
Ger.	*Stuhl*	Russ.	стул		
Eng.	*Vodka*	Russ.	водка		
Fr.	*jardin*	Sp.	*jardín*		

4. The tape-recorder contributes to the learning of pronunciation by letting the learner hear what he is actually saying rather than what he thinks he is saying. But there is no substitute for hearing the clear, embodied voice of the teacher – the learner can actually see him, his lip movements and his gestures. It was striking during the recent BBC Russian course Очень Приятно how much one was helped by seeing C. V. James making the sounds in the television programmes after one had struggled in vain with the verbal instructions of the radio part of the course.

5. The teacher can have no effect on pronunciation if the learner does not pay close attention to what he says. This seems too obvious to state, but there is clearly no room for constant chatter in the classroom during serious oral work. Technique is important:

– naming the pupil who is to answer a question **after** the question is put and not before, so that everyone has to listen;
– re-using pupils' answers so that the whole class has to listen to what each individual says, a situation which forces children to speak distinctly if they are not to impede the progress of their own friends:

T. *A quelle heure vous levez-vous? Brian.*
B. *A sept heures et demie.*
T. *A quelle heure est-ce que Brian se lève? John.*
J. *A sept heures et demie.*
T. *Que fait Brian à sept heures et demie? Simon.*
S. *Il se lève.*

T. *Qu'est-ce que Simon a dit | vient de dire? Wendy.*
W. *Il se lève.*

– not allowing oral work to degenerate into dialogue between teacher and one pupil only, so that the rest of the class 'switches off'.

6. Reading aloud can have a role to play, but it is a limited one. Obviously you can only read well what you understand, yet too often the text is read aloud by a pupil as the **first part** of work on it, before it is understood. The reading is poor, thirty other pupils have to listen and the one person who could read it well – the teacher – is silent.

7. Shy pupils can be helped by allowing them to record in private. In the classroom they can be encouraged by being asked questions relatively late in the teaching process – after the more sociable have had their say. Chorus work can help, but it is notoriously self-defeating if over-used: it encourages a **choral** rhythm and distorts intonation.

8. Intonation is not easy to teach. Pupils may be helped by seeing blackboard sketches of the rise and fall of sentences. Another possible aid: let the learners listen to recordings of the language at the beginning of the course without their having to answer questions or do anything other than listen. This allows them to hear characteristic rhythms. The intonation of interjections, exclamations, commands can only be learned if the teacher uses these where appropriate during the lesson:

Du meine Güte!
Guten Tag, die Klasse (with characteristic non-English stress)
Excellent!
Ça y est
вот и хорошо!

9. Some of the brightest children might be helped by limited use of phonetic script, although they do seem to have enough difficulties with orthography without our adding another script. For many phonetic script is an unnecessary burden. The teacher, however, certainly needs to be sufficiently aware of the difficulties to be able, for instance, to give physical help to children who cannot produce certain sounds – by indicating the position of the tongue after saying,

for example, a German *l* or by showing the shape of the mouth, lips, etc., in making a French *u* or *t* or the nasal in *fin*.

10. We cannot hope for perfect pronunciation, but we do have to decide where our priorities lie. Each teacher will make his own list and decide that he will not compromise on the sounds in it, while accepting near approximations to other sounds. Such a list might include:

é (Fr.) *donné, et, arriver* (notoriously diphthongized in south-east England)
ē (Ger.) *stehen, Weg*
ō (Fr. and Ger.) *bureau, pot*; *ohne, Hof*
r (Fr., Ger. and Sp.)
rr (Sp.)
j (Sp.)
glottal stop (Ger.) *er ist* (not *erist*), *vereinigt* (not *verreinigt*) (unless the latter is really intended)

11. Sentence rhythms and stress and even the pronunciation of individual words can all be hampered by the teacher's constantly insisting on full-sentence answers. Thus if the teacher asks: *A quelle heure l'homme à la barbe grise est-il arrivé au cinéma?* and expects immediately: *L'homme à la barbe grise est arrivé au cinéma à six heures et demie*, he must expect that the struggle to produce these twenty syllables will result in serious distortion of intonation, will probably throw up problems of pronouncing, for example, *r* (in *grise*), *cinéma, six* and will even make such a demand on short-term memory that bits of the sentence will be missed out. If, however, questions have been graded to eliminate potential mistakes, to make the content familiar and to practise some of the difficulties, then such a sentence might be produced with some cause for satisfaction:

Qui est arrivé?	*Un homme.*
Lequel?	*L'homme à la barbe grise* (practice of *r*, statement of facts, use of *à*).
Où?	*Au cinéma.*
A quelle heure?	*A six heures et demie* (facts and /siz/).

*Qu'est ce que l'homme a fait à
    six heures et demie?*   *Il est arrivé au cinéma.*
Qu'est-ce qui s'est passé?   *L'homme à la barbe grise est
                                      arrivé au cinéma à six heures
                                      et demie.*

ALEXANDER BAIRD

University of London Institute of Education

Teaching pronunciation

Why do it the hard way?

The school of Stratford atte Bowe dies hard and there are still those who on patriotic grounds would prefer not to pronounce a foreign language as the native does. This is an argument used by the inhabitants of countries where English is used as a second language to defend their own particular brand of English pronunciation. But French, German and Russian are not second languages in that sense so far as this country is concerned. We do not learn French in order to communicate with other speakers of British languages. There is no real reason, therefore, for insisting on speaking it in the British way.

If we can agree, then, that it is preferable to base our pronunciation on native models, the question of learning to speak a foreign language becomes a straightforward one: can we deploy a sufficient number of teachers whose pronunciation of foreign languages is up to the native standard? Probably not. The teaching of modern languages in our universities has tended to place insufficient emphasis on oral proficiency. Presumably the argument is that that sort of thing ought to have been done at school. It might be done at school too, if the schools were their own masters in this matter. The truth is that the universities impose upon the schools the very policy which they profess to deplore. Entrance examination requirements direct the learner to the written word and his teacher, pressed for time in a crowded curriculum, soon gives up the struggle to achieve an adequate standard of pronunciation among his pupils. The means are there, even if the teacher's own pronunciation falls short of the ideal. The time, however, is not there.

Still something can be done. It would be pusillanimous to give up simply because the task was difficult. But since time is precious, the teacher is bound to use the most efficient methods available for pronunciation teaching. The question whether or not to make use of phonetics does not arise. The teaching of pronunciation involves phonetics whether we like it or not. Either the teacher has mastered the sound system of the foreign language or he has not. Even if he has only partially mastered it, he knows that the sounds of the foreign language are different from those of English. If he has not even achieved partial mastery, then he has no right to be teaching the language. If he continues, he can only lead others into error.

Phonetics is the study of human speech sounds. It follows that a knowledge of phonetics is necessary to the language teacher. He may have learnt about the phonology of the foreign language as an undergraduate. What he is unlikely to have learnt is the phonological system of his own mother-tongue. He has mastered this, of course, if he is an English speaker, but he has no real insight into it. Nevertheless, this is the language which his own pupils speak and this is the source of the phonemic substitutions which his pupils are likely to make in learning to speak the foreign language. The language teacher, therefore, needs to know about two phonological systems, that of his pupils' mother-tongue and that of the foreign language.

This is the necessary basic equipment for the language teacher. With this equipment he may not necessarily succeed in teaching others, without it he will certainly fail. The practice of using phonetically untrained native speakers of foreign language to teach pronunciation is to be deplored; better a teacher who shares the pupils' mother-tongue and understands the difficulties which a speaker of that language has in learning the sounds of the target language. Sensible of their own deficiencies as speakers of French, heads of French departments in many schools hopefully hand over the teaching of pronunciation to the *assistant*. They are frequently disappointed by the results. They have usually assured themselves that the *assistant* knows French, but not that he can teach! Perhaps they themselves are only dimly aware of how pronunciation is taught and are under the impression that regular imitation of a good model is the only way.

Of course, a good model is necessary. Fortunately nowadays there is an abundance of acceptable recordings – acceptable, though perhaps not ideal. There are problems here, but they are not insurmountable. It is not necessary, for example, to have a fully equipped language laboratory. The point is that we do not have to have a live model. But we do have to know what we are doing.

The imitation method, we are reliably informed, works very well with mynah birds. All that is needed is consistent and regular repetition. We cannot, of course, invite the mynah bird to compare two sounds, one in the mother-tongue and one in the foreign language. We cannot administer to him a same-or-different test. We cannot distinguish effectively between his ability to perceive what we say and his ability to reproduce it. Fortunately we are not in a hurry where he is concerned.

But where human beings are concerned we are certainly in a hurry.

Phonetics, phonemes and phonology

Most people who know about languages can agree how many distinctive sounds there are in a given language. They can agree, for example, that there are twenty distinctive vowel sounds in English and twenty-four consonant sounds. We call these the phonemes of English. Each of these phonemes is subject to a large number of variations both of length and quality, depending on where it comes in the stream of speech and what sounds are adjacent to it. As native speakers we make these changes without knowing that we do. The science of phonetics exists to describe these changes and to discover the conditions which govern their occurrence.

Now there is a limit to how much of this the foreign learner can grasp. It looks as if we can only learn these variations by prolonged association with native speakers of the language. And even then a great deal depends upon our own level of perception of sounds. A trained phonetician can draw our attention to certain aspects of the sound system of the language we are studying; he can teach us what to listen for. With that kind of preparation we may benefit from a year's sojourn in the country where that language is spoken. Without that preparation the year's study abroad, which many language departments consider an integral part of the university course, is unlikely to be of much value so far as the student's pronunciation is concerned.

The phonology of a language is the system of its distinctive sounds or phonemes. The statement made above that a knowledge of the phonology of the learner's mother-tongue and of the target language is basic equipment means this: we would expect a learner of English to be able to distinguish orally between words like *cot caught* and *coat*.[1] If he cannot do this, then he has not mastered the vowel phonemes of the language and he is likely to have difficulty in understanding what a native speaker says.

As a matter of fact there is more to these sounds than their fundamental distinctiveness. If instead of *cot caught* and *coat* we were to say *cod cord* and *code*, we would find that the change in the final consonant had brought with it a lengthening of the preceding vowel. If we were to say *god gored* and *goad*, we would find that the vowel had become even longer. We would also discover that whereas the initial consonants in the first six words were all aspirated, those in the last three were not.

This additional information can be useful to the language teacher, but he has to know how to apply his knowledge. It may well be that the presence or absence of aspiration in English stop consonants is a crucial factor in the recognition of those sounds. It is possible, indeed likely, that the substitution of an unaspirated for an aspirated /k/ sound at the beginning of the first six words would lead an English listener to mistake them for *god gored* and *goad*. French learners of English must learn to aspirate stop consonants in initial position in stressed syllables. English learners of French must learn not to aspirate the same consonants when they speak French.

So while we may say that at the phonemic level the /k/ sound of English will do very well for the /k/ sound in French and that therefore we do not have to teach the English learner a new sound, we have to bear in mind that the English learner's aspirated variant of the same sound should not be used when he speaks French.[2]

Phonetics, then, provides us with a great deal of detailed information about a language. It is up to the teacher to decide how much of this information to impart to his pupils. He may need, then, to know more than he teaches both about the language he is teaching and the language his pupils speak. In other words, we may consider his phonological knowledge to be absolutely essential if he is to teach his pupils to discriminate between the phonemes of the target language, and we may consider a knowledge of phonetics at a more advanced level to be desirable.

So what do you expect me to do?

The first question which many teachers ask is whether they are expected to teach pronunciation separately from other aspects of the language. The answer to that is that in general they are not expected to do this. The ideal situation is where the teaching of pronunciation proceeds simultaneously with the teaching of everything else in the language. If we give oral practice we are bound to insist that pronunciation is as accurate as it can be. An oral response is not correct if the pronunciation is unacceptable.

But from time to time it will be necessary to spend a few moments in drilling a particular sound or sequence of sounds. To do this efficiently we must have recourse to different techniques. Let us suppose that we have noticed that a number of pupils in the class are confusing two sounds in the foreign language. Our first step is to make sure that they are hearing them properly.

For this we need a number of minimal pairs of words in the target languages, words, that is, where the distinction between them depends on a single phonemic difference. We have already had examples of minimal pairs,[3] and indeed triplets, in English. We arrange these words in two columns on the board, labelling the columns A and B. Then we say one of the words and invite the class to tell us which column it came from. Responses can be oral or written. In a language laboratory it is perfectly simple to install a press-button flashing-light system. We can vary this method by giving two words from the list and asking the class to decide if they are similar or different. Again a simplified code can be devised for the responses.

This is only the beginning, however, for the teacher must now discover whether his pupils are able to produce the words in such a way that he can distinguish between them. It is useful if at this point he puts himself into the place of the pupil and offers to identify any word from the list of minimal pairs which the pupil decides to say. As a check he should ask the pupil to write down the word or at least the column from which it comes. This the teacher does not see. If he fails to identify the word uttered by the pupil he asks the pupil to repeat it. If necessary the word may be repeated several times.

This technique resembles what the neo-behaviourists call operant conditioning. The idea is to 'shape' the pupil's response in the direction of the required combination of sounds. At each repetition the pupil adjusts his pronunciation slightly until the word becomes identifiable to the teacher's satisfaction.

Exaggeration is another technique which is aimed at shaping the pupil's response. However, to do it properly the teacher needs to have some idea of auditory distances. The technique is analogous to the system which artillerymen call 'bracketing'. If the pupil's response falls short of the target sound, he is invited to aim for a sound at an approximately equal auditory distance on the other side of the target sound. The locations referred to are to be thought of in terms of the conventional vowel-chart quadrilateral. Thus if the target sound is a half-open back vowel and the pupil repeatedly gives a fully open back vowel in place of it, he is asked to aim at a half-close back vowel instead. The theory is that he will fail to realize this by about the same degree of error and will thus produce the original target sound.[4]

It is clear that this technique has to be used with caution. It is particularly useful for the correction of vowel sounds where the crucial factor is the location of the highest part of the tongue. It will not do where such factors as nasalization or voicing are concerned, since it is debatable whether one can have more or less of these features.

One thing is very clear. The technique of imitation of sounds has severe limitations. In the average classroom a sound can be perceived very differently by pupils sitting some distance apart. What they will produce depends on what they think they hear. But more important than this is the fact that we perceive the sounds of a foreign language in terms of the phonology of our mother-tongue. Thus what we hear and what we think we hear may be wildly divergent. The French teacher will say *vu* / vy / , but his English-speaking pupil will perceive it as *view* / vju /; the German teacher will say *geh* / ge /, but his pupil will perceive it as *gay* / gei /.

'They can say it on its own, but when it comes to putting it into a word. . . .'

There is a limit to the amount of time we can spend on isolated sounds. We ought not to be satisfied to leave matters there. When we have practised a sound in isolation we must put it into a word – or better still into several words. Linguistic habits are very strong and the learner of a foreign language may be perfectly capable of putting a sound in medial or final position in a word and may appear completely unable to put it in initial position. For example, the single consonant at the end of the English word 'sing' as pronounced in the south of England occurs quite frequently in medial and final positions but never in word-initial position. If an English learner of a foreign language is asked to make this sound in that position in a foreign word he will have great difficulty in doing so, even though the articulation of the sound itself presents no problem to him. Similarly the consonant cluster /dn/ may present no difficulty in itself, but if the learner is asked to put it in word-initial position he will often fail.[5]

The concept of the single sound segment is something of an abstraction. It is a mistake to regard language as being constructed of single sounds in the same way that a house is built of bricks. Spoken language is more of a prefabricated structure, and if there is one linguistic unit that lies at the base of speech it is probably the syllable. Remember that many languages have based their script on the syllable rather than on the phoneme.

A study of the more common monosyllabic words in a language will give us some idea of the syllabic structure of that language. Of course, some languages contain very few monosyllables and in their case we may have to think in terms of morpheme structure rather than word structure. There is not much pleasure or profit in reciting isolated words, and we are bound to provide practice material for pronunciation teaching in the form of short sentences or perhaps pieces of dialogue. The sentence is, after all, a unit of the written language and much of what we say is not in sentence form.

But immediately we embark upon the use of complete utterances we come up against two difficulties – rhythm and intonation. These are as much part of the phonology of a language as the segmental sounds are.[6] Phoneticians and teachers of foreign languages are all careful to emphasize that we must master these aspects of the foreign language if we hope to speak it intelligibly. For English learners of French and for French learners of English the distinctive rhythms of the two languages probably constitute the greatest barrier to intelligibility. The syllable-timed rhythm of French seems almost unnatural to the English speaker, who is used to the stress-timed rhythm of his own language. The nature of the metrical conventions in the poetry of the two languages is a clear guide to the different nature of the two rhythms. It is a fairly simple thing to provide simple rhythm exercises in a foreign language.

Intonation presents more of a problem. The truth is that the intonational systems of different languages diverge greatly. Hitherto teachers of foreign languages have seen fit to ignore these differences despite the fact that the unsophisticated are quick to resent what they take to be an offensive 'tone of voice' on the part of a foreigner speaking their language. They assume, of course, that, whereas different languages all use different sounds, intonation is somehow universal. Thus they are ready to forgive the foreigner who makes a mistake over a segmental sound and implacable in their resentment of his failure to use the right intonation!

The intonational systems of the major European languages have been analysed, at least so far as fundamentals are concerned. But there are still very few foreign-language teachers who feel confident to undertake the instruction of their pupils in the intonation of the foreign language. Still, they are usually quite capable of distinguishing the intrusion of the mother-tongue intonation into the foreign language. More recorded dialogues of everyday speech in the foreign languages taught in our schools would be a great help here, especially dialogues where the pupil is required, after hearing the complete dialogue a couple of times, to take the part of one of the speakers.[7]

Should I use transcription?

There are many people who imagine that the term 'phonetics' is synonymous with transcription. Thus one may meet experienced teachers who say that they do not use phonetics in their teaching. Of course, this does not mean what it says – that they do not undertake the teaching of the sounds of the foreign language. What they intend to say is that they do not use **phonemic transcription.**

Phonetic transcription is for the professional linguist who concerns himself with the recording of unusual languages. It involves a huge inventory of symbols and diacritics designed to cover all the variations in human speech sounds. The language teacher has little use for this. But he does need some unequivocal way of representing the separate phonemes of the target language. If he is teaching a language in which the orthography is a more or less accurate guide to the pronunciation – German or Spanish, for example – he may not need to make much use of **phonemic** transcription. If he is teaching a language like French or English, however, he may well find it necessary to use transcription at the phonemic level.

There are even features of French and English which cannot be represented by phonemic transcription and where the teacher may find it necessary to draw upon the resources of the professional linguist to represent visually such phenomena as the devoicing of final 'r' in certain contexts in French or the distinction between clear and

dark '*l*' in English. But there is no law that says that we have to
follow the conventions of the International Phonetic Association if
we do not want to. There are other devices that we can use in combination with the traditional orthography of a language. Examples
are the use of numbers for different vowel sounds or the placing of
a dot under or over 'silent' letters.

The thing to bear in mind about transcription is that it is no more
than a visual aid and, like other visual aids, it is there to be used
or rejected by the language teacher as he feels appropriate. Transcription is likely to be useful from time to time and should not be rejected out of hand. It can, for example, offer a quick means of
identifying different nasal sounds in French or of stressed syllables in
Russian. But it can become a hindrance if used too often and the
learner must not be allowed to grow too dependent on it – the printing of liaison signs in French or of stress signs in Russian can provide
a crutch for the beginner, but he will have to learn to walk without it.

The argument that to teach phonemic transcription is to impose
an unnecessary burden on pupils who may be already hard pressed is
a good one if the learning of a foreign language involves learning a
new system of orthography. But when the mother-tongue of the
pupils and the target language use related forms of the Roman
script, it is arguable that judicious use of phonemic transcription
helps to pinpoint areas of difficulty in pronunciation and serves to
overcome the negative transfer of sound-symbol correspondences
from the mother-tongue to the target language.

'Do I need a tape-recorder?'

We do not hear ourselves very well. Other people's voices usually
reach us through air and we are able to perceive such aspects of their
speech as pitch range, timbre and voice quality fairly clearly. The
only limitations which operate here are the result of extraneous noise
or deficiency in our own hearing. But when we speak we hear our
own voices partly through air and partly through the bones of our
skull. Thus we obtain a rather distorted impression of what our
voices really sound like. Everyone who has used a tape-recorder has
experienced the sense of shock involved in hearing one's own voice
as it sounds to others.

This is relevant to the teaching of languages. The teacher who
provides a model for his pupils' pronunciation has to accustom him-

self to monitoring his own voice through the somewhat inefficient channel of his own hearing. It is to his advantage to check his own pronunciation from time to time with the help of a tape-recorder. If he proposes to administer a fairly formal test of perception, he would be well advised to record the test beforehand. This serves two useful purposes: it enables him to present the best possible version of the test material, and it provides a means of unlimited consistent repetition if this is required.

The learner likes to hear his own voice. In this respect the tape-recorder can act as an inducement to him to use the foreign language. It may also help the teacher more directly by enabling him to present the pupil with a clearly audible example of his mispronunciation. There are times when a pupil needs convincing that he failed to pronounce something correctly.

Apart from these direct uses, the teacher may find that he can record broadcasts in the foreign language for use and re-use in the classroom.

The disadvantage of most tape-recorders is that reproduction in the classroom is often poor. Few classrooms have ideal acoustic qualities. A little expenditure on multiple connections for headsets may improve hearing conditions for small groups. With larger classes it may be necessary to install well-placed amplifying equipment in the classroom. This is all very well if language teaching always takes place in the same room. Otherwise it is not feasible.

The language laboratory has many forms and many uses. To make adequate use of it there must be a supply of well-prepared language-teaching material for library use as well as class use. Every institution where foreign languages are taught will have to make its own decision on whether such facilities can be provided and whether they are worth the expenditure involved. A language laboratory is not essential for pronunciation teaching, but properly used it can be a great help.

Notes

1. Cp. Ger. *spuken, spucken*; Fr. *son, sans*.
2. Holding a piece of lightweight paper in front of the mouth while saying *père* or *tête* will show the learner whether he is aspirating the initial consonant. French children learning German have been told to pronounce the word *Kind* like *Khind*.

3. Cp. Fr. *vu* / *vous, tu* / *tout, bu* / *bout*, or Ger. *in* / *ihn, bist* / *Biest, bitte* / *biete*.

4. The learner of French who insists on saying /u/ instead of /y/ could be encouraged to aim at /i/ (*tout, cru, vite*).

5. Cp. German *z* /ts/, which occurs in English *it's, that's awful*, etc., but does not occur initially in English. Hence the tendency to pronounce *zu* /tsu/ as /zu/.

6. Professional linguisticians refer to stress, rhythm, intonation as 'suprasegmental' phonemes.

7. Assuming, of course, that he **understands** what he is saying, since intonation is very dependent on meaning.

PART 7

Reading

Many children, once they have left school, lose all contact with the foreign language they have been learning. For the rest, the most common contact they will have will be with the written word: to find information in books, articles, letters or brochures in the foreign language. It is to the problem of helping learners to seek this kind of information effectively that the writers in this section address themselves.

The most usual starting-point in teaching reading is the 'reader'. Selecting a suitable one is difficult because its content must be appropriate to both the intellectual and linguistic maturity of the learner. Many of the readers available are not appropriate; they are either dull or too difficult to read. Sometimes, in an attempt at simplification, they are written in unauthentic language with inappropriate tenses and choice of vocabulary.

Michael Buckby gives us a good deal of information about pupils' likes and dislikes in reading, and then goes on to suggest ways of helping them to overcome the practical difficulties of reading what they want to read in a foreign language. He warns against activities, such as reading aloud and constant translation, which can actually hinder progress in intelligent reading. Nicholas Beattie distinguishes different types of reading and asks that we adopt procedures to suit the type which is our objective at any given time. He regrets the tendency to relegate reading skills to a minor role because oral work is currently so fashionable. Like him, Ann Davies, working with unselected pupils in a South London middle school, insists on the importance of reading as a personal activity and therefore suggests libraries of readers rather than the single class reader. She describes work-cards and their contribution to making reading private and to pacing work to suit individual children in mixed-ability classes.

MICHAEL BUCKBY

Language Teaching Centre, University of York

What is to be read?

It is generally agreed today that the ability to read efficiently over a wide range of topics is one of the most valuable skills the foreign-language teacher can give his pupils, whether or not they go on to become specialist linguists.[1] It is important, however, in accepting this, not to equate efficient reading with barking at print, even when this is followed by a correct bark at questions designed to test literal comprehension. The aim should rather be for the young people learning foreign languages in schools to develop the attitudes and skills which enable them to read silently, with understanding, over a range of different types of materials and topics which they find interesting and worth while, adapting their reading strategies to suit the materials and their own intentions. This statement of aims begs at least two questions: (1) What **do** young people in schools today want to read? (2) How can they learn to read these materials in a mature and flexible way? This chapter will attempt to answer these questions, with particular reference to British pupils aged 13–16. It will be based on an analysis of the content and methods of the reading programme of the Nuffield/Schools Council French Course, *En Avant*.

There have been a number of interesting surveys of what young people of this age read from preference.[2] The most important of these are summarized in tables 1 and 2 (table 1 summarizes the types of comics and magazines most commonly read by boys and girls aged 13–16, table 2 shows the themes most favoured by them in books). It is, however, important to note that with both boys and girls, over a wide range of ability, magazines and comics are consistently more popular than books, and that fiction is overwhelmingly preferred by boys and girls of all ages to any kind of non-fiction.[3] It is also worth noting that boys and girls who read magazines and comics also read more of everything. The main points to emerge from these surveys which are relevant to the foreign-language teacher are:

252

Table 1: Comics and magazines

	Boys	Girls
Jenkinson (1940)[4]	1. 'Bloods', e.g. *Wizard*, *Hotspur*	1. 'Bloods', e.g. *Schoolgirls' Own, Crystal*
	2. Hobbies and sports	2. Stories and entertainment
	3. General information and comment	3. General information and comment
	4. Stories and entertainment	4. Women's magazines
Pickard (1952–61)[5]	1. *Beano*	1. *Dandy*
	2. *Dandy*	2. *Beano*
	3. *Eagle*	3. *Girl*
	4. *Rover*	4. *Girls' Crystal*
NATE (1967)[6]	1. 'Bloods' and comics	1. Girls' magazines
	2. Hobbies	2. Women's magazines
	3. Sport	3. Comics
	4. Radio and television	4. Hobbies
		5. Radio and television
Alderson (1968)[7]	1. *Victor*	1. *Trend*
	2. *Beano*	2. *Jackie*
	3. Car and motor-cycle magazines	3. *Valentine*
	4. *Boys' Own* and *Eagle*	4. Pony and riding magazines

Table 2: Books

	Boys	Girls
Jenkinson (1940)	1. Adventure stories	1. Adventure stories
	2. Detective stories	2. Home-life stories
	3. School stories	3. School stories
	4. Home-life stories	4. Love stories
	5. Historical stories	5. Historical stories
	6. Technical books	6. Detective stories
Pickard (1952–61)	1. Mystery	1. Mystery
	2. Westerns	2. Westerns
	3. Love	3. Humour
	4. Humour	4. Love
Carsley (1957)[8]	1. Adventure	1. Adventure
	2. Mystery	2. Mystery
	3. Sport	3. School stories
	4. Encyclopedias	4. Biblical stories
	5. Humour	5. Encyclopedias
	6. Biblical stories	6. Poetry
NATE (1968)	1. Adventure	1. Adventure ⎫
	2. War	Love ⎭
	3. Science fiction	3. Humour
	4. Detective stories	4. Animal stories
	5. Humour	5. Detective stories
	6. Westerns	6. Family-life stories

NOTE: The Pickard survey was carried out with children aged 9–11; it is interesting for the reasons given by them for choosing something to read, i.e. (i) exciting, (ii) funny, (iii) interesting facts and puzzles, (iv) story resolution (the cowboy wins in the end), (v) mixture of reality and unreality.

1. Preferences have remained surprisingly constant since 1940, which would suggest that they can be considered as reliable indicators.

2. Boys and girls of every level of ability enjoy reading comics and magazines, whether or not they read anything else; ability does not appear to be a very important factor in what boys and girls of this age want to read.

3. The high degree of similarity between the expressed interests of the boys and girls suggests that it should be possible to prepare a reading programme of which the core can be enjoyed equally by girls and boys. Points 1 and 2 indicate that this core should be based on a series of magazines.

4. There is a very wide variety of interests summarized as 'hobbies' or 'sports', for example; there are considerable divergencies within and between the sexes in these categories, particularly in the case of the boys, who show interest in a much wider range of topics than the girls. This seems to indicate clearly the need to make available to pupils of this age an enormous range of materials on these and similar categories from which they choose freely to supplement a common core.

The available evidence also indicates that what young adolescents really want to read in the foreign language is the foreign equivalent of what they read in English.[9] The teacher who is planning a reading programme based on his pupils' interests will, therefore, look at these foreign equivalents and, first of all, at the magazines and comics most commonly read by young people of the same age in the foreign country in question. In the case of French, this has been done by the French Section of the Schools Council Modern Languages Project.[10] Samples of the most popular French teenage magazines were analysed to establish the topics most frequently dealt with in these publications. The results of this analysis are summarized in table 3. When these are compared with the findings of a similar analysis of British teenage magazines,[7] it emerges that the topics and their respective importance are very similar in the French and British publications.

Table 3: French teenage magazines – topic frequency

1. The pop scene	70
2. Sport	20
3. Cinema	19
4. Fashion	18
5. Beauty hints	15
6. Correspondence columns	12
7. Fiction	11

8.	Current affairs	9
9.	Adolescence	7
	Travel	7
	Science	7
12.	Fortune-telling and horoscopes	6
	Careers	6
	Quizzes and games	6
15.	Art	3
	Humour	3
	Photography	3
	Medicine and health	3
	Psychology	3
	Literature	3
21.	Misc. celebrities	2
	Music (classical)	2
	Aviation	2
24.	Emotion problems	1
	Motoring	1
	Theatre	1
	History	1
	Do-it-yourself	1
	Crime	1
	Religion	1
	Social problems	1
	Language	1
	Human relationships	1

The core of a French reading programme based on what teenagers **do** and **want to** read would, therefore, consist mainly of a series of magazines containing the most popular features of the most commonly read French teenage magazines. These magazines, written specifically for British teenagers learning French, would gradually introduce the vocabulary and structures necessary for an understanding of authentic French magazines. The aim would be to equip teenage pupils to pick up almost any popular French teenage magazine and find in it at least two or three items which they could read and enjoy. Gradually the range of topics within a pupil's reach would increase. The Schools Council French Continuation Course for pupils aged 13–16 has been developed along precisely these lines:[11] a series of magazines called *Dans le Vent* forms the main core of the reading programme and the success which they have enjoyed with teachers and pupils, in both their trial and published versions, seems to confirm the validity of the principles on which they were based.

Many pupils and teachers would not be satisfied, however, by a reading programme made up exclusively of these magazines. There remains the need for a large number and variety of branches, including newspapers, books and more specialist magazines, to cater for individual interests. It is most important that these individual needs be met, and it therefore follows that an essential part of a foreign-language teacher's job is to make his own inquiries about the interests and reading habits of each one of his pupils. It follows equally that he should also make a point of acquainting himself intimately with appropriate publications produced for French readers and for readers of French as a foreign language and that these materials should be made available to his pupils. The teacher should constantly bear in mind that reading can only be successful if what is read communicates something that is meaningful and relevant to the reader.[12]

If a major advance in foreign-language reading skills is to be achieved it will not be enough, of course, to change merely the content of the reading programme. It will be equally important to change the methods used.

The methods employed in a reading programme will clearly be determined by what is perceived to be the nature of reading. If our pupils are to develop the habit and skills of reading in the foreign language, it is vital to move away from the view of reading as being merely a decoding process, as consisting only or mainly of the recognition of words or letters or the ability to answer questions on the factual content of what is read, and to see it as an activity which essentially involves judgement, interpretation and analysis.[13] What the teacher must aim at is the development of **responsive reading**, where the reader 'finds himself involved in relating the text to his own experience of life and to his own hopes, fears, expectations and system of values'.[14] Any method used to introduce and develop reading must be chosen in this light. Responsive reading is not something that can be put off or added on at the end like the icing on a cake. The methods used must ensure that from the beginning and throughout the programme the emphasis is on the reader making an active mental response to the message conveyed by the printed words; this is vital, as the habits and skills developed in the early stages of reading will permanently influence the individual's skills and habits in the use of printed materials and his attitude to himself as a reader. It is therefore necessary to plan a reading programme as a whole; pupils of 13 to 16 will obviously not achieve the aims stated above unless the content and methods of the reading programme they have followed up to the age of 13 have been appropriate.

What, then, are the essential features of a programme designed to prepare pupils aged 13 to 16 to read responsively what they want to read in the foreign language? The first essential is that reading should not be introduced until the pupils have had considerable experience in listening to and speaking the foreign languages. When the pupils do start to read, the texts used should contain only known language items and the content should be based on something that the pupils are interested in and that they have recently been talking about in the foreign language. All of these features are essential if the pupils are to read responsively and with confidence. An example of this approach which can be adapted for use with any course and older pupils can be found in stage 2 of *En Avant*,[15] which is aimed at children aged from 9 to 11. The pupils first listen to, discuss and act out their own variations of a story based on a series of pictures (fig. 1). After this oral stage, the same pictures are presented, one at a time, along with sentence cards which summarize the story, using familiar language (fig. 2). The pupils first listen to the teacher (or a tape) reading each sentence card and repeat the model, with the appropriate picture visible to give context-support. They then read the sentence cards, with the picture still visible, but without the immediate verbal model. They are next shown the sentence cards on their own, with no visual or verbal support, for them to read. Finally, the sentence cards are presented in random order to ensure that the pupils really are reading them and not merely repeating a story they have learned by heart. As a follow-up to this work the same story is presented in a slightly different version, but still with no new words, in a reader. In the reader the pupils learn to cope not only with single sentences but with several sentences together on one page. The pupils are asked to respond to what they read not only on a linguistic level; they are also asked to complete, colour and draw pictures to illustrate what they are reading (fig. 3).

There are certain features of this introduction to reading which merit close attention:

1. All the reading material is orally very familiar and the content is already alive in the minds of the pupils before they start to read it. Nearly all of it consists of simple dialogues written down, a sort of *style parlé écrit*.

2. From the beginning the pupils deal with whole sentences and no attempt is made to emphasize words or parts of words.[16] From the beginning the pupils are encouraged to read lively stories that they

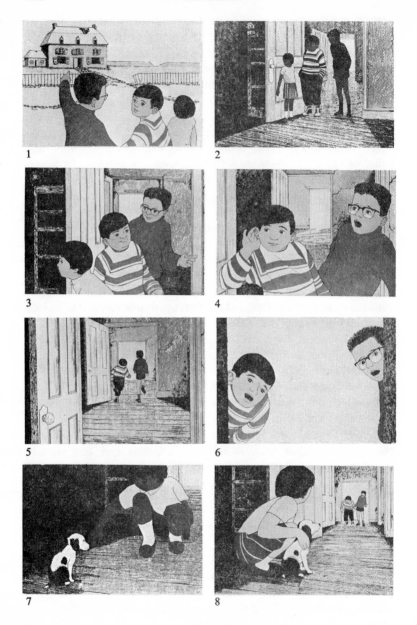

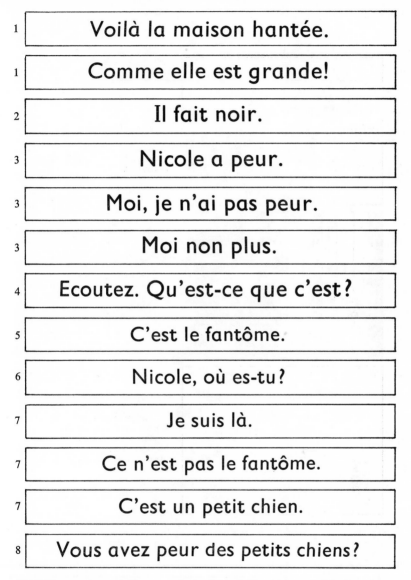

1 | Voilà la maison hantée.

1 | Comme elle est grande!

2 | Il fait noir.

3 | Nicole a peur.

3 | Moi, je n'ai pas peur.

3 | Moi non plus.

4 | Ecoutez. Qu'est-ce que c'est?

5 | C'est le fantôme.

6 | Nicole, où es-tu?

7 | Je suis là.

7 | Ce n'est pas le fantôme.

7 | C'est un petit chien.

8 | Vous avez peur des petits chiens?

Fig 2 The numbers on this page refer to the matching pictures in Fig 1.

–Regardez la maison.
 C'est la maison hantée.
–Comme elle est grande!
–On y va?
–D'accord.

–Ecoutez. Qu'est-ce que c'est?
 –C'est le fantôme.
Les deux garçons ont peur.
Ils se sauvent.

–Nicole, où es-tu?
 –Je suis là. Ce n'est pas le fantôme, voyons.
Voilà Nicole avec un petit chien.
Elle n'a pas peur.
La maison n'est pas hantée.

enjoy in sense groups or 'meaningful mouthfuls'.[17] The pupils do identify individual words, but they do so within this context.

3. The introduction to reading is so graded that pupils over a wide ability range enjoy it and succeed; they perceive reading as something that is worth while and that they can do.

The next major step in this reading programme comes in stage 3 of *En Avant*,[18] with the introduction of silent reading. There are fifteen short readers with this stage, which is designed for children aged 10 to 12, the first seven of which are based on stories the pupils have already worked on orally and which contain no new words. The readers contain a large number of illustrations to give context-support and to make the books appear more interesting and approachable. Before the pupils start to read, the teacher can use the illustrations to arouse their interest and to discuss with them what the book might be about – without revealing the story. This approach helps all pupils, and particularly those with reading problems, to read the books responsively. The readers are also recorded by native speakers, and the pupils can listen to this recording as they follow the text. All of the readers are quite short (500–1,000 words), which permits the pupils to enjoy the feeling of success which comes from reading 'a French book' in a few minutes, with ease and understanding.

Eight of the readers consist of stories which are completely new to the pupils. This is one step forward. They also contain a small number of new words, although there are no unfamiliar structures: about one word per hundred is new. This has been done deliberately to introduce a skill which will be vital if the pupils are ever to learn to read widely in French: the skill of coping with new words. Readers not trained to deal with this are unlikely ever to achieve responsive reading with authentic foreign-language publications. The pupils are, therefore, gradually taught a number of techniques to cope with this eventuality, and these techniques are practised and developed throughout the reading programme.

The pupils learn first not to worry about unknown words which are not crucial to an understanding of the main points of a text. This is one of the signs of a skilled reader; the teacher who persistently expects his pupils to understand every single word of everything he reads is encouraging habits and attitudes which will constitute a barrier to fluent reading. This is one of the arguments against foreign-language reading programmes based on translation. There are, of course, occasions when the reader will need to understand a new word in order to understand one of the main points in a text and, when this is the case, there are several techniques which he can be trained to use. One of these techniques is the use of clues in the context in which the new word occurs. Some readers may, for example, be unable to recognize at once *une mancienne* in French. However, if a mature reader met it in such a sentence as *Il s'est assis à l'ombre d'une mancienne; dans ses branches un oiseau chantait,* he would appreciate that *une mancienne* was a sort of tree and this knowledge would probably suffice. Similarly pupils can be trained to make use of cognates and near-cognates, of which there are very many between French and English. The skilled reader would not be disturbed if he met in a text, for the first time, such words as *une cover-girl, l'oxygène, la panique, abandonner, l'autorisation.*

Pupils can also learn to discover the meanings of new words by using parallels within the foreign language. For example, a well-trained pupil who knew *gai* and *gaieté* and also *bon* would be able to use this knowledge to understand *bonté* if he met it in a text. He would be able to use this technique to recognize easily such words as *un villageois, la hauteur, fatigant.* It is inevitable that the young reader of foreign-language publications will meet many unknown words and if he had to look up in a dictionary every one, he would find progress so slow that he would soon give up: it is a well-documented fact that people who read slowly soon stop reading altogether.

To develop these techniques, the teacher can regularly give his pupils a text to read which he is sure will interest them, which is written at a level that is generally well within their reach but which contains a number of new words (a maximum of one in fifty, regularly spaced), that can be dealt with using these techniques. The pupils should not be allowed to look up anything in a dictionary. When they have read the text, the pupils (**not** the teacher) should discuss the text and ask questions about it; if a pupil asks about one of the new words, the teacher should not simply explain what it means but help the pupil to answer his own question by drawing his attention to the clues in the context or in the form of the word itself which will enable him to discover the meaning of the word. In this way the pupil will not merely learn the meaning of one word but will develop his capacity to cope with many new words. Another device that can be used to develop the technique of the use of context is to prepare crossword puzzle clues where the word to be found is represented as a gap in a sentence made up of familiar words and structures, e.g. *Où est mon stylo? Je veux (. . .) une lettre à mon oncle* (6).

It is the need to develop these techniques which justifies the reluctance with which many foreign-language teachers accept dictionaries. Provided that suitably graded and interesting texts exist in sufficient quantities, there are strong arguments for not allowing young readers to use dictionaries until they have mastered these techniques. There comes a time, however, once a pupil starts to read widely and according to his own interests, when he will occasionally meet words which he needs to understand but which none of the above techniques will help him to understand. The most effective step is for him then to use a bilingual dictionary. Once again, however, it is important that the pupils be given adequate training in the use of a dictionary. In the Nuffield/Schools Council French materials there is a graded introduction to the use of a bilingual dictionary, which teachers using other materials can adapt to meet their own requirements. There are no French–English glossaries for the pupils until they are 13 or 14, when they start on the *Dans le Vent* magazines. Then no word is included in the glossary if a pupil can be reasonably expected to work out its meaning by the application of the techniques described above. When a French word is included in the glossary, the English equivalent given in the first months is deliberately context-specific: it relates only to the sense of the word in the context in which it occurs. Gradually, however, some of the other possible English equivalents of French words contained in the glossary are given, and the pupils have to learn to refer back to the context to see which of the possible English equivalents is most appropriate. In this way the pupils work towards the point when they can graduate to a dictionary and use it with skill and confidence.

The pupil whose introduction to reading the foreign language has taught him to read in a responsive way, in 'meaningful mouthfuls', to cope with new words and whose confidence in himself as a reader has been developed has had an excellent start. Before he can be said to be a mature reader, however, he must also learn how to adapt his approach to what he is reading according to the nature of the material and to his own intentions.[19] A mature reader would not, for example, read a James Bond novel in the same way as he would read a Shakespearian sonnet. He would also adopt different speeds and procedures when reading a newspaper, a legal document of importance to him or a motor-repair manual after he had taken his car engine to pieces! It is clearly not possible for our pupils to develop all the strategies of a fully mature reader by the age of 13 or even 16. They can, however, learn to distinguish between what can be called extensive and intensive reading strategies, and these strategies should certainly be developed with pupils of 13 to 16. In the case of extensive reading, which accounts for most of the reading done by most people, the aim is for the reader to grasp the main points in a text without necessarily understanding every word or every sentence. There are occasions, however, when one needs to read a text or a part of a text intensively, with a very high level of comprehension and retention. When this is the case, different strategies are called for.

The best way, without doubt, for a teacher to help his pupils to develop what is probably the most important of all the reading strategies, that of extensive silent reading, is to persuade them to read a large amount of material which they find interesting, thought provoking and well within their linguistic grasp.[20] The surveys quoted earlier also show that the more a pupil reads, the more likely he is to acquire powers of discrimination and appreciation for himself. Very few teachers, in fact, give their pupils nearly enough appropriate silent reading material from which they can choose freely, to enable them to build up the necessary skills and attitudes. And all too frequently, even when the pupils are given something appropriate to read, the teacher takes steps to prevent them from reading it in a mature way, but rather forces them to read it in a way which will encourage bad reading habits. Reading texts aloud round the class, for example, develops habits of vocalization and subvocalization which can be a permanent obstacle to efficient silent reading.[21] Furthermore, 'the vice of the poor reader is to say the words to himself without actively making judgements concerning what they reveal. Reading aloud or listening to one reading aloud may leave this vice unaltered or even encouraged.'[22] Even those teachers who do encourage their pupils to read silently and at their own speed often reduce the good this does by bombarding them afterwards with oral or written questions, by quizzing them about every detail of the factual content of the text. This can have a harmful effect in two respects: first, it can shape the reader into trying to give equal attention to every detail in the text – whether or not it is relevant or interesting – and thus prevent the development of a personal response from the reader to the text; second, this approach can rapidly convince pupils that the only reason they are asked to read anything in the foreign language is to equip them to answer the teacher's questions, not for any pleasure or satisfaction they may derive from it. It is obviously important for a pupil to discuss with his teacher as often as is possible what he is reading; but the teacher should attempt to make this a very personal discussion, to help and encourage the pupils, individually or in small groups, to react in their own ways to what they have read.[23] Whenever possible, during this discussion, any detailed factual questions that are asked should be asked by the pupils and not the teacher. In short, the teacher can most effectively help his pupils to read extensively by making available adequate time to permit them to read widely and by providing enough material which they will want to read and which is well within their linguistic grasp; he will impede his pupils by over-questioning them.

As regards intensive silent reading, there are a number of possible approaches,[24] the essential features of which can be summarized by reference to the procedure suggested for developing the following passage from stage 4A of *En Avant*,[25] which is intended for pupils aged from 11 to 13 (see p. 266).

It is suggested that the passage should first be read quickly and a general idea of its contents understood. To help the pupils do this, there are a few questions about key points in the text which the pupils read before they read the text itself; the pupils then read the text as quickly as they can, simply in order to find the answers to the initial questions. When these questions have been discussed, the teacher asks a few more questions which call either for a more detailed understanding of the text or for a personal response to various aspects of the text. When these questions have been discussed, the pupils are encouraged to ask questions of their own and to comment on any aspect of the passage which is of particular interest to them.

This example serves to illustrate the main steps which a reader should go through when, for whatever reason, he wishes to read a text intensively. It is important to note, however, that the teacher should gradually take a less active part in the operation. Gradually the pupil should learn to take all these steps without help. He should, on his own initiative, glance quickly over a text and use this brief survey to form questions of his own to direct his reading; he should then read the text in order to answer his questions and perhaps to find some new questions (the important thing to note here being that

Aventure au Pays Basque Episodes 3 et 4: petit résumé.

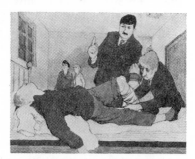

Où vont Roger et Claudine avec les deux contrebandiers ?
Est-ce que le chef veut appeler le médecin ?
Qu'est-ce que les enfants mangent ?
Pourquoi est-ce que Roger et Claudine suivent le petit chemin ?

❉❉❉❉❉❉❉❉❉❉❉❉❉❉❉❉❉❉❉❉❉❉❉❉❉❉

Roger et Claudine doivent partir avec les deux contrebandiers. Ils vont dans une maison abandonnée. Les contrebandiers enferment les enfants dans une chambre.
Henri est blessé. C'est grave mais le chef ne veut pas appeler le médecin. Claudine et Roger veulent aider Henri. Mais que peuvent-ils faire pour lui ?
Les enfants mangent des champignons. Puis ils crient : "Aïe, nous sommes empoisonnés !"
Ils enferment les contrebandiers dans la chambre. Puis, ils vont chercher les gendarmes.
Quand les gendarmes arrivent, le chef est parti. Il veut aller en Espagne. Il y a un petit chemin qui est plus direct que la route. Mais les gendarmes ne peuvent pas suivre ce chemin avec leur voiture. Qu'est-ce qu'ils vont faire maintenant ?

the reading is not the reader's first contact with the text); he should then answer his questions in his own words, giving his own examples where appropriate; he should finally revise this some time later by trying to answer again his own questions. This technique is often referred to as SQ 3R (Survey, Questions, Read, Recite, Revise). The most important point to notice is that the efficient reader does not merely read more slowly when he wants to read something intensively, but he adopts a well-planned searching strategy; merely reading a text more slowly is ineffective and can, in fact, make comprehension more difficult, as frequently the reader has forgotten how a paragraph began by the time he reaches its end and so has to regress and read it all again.

It is the experience of many teachers that pupils who have followed a reading programme along these lines are, to use the words of the song, ready, willing and able to read enormous amounts of French of many sorts between the ages of 13 and 16. This wide reading is, in its turn, the best possible preparation the pupils could have for whatever uses they later choose to put to the reading skills they have developed.

It is not possible, within one short chapter, to give a complete survey of even one aspect of what is involved in learning to read a foreign language. Few language teachers would disagree, however, with the statement that one of their main aims should be to ensure that as many as possible of the 95 per cent of those pupils who study a foreign language to the age of 16 without going on to become specialist linguists will want to, and be able to, remain in contact with the language and its culture through reading. Teachers would also be happy to see sixth form pupils who were willing and able to read more widely in the foreign language than is generally the case now. There can be little doubt that these aims will only be achieved if the pupils' experience of reading the foreign language before they reach sixteen is enjoyable, fruitful and successful. This in turn can only come about if the content of the reading programme is firmly based on what seems relevant and interesting to the pupils, and if the methods employed enable them not merely to decode the printed word but to react to it in a responsive and mature way. There is no simple solution but the successful programme will, first of all, offer opportunities for extensive practice in reading with the emphasis on responsive comprehension. It is also important to bear in mind at all stages that for both teacher and pupil attitudes are as important as techniques; at all times a reading programme should aim at least as much at increasing the pupils' **willingness** to read as at developing his **ability** to read.[26] The teacher should attempt to ensure above all that his pupils learn to enjoy reading in the foreign language, for, if they do, reading in the foreign language will not be something they stop doing as soon as they can choose for themselves.

References

1. RIVERS, W. M. (1968) *Teaching Foreign-language Skills*. Chicago and London: University of Chicago Press.
2. D'ARCY, P. (1973) *Reading for Meaning*, vol. 2. London: Hutchinson Educational.
3. WILLIAMS, A. R. (1951) 'The magazine reading of secondary school children.' *Br. J. educ. Psychol.*, **21**, no. 3, 186–98.
4. JENKINSON, A. J. (1940) *What do Boys and Girls Read?* London: Methuen.
5. PICKARD, P. M. (1961) *I Could a Tale Unfold*. London: Tavistock.
6. NATE (NATIONAL ASSOCIATION FOR THE TEACHING OF ENGLISH) WARWICKSHIRE BRANCH (1968) *Children as Readers*.
7. ALDERSON, C. (1968) *Magazines Teenagers Read*. Oxford: Pergamon.
8. CARSLEY, J. D. (1957) 'The interest of children aged 10–11 years in books.' *Br. J. educ. Psychol.*, **27**, no. 1, 13–23.
9. CLARK, J. (1968) 'French in the primary school.' *Audio-visual Language J.*, **6**, no. 2–3, 96–9.
10. SCHOOLS COUNCIL MODERN LANGUAGES PROJECT, FRENCH SECTION (1970) *A Study of and Concordance to Five High-frequency Topics occurring in a Selection of French Magazines and Newspapers*. Mimeographed.
11. SCHOOLS COUNCIL (1972) *A votre avis*, stage 5; (1973) stage 6; (1974) stages 7 and 8. Leeds: E. J. Arnold.
12. WALL, W. D. (1968) *Adolescents in School and Society*. Slough: National Foundation for Educational Research. FADER, D. N. and MCNEIL, E. B. (1968) *Hooked on Books*. Oxford: Pergamon.
13. FRIES, C. C. (1965) *Linguistics and Reading*. London: Holt, Rinehart & Winston. AUSTIN, M. C. and MORRISON, C. (1963) *The First R: the Harvard report on reading in elementary schools*. London: Macmillan.

14. MORRIS, R. (1973) *Success and Failure in Learning to Read,* 2nd edn. Harmondsworth, Middx: Penguin.

15. NUFFIELD FOUNDATION (1967) *En Avant,* stage 2. Leeds: E. J. Arnold.

16. FRASER, H. and O'DONNEL, W. R. (eds) (1969) *Applied Linguistics and the Teaching of English.* London: Longman.

17. NIDA, E. A. (1964) *Towards a Science of Translating.* New York: Heinemann.

18. NUFFIELD FOUNDATION (1968) *En Avant,* stage 3. Leeds: E. J. Arnold.

19. ELLIOTT, A. V. P. (1962) 'The reading lesson.' *English Language Teaching,* **17**, no. 1, 9–16, no. 2, 67–72.

20. THORNDIKE, E. L. (1934) 'Improving the ability to read.' *Teachers College Record,* **36.** MACMILLAN, M. (1965) *Efficiency in Reading.* ETIC Occasional Paper 6.

21. WEST, M. (1955) *Learning to Read a Foreign Language.* London: Longman.

22. THORNDIKE, E. L. (1917) 'Reading as reasoning: a study of mistakes in paragraph reading.' *J. educ. Psychol.,* **8**, no. 6, 323–32.

23. BARNES, D., BRITTON, J. and ROSEN, H. (1969) *Language, the Learner and the School.* Harmondsworth, Middx: Penguin.

24. FRY, E. (1963) *Teaching Faster Reading: a manual.* Cambridge University Press. WOOD, E. (1962) *Reading Dynamics: notes on study reading, passing tests and 'hard reading'.* Evelyn Wood Reading Dynamics of New York.

25. NUFFIELD FOUNDATION (1970) *En Avant,* stage 4 A. Leeds: E. J. Arnold.

26. MCCRACKEN, R. A. (1969) 'Do we want real readers?' *J. Reading.*

NICHOLAS BEATTIE

School of Education, University of Liverpool

The uses of reading

Introduction

Schools are curiously moral institutions. Any conscientious teacher tends naturally to invest his work with a certain moral value. Thus in the area of foreign-language teaching some zealots have argued so passionately for the primacy of speaking and listening skills that many of us have experienced terrible pangs of conscience at introducing reading sooner than the experts recommended, even though a piece of research recently completed on Merseyside[1] shows that in thirty-three primary schools studied **not one** teacher was introducing the printed word at the point suggested by the course being used. Less urgently than the oralists, but still with a certain tone of moral fervour, other teachers will proclaim that they 'believe in reading', as though reading were an end in itself, an activity whose usefulness or appropriateness need not be argued. The position taken in this chapter will be that whatever reading goes on in foreign-language classrooms is unlikely to be effective in promoting language mastery unless the teacher is able to consider clearly the 'uses of reading': to break down the unrevealing blanket term 'reading' into different **kinds** of reading, to view these varied activities in relation to a wide variety of other techniques at his disposal, and to attempt to relate different types of reading to his objectives at various stages in the language course. This argument will be presented mainly in relation to the intermediate stage of language learning – what the French have usefully christened *Niveau 2* (*Le Français dans le monde*, no. 73, June 1970). It will deal with the initial introduction of reading and with reading at the post-O-level stage only *en passant*. The examples will be drawn from French, though the general principles should apply to other European languages.

270

Reading aloud

It is my guess that if one had an objective record of what actually goes on in the average foreign-language classroom (as opposed to what the teacher thinks goes on) it would reveal a surprising proportion of class time taken up by **reading aloud**. This is, in fact, what many teachers mean by reading. It is not surprising, therefore, that many learners come to share this simplistic view. The unhappy results may not infrequently be seen in the sixth form, where students are understandably disoriented when for the first time they are faced with a text too long to be read in any other way than silently.

This is not to say that reading aloud is a disreputable activity – far from it; but it is a technique like any other and as such must be deployed intelligently. The reason why it is so frequently used is that it is easy to plan, mount and control. A printed text is a supremely manageable stimulus, requiring a minimum of teacher vocalization, little planning, no blackout, power-point, or manipulation of film-strip or tape. But what is easy for the teacher is not necessarily easy for the learner. To read a passage aloud is **harder** than to read it silently: the reader has, so to speak, not only to infer meaning from print, but further to infer sound from meaning. If the passage is one which he has not seen before, and is written in a foreign language whose orthography differs from that to which he is accustomed in his everyday first-language reading, the learner's performance will naturally be laboured and mispronounced. Even though somebody is uttering, it is not in any proper sense of the term 'oral work'. So many elements conspire to complicate the task of the reader that the teacher cannot even obtain much useful feedback about the learner's progress. If reading aloud is to be of value, surely it must be done briefly – perhaps just a sentence at a time – and only on texts which are already well known orally.[2]

A further major practical drawback to reading aloud is that either it must be done by one pupil with the rest sitting passive and often absorbing the halting mispronunciations of the reader, or it must be done chorally – often useful in short bursts, but difficult and tiring for the teacher to orchestrate, and producing a volume of sound amid which it is not easy to discriminate individual errors.

Other types of reading

We are thus led to shift our attention from reading aloud to silent reading. Quite apart from the classroom considerations so far advanced, it is surely clear that in the world outside the classroom we are rarely called upon to read aloud, while the rapid silent scanning of a text for information can be of great practical use. If this is so, then we need to write silent reading into our course objectives (as many more or less audio-visual courses have in fact done over the past few years) and presumably to adopt classroom teaching techniques which will encourage learners to develop appropriate reading skills.

Some teachers may feel that to teach learners to read silently is either unnecessary or undesirable, a form of spoon feeding. Ten or fifteen years ago, when dealing with a selective intake of able pupils from backgrounds which valued books and reading, they may have been right. But the average teacher of French in a comprehensive school can hardly allow a major objective of this kind to be attained by mere chance: he knows all too well that it will not happen. What, then, must he do? How can the teacher who has recognized 'the uses of reading' encourage development of reading skills in his classroom?

First, having clarified the distinction already discussed between reading aloud and silent reading, he must distinguish in his own mind between **initial** reading, **intensive** reading and **extensive** reading.

By initial reading I wish to characterize the very early stages of moving from oral and aural work to presentation of the printed word. It is not my purpose here to discuss this complex question at length: it is dealt with elsewhere in this handbook. I will only point out that if skills of silent reading are to be naturally developed later on in the course, it will be necessary for the teacher (a) not to treat the graphic medium as something sinful, and (b) to present at an early stage brief snippets of written or printed material – initially just the odd sentence. They may be presented in printed or duplicated form, on the blackboard or overhead projector, on flash-cards, etc. They will be read aloud individually and chorally as a support for and extension of oral work which has already been done. In this way familiarity with novel spelling patterns can be progressively built up.[3] Nothing should be presented which is not already known through the oral medium. In the early stages of learning a language confidence is easily sapped and it seems important that children should not come to associate print with that feeling of bewilderment, of having to work out a text like a crossword puzzle, which many of us recall from learning Latin. No doubt it did us no harm; but I suggest that a living language is a different beast from a dead one.

The stage of initial reading ought to pass fairly rapidly. By intensive reading I wish to designate an activity which may (and does) go on at all levels of language learning. One of the central activities of all language teachers, whatever method they may espouse, is to take a passage – a chapter of a course-book, a dialogue already heard on tape, a paragraph from a newspaper, a literary passage, and extract from it whatever linguistic and/or cultural content they judge to be appropriate to their pupils' needs. This is then drilled, practised, tested or otherwise extended and deployed. Again, I do not wish to discuss all these various techniques which may be involved when a teacher says simply 'We read the passage on page 25 this morning'; I do want to distinguish rather sharply between these activities and those characterized by the label 'extensive reading'. These distinctions are important if the teacher is to plan his work intelligently so that these different types of reading are seen as **preconditions** of the distinct activity of extensive reading rather than **substitutes** for it.

Extensive reading

By extensive reading is meant the rapid silent scanning of a text for meaning, the kind of reading which is in fact the norm in first-language work, the process involved when we say 'I read the newspaper / menu / letter / novel'. There are many language classrooms where this never happens, where reading means only reading aloud and particularly the cluster of techniques used in connection with intensive reading. Why this reluctance to embark on extensive reading? I believe that many teachers have understandable fears about this which need to be discussed openly.

1. Some teachers feel oddly **guilty** because they are not performing. There are several answers to this. Much foreign-language work at *Niveau 2*, which is essentially the level at which the learner begins to use language on his own account, is far too teacher centred anyway. The point of a lesson is that the **pupil** should be active: the teacher's activity is incidental. Silent reading is real mental activity, real

practice in processing the foreign language, even if no movement of lips or hand is visible. In any case, language teachers desperately need periods of relative rest throughout the day as well as opportunity to attend to the problems of individual learners.

2. Some teachers claim they have not enough **time** to allow children to read. This is partly a question of how you rate your objectives. If silent reading seems important and is believed to be not just a restful interlude but a positive activity, then (say) one period out of five in the last three years of a five-year French course does not seem difficult to justify. Teachers conducting two- or three-year courses to the first examination are in much more difficult circumstances, though even here judicious use of homework must surely permit of some practice in extensive reading.

3. Some teachers shrink from the exercise because they feel their pupils will not react well to being asked 'merely' to sit down and read a book, and that **idleness** or **disorder** will follow. If relations between teacher and class are strained and tense this is probably true, and a more directive approach may be necessary. In more normal circumstances, however, a teacher should be able to move round the room chatting and questioning quietly, even just looking over shoulders, to obtain feedback about pupils' progress and problems and to remind them tacitly that they are not simply being left to their own devices. For teachers who favour group work, reading is one foreign-language activity which readily conforms to this mode of class organization, and which (in a middle school, for example) may help foreign languages to seem a little less of an eccentric teacher-directed domain.

4. Some teachers fear that time spent on extensive reading will be wasted because pupils will find the task either too **difficult** or too **dull.** This will certainly be true if the texts available are inappropriate. Extensive reading is particularly vulnerable here because unlike most of the activities pursued at *Niveau 2* the pupil is in a real sense on his own. If he perceives his task as boring or impossible, his thoughts will rapidly turn elsewhere. It is therefore crucial that the teacher should select reading material which is well within the pupil's linguistic grasp – in the early stages simpler than what the pupil can manage orally, so that the pupil can read rapidly; he must acquire the habit of looking at sentences as wholes (so that to begin with sentences must be short) and guessing intelligently rather than laboriously construing from left to right. Texts should be quite brief

(to give the satisfaction of 'finishing a book'). Subject-matter should be varied and as no single text is likely to appeal to thirty individuals, they should as far as is practicable be encouraged to select their own, rather than all thirty being issued with one identical book to be processed at uniform speed. Initially illustrations and lay-out are important both for motivation and for establishing meanings. As learners become more confident in their reading skills and their linguistic knowledge grows, the teacher must select longer texts which offer progressively less support to the learner and which in content approximate more and more to the kind of material he reads in his first language.[4]

The values of extensive reading

'The uses of reading' is a deliberately ambiguous phrase. As already suggested, teachers may 'use' reading in varying circumstances, but they do so because they judge reading to be 'useful' to the pupil. It seems worth summarizing this brief account by stating clearly why reading is useful to a learner in extending his control of a foreign language.

First, reading gives the learner **practice**. He is obliged to process for himself a much greater number of foreign-language sentences than he will normally get an opportunity to process orally. He will extend his vocabulary and acquire the essential habit of intelligent guessing. One hopes, too, that he will begin to learn habits of intelligent dictionary use, starting perhaps with a simple monolingual dictionary such as the *Vocabulaire fondamental illustré*.[5] And when he leaves school, reading may be his only means of maintaining his language in reasonable working order.

Second, reading gives **confidence**. Silent reading is a manageable, private activity offering immediate rewards even to the shy and tongue-tied. So many of our methods assume that both teacher and learner are extroverts.

Third, reading provides **interest**. The chief reward of being able to read is that you can obtain information which is not available in other ways. In this sense, reading can eventually be a 'first-hand' activity, as opposed to so many language-teaching situations which are simply contrived as a means to the practice of lexis or structures. For the majority of learners, who either do not go abroad or do so very infrequently, the skills of reading are those which can really begin to open up the reality of a foreign civilization. Thus the ultimate 'use' of reading is the same as that of all other parts of the foreign-language course: first-hand contact with foreign people and a foreign culture.

Suggestions for further reading

Kellermann and Norledge[6] provide a useful basis for further inquiry, and list all the major references. The position briefly presented in this chapter is argued at greater length in three papers covering particular aspects of the problem: choice of readers,[7] moving from intermediate to advanced work[8] and reading aloud.[9] The C I L T lists[10] are those in print in December 1973.

Notes and references

1. HILLS, R. J. (1973) 'An analysis of the way in which teachers . . . of primary school French introduce (or not) the written word.' Unpublished dissertation for the Diploma in the Advanced Study of Education, University of Liverpool.
2. The exception would be reading aloud as a histrionic performance, but this seems generally inappropriate to the objectives prevailing at *Niveau 2*.
3. This familiarity will, of course, be further reinforced by the gradual introduction of writing – initially through simple activities such as copying or more complex ones like dictation.
4. The problem of selecting texts appropriate to particular stages is difficult, and I would urge any conscientious teacher to read books carefully before purchasing them. Distinguish between simple initial readers (e.g. the *Bon accueil les gosses!* series, edited by D. J. Jenkins from Ginn, whose illustrations are a model for books at this level), longer and more complex, but still artificially devised texts (these constitute perhaps the bulk of the market and vary enormously in quality), longer texts which could be read rapidly but seem to be designed more for intensive work (e.g. P. Symonds' *Let's Read French* series from Oxford University Press or the Longman series of which R. Leeson's *Voyage à Paris* is an example) and texts (of which there is a great dearth) providing both information and a manageable linguistic content for a fourth- or fifth-year pupil. Examples of this last category might

be Longman's *Les Jeunes travaillent* series or the reading
material attached to stage 5 of the Nuffield/Schools Council
French course but purchasable separately, or (in briefer and less
permanent form) the language magazines published by Mary
Glasgow, Hachette, etc. At this point actual French texts,
whether simplified or selected, begin to be accessible – trans-
cribed interviews, newspaper extracts, etc. Teachers planning
seriously should begin their inquiries long before the order
needs to be submitted. They should consult the publishers'
catalogues and also the relevant CILT lists.

5. KROPMAN, A. *et al.* (1972) *Vocabulaire fondamental illustré.*
London: Harrap. For a much fuller discussion of dictionaries
and glossaries in the reading process, with lists of currently
available dictionaries, see BEATTIE, N. M. (1973) 'Teaching
dictionary use.' *Modern Languages*, **54**, no. 4, 161–9.

6. KELLERMAN, M. and NORLEDGE, G. (1972) 'Second language
literacy.' *Modern Languages*, **53**, no. 2, 80–6.

7. BEATTIE, N. M. (1970) 'What constitutes a good reader?'
Modern Languages, **51**, no. 3, 108–15, 129.

8. BEATTIE, N. M. (1971) 'Reading as a preparation for sixth form
work.' *AVLJ*, **8**, no. 3, 127–33.

9. BEATTIE, N. M. (1973) 'Reading aloud.' *AVLJ*, **11**, no. 3, 201–5.

10. CILT Teaching Materials Lists: *Italian Supplementary Course
Material and Readers* (1971); *Russian Readers* (1971); *Spanish
Readers* (1971); *German Readers* (1971–2); *French Pictorial
Readers, Classroom Magazines, etc.* (1973); *French Readers in
Graded Series* (1973).

ANN M. DAVIES

Islington Language Centre, London

Organizing reading work

The reader has been used for many years as part of a modern language course. Traditionally it was read aloud, paragraph by paragraph, round the class and/or by the teacher. This meant that frequently it lasted perhaps half a term, sometimes a whole term or even remained unfinished at the end of term because by that time no one, not even the teacher, was interested any more. Adults would never submit themselves to such prolonged boredom when they read, and yet they have expected children to undergo this agony, often in the name of light relief.

A work of fiction at any level should be a source of enjoyment and relaxation. A reader in a foreign language should be read primarily because the pupil is interested in the story, the characters, the way of life depicted, not as an exercise in public reading. It should be read for relaxation, not with the dictionary at hand, looking up every new word and painstakingly noting it in a vocabulary book. It should be read to gain new insight into another culture, not as a prelude to the inevitable list of questions. Modern language teachers need to help their pupils to realize that the foreign language is a medium as adequate as English for expressing ideas on all aspects of life. The ultimate aim of the reading lesson may be to gain information from journals or newspapers, or an intensive study of literature, or an ability to cope with correspondence in the foreign language or the capacity to read it for a variety of other reasons. The seeds for all these activities are sown when the pupil reads his first passage in the foreign language.

Each class should have a stock of readers which can be borrowed and read for pleasure. As in a good library, the books should reflect the interests of the children themselves. Readers are written to suit certain levels of language competence, and although it is very difficult to find any reader which fits a particular group of learners, the teacher should give the pupils access to those readers in which

278

most of the vocabulary and structures are known. If careful attention is not paid to this, then what is intended as a pleasurable activity by the teacher turns into a long boring memory game with the dictionary. Readers could reasonably contain a few unfamiliar vocabulary items, since in any reading there are previously unknown items which become obvious from the context. No teacher, however, can assume that pupils will automatically work out the meaning from the context on their own. The pupils from the earliest stages of reading are making assumptions about the meanings of words, but they need training and encouragement from the teacher if they are to read fluently without worrying about the precise translation of each new word. The teacher needs to show the pupils how in a continuous piece of prose certain words have to mean certain things, although they may only gain an approximate idea of the meaning and be unaware of the English equivalent. The teacher needs to go through many examples with his class, showing them how ideas unfold and the meanings of new words become clear. If this is done, pupils will learn to trust their own understanding of the passage and will not feel so insecure that they have to turn to the dictionary for reinforcement. A dictionary – preferably a picture dictionary or an illustrated dictionary in the foreign language – has a place in the language room, but again the pupils need to be trained to use it and to know when it will be useful. For their individual reading it should be almost redundant. If it is not, then it is likely that the reading matter is too difficult.

When the pupils have learned to read with some confidence, their vocabulary will be extended through the language itself. They will begin to see certain structures always used in a certain way, and they will become familiar with the most frequent words of the language. They assimilate these without making a conscious effort to remember long lists of words, and frequently the phrases that have recurred in their reading will start appearing in their own speech and writing.

If a class has a stock of as many readers at the relevant level as the teacher can find (not an easy task, but one has to remember that the only 'perfect' readers are those that the teacher makes for his own class), say twenty, then each pupil in that class has the opportunity to read twenty different readers in the course of a year. In terms of expense there is little difference between two copies of twenty books and forty copies of one, but in terms of interest, variety and sense of achievement, the pupils' gain is enormous. The library packs that were introduced by Mary Glasgow have faults but they have been found very good for pupils in their second or third year of French. They are interesting and short, and the younger pupils in the secondary school can easily cope with them.

With a large number of different texts in circulation obviously a check needs to be kept. This can be done, with very little paper work involved, if a chart is kept for each class and pupils are appointed to look after the books. A list of titles can be shown vertically and a list of the pupils' names horizontally thus:

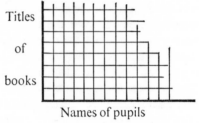

The date on which a pupil borrows a book can be entered against his name and the title of the book, and crossed out when he returns the book. Initially it may be worth asking the pupils to write down their thoughts in English about the books they read, as this may help to plan for future classes. An extensive questioning in the foreign language seems unnecessary and may be detrimental in that it puts an added strain on the weaker pupils. A duplicated questionnaire to be answered in English could be filled out when the pupil has finished the book. This could also be given out by the pupils who are looking after the books and the results recorded very simply in a chart by the teacher. If this type of extensive reading is to be encouraged a lot of it may well be done at home, but it may well be done in class if the teacher wishes.

The other type of reading which is very important is intensive reading of an article or passage to gain information, sometimes, as in scientific journals or brochures, very precise information. Some readers which do not contain simply a story but depict a certain way of life or give geographical or historical information can be used for intensive reading. There are some low-level readers in the *Bon accueil les gosses!* series which are short enough to be used for both intensive and extensive reading. Often the teacher will have to choose his own reading passages and duplicate them. If he also prepares work-cards to accompany these passages or readers, he can use them in the classroom – perhaps one lesson every two weeks – and leave himself free to help those pupils who have missed work or who need extra coaching. Often questions are printed in readers at the end of chapters, but because every teacher teaches in a different way it is usually impossible to find a reader in which the questions are geared to elicit the language which the teacher wants from that particular class. It is better, therefore, to devise one's own work-cards, concentrating on the areas of language which are relevant to that class at that time. For example, the reader *Chauffeur de taxi à Paris* could be used to elicit vocabulary and structures indicating direction, or to consolidate prepositional phrases, or for definitions of people and buildings, depending at which stage the teacher feels he can introduce that reader to a class.

Work-card for *Chauffeur de taxi à Paris* (for pupils in their first or second year of French)

Side 1

1. *Qui est Joël Bret?*
2. *Où est-ce qu'il habite?*
3. *Est-ce qu'il habite avec sa famille?*
4. *Où est-il à sept heures moins le quart?*
5. *Est-ce qu'il prend le petit déjeuner à l'appartement?*
6. *Est-ce qu'il gare sa voiture dans la rue pendant la nuit?*
7. *Où est la Gare du Nord?*
8. *D'où viennent les trains qui arrivent à la Gare du Nord?*
9. *Qui travaille à la Bourse?*
10. *Qu'est-ce que c'est que Notre-Dame de Paris?*
11. *De quand date-t-elle?*
12. *Où se trouve-t-elle exactement à Paris?*
13. *Qu'est-ce que c'est que la Sorbonne?*
14. *Dans quelle rue se trouve-t-elle?*
15. *Qu'est-ce qu'on trouve au Louvre?*

Side 2

Choose one or more of the following to write about:

1. Find out precisely where the Arc de Triomphe is, and when and why it was built.

2. Write a paragraph about Gustave Eiffel and find out why he built his famous tower.

3. Many famous artists have lived and worked in Paris. Choose one and write about his life and work.

4. Find out as much as you can about the Seine and describe a journey on the river from Le Havre to Paris.

5. The Parisii gave Paris its name. Find out who these people were, where they came from, and briefly describe the expansion of Paris to the present day.

A reader such as this can also be used as a springboard for further areas of inquiry. The teacher has to decide whether the foreign language is to be used or whether English is more suitable at that stage of learning. In the early stages when pupils do not have sufficient command of the foreign language to express their own ideas and feelings, it is important to make demands on them intellectually by requiring them to carry out some work which can be recorded in English.

If the reading lesson is to leave the teacher free, then the work-cards for the readers and the reading passages must be quickly available and comprehensible to the pupils. A method which has been successful is to make work-cards which are slightly smaller than the reader to which they refer. A rectangle or triangle of card can be stuck inside either the front or back cover of the book and the work-card can be kept in this pocket. Teachers often spend hours sticking duplicated sheets of paper on to card to make the work-cards more permanent but most spirit duplicators will print directly on to card, which, because it is thicker than paper, can be backed, thus reducing the amount of card used. The size of the work-card should first be decided upon, then the card cut on a guillotine, then the master copy cut to fit this. Spirit duplicators have flexible guides for feeding in the paper or card, and if these are adjusted accordingly there is no fear of printing only part of the required stencil. Some schools and most teachers' centres now have facilities for laminating work-cards and this makes them even longer lasting and less susceptible to 'decoration' by the pupils, since they can be wiped clean.

Where a reader is not used but the teacher is choosing his own reading passages, it is better if the passage and questions are both on the same card but on different sides of it. Quite a long passage can be typed on to a stencil to fit a card 16×16 cm, or if the school has a stencil-cutter, articles from newspapers and journals can be fitted into this space. These cards can then be backed by the relevant questions and can be stored in a box. Shoe boxes are the right size and are extremely useful for storage. Levels of language complexity or areas of interest, or both, can be shown by the colour of the card used (most schools have a large selection of different colours) or by self-adhesive coloured circles in the corner of the card. In this way the teacher can keep a check on the suitability of certain cards for certain pupils – especially useful in the mixed-ability class.

Helping pupils to read both intensively and extensively in a foreign language does put an extra burden on the teacher. It does mean extra time spent looking for suitable readers, preparation of work-cards and organization of the classroom. This time is, however, very well spent, for if pupils can be encouraged to read on two levels from the very beginning, the teacher has made an important contribution to the language-learning skills of his pupils.

PART 8

Writing

Writing in foreign-language lessons is sometimes postponed for long periods or avoided altogether because of a belief that it hinders the progress of less able children and interferes with good habits of pronunciation. The first three chapters in this section all question this belief and see writing as having a valuable role to play. In the two chapters on composition it is seen as enabling the learner to use, under careful guidance, the language he has learnt for coherent and extended expression.

Writing is an additional form of language expression, providing activity for all the class at once and a change from non-stop oral work. Some children do not have an oral/aural style of learning and most need a visual support as an aid to remembering what they are learning. Writing can also be a useful form of assessment, indicating to the teacher what the learner is **seeing** when he is reading.

At first, writing will be largely a matter of copying from the board, of labelling pictures. Then it will involve reformulation in altered circumstances (*J'ai douze ans. Et ton frère? Il a dix ans*) and, in the initial stages of composition work, will advance to reorganization when the learner links what he has been learning into a coherent whole – under headings such as *moi, mon ami(e), mon trajet de la maison a l'ecole*. Eventually it will involve real creation – in letters and reports. This journey through writing will be comprehensively supported with written question and answer work, with the construction of written data (school timetable, personal dossier, recipes, etc.), with dictation (in which the teacher provides models of short, coherently linked passages) and with projects (a scrapbook on the home town of the French family on which the early language work is based) – in short, writing activities which support and supplement the rest of the language-learning work.

C. J. DODSON

Department of Education, University College of Wales, Aberystwyth

Introducing the written word

There is still a great deal of controversy about the point in time at which foreign-language (FL) writing work should be introduced in a modern languages course. With more traditional indirect grammar-translation methods, which deliberately tend to ignore the spoken word, pupils are required to write in the foreign language almost immediately at the beginning of a course, whilst with direct method approaches, which lay stress on oral fluency and accuracy, it is frequently advocated that writing work be postponed for at least the first term and in many instances for the first year.

Teachers of the latter school argue that as FL writing work cannot be introduced before pupils have been presented with the FL printed word, and as pupils' spoken responses deteriorate if the printed word is introduced too early in a course, postponement of writing work is both justified and necessary. It is held that the connections already made by pupils between mother-tongue (MT) sounds and the MT printed word system are transferred to the new connections they have to make between FL sounds and the FL printed word. This transfer causes immediate spoken word interference, which it is very difficult, if not impossible, to eradicate. It would, therefore, seem most prudent to postpone both the FL printed and written work until the pupils' FL speech has become firmly consolidated and is no longer in danger of being modified by the outside influence of the spelling system. In addition, this postponement seems to coincide neatly with MT learning procedures, where mastery of the spoken word precedes the introduction of the printed and the written word by a matter of years.

Yet there are dangers which, though initially hidden, can cause perhaps greater havoc amongst pupils than the apparent advantage gained by postponing contact with the printed and written word. When a pupil hears an FL sentence for the first time during the initial imitation exercise for any language unit and is then required to

284

repeat this F L sentence (either individually or in chorus) a number of times in order to achieve accuracy in pronunciation and fluency, it should not be assumed that he is able to complete his F L response merely by relying on the **sound** image of the F L model. The average pupil finds it impossible on most occasions to cope with new sound chains consisting of more than five syllables if forced to rely on only the sound image of these chains. (Let the reader, who by definition is a language specialist with a high I.Q., a good memory and years of training, attempt to imitate chains of nonsense syllables **without** relying on outside associations, and score his performance in such an exercise.) In order to satisfy the demands made on him by the teacher, the pupil must rely on outside associations to complete his spoken response satisfactorily. The association most readily available to all pupils learning a foreign language in our educational system is the association between speech sounds and the printed word or letters of the alphabet. It is safe to assume that there are hardly any pupils who cannot recognize letters and their associated sounds and yet are taking part in foreign-language lessons in our secondary schools. Illiterate pupils should not be confused with those who cannot spell very well, especially as bad spellers tend to spell correctly from a phonetic point of view.

The majority of pupils, therefore, reinforce the sound image of the F L models by inventing their own spelling system to help them retain the sound image long enough to make a satisfactory response. Some pupils even go so far as to write this invented system with their index finger in the palm of the other hand. This phenomenon has been observed with children as young as eight years of age, where one would not have expected it, as these children were to some extent still involved in the process of establishing associations between sounds and spelling systems in their first language. Other pupils use different ways in their endeavour to form associations, from tongue-writing on teeth to the creation of letter images in their minds.

The fact that the teacher has withheld from his pupils the F L printed word does not mean, therefore, that the pupils have learnt to pronounce correctly without the aid of any form of spelling system whatsoever. However, the spelling systems invented by the pupils normally conflict with the accepted spelling system. Unfortunately, these invented spelling systems become progressively more fixed and consolidated with every spoken response made by pupils, so that by the end of a term the association between sound and imagined spelling is absolutely firm.

When after the first term or year the teacher introduces the actual FL printed word so that his pupils can progress from reading to writing, he often finds that his pupils have difficulty in learning how to spell correctly. He is, in fact, faced with the task of having to eradicate previously learnt unacceptable letter combinations before he can begin to teach his pupils the correct forms, and every teacher knows how difficult it is to eliminate well-consolidated errors.

The dilemma can be defined as follows: the teacher keeps the FL printed word from his pupils, thus ensuring good pronunciation (though not without the pupils' invented spelling system) but causing difficulty when reading and writing are introduced at a later stage **or** he introduces reading and writing at the beginning of a course, thereby creating a situation which interferes with his pupils' attempts to pronounce correctly.

There is, however, a third way in which this dilemma can be overcome: the teacher makes available the printed word at the beginning of the course, but ensures that the spoken FL model remains the **primary** stimulus. Pupils are only allowed to scan the printed sentence (on the board or in course-book) whilst they are **listening** to the spoken model, but must look at the teacher or visual aid when making a spoken response. They therefore have to rely on a **mental** image of the printed word, which is sufficiently strong to help them complete their responses (as was the writing in palms) yet sufficiently weak not to diminish the sound image of the spoken stimuli or to cause interference. Teachers should take immediate steps if any pupil looks at the printed word during his response by encouraging him to look elsewhere. It is, therefore, important not to have the printed word next to any visual aids at the beginning of a course; pupils' eyes will be drawn to the printed word rather than to a picture during a response.

Once sentences of a basic situation can be spoken fluently and accurately, the printed word can be withdrawn before starting on oral substitution, extension and question and answer work. It will be found that after the oral steps for any situation have been consolidated, the printed word for this situation can be re-introduced without causing interference. In fact, the availability of the printed word as a secondary stimulus at the beginning of a situation cycle helps the pupils in their spoken work, and reduces the number of times a teacher has to give spoken models for any sentence.*

When the printed word is re-introduced at the end of a situation cycle at the beginning of a course, the teacher should not make his pupils read aloud, as this converts the printed word into a primary stimulus during a spoken response, thus leading to possible interference in FL speech. Instead he should utilize the pupils' acquaintance with the printed word for silent reading and for introducing writing work. It is, therefore, possible that a class could be writing FL sentences at the end of the first week without in any way interfering with the acquisition of good FL speech. Obviously this writing work should be kept to a minimum (perhaps ten minutes per lesson) in the early stages, so as to give pupils an optimum number of spoken contacts. Pupils should not be expected, however, to write any sentence which includes words and phrases not thoroughly consolidated in their spoken forms, or else these are likely to be mispronounced subsequently.

Depending on the general ability of the class, writing should be introduced through copying or dictation work. It is wise before giving a dictation to allow pupils to look for a few minutes at the text to be given, and encourage them to copy out the words or phrases they think they will find difficult to write. Dictations at this stage are not tests but exercises to help pupils learn how to spell correctly what they can already say fluently and accurately. Pupils should correct each other's work by referring to the original text (in a book or on the board), whilst the teacher supervises the marking to ensure that pupils do not miss too many of their neighbours' errors. Corrections should be made in a downward column and not in the traditional horizontal line. For the first correction pupils should look at the original text, then hide the written correction with their non-writing hand whilst attempting a further correction underneath. If they have forgotten the correct form, they can look at the first correction before making a second attempt, and so on. When they find it easy to write the correct form, several additional corrections should be made in the vertical column for consolidation purposes.

Once pupils feel confident that they can write correctly what they can already say, the teacher should branch out and allow them to write first in response to various stimuli already used during oral

* Cp. DODSON, C. J. and PRICE, J. E. (1966) 'The role of the printed word in foreign-language teaching.' *Modern Languages*, **47**, no. 2, 59–62.

work, e.g. picture-strips, composite pictures, miming cues, etc., and second, about global topics, which could be either basic or extended situations, without external aids so that pupils have to rely on their own imagination. Learning how to control this imagination by expressing ideas within the confines of known vocabulary, phrases and patterns should be accomplished during oral work preceding any written composition work.

As far as primary school children are concerned, the printed word should be introduced at the beginning of a course as described above, but F L written work should be delayed. A young child takes such a long time to write a sentence and achieve correct spelling, that there will be insufficient time to consolidate the oral work on which the written work should be based.

FRANK CORLESS

School of Education, University of Southampton

Writing in an oral lesson

In many French teaching-practice lessons at which I have been present, the student, after a lively start, has chosen to carry on teaching orally throughout the time allotted to the lesson. Even as an observer I have felt, after twenty minutes or so, my concentration waning and my head beginning to spin, whilst the pupils have started to get restless, their sparkle has disappeared and the accuracy of their answers has diminished. The fact that a potentially promising piece of teaching has undermined itself has often been confirmed on my next visit, when the student has complained at how poorly the class seemed to remember, two or three days later, the material taught during the lesson in question. Generally speaking, the root of the trouble is quite simply that the student has failed to see the point at which he might profitably have introduced a different activity into his lesson. And provided that the class in question had already been introduced to reading and writing in French, I would suggest that the new activity might essentially have involved these two skills.

It is not within the scope of this chapter to consider the case for or against an early introduction of reading and writing in a foreign-language course. Suffice it to say that in our culture, from five or six years on, the written word plays a principal role in the educational process, and the child learns more and more to rely on it as a vital learning tool. Once the activities of reading and writing have been carefully introduced, the timely appearance of the written word in an oral-based foreign-language lesson performs, I would claim, four functions for the learner:

1. It offers him a relief from intensive oral work and helps dissipate the tensions that this generates[1] ('What **is** he getting at?' 'How will I **ever** remember all this stuff?').

2. It helps him to identify and then organize for himself any new piece of language being taught.

289

3. It reinforces the aural/oral mastery that he has achieved of a new piece of language or one that is being revised, both visually, by reading, and kinesthetically, by writing.

4. It helps him to remember the new material, and enables him to recall it more easily at a later date.

Having put forward my case, I would now like to look in detail at one possible procedure for making use of reading and writing to reinforce and supplement the oral work done in a foreign-language lesson, both in teaching new structures and in revising or extending material already taught. I am taking as an example the introduction of the perfect tense to a class of moderate ability in a lesson which is, say, forty minutes long. In a previous lesson the teacher will have introduced or revised the lexical items involved, and in the lesson in question he will be aiming at establishing these items:

> *Il (Jean) a dessiné une maison.*
> *Il (Marc) a mangé un bonbon.*
> *Il (Paul) a coupé une pomme.*
> *Il (Alain) a fermé une fenêtre.*
> *Il (Pierre) a gonflé un ballon.*

It is important that each of these activities can be performed fairly quickly and can therefore be clearly seen to have been done.

The initial oral phase of the lesson, lasting for some twenty minutes, will start by the teacher giving a series of commands to various pupils in relation to the appropriate objects (e.g. *Marc, venez à la table. Prenez le bonbon. Mangez-le. . . . Asseyez-vous.*) The teacher will then aim at enabling the class to produce the new material accurately by a sequence of questions and answers, comparing first the pupils involved (*Qui a dessiné une maison, Jean ou Marc?,* etc.) and then the activities (*Est-ce que Paul a fermé une fenêtre ou est-ce qu'il a coupé une pomme? Est-ce que Pierre a mangé un bonbon?,* etc.). As he feels that each example in turn has been mastered orally by the class, the teacher, first perhaps asking another question to evoke it orally (*Qu'est-ce que Jean a fait, alors?*), will then write it clearly on the board, and draw the pupils' attention to it by getting them to read it aloud, first in chorus and then perhaps two or three individuals. As each of the five examples is dealt with in this way, he will thus have made an initial link between its spoken and written form. When all five examples have been mastered and written up, he might well choose to get them all read through again, and even isolate the new tense forms *Il a dessiné . . . Il a mangé . . .*, etc., for oral reading in order to draw special attention to them for the particular benefit of slower pupils. This is perhaps all the more important in the case of an example such as I have chosen, since this will no doubt be the first time that the pupils have met a compound tense in French.

Having had an initial link established for them between the new oral forms and their written equivalents, the pupils should now be in a position to make their first attempt at writing the new forms themselves, and for this they will need to have rough books or pieces of paper quickly available. The teacher will begin by erasing just the new tense pattern in, say, two of the five examples written on the board (e.g. *Il a dessiné, Il a mangé*). He will then, for the first example, ask a question to evoke the correct oral response, the question offering the class more or less information as he judges appropriate (e.g. *Est-ce que Jean a fermé une fenêtre ou est-ce qu'il a dessiné une maison?* or simply *Alors, Jean, qu'est-ce qu'il a fait?*). When the answer to the question has been elicited orally, the pupils will be asked to write it in their rough books (or on their pieces of paper), whilst one of them fills in the appropriate blank on the board. (While the class is writing, it is, of course, important that the teacher looks quickly at some of the efforts being produced by the pupils, particularly by those he suspects may be having some difficulty; this is a point which also applies to the later phase of the written work described below.) When both teacher and pupils are satisfied that the correct form has been written on the board, the pupils can check their own answers against it and individual difficulties can be sorted out. The second erased item is then treated in the same way, and the whole process is repeated one by one for the other three examples being taught.

Apart from getting the pupils to produce in writing the five examples of the new tense-pattern – without overtaxing their memories – the teacher has also been strengthening the bond between oral and written forms and helping the pupils to develop an awareness of the new pattern, since two or three examples of it will always have been visible on the board. It needs perhaps to be emphasized at this point that this procedure takes considerably longer to describe than to carry out, and that its aim is both to reinforce oral command and to bring about written mastery of the new material.

The pupils should now be ready for a more comprehensive piece of written work on the new material – not so much a 'test', let it be added, as a further attempt to reinforce their command of it and to facilitate their memorization and recall of it. At the stage in a French course when the perfect tense might profitably be introduced, the written work in question will perhaps best be a series of, say, five questions written on the board, resuming the oral work done earlier in the lesson, with the early questions providing some information (e.g. *Est-ce que Marc a coupé une pomme ou est-ce qu'il a mangé un bonbon? Est-ce que Jean a gonflé un ballon?*), and the later ones challenging the pupils to provide all the information for themselves (*Qu'est-ce que Pierre a fait? Et Alain, qu'est-ce qu'il a fait?*). Once the questions are written on the board, the teacher may well find it valuable to have each question read, both chorally and even by one or two individuals, in order to draw the pupils' attention to details that he feels may be misunderstood or badly copied. Depending on the time available and the teacher's wishes, the questions could then be copied out and answered in the pupils' French notebooks in order to provide a permanent record of the new material, or they could simply be answered in rough books. In the latter case, the answers, once the pupils have finished working, can be written on the board by either the teacher or individual pupils; the work can then be checked and difficulties discussed. The value of such 'on-the-spot' correction lies in the immediate feedback that it offers to the teacher. If particular errors abound in the pupils' work and appear to stem from the teaching of the material, the teacher can, if time permits, review the material there and then or plan his next lesson accordingly. For the same reasons, if the pupils have done the work in their French notebooks, it is important that the teacher checks through them as soon as possible.

At an earlier stage in the French course, this latter phase of the written work might involve, for example, drawing and labelling things that have been used in classroom, or copying and answering questions relating to pictures provided on a duplicated sheet. As the course develops, it might involve a short dictation resuming the material taught in the preceding part of the lesson. (If, for example, to extend the pupils' experience and control of the perfect tense, a particular shopping expedition to the near-by town by Mme Dupont has been worked on, her major activities can be presented as a short dictation.) Moreover, a similar use of reading and writing as a support to oral work plays a part in the development of guided compositions, as a later chapter indicates.

The procedure I have described here can be accelerated or developed even more slowly in accordance with the wishes of the teacher or the ability of any given class. I would not, of course, claim that it is the only possible way of making use of the written word in an oral foreign-language lesson, but I would claim that it goes some way towards performing the four functions for the learner that I outlined earlier on. In a chapter which she sums up as being a plea for the readmission of the written word to the classroom in the early stages of foreign-language learning, W. M. Rivers quotes Saussure: 'Writing . . . is used continually to represent language. We cannot simply disregard it. We must be acquainted with its usefulness, shortcomings, and dangers.' She goes on to say: 'There is no reason why this should not be as true in the early stages of learning a language as in the later stages, so long as the written script is regarded merely as a help to memory and understanding and not as an end in itself'[2] (pp. 113–14). It seems to me that both her insistence on the value of the written word and her note of caution about its functions can be reiterated with profit at the end of an article such as this.

References

1. Cp. TITONE, R. (1973) 'Some factors underlying second-language learning.' *English Language Teaching*, **27**, no. 2, 114.
2. RIVERS, W. M. (1964) *The Psychologist and the Foreign-language Teacher*. Chicago and London: University of Chicago Press.

JENNIFER M. FORD

Avery Hill College of Education, Eltham

The place of dictation

'*Aujourd'hui nous allons faire une dictée*' is a well-known preliminary to many French lessons. Forty minutes later the teacher departs with a sheaf of papers to correct, leaving behind an exhausted and dispirited class, whose only achievement has been to produce a page of crossed-out and rewritten French often quite unconnected with any material studied before in class. The dictated material is frequently devoid of context, and sometimes is only administered as a device to quell a noisy class.

Such is the picture of dictation at its most dismal. And the culmination is the O-level test:

> *Depuis l'arrivée de l'hiver, dans la ferme isolée, on avait souvent parlé des fêtes, et voici qu'elles approchaient.*
>
> *– Je me demande si nous aurons de la visite le jour de l'an, fit un soir la mère. Un soupir montra qu'elle songeait encore à l'animation des vieux villages à Noël, aux repas de famille, aux visites de ceux qui arrivaient en traîneau, cachés sous des couvertures à cause du grand froid.*
>
> *Marie pensait à autre chose.*
>
> *– Si les chemins sont aussi mauvais que l'an dernier, dit-elle, on ne pourra pas aller à la messe de minuit. Pourtant j'aurais bien aimé.*
>
> *Dans cette région du Canada, au milieu de décembre la neige tombait sans cesse. Deux semaines plus tard le vent du nord se leva et on ne pouvait plus voyager par les routes. Il fallait se résigner.* (London, January 1968).

Despite the stilted register, the literary style and the difficulty of following what the passage is about, there are many who would regard this as a normal and useful exercise, a test presumably of mental discipline and of the ability to spell what has not necessarily been seen before and a check on the ability to cope with the agreement in *qu'elles approchaient* and other grammatical forms. So pervasive is this view of dictation that relatively few teachers seem to consider it as functioning in any other way. Boards of examiners themselves see it as a measure of a skill of those 'who have followed a normal secondary school course' (East Anglia, 1974), but do not offer any reasons why such a skill should be acquired. It is not surprising, therefore, that, dictation should be seen as **only** a test of spelling, unrelated to the general language development and needs of the learner, or even as an exercise in phonetics, destined to quicken the pupils' faculties of auditory perception. Such a view would justify the giving of nonsense dictations in phonetic script. All such views ignore the value of dictation as a useful teaching device which:

– quickly checks the ability of the learner to spell words he has **recently** heard and seen written;

– brings together into a short coherent statement some of the strands of recent oral work;

– allows the teacher to show the learner how to link pieces of language, using words like *et ensuite, donc, puis* or *wohl, doch, zunächst*;

– forces the learner to take an **active** interest in what the teacher chooses to write on the board;

– encourages the habit of attentive listening – essential for good oral work.

If we ask ourselves what is happening to children during dictation, it seems that the child's ear is operating on the acoustic waves set up by the transmitter of the dictation, decoding the message by making links between the sounds he hears and the meaning he ascribes to them. He searches for the pattern as a whole. At each stage in dictation work he needs to be familiar with the common letter sequences which are included (*-gne*) and he needs to predict likely word structure (aligning plural verb endings with plural subjects, for example: *Marie et Paul mangent une glace*). If this is not the case, then it is particularly the less able child who suffers most – being hampered more by interference from his mother-tongue and taking longer to make up his mind about forms like *mangent* so that he is frustrated by the teacher's ignoring his tardiness and inexorably carrying on with the dictation. For such a child the whole exercise consists in writing a jumble of disparate words with long gaps in between, which he vainly tries to fill during the last reading of the passage. He does not practise his spelling, nor is he able to make analogies with what he has previously learnt. The linguistically able child, who is often the fastest and neatest writer, enjoys practising his skill of spelling, which is one of the principal manifestations of his higher verbal reasoning power.

All children will perform the exercise of dictation better if they can see the relevance of the material dictated to their own interests and their previous language-learning experience. It seems important here to specify 'interests' because few children really 'need' dictation. They do not need to **hear** passages involving manipulation of the past historic, nor is a synopsis of a short story of any particular value to them. A day in the life of the 'Dupont' family does not represent material which anyone ever needs to dictate.

After dictation as a recapitulation of oral work has been largely exhausted, one still has to pose the question: what needs to be dictated? When does the teacher have one copy of information for all the class to transcribe? What is dictated in real life outside the school which can be taken down in the classroom? An employer dictates to his secretary, a friend dictates directions of how to find his house, an employee listens to instructions on how to use the firm's telephone, teenagers dictate the words of the latest pop songs to one another, ways of using a sewing pattern are transmitted orally, a recipe is exchanged, horoscopes are read aloud from the Sunday paper. A song (*Le jour où la pluie viendra, nous irons, toi et moi* (Gilbert Bécaud)) can be useful also for reinforcing the future tense, and even the structure after *où*. Football teams and their fortunes are of real interest to the schoolboy. Practical craft lessons in French will involve some dictation. For example, when one is making Christmas decorations for the classroom in the French lesson, the instructions may be dictated. Likewise when children make a folder to contain their French materials, the instructions, complete with metric measurements, can be given orally.

In giving these less formal dictations, the teacher still needs to attend to clarity of intonation and articulation, to a measured speed, to short and meaningful breath-groups: not separating subject and verb unless this is unavoidable. Liaisons need to be consistent, punctuation given in French and a careful preliminary reading made before the dictation begins. The slowest writer in the class needs to be observed to ensure that he is keeping pace with the rest. After a final reading at normal speed, the class needs five minutes for private revision. Certainly in the early stages short and frequent dictations seem more useful than long passages after protracted intervals. At first, a line or two every lesson using material from the lesson helps to focus the class's attention on certain structures or vocabulary.

Dictation can thus test whether work has been taught and learnt correctly. It is a yardstick for teacher and pupil. It exercises aural comprehension, it helps fix grammatical structures and particles (e.g. *puis*) and it consolidates oral work:

Vouz prendrez la première à gauche et après le stop, la première à droite. Filez tout droit! Au deuxième feu rouge tournez à gauche, alors au rond-point vous trouverez un agent de camp en uniforme qui vous dira où trouver quelqu'un pour mieux vous renseigner. Le gardien pourra vous diriger et vous trouverez un emplacement près de la rivière.

This in the fifth form can be a means of consolidating the recent teaching or revision of the future tense as well as summing up the camping holiday idioms and vocabulary which have been the subject of previous lessons.

In conclusion, dictation is a valuable exercise in that it helps the pupil to consolidate in another form the foreign language he has been learning. It is an active aid in co-ordinating language skills, since listening, understanding, writing and reading are all involved. And, as the course progresses, it can become the natural way in which information is conveyed, without necessarily following the prescribed form of the formal examination test.

F. M. HODGSON

Formerly University of London Institute of Education

The place of composition

The aim of the foreign-language teacher is so to equip his pupils that they are able, over an ever-widening field, not only to understand what is said and written in the language by others, but also to use it as the medium through which they can express their own ideas. The exercise by means of which they acquire the ability to organize the forms and structures of the foreign language into a coherent whole in relation to a particular topic is that of composition. We propose here to consider the problems inherent in the writing of a composition and to examine its role in the learning process.

There are two aspects to be considered: the strands of raw material, i.e. the lexical and grammatical elements which constitute the content of any composition, and the process by which these are woven together in such a way that what emerges is an acceptable and worth-while finished product. Since by definition com-posing is a putting together, it is to be assumed that what is to be put together is already at the writer's disposal. But it is not merely a matter of setting side by side ill-assorted pieces of language. Whatever the topic, there must be some kind of preliminary analysis of the possibilities it offers, selection of those parts which the writer considers relevant to what he wants to say, and arrangement in coherent fashion of what is selected, i.e. finding a suitable starting-point, setting the scene, seeing which elements belong together, what will logically follow what, where it will lead and what will be a satisfactory conclusion. Unless, over the years, in their foreign-language lessons, the pupils are faced with situations which provide them with experience of doing these things, unless they are trained in grasping a total situation as the synthesis of the elements that constitute it, it is not to be expected that at the end of their period of study they will suddenly become able to do so in relation to such topics as an account of some real or imaginary event, a letter, the telling of a story based on a series of pictures, imagining the end of an uncompleted story, or, at a later stage, a literary essay in the sixth form.

298

Since any statement is an answer to a potential question, it is obvious that children who are not able to produce the answers to questions in isolation will not be able to compose them. That there are many who cannot do so after five years of study is evident in what is written in answer to questions set at the O-level examinations on passages designed to test comprehension, where the material on which to draw is given and the question of arrangement of ideas does not arise. Those, for example, who, when asked in relation to a situation in which a man had broken a vase, *Pourquoi a-t-il mis les morceaux dans sa poche?* offer renderings such as: *parce qu'il a voulu à les cachent*; *parce que son femme les verra*; *parce que de Hortense*; *il ne voulait pas à voir les*; *il ne les voulait pas à être trouver,* show that they have understood the facts, that they know what they want to say, but that they cannot find in their repertoire the pieces of language that the situation requires. Their only recourse is to arrange half-remembered bits of 'grammar' in accordance with the sentence patterns of English. It is then no matter for surprise that in reporting on the compositions written at this same level the examiners frequently make reference to inability to manage the basic constructions of the language, to widespread ignorance of verb forms and tense usage, and to failure to make the necessary agreements in the case of pronouns and adjectives. Whatever the previous linguistic experience of these pupils has been, when put to the test it proves inadequate for the purpose it was intended to serve. It is not the place here to discuss methods of language teaching; suffice it to say that, in attempting to compose, pupils whose learning of a foreign language has been by way of general statements about grammatical categories and the application of so-called rules in mechanical exercises devoid of context will be at a grave disadvantage by comparison with those whose learning has been by way of individual instances, met and meaningfully practised in contexts specifically chosen to ensure that the relation between form and function is clearly perceived. For this latter, in any given situation certain parts of their stock of language will be felt to be appropriate to it precisely because they have earlier been firmly linked with other similar situations.

Assuming, then, that composition is not an exercise to be left to the later stages of the course or to be 'set for homework' without proper preparation, and that at each stage of their learning our pupils do possess, in the sense of being able to operate with, what they have been taught, how shall we proceed so that by the end of their course they find themselves able to write competently, in connected fashion, what they want to say?

From quite an early stage, when they have very little linguistic material on which to draw, they can begin to acquire the habit of bringing together and arranging pieces of language with which they are familiar through having met and used them, orally and in written form, on a number of different occasions. These are now to be shaped into a connected whole by means of questions specifically planned by the teacher to that end. The particular lexical items and the particular forms and structures so far mastered will determine the choice of topic. At the stage at which the emphasis has been on learning the names, attributes, spatial relations, physical and other characteristics of objects and persons, and when the sentence structures so far met involve only present tense verb forms, the topics chosen will necessarily be either purely descriptive, of people, of places, of the happenings in a picture, or will relate to the habitual activities and happenings in the children's own families or in the life of a family created by the teacher or met with in the course-book. Whatever the topic, the first step will be to make sure, through appropriate questions, that the pupils can produce the facts, the 'stuff' of which the composition will consist. Let us suppose that the composition is to be based on the happenings in a picture, one which is susceptible of easy analysis, in which there is a focal point, and in which the details are readily perceivable. Here the preparatory work will be by way of questions from the teacher as to who and what can be seen, how many of them there are, what they are like, what they are wearing, where they are and what they are doing. Some of the material will already be familiar to the pupils, some of it will be being met for the first time and will need thorough practice. Not all that emerges will be either necessary or appropriate when the time comes for writing the composition; what is actually selected and the shape it takes will be determined by the teacher's final planned series of questions. If a first draft is gradually built up on the blackboard by the combined efforts of the class – and in particular by those members of it who are likely to have the most difficulty – any mistakes made will be evidence of where these difficulties lie and of the need for further practice by means of which they can be eliminated. If, finally, what has been built up is read aloud so that the pupils get the feel of it as a whole, it can be discussed and evaluated, and where necessary suggestions for tidying up or other improvement can be made.

It is not, of course, being suggested that every composition will need to be written in class as a communal effort, but it is suggested that throughout the course, before children embark on a composition they will need help and guidance through discussion with the teacher of what kinds of thing might be said and of the order in which these things could best be said. If, for instance, they were to write in French an account of an accident, there might be discussion as to whether it would be desirable to set the scene by saying when and where it happened before saying what happened. If so, what suggestions could the children offer, out of their earlier linguistic experience, as answers to *Où* and *Quand?* From, say, a third-year class, these might include *devant une boucherie, près d'un arrêt d'autobus, au milieu de la rue, dans la place du marché, à minuit, la veille de Noël, l'année dernière, au mois de décembre* and much else. Further discussion would elicit suggestions as to who and what might have been involved, what might have happened, why and how, the children being all the time encouraged to find within themselves what they knew and felt to be relevant, and at the same time being steered away from attempts to say what was as yet beyond their powers. In the process it might well be revealed that some of what the teacher assumed he had taught was in fact not known. In that case the opportunity for putting matters right through further practice would be to hand, and mistakes which might have occurred when the composition came to be written could be eliminated before they were made.

With the systematic enlargement of the pupils' linguistic experience through acquaintance with new lexical items, new verb forms and tenses, new and more complex structural patterns, and with the pupils' growing ability to make their own choice among the questions whose answers will provide them with the material they need for a given topic, the composition which earlier was merely a short connected passage built up from simple connected questions will become a much more complex and elaborate entity. The choice of topic also will become much wider, but this does not mean that topics of a very general character, or those demanding reasoning or great imaginative effort will quickly be within the children's capacity. At every stage the ideas to be expressed will be limited by the tools available for expression, and the more precise and definite the circumstances in which the children gain experience in using the tools they have the better. Even in their mother-tongue the task of analysing the situation to be dealt with, of selecting and arranging the relevant material, seeing the relation of the parts to one another and to the whole, is complex enough. It is vastly more so in the foreign language, when the determining factor is not what the writer would like to say but what he knows how to express.

There will be some pupils to whom ideas do not come readily and who, left to their own devices, would find difficulty in thinking what to say; there will be others with much more to say than they can express. Many of us may remember the painful experience, when young, of having to write a letter of thanks to Aunt Mary for a birthday present and of coming to a complete stop when 'Thank you for the book' had been said. They may also remember the relief when some sympathetic adult, weary of our complaints of having nothing to say, came to the rescue with: *Have you told her that . . .? Why not ask her . . .? Wouldn't she like to know that . . .?* Those who do will readily recognize the importance of the period of preparation for the pupil who can't think what to say. It is no less important for those who may be tempted to be too ambitious and who need help in recognizing the limits within which they must operate.

When the composition is written it will provide the teacher with evidence as to how far the verbal tools his pupils have been learning to manipulate over the years have truly become their own, readily available in the situations that call for their use. The mistakes made – and there will inevitably be some – will be both an indication of what needs further practice and a pointer to the direction his teaching could most profitably take in the immediate future.

Time spent in writing, and later attempting to correct a so-called composition bristling with elementary mistakes is time wasted. The following example, written at an O-level examination, offers food for thought:

> *Quand je n'ai que douze ans, j'ai un malade sérieux et était dû rester au lit pendant près de sept heures. Le médicin eut venu deux fois pendant la jour et je ne mangais que la soupe qui j'ai n'aime pas à tout. Ma mère et ma soeur passerent heures asseyant à côté de ma lit de m'accompagner. Quelquefois ils ont me lu de un grand livre qui j'ai reçu à Noel. Quand j'étais commençement de porter me bien je permettais de voir un et deux de mes camarades qu'eurent me porté petits ∧ et m'ont dit de les incidents à l'école. Afin, après midi un jour, ma mère a ouvrit la porte de ma chambre et m'a dit 'Géorge,*

*j'ai vous ammené quelqu'un qui vous serai très heureux de voir.' Il
était mon oncle Jean qui a venu de Londres. Il a assit sur mon lit et a
dit 'Je n'ai pas connu que vous eûtes malade, mon garçon, mais le
médicin a dit que vous pourrez sortir au semaine, puis nous pourrons
faire à monter dans mon auto. Combien aimez-vous que?'*

We can only speculate as to what his teacher's reaction on reading
this would have been. It may be that, echoing Uncle Jean, though
expressing himself more adequately, he would have asked himself
'How do you like that?' Would he also, we may wonder, have seen it
as an example of his pupil's inability to learn or as the occasion for a
critical re-examination of his own teaching procedures?

D. HARRIS

University of London Institute of Education

Teaching composition

This chapter is about what a teacher can do to prepare his class for written composition in a foreign language before the stage of 'free' composition is reached.

To take French as our example, composition involves the putting together, in accurate French, of coherent ideas relevant to a given topic. The pupil's task is a dual one: it requires, first, that each piece of language be accurate (in so far as it is inaccurate it ceases to be French) and, second, that the component ideas fit together satisfactorily. These demands are bound to influence the procedures adopted by the teacher, whose job it is to ensure that the pupil is adequately prepared for what he is called upon to do. The latter will not be prepared if the set composition has little structural or lexical connection with the work that has preceded it. Nor will he be likely to succeed if he has received only scant guidance in writing compositions as such

Failure to have mastered the necessary grammar and vocabulary tends to lead to desperate resort to the mother-tongue which, with the help of a dictionary, all too often produces the writing of nonsense. For example, the sentence *Il était réputation derrière le mur* was the product of a schoolboy composition writer who was trying to convey the idea that someone was standing behind a wall. At this point in his composition the boy's learning failed him and the whole of this sentence was, as a result, incomprehensible. Similarly, those who have little control of **any** of the component structures and lexis are bound to fall back on translation from the mother-tongue at every stage.

To have mastered the necessary structures and vocabulary is, however, insufficient. The pupil needs to be shown how these can be built up into a composition, and this means that in the first instance (i.e. the first few years in most cases) the form of the composition will be determined by the teacher. Some of the essential groundwork

304

should consist in the reproduction of information or anecdotes chosen and presented, verbally or through texts, by the teacher. In other words, 'free' composition is out of the question until the learner has had practice in writing compositions under close guidance. Only under the closest supervision can he prove to his teacher and, more important, to himself that he is capable of writing a passage of accurate French that makes sense both as a series of sentences and as a whole. It is only after the learner sees that he has **already** written (with help) a number of successful pieces that the full force of the injunction, 'Keep within the limits of what you know' can be appreciated. Only then is it reasonable to expect him to cope with a composition from which some of the supporting props have been removed.

At the point where pupils can, with reasonable expectations of success, be given a title and a few sub-headings and told to write a composition on this basis, it can be said that the teacher is engaged in a form of testing rather than teaching, or that he is exploiting a previously learnt technique. Extreme variations in ability make it impossible to say when this point is reached. Suffice it to say that, even though the following story happened to be inspired by picture material in a fifth-year course-book[1] (p. 294), the actual procedures which will presently be described are deemed to be suitable, not to the later 'free' stage, but to the earlier, teacher-directed, one.

How can a teacher prepare a composition of the reproduction type, in the knowledge that it will be within the limited powers of the learners? Consider the following story:

Monsieur et Madame Masson habitaient dans les Alpes, à vingt kilomètres de Grenoble. Monsieur Masson, qui avait soixante-dix ans, souffrait du coeur et de temps en temps il devait rester au lit.

Un jour, en déjeunant, il s'est senti malade et il s'est couché. Sa femme a téléphoné au médecin qui a appelé une ambulance.

Au bout d'une heure l'ambulance est arrivée. Mais, comme il neigeait depuis plusieurs jours, il y avait beaucoup de neige devant la maison et l'ambulance a dû s'arrêter à cent mètres. Heureusement les ambulanciers avaient des pelles et ils ont pu dégager la route jusqu'à la porte.

Après avoir fini ce travail, les ambulanciers ont mis Monsieur Masson sur un brancard et ils l'ont transporté dans l'ambulance. Enfin l'ambulance est partie pour Grenoble.

Before examining procedures that one might adopt in preparing this story for composition, some assumptions need to be made explicit.

It is assumed that, although the story may contain some new vocabulary, all the grammar and the bulk of the vocabulary will be familiar. For example, the class will already have had considerable practice in using the imperfect tense, as well as the perfect tense of verbs conjugated with *avoir* and *être*, including reflexive verbs. They will be familiar with the masculine preceding direct object pronoun with the perfect tense, and past participle agreement with *être* verbs. Other basic structures will include the present participle after *en* in the sense of 'whilst doing', the relative pronoun *qui* and various tenses of *devoir* followed by the infinitive. In so far as the pupils may have only a nodding acquaintance with any of these grammatical points, any attempt to incorporate them into the composition is certain to cause difficulties. On the other hand, recognition of familiar patterns will underline the relevance of past learning and the importance of each phase in the learning of succeeding phases.

If the pictures on which the story may be based are shown to the class as a first step, they can serve to introduce some of the vocabulary (e.g. *C'est une ambulance, c'est un ambulancier, ils tiennent des pelles, sur un brancard, ils dégagent la route*) and incidentally prepare the pupils for the kind of story they are about to hear. (The subject of the composition could equally well have been the gist of a story **read** in a course-book or reader.)

A second step can then be to tell the story to the class. This is possibly best done if each section is recounted and worked on separately, to avoid excessive strain on the memory. Understanding should not be a serious problem in view of the assumptions outlined earlier and the prior presentation of the new vocabulary through the pictures. Reference to Grenoble can be clarified by the statement *C'est une ville française*, and by reference to a map.

After narration of the story, or part of it, a series of suitably chosen questions will produce answers giving practice in the language that will be needed in the composition. For example, to take the first paragraph only:

Comment s'appelaient l'homme et sa femme?
Ils s'appelaient Monsieur et Madame Masson.
Où habitaient-ils?
Ils habitaient dans les Alpes, etc.

Or, if an easier question is called for,

Est-ce qu'ils habitaient au bord de la mer?
   Non.
Où habitaient-ils?
   (Ils habitaient) dans les Alpes.
Qu'est-ce que c'est que les Alpes?
   Ce sont des montagnes.
Et les Pyrénées?
   Ce sont des montagnes aussi.
Est-ce que les Masson habitaient dans les Pyrénées?
   Non, ils habitaient dans les Alpes.
Où exactement?
   A vingt kilomètres de Grenoble.

Or, if this question is too demanding,

A quinze kilomètres de Grenoble?
   Non.
A vingt kilomètres de Nice?
   Non.
Où alors?
   A vingt kilomètres de Grenoble.
(To another pupil) *Où habitaient-ils? Vous pouvez me dire **deux choses**
à ce sujet.*
   Ils habitaient dans les Alpes, à vingt kilomètres de Grenoble.
Quel âge avait-il, Monsieur Masson?
   Il avait soixante-dix ans.
Avez-vous soixante-dix ans?
   Non, j'ai quatorze ans.
(To another pupil) *Et vous?*
   J'ai quinze ans.
(Pointing to pupil who is fourteen) *Et lui (elle)?*
   Il (elle) a quatorze ans.
Et Monsieur Masson?
   Il avait soixante-dix ans.
Il se portait bien?
   Non, il souffrait du coeur.

Or, if difficulty is encountered,

Est-ce qu'il souffrait (or *Il souffrait* with interrogative intonation)
de la tête?
  Non, il souffrait du coeur.

Or, if still more help is needed,

Qui souffrait du coeur, Monsieur Masson ou Madame Masson?
  Monsieur Masson.
(To another pupil) *De quoi souffrait-il?*
  Du coeur.
(To another pupil) *Comment se portait-il alors?*
  Il souffrait du coeur.
Et par conséquent?
  Il devait rester au lit de temps en temps.

Or, if more help is required,

Qu'est-ce qu'il devait faire de temps en temps?
  Il devait rester au lit.
(To another pupil) *Pourquoi* (*devait-il rester au lit de temps en temps*)*?*
  Parce qu'il souffrait du coeur.
(To another pupil) *Maintenant, que savez-vous de Monsieur Masson?*
  *Vous pouvez me dire **plusieurs** choses à son sujet.*

Questions such as these can be combined in dozens of different
ways, depending on the level of ability of the class, the needs of
individual pupils (including the weakest ones) and the kind of
mistakes made, or difficulties evinced, at any particular moment. If the
work is presented at the right level of difficulty, it should not be
necessary to break down every single sentence into its smallest elements. After all, it is assumed that the pupils have already attained a
certain level of competence. In any case, pupils who from experience
have come to see these procedures as means whereby the teacher
facilitates their learning (as opposed to mistaking them for 'conversation') and who, through repeated oral practice, have become so
familiar with words like *Qui?, Où?, Quand?,* etc., that they have no
doubt about the **kind** of question the teacher is asking,[2] will know that
these measures are more likely to accelerate the pace of a lesson than
to slow it down.

Once the details of the story, or a suitably short section of it, have
been thoroughly practised orally, it is time to see it as a continuous
whole as opposed to a collection of bits and pieces. The teacher can
present the story on the blackboard, or whatever piece of modern

equipment may have replaced it, by writing up successive sentences as the information is elicited from the class. To take an example from the second paragraph of the story:

Qu'est-ce qui s'est passé un jour?
  Monsieur Masson s'est senti malade.
Quand (exactement)?
  En déjeunant.
Qu'est-ce qu'il a fait donc?
  Il s'est couché.

would provide the basic data needed for the teacher or pupil to write, *Un jour, en déjeunant, il s'est senti malade et il s'est couché.* The whole story can gradually be built up in this way. It is now that the pupils begin to see that they have the wherewithal to recount a continuous piece of French. With the story now written up before them, the teacher or a pupil can read the whole passage aloud in order to bring out the continuity.

When the passage has been erased, the teacher can profitably spend a moment checking whether individuals can or cannot spell the new vocabulary, or other items that have caused difficulties in the past. He may, for instance, use 'rough books', with one pupil writing on the board as a focus for general comment. The clause *L'ambulance est partie* is perhaps a good one to test, since it may contain an example of both types: knowledge of both the gender and spelling of a new noun, *ambulance*, and ability to indicate past participle agreement with an *être* verb. Having discovered what spelling mistakes have been made, the teacher can usefully spend a little time enabling the pupils to correct these before passing on. Such time is usually well spent, for it helps to prevent many errors recurring later. A teacher who is unwilling to attend to obvious defects when they appear, on the grounds that 'we have to get on', has little right to complain later when the pupils' finished product reveals that the said defects have not miraculously disappeared in the meantime.

So far the learners have been required to produce oral answers to questions; they have seen and read the complete story; they have eradicated some problems of spelling. A series of oral or written questions on significant points in the story, to be answered in writing, will now test the oral and written skills **together** and, of course, will test everybody at the same time. Here are possible questions to bring out the salient facts:

1. *Où les Masson habitaient-ils?*
2. *Que savez-vous de l'âge et de l'état de santé de Monsieur Masson?*
3. *Qu'est-ce qui se passait, donc, de temps en temps?*
4. *Quand exactement Monsieur Masson s'est-il senti malade?*
5. *Qu'est-ce que Monsieur et Madame Masson ont fait alors?*
6. *Et le médecin?*
7. *Qu'est-ce qui s'est passé au bout d'une heure?*
8. *Quel temps faisait-il?*
9. *Depuis quand?*
10. *Par conséquent . . .?* (*Deux réponses S.V.P.*)
11. *Qu'est-ce que les ambulanciers ont fait avec leurs pelles?*
12. *Qu'est-ce qu'ils ont fait après avoir fini ce travail?* (*Deux réponses S.V.P.*)
13. *Qu'est-ce qui s'est passé quand Monsieur Masson était installé dans l'ambulance?*

When this work has been marked, the teacher should know whether anything further needs to be done. Sometimes a dictation of (part of) the story helps to iron out any spelling difficulties that persist; it underlines the continuity and is a means of keeping in circulation expressions like *de temps en temps, au bout d'une heure, comme, heureusement, enfin*, which can hardly have been practised thoroughly. Alternatively, just a few seconds devoted to testing the spelling of one or two 'difficult' phrases can later prove to have been far from wasted.

The conditions in which the composition is written in its final version will, obviously, depend on the ability of the class. For weaker pupils, it will be appropriate for the teacher to supply the thirteen questions indicated above, but with the instruction that this time the questions are merely a guide to memory, since the composition has to be in continuous prose. If desired, one could add the information that questions 1 to 3 relate to the first paragraph, numbers 4 to 6 to the second paragraph, and so on. It is assumed here that, except in the case of very weak pupils, the earlier written answers to these questions, having been marked and discussed, have been collected up again before the composition is written on a separate piece of paper.

A less helpful guide, for brighter pupils, would be a brief summary of the four paragraphs, for example:

1. *Renseignements généraux sur Monsieur et Madame Masson* (or *Introduction*).
2. *Ce qui s'est passé à l'heure du déjeuner.*
3. *L'arrivée de l'ambulance.*
4. *Le départ.*

More difficult would be the simple instruction *Racontez l'histoire de Monsieur Masson,* and, still more difficult, *Racontez l'histoire comme si vous étiez Monsieur Masson.* Here we depart from a reproduction of the story. Progress from reproduction to 'free' composition is beyond the scope of this chapter, but it may be worth adding that a point somewhere between the two is reached when the pupils are given, for example, a set of pictures and a list of questions like the thirteen we have just seen, **and no other help.**

To sum up, this chapter is an attempt to show how one kind of composition can be written as a result of detailed preparation, and with emphasis on oral and written mastery of the component parts. It is my belief that 'free' composition, in whatever sense, is only possible (except with the very brightest pupils) after years of closely supervised and teacher-directed work.

Some readers will feel that their pupils can do without some of the procedures outlined here; in which case, so much the better. However, as I suspect many O-level script markers will agree, compositions typified by *Il était réputation derrière le mur* are still to be found in abundance. Therefore, any procedures which ultimately help to bring the learner to the conviction that a given piece of French 'sounds right', because it corresponds to what he has successfully used over and over again in a variety of similar situations, are surely worth applying.

A final word on tenses. The perfect tense has been used in preference to the past historic on the grounds that the limited need to **produce** the past historic is quite out of proportion to the amount of time often accorded it in schools; that ability to handle the perfect tense is vital and therefore maximum opportunity to practise it should be given; and, finally, that, apart from the special case of the dictation exercise, a minority of examination boards up to O level require production of the past historic.

Notes and references

1. GILBERT, M. (1972) *Cours illustré de français.* 2nd edn. London: University of London Press.
2. Whether the number of such pupils is as large as it ought to be, after more than a decade of the so-called modern languages 'revolution', is perhaps debatable.

PART 9

Drills and exercises

Exercises and drills are needed to provide the massive practice which seems to be essential to successful language acquisition. None of the contributors to this section would question this need, but they all recognize that it is a difficult one to meet. Thus, in producing a good exercise, the number of variables needs to be reduced so that the learner is not faced with too many difficulties at once, but at the same time this should not lead to an isolation of the language from any recognizable semantic context. There has always been a danger that foreign-language learners practise **forms** without at the same time learning where the form is appropriate. There has also been in recent years a justifiable reluctance to ask learners to engage in exercises which are not 'language-like' – some 'gap-filling' exercises fall into this category and, in particular, exercises which ask the learner to make sentences out of randomly jumbled words.

It is not possible to place exercises in an order of merit or suggest a 'best buy'. The contributions in this section offer possible criteria to help in the choice of worth-while exercises which might help teachers to avoid asking their pupils to engage in activities which make no contribution to language acquisition or which could even erase good habits or muddle sound knowledge.

DERRICK L. MALE

Kelsey Park School for Boys, Bromley

Types and use

A distinction needs to be made between the type of exercise which requires time for thought and checking on the part of the student and which may contain a strong written element and the type of exercise or drill which is meant to be heard and to evoke an immediate oral response. The traditional 'grammar' exercise with its filling in of blanks and/or substitution of particular elements was for too long a time the only exercise available to the student; it is arguable whether such exercises are even of limited use to anyone learning a language, since the thought processes involved are not sufficiently creative. The only excuse for their continued existence is, one would suppose, that they are easy to construct or that the hard-pressed teacher is using a course-book containing a convenient collection of them. They do indeed die hard: the *cahier de l'élève* of *Voix et images de France, deuxième partie – Leçons de transition* (CREDIF, 1971) contains many traditional grammar-type exercises.

A fictitious example will illustrate the essential difference between oral-based and traditional exercises:

Il faut que vous (dormir) un peu.

The traditional exercise prints an inappropriate infinitive and requires it to be replaced with the appropriate person, tense and mood of the verb. An oral-based approach to this particular pattern might produce the following:

Stimulus. *Je dois dormir?*
Response. *Oui, il faut que vous dormiez un peu.*

The oral-based exercise can equally well be used for a written check of the subjunctive element involved, whereas the traditional type can hardly be used in a language laboratory for oral practice. There are, moreover, three distinct advantages presented by the oral-based exercise:

314

1. The student is not forced to read grammatical nonsense in order to produce a correct grammatical point.

2. There is a context (albeit a brief one) to the response and this is supplied by the stimulus.

3. Greater flexibility is possible – for example, one can be rid of what might be termed the 'infinitive' complex that seems to have such a grip on traditional exercises. The grammatical assumption that every student somehow knows the infinitive and that if he does he can work from it, is not only inaccurate but inadequate for any real progress (see pp. 2–13). Indeed, the exercise one could evolve from *Il faut que vous dormiez* as the stimulus, leading to the response *Mais je ne veux pas dormir*, will soon be recognized as equally useful.

One arrives, then, at three basic distinct types of exercise: the immediate response oral drill – probably useful for rapid written checks; the creative response type of exercise where time is needed to think and where the written element may predominate; the traditional 'grammatical' exercise. Since it is the first two categories which expose the student to more of the foreign language in a meaningful context, should it not be with these two categories that we should be concerned in teaching a foreign language and its grammatical phenomena?

The **immediate response oral drill** may be further subdivided into three different types: teaching drills, consolidating a grammatical point; testing drills; remedial drills. Although there can be an overlap between these types, it is as well to have a clear idea of them in mind when one is composing drills.

A **teaching drill** should not attempt to teach too many points at a time, but it is possible to practise more than one element provided that the practice element remains constant. For example, in the drill *Il a réveillé sa femme* (**S**) . . . *il ne voulait pas la réveiller* (**R**), the grammatical element which requires intelligent attention could be the object pronoun (changing to *le, la, les, l'*), but the element *Il ne voulait pas* would remain the same for each example as a practice element worth repetition. Alternatively the object pronoun might remain feminine throughout while the infinitive changed: *Il a bu cette bière* (**S**) . . . *il ne voulait pas la boire* (**R**). Teaching drills should not just be answers to questions or further statements arising from a statement used as the stimulus. I feel strongly that too much of our teaching sometimes is concerned with question and answer, with the teacher asking all the questions. The student of a foreign language needs to be able to ask questions himself in order to survive linguistically if not sometimes physically. An oral approach to drills can easily produce a stimulus which requires a question as a response, e.g. *Demandez à votre ami ce qui est arrivé* (**S**) . . . *Qu'est-ce qui est arrivé?* (**R**) or *Il s'est blessé* (**S**) . . . *Comment s'est-il blessé?* (**R**). Frequently, with minor adjustments a question stimulus with its response can be used in the reverse order. The possibilities are there for the exploitation.

A **testing drill** may very well have more than one element changing provided that one follows the criterion of clarity of comprehension. Much will depend on the student who is using the particular drill. In language-learning work, as in many other spheres of activity, success will bring confidence and encourage further successful attempts. The authoritarian teaching attitude which takes a delight in catching out the students (to establish one's own superiority as a teacher?) has little to commend it. Ideally a testing drill should be composed so that every student can get most, if not all, of the examples correct.

Remedial drills might be defined as drills which counteract interference from the native language. They require on the part of the teacher composing the drill a sensitive knowledge and experience of the equivalent meaning of the two languages concerned. This is not to assume that a parallel pattern in a foreign language will not require practice: *Je vais sortir*, for example, is a pattern that still needs considerable practice in spite of its parallel with the English pattern in grammatical terms. One needs to be on one's guard where a false analogy may be made either from a pattern already learnt or from native interference or a combination of both. For instance, *je refuse de manger* or *je commence à comprendre* need separate practice. *Sans manger* will need considerable emphasis as a pattern especially after a spell of practice of the pattern *en mangeant*. One might include, too, under the heading of remedial drills phenomena which cannot be classified as grammatical I am thinking, for instance, of such examples in French (but no language is lacking in them) as *beaucoup mieux* but *bien pire* and *bien meilleur*, which can easily be included in drills so that the student has some chance of learning them instinctively, since nothing in any grammatical description would proscribe '*beaucoup pire*': it is wrong for the best possible reason, that is that a French person is unlikely to say it. Under this heading, too, might come the numerous expressions which by reason of analogy are often mistranslated or misunderstood. For instance, one might be practising *bien* with the perfect tense, using such a pattern as *Il a mangé?* (**S**) . . . *Oui, il a bien mangé* (**R**). An English person might be forgiven if he assumed that *il a bien fait* was the French equivalent of *he has done well* instead of its more particular meaning *he chose the right course of action*. I wonder how many of us in the past have, at the conclusion of an oral examination at O or A level, heard the examiner say '*Vous avez bien fait*'? A remedial exercise might well be useful in this instance to highlight the correct meaning: *Il a dû prévenir les invités?* (**S**) . . . *Oui, il a bien fait de les prévenir* (**R**). Other examples in this category that spring to mind are *Il prétend que* . . . and *sans doute*. Whatever the language one is teaching one can soon establish a list of such expressions which would benefit the pupils if used in a remedial drill.

The second category of drills is **the creative response type of exercise**, which might also be called an open-ended context drill – open-ended in that more than one reply is possible. These usually require more time for the student to prepare, since more thought, more imagination, hence a more confident fluency in the language is involved. The stimulus is often quite long, giving a more detailed situation and more subtle uses of language become possible, for example, the use of irony in French:

> *Vous vous impatientez dans un magasin parce que la vendeuse au lieu de s'occuper de vous bavarde avec une autre vendeuse. Exprimez votre impatience. . . . Alors, toutes les vendeuses sont occupées?* or *Qu'est-ce que vous attendez pour fermer le magasin?*

The survival situation and role-playing exercises come into this category (what one says or does in a particular set of circumstances described in some detail). Many of the oral exercises in *Voix et images, deuxième partie – Leçons de transition* are on these lines and the reader might do well to examine some of them in detail.

An approach which is exclusively grammatical and rigid can be detrimental in the composition of oral-based exercise material. I would like to give the following personal view of the interdependent criteria which I have found useful in constructing drills.

My first consideration would be the recognition and analysis of the grammatical points I thought of practising in terms of their **grammatical usefulness** generally and for the students concerned. My next consideration, to my mind of equal importance, would be the

credibility of both stimulus and response taken separately and together (why expose the student to a stimulus which sounds unreal?). Native speakers, although notoriously at variance on matters of translation equivalent, will usually give an accurate opinion on whether this sounds right in French or German or Spanish, etc. My other main consideration would be students' **comprehension**: are the stimulus and pattern clear? . . . is the pattern too long or too complicated? . . . is the student likely to get it right **orally**, or at least to be able to pick up the correction he hears? . . . Can the teacher himself do the exercise without any strain? – the help of a qualified colleague here is a valuable and humbling experience!

Spin-off effect might occur and be intentionally included in any drill. For example, in understanding the stimulus the student may well be consolidating an element that he is not required to use actively in his response. In the example *Je ne trouve plus la clé* (**S**) . . . *J'ai dû la perdre* (**R**) the element *Je ne trouve plus* might be called a spin-off effect. Similarly *Que faire?* in the exercise *Que faire? Aller au restaurant?* (**S**) . . . *Oui, nous pourrions aller au restaurant* (**R**). Alternatively this effect can be included in the response as an element which remains constant throughout the exercise. Expressions such as *volontiers, d'ailleurs, pensez-vous!* can be inserted in this way. Examples of this have already been mentioned, but perhaps this one is a good example of what I mean: *Tu n'es pas resté au salon?* (**S**) . . . *À ta place je serais resté au salon* (**R**). Here the student can well be told that *à ta place* is, in the '*tu*' context, the equivalent of *if I were you* or *if I'd been you*. The following diagram will perhaps serve to clarify the above suggestions and underline their mutual dependence.

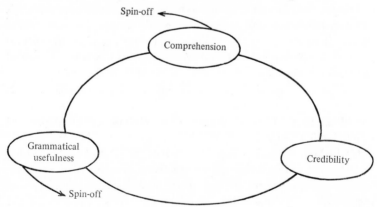

The advent of the language laboratory obviously created a need for oral-based drills and exercises: a language laboratory is essentially a means of intensive, personal practice and has proved particularly effective in 'total immersion' courses in the sphere of adult education, as well as in the longer school type course. These same exercises can, however, be used effectively in the classroom situation in different ways: the traditional teacher-centred method where only one student will be responding while the others listen and learn; the putting of students into pairs or small groups; chorus work with perhaps small classes and younger students, using the tape-recorder. Many drills can be done in a sort of quick-fire practice around the class. One of the main problems of the laboratory, that of boredom, will probably not occur in the classroom, but, of course, one loses the intensity and concentration on the individual that a laboratory can offer. I have found that work in pairs or groups, in the absence of a laboratory, has proved effective with the language laboratory drills of *Ça y est.**
If a working atmosphere is firmly established the noise generated is acceptable, and, indeed, it could be argued that in real life one is often surrounded by other people carrying on different conversations while one is speaking. There would, of course, be the usual balance between written and oral work, since many drills do need a written check for grammatical endings which may be ambiguous orally. Open-ended exercises of the creative response pattern are I believe from my own experience best practised in a group. The dynamic of the group does seem to produce better inspiration, the work is made more entertaining, and the social use of language is thereby given greater emphasis.

One of the main advantages of the laboratory is that our first category of drills, i.e. the immediate response type, can be made into a valid self-correcting exercise on the well-known four-phase pattern: stimulus . . . space on student track for student response . . . correct response on master track . . . student repeats correct response. It is obviously possible for the student to refuse to co-operate and choose the easier course of repeating merely the stimulus in the first space; one needs to bear this in mind while monitoring. Providing the drills are within the student's grasp, the self-correcting mode is undoubtedly effective. Experience seems to have shown that there will be a greater gain in fluency and comprehension than with normal class-work.

* MALE, D. L. (1969) *Ça y est! Twenty audio-lingual lessons.* London: Harrap.

Accent and intonation may need separate remedial exercises and it can be argued that the language laboratory is not necessarily the best place to do these.

One of the problems of language laboratory work which affects both children and highly motivated adults is that of boredom. Whether this arises in spite of the intensity of concentration involved or because of it, I am not sure. For this reason, however, language laboratory sessions are best given at frequent intervals for a relatively short time. With students in further education, where the time available for language work is often two hours at a stretch, it is possible to organize sessions of thirty minutes, which would seem to be a reasonable time (both for the students and the teacher monitoring them) to adopt. The problem of boredom or perhaps fatigue can be alleviated somewhat by a combination of different types of exercise, perhaps on the following pattern:

Teaching drills (four-phase, self-correcting)
Testing drills (four-phase, self-correcting)
Creative response exercises (**not** self-correcting)

where the student can be equipped with a note-pad and will possibly make notes, having stopped the tape to think and prepare the response, which can be discussed later in groups in the class situation. Any drills used in a laboratory should, I feel, be connected with the material already used in class beforehand. Students should be encouraged to think of a laboratory session as a personal, intensive period of work, and improvement should as far as possible be noted and commented upon when work in the class is resumed. The laboratory session should **not** be taken as an end in itself or as rounding off a piece of work, but as a mode of work to help the student prepare himself for what is, in the final analysis, the real situation of language in life: the flesh and blood confrontation with people.

PETER WEXLER

Language Centre, University of Essex

Critique of an elementary lab-drill

This is an exercise in slow reading. The text is a short drill, taken more or less at random from one of the better recent courses (it doesn't matter which). A drill, like any other text but more detectably than most, bears the traces of a large number of assumptions made by the writer, consciously or not. The object of the exercise is to see if we can reconstruct some of these assumptions, and then to see if we can doubt them.

The drill consists of a rubric and eight cues (Q1–Q8), printed and taped; the eight answers (A1–A8) I omit:

You will hear a question addressed to you:

Vous avez mon stylo?

You will answer: **Mais non, je n'ai pas votre stylo.**

1. *Vouz avez mon crayon?*
2. *Vous avez ma lettre?*
3. *Vous avez mes timbres?*
4. *Vous avez mes enveloppes?*
5. *Tu as mon cahier!*
6. *Tu as ma place!*
7. *Tu as mes livres!*
8. *Tu as mes oranges!*

Consider first the rubric. Does it make clear to you what you are to expect and what is expected of you? Are you grateful for the supplementary explanation that all the answers are (a) to begin with *Mais non, je n'ai pas,* (b) to end with the same noun as the cue, and (c) in between, to switch to the appropriate possessive?

As to what you are to expect by way of variation in the cues, the rubric's single specimen can't, of course, give you any idea. It's like saying 'Continue the series: 2. . . .' This situation leaves some pupils with the feeling either that they have no right to expect more or that they have had more and were too stupid to notice; either way discouraging. Fortunately they get much-needed help from hearing Q1, which should count as part of the rubric in this respect.

Is that now clear? Do you think you should have understood all this without the supplementary explanation? But could a single example in the rubric be expected to convey all three aspects of the expected answers – part uniform, part copied, part changed? I'd be sure it couldn't, were it not for the fact that some pupils do cotton on at once. I don't know how they do it, but I don't think enough of them do it for the situation to be satisfactory.

By the end of Q1, then, there are grounds for supposing that nothing in the cues will change except the noun (with minimal consequent changes in its possessive). By the end of Q4 the suggestion is overwhelming that the verb, for example, is not going to change, nor its person. But now one of these well-confirmed expectations is upset, with *Tu* replacing *Vous*; and simultaneously the question-cues, despite the rubric, become exclamations or accusations.

This sort of thing doubtless keeps everyone on their toes, but there must be a better reason than that. Something so odd is surely part of the point of the drill; but what can it be? The incurious pupil may adjust quickly to the switch; the inquisitive pupil will try and make sense of it. Let's hope the outcome doesn't discourage inquisitiveness.

As an inquisitive student, my efforts to impose sense on what seems to be a pattern look like this:

1. 'One can't accuse *vous* as readily as one can accuse *tu*.' Is this true? Was it intended? One must expect guesses of this kind to be stimulated by all kinds of unintended regularities in the material we present. Occasionally the guesses are right; once in a while they teach the teacher (like the deduction by an eight-year-old that 'You say *très grand* but *tout petit*').

2. 'If addressed as *vous*, answer with *je* and *vous*; if addressed as *tu*, answer with *je* and *tu*.' In other words, 'Being addressed as *vous* or *tu* makes no difference in how your answer refers to yourself, and makes a difference in how your answer refers to the other party'. As it happens, both parts of this ingenious deduction are wrong. Outside a language lab *vous* is sometimes answered by *nous*, and both kinds of second person cue can be answered by *vous* or *tu*; in context only one is right and inconsistency is certainly wrong. Is this a case where the rule is too complicated to be taught all at once? Or that we only thought it was because we didn't add to the cost of teaching the bits separately the further cost of correcting the guesses which rushed to fill the gap between the bits? Is it a defence that **all** rules are more

complicated than they pretend, with something, possibly a great deal, left to 'experience', i.e. what the learner has to discover beyond what there is time to tell him. But if that were the case we could be open about it, acknowledging that the route to understanding had better pass through a period of playing with the rules and having intelligent guesses about their implications; though that isn't compatible with some views about the role of intelligence in language learning.

3. '*Mais non* is equally appropriate in response to a question and to an accusation.' I wouldn't need to know much French to suspect rather that, as with *No*, there are important intonation differences concealed here by the inadequacy of our writing system. A5 is more different from A4 than it looks. Perhaps even the most orally fixated teacher is still so conditioned by spelling that he can hardly help seeing problems like *mon* / *ma* / *mes* as more real, somehow, than the distinction between irritated / polite / forbearing *Mais non*. There are drills for the first, not for the second. Is this just because grammarians have thoroughly described the first but not the second? But why should drills be limited to what grammarians have thoroughly described? Of matters like the distinction between irritated / polite / forbearing *Mais non* every learner already knows enough to start doing exercises, if it's important enough – and it may well be. There's no overriding need to wait for some future grammarian to know it all. But, of course, in playing games like this with the only partially known the pupil and his teacher are only doing what that future grammarian will do more elaborately.

The drill has eight questions. Why eight? Not because someone has shown that the average attention span is eight items long, but because French has two genders and two numbers and the exercise is confined to two persons. These ingredients are permuted quite systematically, as if the setter were checking against something in a reference grammar: four *vous*-cues with masc. sing., fem. sing., masc. plural, fem. plural, followed by four *tu*-cues in the same sequence. Some such methodical check-out is very necessary to make sure you have covered all the parts of a rule; though it doesn't follow that the parts must be practised in standard order, and necessarily once each; nor is it by any means self evident what the parts of a rule are.

To illustrate this last point we can reconstruct exactly what the setter must have had in his mind's eye while checking out his drill: a table of two rows and two columns, like a slice of Battenberg, with column 1 (labelled 'singular') containing *mon* and *ma*, and column 2 (labelled 'plural') containing *mes* and *mes*. An alternative version would have erased the line dividing column 2 into two boxes, and entered *mes* just once. The difference seems trivial, and isn't. The latter version makes it easier to see that no further information is needed once you know you are in the plural column; and also makes it easier to see that a table is meant to be read two ways: read inside out, it says 'Knowing the plural doesn't tell you anything about the gender'. Appreciating this, the learner will more readily suspend judgement when he hears something that is either *mes amis* or *mes amies*, and listen harder for some other marker of that interesting difference, elsewhere in the text. If the simpler version had been in the setter's mind his exercise would have been shorter: he would have left out either Q3 or Q4, and either Q7 or Q8. It's not just a matter of saving practice-time: being asked to remember something which turns out to be superfluous slows down reaction-time and is generally bad for morale.

With this minor adjustment made, we'd still have a two-by-two table; but what, come to think, are the labels on the **rows**? In the singular, masculine is always *mon* and *ma* is always feminine; but, of course, the converses don't hold: *mon* isn't always masculine and, feminine isn't always *ma*. Whether the table is read from out to in or from in to out, it's half wrong. Unfortunate; but not the end of the matter. For drill writers are fallible in two ways: the rule they are building on may contain a slip; or they may allow their analysis of the rule into its **constituent difficulties** to be overinfluenced by its conventional layout. I am more worried by the second danger. After all oversights, major and minor, are always to be expected; it's when they've all been corrected that the work starts to become interesting.

What remains is one of the central assumptions of the drill, that the domain of the rule is indeed the three-member set *mon | ma | mes* (and its cousins). This is perhaps the most striking illustration of the influence of convention on a setter's thinking. Though offering the radical modernization of a taped course, what he has unconsciously taken over here is **eye-grammar** – true for reading, not intended to be applicable to hearing. In the corresponding ear-grammar, the possessive adjective has **five** forms – | mɔ̃ | mɔn | ma | me | mez | , three of which give no information about the gender of their noun. Exercising these once each would, of course, make the drill longer; which is to say that some constituent difficulties have been left out, and in such a way as to mislead anyone who wonders how the gaps might be filled. **Oranges** looks like the odd man out in its set of four thefts; is this done deliberately, to suggest that the feminine plural is / mez / and the masculine plural / me /? What is the singular of *mes oranges*? Suspicion begins to fall on the whole scenario: what can the speaker possibly be doing with **more than one orange** in the first place?

In short, we must resist the temptation to suppose that the layout in a reference grammar is a sufficient guide to the **constituent difficulties** of a rule. But this term (which I've just invented) demands explanation. Consider, for example, the definite article in French. It has four forms to the eye, five to the ear. One could either (1) just learn the right form along with the noun in the first place, or (2) learn the noun by itself; plus the fact that it is masculine (or feminine); plus the terminology 'masculine' and 'feminine'; plus the more visible but still separate facts about its number and whether it begins with a vowel or consonant; plus the terminology for those distinctions also; and finally commit to memory the table which, if you pass those qualifying tests, will reward you with the right form of the article – provided you have also mastered the non-trivial conventions governing the construction and use of tables.

If some of us take the grammarian's conventional layout to amount to a recommendation that the learner take the second way, is this absurdity his fault or ours? Both, I think. Look at it from the grammarian's point of view. He describes the definite article on one page and the possessive on another, which may be a long way away; it seems economical to keep the same table-format, with the same rows and columns. But the crux of the matter is that the grammarian **doesn't expect to be read consecutively**. He too has been conditioned, into seeing his typical problem as 'How to describe the possessive'. The learner, in contrast, is necessarily going through the book, in some order; for him the only realistic problem is 'How to describe the possessive **to someone who already knows the definite article**'.

The grammarian's rules all try and go back to first principles; he counts it a merit if the same set of principles (which are the dimensions of our tables) can be re-used to state many rules. The learner's rules are different in kind: they start from some memorized set of facts and proceed via rules for converting that set into each of the related sets (and these into each other). The learner has to make a bigger investment than the grammarian; in return for this his rules **are simpler**. The job of the course writer is to choose that set of initial facts which gives the best starting-point, i.e. has a low initial memory-investment while keeping the conversion rules simple.

In the present case: the oral definite and the oral possessive have five forms each, matching one to one (and mostly rhyming): | 1 / mɔn, lə / mɔ̃, la / ma, le / me, lez / mez |. To convert oral definite to written definite, collapse the plural pair; the rest match one to one. To convert oral possessive to written possessive, collapse the plural pair and two of the singulars. To convert written definite to written possessive, collapse the same two singulars. A constituent difficulty arises whenever two sets don't match one to one.

Every exercise relies absolutely on the setter conveying much more than he can specify. I am sure many such conventions lie still buried in our specimen drill, even in its printed version, and we haven't begun to consider the taped version and **its** different conventions, which seem to have become venerable overnight.

If there are lessons in the above, they hold outside the language-learning context. In every subject exercises become stylized; expositions contain more patterns than the expounder knows; and pupils' misapprehensions are more legitimate, and more instructive, than we allow; and course writers take too much from the experts.

GEOFFREY BROUGHTON

University of London Institute of Education

Paired practice

The language teacher is often faced with the conflicting problems of teaching large classes and the need to give them massive practice in the structures of the language. What is more, few course-books, if any, give sufficient practice material to ensure controlled oral drill to the point of saturation in the patterns that have been taught. Understandably many teachers take the line of least resistance to these difficulties, and limit their oral work to a minimum of class repetition and a few scattered questions.

Yet massive oral practice is possible with large numbers of learners, and one device open to the teacher in such a situation is to set the students working orally in pairs. The present purpose is to suggest how this may be done; whilst the examples relate to the teaching of English as a foreign language, the principle is, of course, applicable to other modern languages.

After all, the essence of language is communication; at its simplest, meaningful verbal intercourse between two people. Common forms are found in seeking information (by question and answer), seeking confirmation (by affirmation and agreement), eliciting disagreement (by affirmation and negation) or eliciting verbal action (by command and obeying). All of these are modes that the teacher can readily harness to paired language practice. This, at the reinforcement stage of language learning, gives a communication situation in its simplest form, yet with an optimum control over the resulting dialogue.

Perhaps an example will best illustrate the advantages and potential of oral practice in pairs. Imagine the situation where the teacher has introduced defining relative clauses – with *who* and *whose* (e.g. *The man who brings the milk. The man whose car is outside.*) The learners have met and understood examples and seen how they work in context. Now is the time for practising them and the teacher who takes the line of least resistance sets a written exercise from the book. But this can hardly be called massive practice, and the ten or fifteen sentences each student writes (even if correct) can hardly be sufficient to drive home the new patterns to the point where they are integrated with the general body of his language mastery. The written exercise certainly has its place as a slightly different kind of reinforcement, but it should be preceded by oral drill.

The paired practice is introduced by the teacher putting on the blackboard:

a nurse
a librarian

and asking: *Where does a nurse work? (A nurse works in a hospital)* and *Where does a librarian work? (A librarian works in a library)*. Then comes the new pattern in the questions: *Which one is the person who works in a hospital? (A nurse)* and *Which one is the person who works in a library? (A librarian)*.

Now the teacher adds to the blackboard list familiar nouns which fit the pattern: *a waiter, a secretary, a cashier, a shop assistant, a teacher, an actor, a hairdresser*. Then he asks the class, *Which one is the person who works in a –* ? He asks five or six questions, if necessary writing up the place of work opposite each noun:

a nurse	*a hospital*
a librarian	*a library*
a waiter	*a restaurant*
a secretary	*an office*
a cashier	*a bank*
a shop assistant	*a shop*
a teacher	*a school*
an actor	*a theatre*
a hairdresser	*a hairdresser's*

Now the class is able to do its first piece of work in pairs. 'Practise in pairs,' the teacher says; 'the person on the left asks the questions, the person on the right answers.' Notice that there is no problem for the learners as to what to ask and what to answer. Notice also that the teacher has made things easy for the weaker and less enterprising students, who will ask the questions they have heard the teacher ask; but the more enterprising will want to start with the questions the teacher deliberately left out.

Watching and listening carefully, the teacher decides when to change the questioners and when he judges that the material has nearly been used up, instructs the persons on the right to ask the questions and those on the left to answer.

After a suitable time for this practice, the teacher stops the activity and prepares the class for its development. So far all the questions have started: *Which (one) is the person who works in a– ?* But we can make the question more general by adding more nouns to the blackboard and giving more choice in the question, though still practising the same pattern.

So a new blackboard list is begun alongside the first, starting with:

a postman
a pilot

As before, the teacher puts the first questions to the class: *Which one is the person who brings our letters? Which one is the person who flies planes?* Now this second list is developed on the blackboard by the addition of familiar nouns, and these are used to frame questions. Again, if necessary, a brief help towards the answer may be added:

a postman	*brings letters*
a pilot	*flies planes*
a bus driver	*drives a bus*
a farmer	*grows food*
an author	*writes books*
a musician	*makes music*
a window cleaner	*cleans windows*
a dentist	*looks after teeth*
a florist	*sells flowers*
a tennis player	*plays tennis*
an architect	*designs houses*

After five or six questions to the class, they are told for the second time to practise in pairs, with one member of each pair being the questioner to start with, and later the other. This practice continues for a suitable period – up to two minutes – before the teacher brings it to a stop and introduces a related pattern. As a reminder, he puts an example of the familiar pattern on the board – *A person who works in a hospital.* Now he asks: *What's a librarian?* eliciting the answer *A person who works in a library* and *What's a postman? (A person who brings letters).* Two or three other examples show the class the new, related, pattern of question and answer (*What's a – ? A person who –*). And the learners are ready for the third short session of work in pairs. Notice how changing the order of the items in the 'brings letters' column, or deleting them altogether adds a further degree of challenge and interest.

This particular set of twenty nouns has been selected to be used with other related patterns, using *whose*. So, after the third paired practice, the teacher reminds the class of one of the *whose* patterns. *Which one is the person whose work is in a hospital? (A nurse), Which one is the person whose work is bringing letters? (A postman).* A fourth paired practice follows, and the fifth, using the same lists and a *whose* answer, is started by sample questions and answers like *What's a waiter? (A man whose work is in a restaurant)* and *What's a farmer? (A man whose work is growing food).*

Set out like this, such an activity appears to be more tedious than it is. Notice that all the sentences are meaningful to the learners, that they are being drilled in making correct sentences, and that the periods of paired practice are broken up by the teacher's exposition and questions. So that, in fact, the learners here have done a total of some eight or ten minutes' very solid practice in two kinds of defining relative clauses, and during that time have themselves either asked or answered up to a hundred questions using the relevant patterns. This is the kind of massive practice which reinforces the active handling of structures in preparation for the written exercise.

The experienced teacher will soon recognize what a wide range of patterns can be practised in this way. There is the obvious range of structures which involve direct questions – What's that? Is that a **noun**? Is that a **noun** or a **noun**? Is that **noun adjective** or **adjective**? Where is the **noun**?, and many others. Question tags, using the anomalous finites (*can, must, may, will,* etc.) are a very profitable area – *You can swim | run | drive | dance,* etc., *can't you? You can't fly | walk on your hands | see an elephant, can you?*

Rather less obvious, however, is a range of traditional exercises which may easily be converted to oral practice in pairs. For example, one course-book, practising *used to*, gives an old school timetable, followed by this substitution table:

		do	French	geography		Monday
The class		have	German	maths		Tuesday
The boys	used to	study	English	science	on	Wednesday
They		learn	history	music		Thursday
						Friday
			play football			

For paired practice the teacher need only start asking, *When did the boys used to have French?* and so on. Then, with the school time-table on the blackboard, the learners can continue in pairs asking each other similar questions. The related pattern, *What did they use to do on– ?*, follows naturally.

Some traditional exercises are more difficult to turn into question and answer, but can be rephrased to give a challenge and its reply. The familiar conversion exercise where direct speech is to be reported can be handled in this way. For example, the following sentences might be set for reporting:

She said, 'I want to see that film'.
She said, 'I'll go tonight'.
She told him, 'I think I'll go in the best seats'.

A way of working these in pairs would be like this:

A. *She said, 'I want to see that film'.*
B. *Yes, I know. She said she wanted to see that film.*
A. *She said, 'I'll go tonight'.*
B. *Yes, I know. She said she would go tonight.*
A. *She told him, 'I think I'll go in the best seats'.*
B. *Yes, I know. She told him she thought she would go in the best seats.*

These short periods of oral work, of course, are intended to give maximum practice for the class and are certainly more demanding on the teacher. Not only must he plan the sequence of the drills with great care, but while the pairs are working he should move around the class to make sure that mistakes are not being made, and generally keeping his finger on the pulse of the class. In this way he knows when to stop the activity as the students are reaching the last examples, or in the rare cases where individuals have not properly understood the procedures. Another advantage of the teacher moving about is that he can control the noise level. Though if he is firmly in control of the learners, he can usually make sure that the general level of noise does not rise above an acceptable hum of interested conversation.

Perhaps these considerations suggest the fundamental secret of the success of this kind of oral activity. It depends completely on the willingness of the class to take part (a matter of discipline) and their understanding of what they are expected to do (a matter of organi-zation). The young or inexperienced teacher may be chary of letting control go out of his own hands and may even encounter difficulties when he tries paired practice for the first time. But, as with most activity methods, its advantages repay the organizational efforts involved. It is worth spending extra time in getting the pairs working well on the first occasion. The earliest drills should be straight repetitions of class practice. It helps when learners always work with the same partner, so that a routine is established for the activity.

Notice, too, how the use of the blackboard as a focal point gives each pair something external to themselves to concentrate on. Not only does it keep them working, but discourages them from drifting into a non-English private conversation. But perhaps most important is the challenge of running correctly through an interesting and meaningful exercise: once it becomes meaningless or tedious it loses interest.

Here, then, is an activity method which the teacher of the largest class can use, one in which no learner need leave his seat, one in which the maximum use is made of the learners' time. And if it is devised with a little imagination from the teacher, one which the learners will enjoy whenever he says, 'Practise in pairs'.

D. HARRIS

University of London Institute of Education

Drill and context[1]

In a well-known book[2] (pp. 118–20) E. M. Stack describes the language laboratory as a 'drill ground' which 'provides the facilities for that solid, concentrated, systematic practice needed to establish the required linguistic habits'. The exercises or drills give 'intensive active practice in application of structural and phonetic principles *previously presented* in the classroom' (author's italics). According to Stack, 'Pattern drills and laboratory exercises of other kinds constitute the spadework of language learning. They release the teacher from the mechanistic process of repetitive practice, making classroom experience relatively free of basic pronunciation and structural problems.'

Before commenting on these claims, it would perhaps be wise to remind ourselves of some of the commoner types of laboratory drill. These include **replacement drills**, e.g. replace the subject by the appropriate pronoun:

> **Stimulus.** *Jean va au cinéma.*
> **Response.** *Il va au cinéma*[2] (p. 143).

analogy drills, e.g. apply the adjective used in the first half of each sentence to the noun suggested in the second half:

> **Stimulus.** *Cette maison est grande. Et l'appartement?*
> **Response.** *L'appartement est grand*[2] (p. 178).

transformation drills, e.g. change to the *passé composé*:

> **Stimulus.** *Mes amis sortent de la maison.*
> **Response.** *Mes amis sont sortis de la maison hier*[2] (p. 148).

These may be said to be typical of drills commonly practised both inside and outside language laboratories to establish what Stack calls 'the required linguistic habits'. The requirements include making the appropriate sounds (i.e. everything included under the

333

headings of pronunciation, intonation, rhythm, etc.) and producing the right grammatical forms. Leaving aside the question of dangers inherent in what may be largely unmonitored laboratory work, I am prepared to accept that, given adequate supervision and a modicum of intelligence, it is perfectly possible to train the person who is working on these drills to produce the right sounds and forms.

But is this enough? Or, to pose a different question, is it worth doing at all? It is not too difficult to see how a learner who has successfully worked through a pattern drill of, say, eight examples, can become adept in doing subsequent drills **of the same type.** Practice improves performance in whatever is being practised. But since no Frenchman outside a classroom or a psychiatric ward will ever feel it necessary to say to our pupil, '*Mettez au passé composé...*' or '*Remplacez le substantif par un pronom ...*', it follows that these pattern drills can only justify themselves if it can be shown that they have transfer value to some other kind of situation, one in which the language used is felt by the speaker to be appropriate to a context that is itself **non**-linguistic.

Since the drills we are discussing do nothing to make the learner aware that a given utterance is valid in certain contexts and invalid in others (he is using the pronoun, the *passé composé*, etc., because the teacher **tells** him to), it is hard to see how, as a result of working through them, he can possibly come to acquire the essential feeling that any of the language he uses is relevant, appropriate or necessary. Such conviction can only come from repeated use of language in contexts that are not merely linguistic ones; and this experience is not provided by the pattern drills. If, after working through dozens of exercises in which he converts nouns into pronouns and present tense into past tense, the learner still does not know **when** to use these forms (how could he?), what purpose has been served by all the 'solid, concentrated, systematic practice'? Structural problems will **not** have been taken care of; they will be only too evident in the pupil's failure to know which structure to use. Drill grounds, unfortunately, are places where people learn **not** to think about the significance of what they are doing, whereas a successful language learner must understand the significance of what he is saying.

If we look again at our examples of pattern drill, we see that the response *Mes amis sont sortis de la maison hier* does not relate to an event which is felt **from the evidence of the stimulus** to have taken place in the past. In the example in which a noun is replaced by what is described as 'the appropriate pronoun', the pupil is required to show that he can see **some sort of** link between *Jean* and *il*, but his production of *il* and his repetition of *va au château*, far from helping him to use pronouns at the right time, is more likely to encourage the belief that nouns and pronouns are interchangeable. In fact, pronouns do not replace nouns in this way; they are not interchangeable. Each has a distinctive contribution to make to the language – though large numbers of third and fourth form secondary school pupils appear to be unaware of the fact, judging by a widespread inability to produce *il, elle, ils* and *elles* at the appropriate time and place.

The danger of producing pronouns only when the teacher asks for them is well illustrated by the example of analogy drills in which the pupil's attention is directed to the form of the adjective. Apart from the fact that the statement *L'appartement est grand* is meaningless, as it appears in the drill quoted, one wonders whether the pupil has had time to notice that he is being mistaught the relation between nouns and pronouns; for the question *Et l'appartement?* calls, in fact, for an answer beginning with a pronoun. The excuse that 'today we are practising adjectives' or that 'I haven't taught pronouns yet' will not do. Certainly it is sound practice to teach one new thing at a time; but to undermine what has already been taught, or to teach something that has to be unlearnt at a later stage, so that a given 'linguistic habit' is 'required' today, only to be dropped tomorrow, is confusing.

All of which leads to the question whether it is possible to produce types of pattern drill or exercise which, while laying stress on a particular aspect of grammar, none the less involve the learner in an appreciation of the meaning of the language used. Let us look first at the following exercise on the imperative:

Instructions: Listen to the following information and say the actual words used by the person involved.

Example provided:

Stimulus. *Le professeur a dit à Jacques de se lever.*
Response. *Levez-vous.*

S. *Le professeur a dit à Paul de sortir.*
R. *Sortez.*

S. *Monsieur Dauche a dit à ses enfants de se taire.*
R. *Taisez-vous.*

S. *Madame Amiot a dit à sa bonne de nettoyer la cuisine.*
R. *Nettoyez la cuisine.*

S. *Madame Amiot a dit à son mari de se lever.*
R. *Lève-toi.*

S. *Monsieur Pasquier a dit à son fils de s'habiller.*
R. *Habille-toi.*

S. *Madame Pasquier a dit à sa fille de ramasser ses jouets.*
R. *Ramasse tes jouets.*

S. *Je regardais deux automobilistes qui se battaient après un accident. Un agent m'a dit de m'en aller.*
R. *Allez-vous-en.*

Although these examples are offered tentatively, in the knowledge that they are probably fairly crude, it will have been seen that production of the right answer depends on an understanding of the meaning of the stimulus, and is not a mere mechanical reaction. Whether both *tu* and *vous* forms can be included in the same exercise, whether reflexive and non-reflexive verbs can be brought together, whether production of *tes jouets* can fairly be expected, will all depend on the stage the pupils have reached; but it seems to me that, inasmuch as the pupil is forced to think about the situation in which the language is operating, to think about the relation between the person giving the command and the person receiving it, to imagine what he would have heard and said if he had actually been present, then he is making sense, not merely producing the right answer.

Here is an example of an exercise to practise *aller* and the infinitive:

Instructions: Make a statement, using the verb *aller* and an infinitive, about the people in the following situations.

Example provided:

Stimulus. *Jean entre dans une boucherie.*
Response. *Il va acheter de la viande.*

S. *Jean entre dans une boulangerie.*
R. *Il va acheter du pain.*

S. *Marie-Claude entre dans un cinéma.*
R. *Elle va voir un film.*

S. *Pierre sort de la baignoire et prend sa serviette.*
R. *Il va s'essuyer.*

S. *Je prends une brosse à cheveux.*

R. *Vous allez vous brosser les cheveux.*

S. *Robert et Michel partent pour la piscine.*

R. *Ils vont se baigner.*

The reader may well be asking whether the instruction to use *aller* and an infinitive is less artificial than the requirement in the earlier exercise to change a verb into the *passé composé*. I think it is because, whilst in the latter case the response does not arise out of the **meaning** of the stimulus and is therefore purely formal, in the case of *aller* and the infinitive the response is a logical or possible conclusion that can legitimately be drawn from the information supplied.

Another kind of exercise is one in which the pupil must react to a set of circumstances as if he were one of the characters involved. Here are some examples requiring use of *venir de*:

Instructions: In the following situations, one of the characters needs to use *venir de* and an infinitive.

Example provided:

Stimulus. *Deux Parisiens sont arrivés à Londres. En sortant de leur hôtel deux heures plus tard ils ont rencontré un ami français. Il leur a dit, 'Vous êtes là depuis longtemps?' Ils lui ont répondu ...*

Response. *Non, nous venons d'arriver.*

S. *Madame Plon est restée seule à la maison quand son mari est sorti. Au bout d'un instant le téléphone a sonné. On a demandé Monsieur Plon. Madame Plon a répondu ...*

R. *Il vient de sortir.*

S. *Dix minutes après la mort d'un malade dans un lit d'hôpital, son médecin a téléphoné à l'hôpital pour demander de ses nouvelles. On lui a répondu ...*

R. *Il vient de mourir.*

S. *Un après-midi le téléviseur de Madame Prat est tombé en panne et elle a appelé l'électricien. La réparation faite, l'homme repartait quand Monsieur Prat est rentré du bureau. L'électricien lui a dit ...*

R. *Je viens de réparer votre téléviseur (le téléviseur).*

S. *Après s'être disputé avec la concierge Monsieur Michaud est rentré dans son appartement où il a dit à sa femme ...*

R. *Je viens de me disputer avec la concierge.*

My final example involves making judgements or comments on data supplied:

Instructions: Comment on the following situations, using *J'aurais dû*, etc., followed by an infinitive.

Example provided:

Stimulus. *Monsieur Pascal était malade. Il n'a pas suivi les conseils du médecin et, par conséquent, il est mort.*

Response. *Il aurait dû suivre les conseils du médecin.*

S. *Chaque matin Monsieur Gide part pour la gare pour prendre le train de Paris. Un jour il est parti trop tard et il a manqué son train.*

R. *Il aurait dû partir plus tôt.*

S. *En cherchant un médicament, une femme s'est trompée de bouteille. Elle n'a pas lu l'étiquette et elle s'est empoisonnée.*

R. *Elle aurait dû lire l'étiquette.*

S. *Un automobiliste a renversé un piéton. Pris de panique, il a continué son chemin sans ralentir.*

R. *Il aurait dû s'arrêter.*

S. *Monsieur et Madame Braux sont allés au théâtre, mais ils n'avaient pas retenu de places. En arrivant au théâtre ils ont trouvé que c'était complet.*

R. *Ils auraient dû retenir des places.*

S. *Un incendie s'est déclaré chez les Dupont. Ils ont essayé de le maîtriser eux-mêmes et, par conséquent, la maison a brûlé.*

R. *Ils auraient dû appeler les pompiers.*

We have seen why I do not think that a person can be trained to speak a language by dint of speaking the non-language of 'mechanistic' drills, even when the latter are carefully structured. We have also looked at examples of exercises in context, in which one is required to grasp the sense of the data, without necessarily attending to every single word, and to make an appropriate and fairly immediate response, something that one has to do in everyday discourse. Several points relating to the contextualized exercises remain to be clarified.

First, I envisage them as material for follow-up work. I assume that the grammar and vocabulary have **already** been practised in other contexts, the nature of which is described by other contributors to this volume. In other words, I see the role of contextualized exercises as being more modest in the scheme of things than that of the 'mechanistic' ones as suggested, for example, by Professor Stack.

A possible criticism of the exercises is that they are sometimes too long and too grammatically complex. Length **is** a problem, in that the stimuli must be short enough to be 'taken in', while remaining long enough to provide adequate context. There is no reason why a printed copy of the stimuli, or possibly the instructions and the first example, could not be provided (e.g. for language laboratory work) to relieve possible strain. As to the claim that the exercises are too complex, this depends on the level aimed at. Some of the examples are possibly unsuitable for anyone below sixth form standard; and it seems to me that in view of the level implied by the need to grasp a context that is possibly conveyed in relatively complex language, exercises of this kind have more to offer in the later than in the earlier stages of a course.

Can the grammar be practised equally well through the exploitation of texts? It might appear so, since texts are one of the richest sources of language practice. But is it not difficult to ensure thorough practice of certain expressions without sometimes resorting to 'unreal' or even silly questions? And what does one do about pupils who have missed lessons or the question and answer work on texts, or those who for some other reason need extra practice? Cannot the exercises help in such cases?

Can one force one specific answer? Does it matter? Are several possible answers a good thing? In the final analysis, I do not see how one can always force one answer without running the risk of reverting to meaninglessness. With the simpler structures it is not too difficult, and the initial example provided is bound to direct a particular kind of response. Furthermore, in the case of laboratory work, it is always possible to run through the exercise first in class to discover what kinds of answer will emerge and establish what is acceptable. With the more advanced structures, where it is almost impossible to force one answer, the drawback is offset by the fact that, whatever the precise terms of a pupil's answer may be, he is at least likely to be using the structure in context, which is one of the aims of the exercise; and since advanced work implies that a certain level of competence has been attained, the pupil must have developed **some** discriminatory sense. Outside the laboratory the possibility of a variety of answers is a positive advantage, for the pupils can take the opportunity to show that they can apply in individually different ways whatever they have learnt. And this is what foreign-language learning is ultimately about.

Notes and references

1. Some of the arguments presented in this chapter have appeared in a paper presented to, and subsequently circulated by, a group of teachers meeting informally at the University of London Institute of Education. Useful suggestions and critical comments were made at the time by Mrs A. Bridge, Dr M. Neale, Mr D. Shotter and Mr O. Williams. My original interest in this subject was aroused by my work with Mr F. Corless and by material in *Voix et images de France*, part 2, C R E D I F, distributed for Didier by Harrap. Other sources of contextualized exercises are now opening up, but 'mechanistic' drills retain a dominant position on the modern languages scene, as an examination of a cross-section of currently used commercial courses will amply show. Whether the exercises discussed in this chapter are practised inside or outside a language laboratory is not my main concern. Granted, the laboratory imposes certain conditions that affect the way one can operate, but this is secondary to the real issue of the educational value of this or that type of exercise.

2. STACK, E. M. (1971) *The Language Laboratory and Modern Language Teaching*, 3rd edn. London: Oxford University Press.

P. F. SANDS

Borough Road College, Isleworth, Middlesex

French drills in the language laboratory

The value of the pattern drill as a teaching technique in the language laboratory remains in question. E. M. Stack has indicated the unsuitability in this context of many traditional textbook exercises. His proposed alternatives, substitution and other drills, have also been widely criticized as being mechanical, monotonous and meaningless. Even drills presented within a meaningful context in natural language have been recently described as involving the practice of 'structurespeech, not communication, and structurespeech without much emphasis on structures'.[1]

Moreover, experience proves how reluctant students are to undertake such work. Few enter the laboratory with enthusiasm. In view of these criticisms and the problems of preparing suitable material, this contribution will propose on the basis of my experience some guide-lines for composing drills, establish criteria for assessing their value and suggest ways of improving them.

Guide-lines for composition

1. The phased drill-form offers up to five phases of practice:

Master: Stimulus – Correction – Confirmation.
Student: – Response – Reinforcement.
The number of phases used then varies according to the type of drill, its degree of difficulty or the learner's stage of progress.

2. Drills are best not used for demonstration or testing. They should be clearly based upon work previously presented and practised in class.

3. With the possible exception of remedial work, isolated collections of drills have little value, for language work should normally be progressive, forming part of an integrated whole.

4. As it is impractical to correct responses individually or modify

341

the programme *en cours*, drills should be self corrective, not offering a variety of possible answers.

5. In devising drills, it is advisable to begin with the response and then seek the appropriate stimulus.

6. The stimulus then provides the information required to formulate the response and the response presents the sentence pattern to be practised.

7. A text of the example and of part of the drill may be required by some students.

8. Each response should offer an acceptable analogy with its predecessor and each pair agree with the convention established by the example. The stimuli may vary in form provided that they give adequate information for the reproduction of the response.

9. Drills should normally be iterative and not progressive, offering an equal degree of difficulty in each pair. The response should preferably proceed naturally and simply from the stimulus and be of reasonable length.

10. To avoid boredom a drill should contain no more than eight pairs. A unit should be varied and not rely on one particular drill-form.

11. More than one example may be provided and should then be repeated at the beginning or the end of the drill.

12. A unit should be short enough to allow practice and playback during one period. A familiar centre of interest allows situations to recur, thus limiting the semantic field.

13. Recording should preferably be done at normal speed by two or more native speakers. Pauses should not be too long, the pause control being available to a hesitant pupil.

14. Instructions should be clear and precise. The use of English may be preferred for beginners.

Criteria for assessment

Criteria for the assessment of the effectiveness of drill-forms in terms of the relations between the stimulus (S) and the response (R) have been established as follows:

1. Complexity: the degree of difference between S and R. A repetition exercise has minimum complexity because $S = R$. A mutation exercise may be more complex:

S. *Sacha Distel habite en France, n'est-ce pas?*
R. *Mais, bien sûr, il est français.*

This involves a change of subject, verb and complement and some general knowledge.

2. Relative length: the degree of difference in length between **S** and **R**. If **S** is short and **R** long, the drill is apparently more efficient, since **R** represents the pupil's contribution.

3. Contextuality: the degree to which **S** and **R** approximate to real-life conversation (Higgins,[1] pp. 49–50).

Conventional drills have been criticized on four counts:

(a) They are mechanical and may be performed without any attention to the form of the structure.

(b) They are meaningless and the learner has no control over the content or form of his response.

(c) They are unnatural and involve response to a stimulus which may never occur naturally. The learner may never learn how to use the structure in a normal conversation.

(d) They may encourage overgeneralization. The learner may imperfectly understand the meaning of the structure or draw incorrect conclusions about the rules for its formation. He may consequently fail to use the rule correctly (Dakin,[1] pp. 55–60).

Evidently, though these criticisms may partly apply to all drills, careful contextualization, where each pair forms a conversation in miniature, may largely obviate them. In consequence contextuality will be the main criterion applied in the following examination of drill-forms.

Examination of drill-forms

Although many drill-forms are available,[2] only the principal types will be examined and improved alternatives suggested.

1. Repetition
This simple drill has a good ratio of relative length ($\mathbf{S} = \mathbf{R}$) but it is uncontextual except as a teaching technique. It may be useful as a pronunciation exercise but is mechanical and monotonous. Structures are better practised in other ways.

2. Substitution

S. *Il est chez moi – vous.*
R. *Il est chez vous.*

This has low complexity, a good ratio of relative length but is uncontextual. Though easy and apparently suitable for beginners, it is monotonous and can be performed with little understanding of meaning.

Alternative:

S. *François est chez moi ou chez vous?*
R. *Il est chez vous.*

This, in turn, would be improved by the provision of a relevant context.

3. Transformation or mutation

(a) By substitution

S. *Je m'en vais. Nous . . .*
R. *Nous nous en allons.*

Alternative:

S. *Vous restez un moment?*
R. *Non, nous nous en allons immédiatement.*

(b) By addition

S. *Nous nous en allons immédiatement – il faut.*
R. *Il faut que nous nous en allions immédiatement.*

Alternative:

S. *Vous vous en allez tout à l'heure?*
R. *Non, il faut que nous nous en allions immédiatement.*

(c) By combination

S. *Il pleuvra. Je resterai à la maison.*
R. *S'il pleut, je resterai à la maison.*

Alternative:

S. *Regarde, il va pleuvoir. Je vais rester à la maison.*
R. *Moi aussi, s'il pleut, je resterai à la maison.*

(d) By analogy

S. *Attends pour sortir.*
R. *Ne sors pas tout de suite.*

Alternative:

   S. *Vous voulez que votre ami ne sorte pas tout de suite. Que lui dites-vous?*

   R. *Ne sors pas tout de suite.*

The uncontextuality of these examples is obvious. The alternatives gain in value when based upon a familiar situation. They are contextualized in so far as any natural linguistic exchange used in class or encountered in a dialogue can be used as a basis for a series of analagous 'micro-conversations', provided that all the data required for **R** is provided in **S**. *D'après les données devinez la profession de l'interlocuteur*:

   S. *Je porte les bagages à la gare.*

   R. *Ah, vous êtes porteur, alors.*

'Stimuli affectifs' add realism to the sequence of analagous exchanges.

Exprimez la surprise:

   S. *Vous regardez le bébé de votre soeur. Il est mignon. Que dites-vous?*

   R. *Comme il est mignon!*

Exprimez votre désaccord:

   S. *Il va venir, tu sais.*

   R. *Ah non, je n'ai aucune envie qu'il vienne.*[3]

The imperative and interrogative, normally used only by the teacher, can be practised:

   S. *Vous voulez partir. Que diriez-vous en parlant avec politesse?*

   R. *Je pourrais partir?*

Consentez à ce qu'on vous demande:

   S. *Je pourrais partir maintenant?*

   R. *Oui, partez tout de suite.*[4]

The student thus assumes a role in the dialogue:

Dans un magasin, Françoise, timide, ne veut rien demander à la vendeuse. Ecoutez:

   S. *Michel, demande à la vendeuse le prix de la jupe.*

   R. *Pardon, mademoiselle, c'est combien cette jupe, s'il vous plaît?*

Paul tombe en disgrâce. Ecoutez cette conversation entre lui et sa mère et puis continuez de même:

S. *Veux-tu ne pas te réveiller si tôt.*
Comment, maman?
R. *Ne te réveille pas si tôt.*

This role will become meaningful when the exchanges relate to a single situation or centre of interest:

Françoise réveille les enfants qui n'obéissent pas. Ecoutez:

S. *Réveillez-vous, les enfants! Après quelques moments:*
R. *Alors, vous vous réveillez, ou pas?*
(Continue with *se lever, se laver, s'habiller*, etc.).[5]

4. Questions and answer
(a) By analogy
S. *Michel est dans le jardin. Et Françoise?*
R. *Françoise est dans le jardin.*

Alternative:

S. *Michel et Françoise sont toujours ensemble. Michel est dans le jardin maintenant. Où donc est Françoise?*
R. *Elle est dans le jardin, aussi.*

(b) *'Oui' or 'non'*
S. *Michel est dans le jardin?*
R. *Oui, Michel est dans le jardin.* Or *Non, Michel n'est pas dans le jardin.*

Alternative:

S. *Michel aime cultiver son jardin. Aujourd'hui c'est dimanche. Il fait beau. Michel est dans la maison?*
R. *Non, il est dans le jardin.*

Though question and answer should be contextual, the original examples are mechanical, unnatural and largely meaningless. The alternatives are contextualized but have a high ratio of relative length and, like the mutation drills described, they are complex. Consequently both may be best used with older students. With younger learners, information can be supplied economically by using texts and situations already familiar as a basis for questions. Take an example from the *Cours illustré de français*.[6] Drills could be composed practising *sur* and *sous*, either in a homogeneous progression or in a varied sequence of question forms:

(a) Homogeneous

Image A

S. *Où est Madeleine?*
R. *Elle est sur la chaise.*
S. *Où est la souris?*
R. *Elle est sous la table.*

Image B

S. *Où est la souris maintenant?*
R. *Elle est sous la chaise.*
S. *Où donc est Madeleine?*
R. *Elle est sur le piano.*

(b) Sequential

Image A

S. *Madeleine est sur la table ou sur la chaise?*
R. *Elle est sur la chaise.*
S. *Et la souris?*
R. *Elle est sous la table.*

Image B

S. *Est-elle sous la table, maintenant?*
R. *Non, elle est sous la chaise.*
S. *Où donc est Madeleine?*
R. *Elle est sur le piano.*

Alternatively a series of pictures with or without a text or dialogue can stimulate a number of disparate but carefully structured questions which reveal the student's ability to understand and to formulate accurate responses:

Maintenant répondez pour Jacques. Les numéros se rapportent aux images du livre de l'étudiant.[7]

1–2 **S.** *Vous habitez rue de la Gare?*
     R. *Non, j'habite rue de la Poste.*
3   **S.** *La maison est en face du théâtre?*
     R. *Non, elle est en face du cinéma.*
4–5 **S.** *Vous habitez au numéro douze ou au numéro treize?*
     R. *J'habite au numéro treize.*
8–10 **S.** *Vous avez un appartement?*
     R. *Non, j'ai seulement une chambre.*

5. **Other stimuli**

The drills so far described largely rely on a verbal stimulus providing the data required to form the response. Most are uneconomical in the time taken to provide the information, offer problems of comprehension and may generate a complex linguistic transformation. Drills may, however, be prompted by other types of visual or aural stimulus.[8]

(a) Visual prompts

S.   *Michel est en train de monter l'escalier.*

R.   *Il vient de le monter.*

S. | *Défense de fumer* |

R. *On ne peut pas fumer ici.*

S. | *Pelouse interdite* |
R. *On ne peut pas marcher sur cette pelouse.*

(b) General knowledge prompts

S. *Napoléon habitait en France.*
R. *Oui, il était français.*
S. *Churchill habitait en Angleterre.*
R. *Oui, il était anglais.*

(c) Sound effect prompts

S. Dog barking.
R. *J'entends aboyer un chien.*
S. Crowd clapping.
R. *J'entends applaudir des gens.*

The language laboratory drill is intended to encourage the practice of a wide variety of structures. It can be presented as a meaningless piece of verbal gymnastics or can be used to add realism to an artificial activity which is difficult to make interesting and towards which the learner is not easily motivated. If, however, the acquisition of a foreign language depends upon the frequent practice of sentence patterns in a meaningful situation, these suggestions may contribute by encouraging a more flexible, varied and natural approach to the composition of laboratory drills.

Notes and references

1. DAKIN, J. (1973) *The Language Laboratory and Language Learning* (p. 88). London: Longman. See also DELATTRE, P. (1971) *Les exercices structuraux pour quoi faire?* Paris: Hachette; HIGGINS, J. J. (1969) *A Guide to Language Laboratory Material Writing.* Oslo: Universitetsforlaget; REQUEDAT, F. (1966) *Les exercices structuraux.* Paris: Hachette/Larousse; STACK, E. M. (1971) *The Language Laboratory and Modern Language Teaching,* 3rd edn. London: Oxford University Press. Stack's book is overrated in its chapters on preparing materials, but the others, particularly those by Dakin and Higgins, are useful.

2. Seventeen different types are described by ETMEKJIAN, J. (1966) *Pattern Drills in Language Teaching,* pp. 7–21. London: University of London Press.

3. REQUEDAT, F., op. cit. in 1, pp. 46–7. The *Livre du maître* of *Voix et images de France* (Paris: Didier) contains material readily adaptable to the laboratory; RIVENC, P. (ed.) (1967) *Voix et images de France, premier degré – Exercices pour le laboratoire de langues – Livre du maître;* GUBERINA, P. (ed.) (1966) *Voix et images de France, deuxième degré – Livre du maître.*

4. GUBERINA, P. (ed.) (1962) *Voix et images de France, premier degré, leçon* 11, p. 48. Paris: Didier. My examples.

5. Op. cit. in 4, *leçons* 14 and 15, pp. 60–7.

6. GILBERT, M. (1966) *Cours illustré de français,* bk 1, pp. 46–7. London: University of London Press.

7. Op. cit. in 4, *leçon* 3, p. 10.

8. DAKIN, op. cit. in 1, pp. 61–90; HILL, N. (1969) 'Exercices sur l'imparfait et le passé composé.' *Le Français dans le monde,* **66,** 49–51. Dakin includes many mutation drills under the headings of application, collocation and implication drills.

PATRICIA C. C. HEAP

Chesham High School

Games in Italian

Learning is fun, or should be. In the annual routine of working through the appropriate chapters and grammar points of the year's syllabus, sometimes the fun can be lost, to the disadvantage of pupils and teacher alike. But by means of games the fun can be easily brought back. Several of the following suggestions involve the whole class, whilst others are more suitable for small groups – working, for example, with an assistant, or permitting several different activities to take place at once when a whole class is being taught.

The teaching points practised by playing are clearly evident, and I begin with ideas giving experience in everyday situations likely to be encountered on a visit to Italy.

Map game

We are staying in the *Pensione del Sole*, in an imaginary or real town. Confronted with a street plan, we wish first of all to find the shopping centre. (Real town maps may be used if resources permit, but a blackboard diagram offers more versatility.) The children first have to ask the hotel receptionist (appointed arbitrarily from the class) how to reach the shopping centre. Various details are on the map, such as traffic lights, one-way streets, pedestrian precincts, the weekly market, and road works, and the *Pensione* is situated some distance away from everything of interest to give opportunity for more complicated directions.* The hotel receptionist will explain the route to be followed, (thus practising imperative forms). Whichever form of address is used (*tu, voi, Lei*), other persons staying in the hotel are introduced to practise the other imperative forms, e.g.:

* Cp. HORNSEY, A. W. and M. and HARRIS, D. (1970) *On parle français 1, Teacher's Handbook*, pp. 23–4. London: Heinemann.

due bambini: '*Può indicarci dove si trovano i negozi, per favore?*'
segretario: '*Prendete questa strada qui, fino al semaforo, poi andate a sinistra. . . .*'
vecchia signora: '*Può indicarmi. . .?*'
segretario: '*Lei prenda. . . . poi vada . . .*'

After receiving the directions, someone repeats them in the present tense to ensure they know where they are going:

Prendiamo questa strada, andiamo . . .

Then the route is followed on the map, with queries and unexpected obstructions such as a typical pile-up at the traffic lights and the immediate Italian audience making the route impassable. Once the shopping centre has been reached, one can either change to the 'shopping game', or continue with a visit to the market, requiring further directions. After all the shopping refreshment is required, so one must find the nearest café, and finally work out a route back to the hotel.

Shopping game

There are many variations on this theme, which enables the children to become accustomed to Italian money and how to explain what they want. If a form enjoys acting, then small groups can each present a scene in a different type of shop. More able groups can point out typical English blunders themselves, as in one example:

Nella Farmacia:
Inglese: '*Buon giorno, vorrei una camera, per favore.*'
Farmacista: '*Sissignore, lei vede quella pensione all'angolo? Ce ne sono tante.*'

Then followed a short argument on the meaning of '*camera*' and the *farmacista* finished:

Questi Inglesi, vengono sempre qui per le camere, mentre io vendo macchine fotografiche.

With a less active group the scene can be a large store, where each member has to ask for something, the teacher or another pupil states the price, and the bill is totalled on the blackboard. A sum of money is offered and the change is worked out. Later the wrong change can be given and the customer then has to argue for the correct amount with the cashier. For the younger ones a toy shopping game can be purchased in Italy, with imitation currency.

A popular variation on this is a visit to a café, where each pupil has to decide on what to order. When the first one attempts to do so, his attention is drawn to the sign:

Si pregano i sig. clienti di munirsi dello scontrino

which is then explained. Having settled the order, it must be totalled up by the cashier, who, according to ancient Italian custom, gives the change partially in sweets. (More enterprising pupils later try to make small purchases with accumulated sweets, and the ensuing dialogue can be very amusing.) Finally the order is placed and the *cameriere* succeeds in confusing everything and everybody to involve further essential travellers' phrases.

Other situations may be a visit to the cinema, art gallery, football stadium, the beach, and the final journey back involving losing luggage, buying tickets, the frequent disregard for the railway time-table and the announcements of expected arrivals and departures:

Il direttissimo per Livorno sta arrivando al binario quattro.
Il rapido proveniente da Napoli arriverà 120 minuti in ritardo.

In order to practise vocabulary and spelling, a variety of **word games** can be played. These can be started with complete beginners, once the alphabet has been learned, an essential when trying to explain awkward English names to Italians. *Io vedo* (I spy) practises classroom vocabulary, and a simple competition is trying to find the maximum number of words starting with the same letter. Old-fashioned Spelling Bees and Hangman acquire a new interest, with points scored against for wrong letter names as well as letters. Crosswords can be invented or simple ones found in books of puzzles and magazines (see 'Teaching materials,' p. 355),   and a favourite at all levels is Scrabble.

Another very simple way of enlarging vocabulary is by using **card games** re-labelled in Italian, such as Happy Families, Animal Snap, Farmyard Donkey, etc. Happy Families in particular trains the pupils to remember the definite article before the name, e.g. *Il signor Fuliggine è a casa?*

To increase general knowledge and vocabulary various games can be purchased in Italy and prove to be very popular. One I found consists of placing one wire on the question and the other on the answer. If this is correct, a battery-operated buzz is emitted. The questions have endless variety and can suit all levels.

Quiz games can be invented for every class, with both questions and answers in Italian. If the questions are simple enough, even the most reluctant language learner will enjoy counting the number of windows in the maths room (to the consternation of the teacher), and finding out what colour is the car with a certain number plate. Italian geography, which is otherwise completely ignored throughout the school, provides much quiz material and many howlers, such as Genoa being listed as a southern city, and Turin as a port, but with the incentive of some *baci* as a prize, Naples rapidly moves from the Venetian lagoon to its rightful place in Campania.

Useful quizzes for verb practice are those involving people. One member of the group thinks of a well-known person, and the others have to discover who it is by asking questions about him or her. An alternative is for the others to attach a name to one member's back, and he must then find out who he is, thus practising the first person verb forms. Historical characters involve the past tenses.

The present tense may have been taught either by direct method or traditional approach, but this means of practising the different forms is very simple and can be started as soon as a few basic verbs have been learnt. The important point is to stress the **ending** of the verb to indicate the **person**, as the subject pronouns are so little used, so *canto* means *I sing*, *canti* means *you sing*, but one must avoid any confusion with masculine and feminine endings for nouns and adjectives. The verb persons can be varied, with the pupils asking the teacher directly, using the polite form *Lei*, e.g.

Lei canta? Lei scrive?

or asking each other, and therefore using the second person singular:

Canti? Scrivi?

In both these cases the reply must be given in the first person:

Non canto. Non scrivo.

Alternatively to practise the first and second persons, one pupil may be sent out while the others decide who he is. On returning, he must ask the others:

Scrivo? No, non scrivi.

For ordinary third person singular the teacher picks a subject:

Penso di qualcuno.
È un uomo? È un uomo.
È vivo o morto? È vivo.
Canta? Gioca a calcio? È attore?

This also practises adjective agreement and omission of the definite article before a profession.

To practise the agreement of adjectives at a very early stage, a member of the class can be used as the subject, and only use the verb form *è*, e.g.

È un ragazzo o una ragazza? È una ragazza.
È alta? È piccola? È bionda? È intelligente?

The adjectives and agreement are very easily taught by direct method, by finding examples in the class or room; *la porta è azzurra, Giorgio è alto.*

Free composition can be encouraged by each member of the class contributing a sentence to a story. This may need some prompting from the teacher, or more often controlling before the story gets out of hand. *C'era una volta* when Snoopy, travelling from Milan to Rome by train, partook of too much liquid refreshment in Florence and was arrested for being drunk and disorderly. He escaped from custody by knocking out the *sbirro*, met a very attractive French poodle *en route* for Sicily, where he sought protection from the Mafia

e tutti vissero felici e contenti.

I have left until last the important part played by **magazines** and **cartoon books** because it is often so difficult to obtain them in England. The most popular amongst my pupils and most unobtainable outside Italy is *Linus*, with so many of their favourite cartoon characters in Italian. One second-year class, always with five minutes to spare at the beginning of one lesson due to internal organization, settle down happily with their *Linus* and are very reluctantly separated when the lesson proper begins. Also in the cartoon line are translations of Snoopy, Tom and Jerry, Bristow and Andy Capp, as well as original Italian cartoons, where the meaning can easily be gathered from the picture. Cartoons and advertisements from Italian magazines help to decorate the formroom.

The more serious reading, with articles on politics, regional problems, national and international news, giving an excellent picture of contemporary Italy, can be found in the more readily available weekly magazines, along with scandal, problem pages, and pictures of Italian football players.

Italian newspapers, however, apart from selected articles for interest and translation, and giving a brief outline of the Italian press, are not as useful as magazines for news items, because by the time they have reached England they are usually out of date.

In the deplorable absence of suitable teaching materials for Italian in schools I have tried to make suggestions to bring the language and the country to life within the four classroom walls, and perhaps some of these may be helpful to teachers of subjects which are more favoured by publishers, but whose resources are limited.

Teaching materials

MAGAZINES

Most easily obtainable are *Domenica del Corriere, Oggi, Gente, Epoca, Grazia, Annabella*. *Grazia* and *Annabella* are more women's magazines, the others contain current affairs, cartoons, crosswords, etc.

NEWSPAPERS

La Stampa, Il Tempo, Il Messaggero, Corriere della Sera, La Nazione, Il Resto del Carlino, Stampa Sera.

CARTOON MAGAZINES

Linus, Eureka.

CARTOON BOOKS

Jacovitti (illustrated short stories, i.e. *Pinocchio*); *Mafalda*; *Timbra il suo Cartellino,* Bristow; *È Domani,* Charlie Brown; *Era Una Notte Buia e Tempestosa*; *Il Bambino a una Dimensione*; *Snoopy e il suo Sopwith Camel*; *Il Libro Dell'Elefante*; *Andy Capp Autunno Sbronzo*; *Andy Capp Controvento*.

CROSSWORD PUZZLES

Facili Cruciverba. Weekly magazine. Florence: Corrado Tedeschi Editore.

BARRIE K. JOY AND J. M. MCNAIR

Department of Education, University of Manchester

A review of written exercises

In this chapter we do not attempt to provide some sort of vade-mecum of instant and universally applicable prescriptions for written exercises in any foreign-language course. To do so would be not only pretentious but fundamentally mistaken. Written exercises cannot be divorced meaningfully from other aspects of work in the foreign-language course: both their functions and their efficacy must be determined largely by the teacher's assumptions as to how the language is best learned and, therefore, best taught. These considerations dictate the structure of this chapter. First, there is a brief discussion of the functions of written exercises in relation to other aspects of course work. Then we suggest criteria for written exercises. The final section is concerned with a critical review of various types of exercise.

The chapter focuses on exercises designed to produce written work up to paragraph length and particularly on those which strengthen command of syntax or morphology. Only exercises requiring written response in the foreign language are considered. Examples are given in the languages most commonly taught in British schools, but the points would, in principle, apply to written exercises in other languages.

The functions of written exercises in the foreign-language course

For a considerable part of its history foreign-language teaching was influenced by 'the suggestion that spoken language is an impoverished relation of the written language',[1] that one only really knew the foreign language if one was able to write it. More recently this imbalance has been redressed considerably. Increasingly the importance, even the primacy, of the spoken over the written language is gaining recognition. This is evidenced partly by the move from the deductive, grammar / translation-based course-book to the more inductive skill-based model of foreign-language learning on which

356

most audio-lingual and audio-visual courses are based. But there has also developed in some quarters an enthusiasm for spontaneity, sometimes in direct opposition to accuracy of expression. This has led to some uncertainty and, at worst, to a positive rejection of the functions of written exercises.

But oracy and literacy are not alternatives: both are required, and they must be closely related to each other in a well-designed language course. Briefly language is primarily speech, and the written word is the symbolic representation of speech. Meaningful speech does not depend on the ability to read or write, as the average three-year-old will show. To read requires the learner to interpret symbols and to articulate, aloud or silently, the sounds associated with them – in short, to decode. To write the foreign language requires knowledge of the symbols related to the sounds of the language and the ways in which they are arranged in order to convey meaning. This essential link between sound and symbol requires constant strengthening if errors like the following are to be avoided: *Quand il l'avais fais.* The pupil who wrote this clearly has a good grasp of the language but not of its correct written form.

The precise function of written exercises will vary greatly according to the level of language involved. The first exercise of writing skills will be an introduction to and copying of the symbols representing short sentences or phrases already mastered orally. In copying in this way the pupil will be further practising the sentences and also recording them for reference. At a more advanced stage exercises will require learners to recast elements already familiar into what, for them, will be new and original units. Gradually the emphasis will be on providing practice, which leads to the development of continuous writing as a skill in its own right, with the ultimate aim of not merely getting an answer right but of producing good original language. Later work requiring the writing of passages longer than a paragraph will reflect a difference in degree and emphasis rather than principle. But the ultimate ability of the pupil to write creatively in response to more open stimuli will depend essentially on his having already acquired the necessary elements of the language through carefully guided exercises based on closely controlled stimuli and predictable responses. This move from guided control to open specification is paralleled by a shift of emphasis from the teaching to the testing function of written exercises.

It is important for the teacher to be aware of the intended teaching-testing emphases of any exercises he sets. Clearly some exercises will perform both functions, but pupils must not be discouraged by being tested at too early a stage. This is particularly liable to happen with French, which shows a higher degree of redundancy in its written form than, say, German or Spanish, as shown in the agreement of adjectives and past participles. Generally, however, if the material to be written is wholly familiar to the learners in its oral form, they will be in a better position to produce the written form. The link between systematically drilled oral work and written follow-up will therefore be retained whenever possible. For although written exercises will usually provide more time for critical reflection before committing oneself to a final version than would oral work, this 'extra time' should provide opportunity rather to check the appropriateness of the intended responses against an internalized and meaningful directive system of language patterns than to suspend the meaning of language while puzzling out the appropriate form by referring to grammatical rules and paradigms. If this is so, then the homework exercises ritualistically 'solved' by generations of foreign-language learners are of little value.

So the noun 'exercise', defined by Chambers' Dictionary as 'a set of problems, passages for translation, etc., in a textbook' is here rejected. As language teachers begin to dispense with textbooks and develop a more active approach to teaching languages perhaps the verb 'exercise' meets the language learner's requirements: 'to drill: to train by use: to improve by practice: to give exercise to'. If to each of these is added the words 'in writing', a comprehensive definition of the functions and range of written exercises emerges.

Criteria for exercises

1. All exercises should derive from or present a meaningful situation. The situation may be real or imagined, text, narrative or visual based, provided it is significant to the learners.

2. Exercises should not demand so much attention to form that meaning becomes of secondary importance.

3. The language contained in exercises and the expected responses should exemplify natural and authentic usage.

4. The language involved should be within the capabilities of the learners – particularly in relation to structure. It should reflect clearly the priorities operating in oral work.

5. The content-matter should be as interesting and relevant to the learners as possible.

6. Over a period a balance should be struck between the boredom of repetition and the overstretching of analogy. Predictability is important but challenge is needed too. Exercises should provide systematic rather than random coverage.

7. They should, as far as possible, exercise or test specified items and not others; e.g. there should be no difficult lexical items in exercises focusing on structures.

8. The aim should be explicit and instructions clear; there should be no ambiguity of interpretation, especially when instructions are given in the foreign language. Models should be included where appropriate.

9. Exercises should be easily checkable. In accordance with criteria 7 and 8 it is important that learners are aware of both the aim of a particular exercise and of the means of its assessment. This will encourage them to concentrate on the element or elements to be tested.

Important though these criteria are, it must again be stressed that ultimately any exercise can only be evaluated in relation to its function within the course as a whole. Written exercises which divorce form from meaning in language work, however varied and novel they may be, can quickly reach the point where they are scarcely concerned with language at all.

Types of written exercise

WRITING UP WORK ALREADY MASTERED ORALLY

Learning to write. In the early stages of writing the pupil has to master for the foreign-language conventions of graphic form, some of which will be quite new (accents, letters, some punctuation marks), some of which will seem familiar but will turn out to be used differently (e.g. French *lit*, German *zwanzig*, Spanish *cinco*). He has to learn to associate these symbols with the foreign-language sound system. To make this association securely he must have a confident command of the sounds represented, and this presupposes ample oral practice of any material he is asked to write. He must also have had ample opportunity to see and study (on blackboard, duplicated sheets or in textbook) the visual representation of this material.

A pupil who has not had this experience, both oral and visual, of the language material he is asked to write will be in difficulties with such sentences as:

Qu'est-ce que c'est?
¿Cuántos años tiene Vd.?
Wie heißt der Mann draußen? Er heißt Herr Müller.

The systematic acquisition of writing skills will be helped by getting pupils to copy into work-books much of the language practised orally in class. This will have been presented and practised in question and answer work, and it will be helpful in the early stages for pupils to copy not just sentences or items but the question and answer series they have already used – a practice which has the advantage of giving a context to structural items. This also ensures that the material is then available to the learner for subsequent reference and revision. The inclusion of the question forms will help pupils to free themselves from their dependence on the teacher to initiate communication.

The link between question and answer is as important in the early stages, e.g.

Qu'est-ce qu'il y a dans le jardin?
   Il y a deux arbres.
Qu'est-ce qu'il y a sur la table?
   Il y a trois livres.
Combien d'arbres y a-t-il dans votre jardin?
   Il y en a cinq.
Combien de livres y a-t-il dans votre serviette?
   Il y en a sept.

as later on with such material as:

A quoi sert un pardessus?
   Il sert à nous protéger contre le froid.
A quoi sert un parapluie?
   Il sert à nous protéger contre la pluie.
A quoi servent les lunettes de soleil?
   Elles servent à nous protéger contre la lumière.

After the initial stages such writing up of the question and answer patterns will necessarily become selectively illustrative rather than exhaustive. But at all times their teaching function will be in direct accord with the aims and emphases of the main programme of work.

Learning to manipulate. As written exercises begin to demand the production of the response from the pupil, their testing function becomes more emphasized. But such exercises still have an essential teaching function in that, in so far as they operate within the learner's range of language competence, they require him to use and thereby reinforce language with which he is already familiar. Only when the level of demand exceeds his competence do written exercises begin to acquire more negative characteristics. The learner who begins to answer the question *Seit wann lernst du Deutsch? / Depuis quand apprenez-vous le français? / ¿Cuánto tiempo hace que aprendes el español?* by **Ich bin lernen / *J'ai appris / *He estado aprendiendo . . .* is practising incorrect language: for him the exercise fails to teach in any positive sense. What is needed is teaching or further guided practice of the structure, not further practice of an incorrect form.

The stuff of such exercises will vary considerably in accordance with aims. Initially there might be a bringing together of critical language elements relating to personal details, home, family, etc., under the heading *Moi, Ma famille, Ma maison*, copied, with the necessary individual adjustments, from the blackboard, with or without the key question forms which were the basis of its patterns. To consolidate the third person pronoun and verb forms, and possessive adjectives, this text, after any necessary correction, could act as a basis for a short description of *Mon ami*.

Learning to create. This approach will be maintained as the work develops: so, for example, in the presentation of the past tense (which in French involves problems of choice of auxiliary and past participle agreements, in German auxiliary and word order, in Spanish selection of preterite or perfect, in Russian perfective or imperfective aspects) all the relevant features will have been shown in written form by putting on the blackboard some or all of the actual sentences used in oral presentation. These can then be rubbed out, and the pupils asked to write them again on the board, with appropriate help from the teacher, either as separate examples or as a complete narrative, for public correction if necessary in the class before the individual pupils write them in their work-books. This final version can be copied, or reconstructed on the basis of answers to key oral or written questions.

Guided composition at a later stage will involve a difference in range rather than principle: meaningful written practice of language requires that pupils already possess the elements and organizing ideas to be exercised; these they will then be able to formulate in a way appropriate to more or less specific stimuli.

First attempts at letter writing will serve as an illustration. However brief, a letter requires certain conventions, e.g. *Mon cher Paul, Liebe Mutti und Lieber Vati, Muy señor mío.* The elements of language which need to be combined in a particular way will have been learned already. Pupils are now required to recast these elements into a form appropriate to the particular letter (Thank you for . . . I am glad/sorry to hear that . . . When are you coming . . .? My regards to . . . I hope that . . . Please send me . . .).

After exposure of this sort to the language of letters, the learner will be capable of writing letters freely. He will be able to combine familiar elements of language in a manner appropriate to a specific context.

PATTERN PRACTICE AND MATCHING EXERCISES

There are several forms of this exercise; essentially they are all intended to restrict the range of appropriate responses from which elements may be combined. Thus all the possible elements are given, comprehension is assumed and there is little puzzling over the forms of individual words. This allows the learner to focus on deciding which elements may be meaningfully combined. These exercises offer a useful way of reinforcing a particular pattern of language in visual and written form. Ideally they should be based on a prior context, established through textual materials, oral narratives, picture series or events (connected with the learner's own experiences) – either real or imaginary. Otherwise there exists the real danger that, although the aim is to reinforce forms within contexts, these contexts can easily become so superficial and unrelated to the experiences and interests of the learners that they are empty of meaning.

Learners might be asked, for instance, to construct as many sentences as possible from the following chart, using four units – one from each block – for each sentence.

Gestern nachmittag	habe ich	ein neues Haus	gesucht
Letztes Jahr	hat Christoph	einen Sportwagen	gekauft
Vor einem Monat	haben Petra und Johann	eine Kamera	gewählt

e.g. *Letztes Jahr haben Petra und Johann ein neues Haus gesucht.* This pattern chart is virtually learner proof; it almost guarantees correct formulations. Indeed, its very predictability is probably its greatest weakness. The production of sentences becomes automatic, similar to balancing an algebraic formula, except that when who did what becomes insignificant. The end product looks like language but has lost significant meaning for the user.

The next example is essentially different. Learners are asked to match the elements in accordance with a context already established. They practise in written form patterns already established orally and because there is a consensus as to what took place selection of the correct elements is essential to both meaning and form.

Quand vous êtes entré	*je*	*travaillais.*
		lançais une orange à la tête de. . . .
A ce moment-là	*nous*	*cherchions nos livres.*
		finissions nos devoirs.
		dormais tranquillement.

EXPANSION EXERCISES

In these exercises pupils are given a basic statement which they are encouraged by judicious questioning to expand into a fully developed sentence. Thus, starting with

Jean est allé au cinéma

the teacher asks such questions as:

Quand est-il allé au cinéma?
Avec qui est-il allé au cinéma?
Comment s'appelle le cinéma auquel il est allé?
Où se trouvait le cinéma auquel il est allé?

to lead to the production of such a sentence as

Jeudi passé Jean Lemaire est allé avec son amie Marie-Claire au cinéma Rex, qui se trouve dans la rue de Lyon.

This type of exercise is particularly suited to written work, as it allows the thinking time necessary to originality – even within a restricted area of content and structure. Moreover, it can form a useful step forward from the specificity of content and structure required, for example, in answering questions on a text, to the openness of free composition. The teacher, using carefully sequenced questions, can control the guided but creative use in meaningful contexts of elements and structures already known to the learners.

The accumulation of a stock of these structures will in time make free composition possible.

A further advantage of this type of exercise is that the question forms prompt patterns of language without reference to the mother-tongue.

EXERCISES BASED ON A WRITTEN TEXT

Three levels of question, each with a slightly different function, can be used with printed texts:

(a) those which elicit answers lifted unchanged from the text;

(b) those which require alterations or reordering of the language of the original text; and

(c) those which require language not used in the text.

The three categories are illustrated below in relation to this text:

Après avoir bu son café et remis son journal dans sa serviette Mercier est sorti du restaurant. En route pour la gare il a remarqué le voleur qu'il recherchait: il travaillait dans une station-service. Mercier s'est caché derrière un arbre et a sorti son appareil de sa serviette. Agent secret depuis deux ans, il était expert en photographie.

(a) Answers lifted from the text

1. *Qu'est-ce que Mercier a remis dans sa serviette?*
2. *Où le voleur travaillait-il?*
3. *Depuis combien de temps est-ce que Mercier était agent secret?*

Written questions of this sort test comprehension and the ability to select the appropriate piece of the text and transcribe it correctly.

(b) Answers requiring manipulation of language elements

1. *Qu'est-ce que Mercier avait fait dans le restaurant?*
2. *Qu'est-ce qu'il avait fait de son journal avant de quitter le restaurant?*
3. *Pourquoi est-ce qu'il s'est caché derrière l'arbre?*

Such questions test comprehension, the ability to recast given material into an answer form appropriate to the form of the question, and to write it accurately.

Question 2 illustrates certain aspects of marking exercises. Possible answers will include:

Il avait remis son journal dans sa serviette (correct but artificial)
*Il le avait remis dans sa serviette⎫
*Il l'avait remise dans sa serviette⎭(natural but containing error)

The marking scheme should give credit to the pupil who successfully handles the critical features of the exercise (in this case the tense of *remettre*, which in all three examples is correct), while not at this moment overstressing errors not of central concern. The teacher will also want to reward enterprising attempts to use natural language – in this case the replacement of noun by pronoun, and the opportunity will be taken to encourage this. So a testing exercise becomes a springboard into further teaching examples.

(c) Answers requiring language not used in text

1. *Qu'est-ce qu'on fait dans une station-service?*
2. *A quoi sert un appareil photographique?*
3. *Qu'est-ce qu'un agent secret?*

Questions such as these test not only comprehension – including implicit meaning, but also the learner's possession of the necessary elements of language and his ability to formulate them in a manner appropriate to the question and to write them accurately. They require, therefore, considerably more than questions of type a and b and quickly become counterproductive if they demand the use of language unfamiliar to the learner.

Questions based on oral narratives

The three types of question just listed may also be based on oral narratives. This demands more of the learner, since he has no access to the written form to check spellings, genders, word groupings and punctuation.

Both written texts and oral narratives provide bases for a more exacting type of writing in response to stimuli of the *'Qu'est-ce qui se passe?'* or *'Racontez'* type. Learners may either be left to their own devices, or memories may be helped and structures prompted by a few leading questions, e.g.

Quelle est la première chose que Mercier a faite?
Qu'est-ce qu'il y avait dans sa serviette?

EXERCISES BASED ON VISUAL MATERIALS

Visual materials provide an excellent basis for exercises derived from content areas outside the classroom. Unless accompanied by short descriptive texts they make considerable demands on the learner, since he has to produce the necessary language from memory without direct access to its written form.

It is, of course, essential for the teacher to ensure that all agree about the meaning intended to be conveyed by the pictures being used.

Single pictures. Depending on their composition, pictures clearly provide opportunity to practise and test aspects of place, descriptions of persons and things, people's actions, etc. They also offer a sound basis for contrastive tense work: while the picture is exposed to the learner the tense normally used is the present (in Spanish, the present continuous); in a complex picture certain states exist – people have already done certain things, some are involved in doing, others are about to do, or will do, other things. One person may act as a focus for a range of tense usages. Imagine a lady standing at a bus-stop with her basket on the ground beside her. The following questions are immediately appropriate:

Que fait la dame? | Was macht die Frau im Augenblick?
Où est-ce qu'elle a posé le panier? | Was hat sie mit dem Korb gemacht?
Qu'est-ce qu'elle va faire quand l'autobus viendra? | Was wird sie tun, wenn der Bus kommt?

The range of tense coverage can be further increased, once the content is clear, by removing the picture. Appropriate questions are now in the imperfect and pluperfect:

Qu'est-ce qu'elle avait fait de son panier?
Qu'est-ce qu'elle faisait sur le trottoir?

Such situations usually can lead to the eliciting of causal relations:

Pourquoi est-ce qu'elle avait mis son panier par terre?

If several characters are included, it becomes possible to ask defining questions requiring the use of relative clauses or expressions of comparison.

All questions will force the learner to produce patterns of language from within himself. These may be at an elementary level –

> *Combien de personnes y a-t-il? | ¿Cuántas personas hay?*
> *Le garçon, qu'est-ce qu'il achète? | ¿Qué está comprando el chico?*

or of a more advanced, structure-specific type:

> *Qu'est-ce que l'agent de police vient de faire?*
> *Qu'est-ce que le jeune homme vient de saisir?*

or of a less controlled, more open type:

> *Décrivez l'image | Vergleichen Sie die zwei Damen!*

In this last case leading questions may be given, around which the learner is required to organize his written description. But to a great extent the learner will need to rely on those elements which he has mastered.

Picture series. Picture series depicting a sequence of events are susceptible to treatment similar to the single picture. They also provide useful stimuli for the sequencing of events based on adverbs of time, conjunctions, and so forth, e.g.

> *Zu Beginn der Geschichte . . . Dann gehen sie . . . Nachdem sie . . .*
> *besucht hatten, . . . Schließlich fuhren sie nach Hause.*

Because the actions are connected, causal links are also available to the willing learner:

> *Comme ils avaient déjà vu le film, ils ne voulaient pas . . .*
> *Weil sie den Film schon gesehen hatten, wollten sie nicht . . .*

Picture series do allow a very wide range of response – sometimes rather too wide from the marker's point of view: precisely because of the potential complexity of the language many learners operate at a minimal level but almost without error, whereas other more ambitious learners attempt far more difficult structures with, in many cases, a considerably higher incidence of error. This situation is further aggravated by the attraction of the present tense for the weaker learner, while the stronger pupil tends to incur more penalties through operating in the past tense. Clear instructions about the tense or tenses to be used should always be given, with the learner knowing precisely whether he is expected to describe the pictures or tell the story suggested by them.

FORM-CHANGING EXERCISES

Such exercises may be of various kinds. Pupils may be asked to replace an infinitive by another verb form, to substitute a pronoun for a phrase, alter a case, change a main clause into a subordinate one, an affirmative statement into a negative one, an active into a passive sentence, and so forth.

In many of these exercises the visible stimulus sentence itself presents incorrect forms of the language, e.g.

Les jours de fête, on (pouvons, peuvent, peut) voir des danses basques.
La muchacha (estar Imp.) en la cocina.
Der Mann (halten) (der Bleistift).
Er (geben) es (ich).

Moreover, the student tends to further reinforce the incorrect form by uttering it, either aloud or subvocally. It might be argued that the learner benefits so much from consciously choosing correct forms that the original exposure to incorrect forms does not matter. But any reinforcement of the correct pattern is obtained at a high price – the continuous and cumulative use of meaningless language. The examples arise from no real situation – they are basically unimportant; they are presented not with a view to giving information but in order to be promptly changed for something else. Form is emphasized to the detriment and even the neglect of meaning. They may provide practice for the working out of grammatical rules, but they imply the production of language as rule-bound forms rather than as meaning expressed spontaneously through form. When worked with reference to formal grammatical summaries and tables, such exercises often involve pupils in a process of looking up, writing down, and forgetting. The patterns did not exist within them before the exercise, whence the need to refer, and the actual form is produced by short-term reference to a page of grammatical rules rather than prompted from within.

Such an exercise can, however, be legitimate when it amounts to a fresh formulation of the original sentence. Thus to ask a pupil to express a given idea in a different way without significantly altering the meaning is quite different from asking him to negate, refute, or change arbitrarily the meaning of a sentence. Paraphrasing or the reformulation into indirect speech of an oral narrative told originally in direct speech are of a different order: they stem from merely different perspectives and illustrate, therefore, alternative possibilities of expression. Thus the two forms, the original and the form used in the pupil's answer, remain secondary to the primacy of the idea, e.g.

Ich esse gern Äpfel.
(*Äpfel schmecken mir.*)
Nach langem Warten haben wir endlich Eintrittskarten bekommen können.
(*Nach langem Warten ist es uns endlich gelungen, Eintrittskarten zu bekommen.*)

A son arrivée il a trouvé la ville déserte.
(*Lorsqu'il est arrivé il n'y avait personne dans la ville.*)

– Lo he visto todo, dijo Roberto.
(*Roberto dijo que lo había visto todo.*)

COMPLETION EXERCISES

There are two quite different types of completion exercise:

1. *Ein Bäcker ist ein Mann, der. . . .*
   Le boulanger est un homme qui. . . .

The first part of a basic pattern is given; the learner is then asked to complete it. This assumes a thorough familiarity with the total pattern. The first part of the sentence should trigger off the second part, to which it is functionally related. The learner should not need to suspend concern for the total meaning of the unit while struggling to find the correct form.

Either the correct pattern is suggested readily from within, leaving the learner to concentrate on writing the known form accurately, or the meaning of the unit is overshadowed by emphasis on the form, which he is obliged to seek by referring to rules or paradigms concerning relative pronouns. The exercise has point only if the given part of the sentence prompts a form already present in the learner, a form which would be equally readily produced by the question *Was ist ein Bäcker? / Qu'est-ce qu'un boulanger?*

2. A different type of completion exercise is of this nature:

– großzügig – Tante gibt – klein – Jung – ein – Apfel.
Les enfants grimp . . . à l'arbre.

In filling the gaps the learner's attention is focused on form to the point where meaning is secondary, even trivial. Only by hypothesizing the missing forms can one arrive at a point where meaning becomes clear. Real language does not function in this way – intended meaning indicates the form or forms of expression available, not vice versa. Cumulatively such exercises can become conundrums militating against an intuitive feel for the language instead of promoting it. Moreover, this type of exercise often contains ambiguity – e.g. are the forms intended to be singular or plural (*dem kleinen Jungen or den kleinen Jungen?*), accusative or dative (*in das* [*sein* / *ein?*] *alte*[*s*] *Münster* or *in dem* [*seinem* / *einem?*] *alten Münster?*).

If visual reinforcement is to be employed positively, such exercises are best avoided. Exercises in language should aim to present language as a patterned phenomenon, not as a series of dismembered and imperfect pieces.

DICTATION

Dictation is basically concerned with recording or testing and has only incidental teaching value. It has more point in those languages where because of redundancy in the written form the same sound can be represented in several ways with differences in meaning.

Thus, whereas in German and Spanish dictation is largely a matter of writing down symbols which correspond unambiguously with the sounds heard, in French a good deal more is involved.

In order to write the language accurately the learner must have some knowledge of the patterning of the language, which will enable him to group sounds meaningfully and ensure that redundant written elements (unpronounced adjective agreements, plural markers, verb forms) are duly marked down. Ideally the concern with form should still be subordinate to awareness of meaning, and in dictation there is a danger that content is only important in so far as it permits the student to produce the correct form. This can lead to learners becoming more alert to the 'tricks' of transcription than to the meaning of the language dictated: language then becomes impersonal and irrelevant to the learner.

Dictation need not be restricted to the typical examination format which samples a whole range of language. It can be more usefully restricted to the recording, practising and testing of work recently done, which is therefore more meaningful to the learner. Unless the passage has meaning for the pupils and is related to their main course work, dictation can be a sterile written exercise.

Nor need the passage be dealt with according to the full ritual of reading and re-reading, in units and sub-units. If pupils are familiar with the material, then one or two readings at a speed which enables them to mark down accurately what they hear should suffice. Thorough and systematic writing up of work covered orally will give more meaningful practice than passages which are full of traps for the unwary.

TRANSLATION

Translation from English into the foreign language is essentially a testing device, although it is often used as a teaching method in foreign-language learning. It emphasizes mother-tongue usage at precisely the point where interference should be reduced to a minimum in order to allow a feel for the language to develop. It can easily lead the learner to view the foreign language as merely an optional way of expressing ideas conceived in the mother-tongue; in time it will seem not merely optional, but inferior as a means of expression.

Because the starting-point is the mother-tongue, it is highly likely that interference will occur, and the less the learner knows of the foreign language the more serious the interference will be (*Il donne Jean le livre*). Because the meaning is already given, the learner has to concentrate on form (gender, tense, agreements), so that language becomes not a means of saying something interesting, but a series of puzzles to be solved. Because translation requires the learner to select from among several possible ways of expressing an idea in a foreign language, and he usually has few alternatives within himself, he is forced into relying on, and learning, a series of mechanical word for word equivalences (*Papa nous a pris à Paris. *Nous sommes allés à les magasins*). These will be a hindrance to later learning.

Practical considerations

1. Since it is common for written work to be done at home, it is important that students have some form of reference material available to them. Some teachers may take this to imply paradigms and rule formulations, but it is more consistent with the sort of work

advocated here for the learners to build up in their work-books a stock of examples of the language uses they have learned, and to be encouraged to use this stock when it is appropriate.

2. If exercises have been properly prepared and pupils know precisely what is required of them, the amount of error to be corrected should not be great, and pupils will not experience the discouragement of finding their work submerged in red ink. It is worth considering whether when correcting an exercise dealing with a particular grammatical feature it is to everyone's interest (the pupil's since he wants to learn; the teacher's, since he needs to diagnose errors) to distinguish between the errors critical in **this** exercise and other mistakes.

3. There is a need to see that over the course the learner is exposed to **all** the forms he will need to use (persons of the verb, interrogation forms, word order) and not just a few which it is convenient to practise.

4. Revision in the form of planned re-use of the learned material should be incorporated into the ongoing programme.

Conclusion

Certain basic themes have recurred throughout this chapter; they can be summed up in the positive rejection of exercises as ready made devices which the teacher simply picks off the page and administers. If written work is to help the learner to progress in the foreign language, it will be work which the teacher himself devises, which has meaning and interest for the learner, strikes a happy balance between excessive difficulty and enervating easiness, and allows the learner the amount of freedom appropriate to his level. But, above all, it will arise from the whole language-learning programme of the class, and will be an integral part of that programme.

Given this, it may yet be possible to reverse John Storm's statement, quoted over fifty years ago by Harold Palmer: 'The worst and most unfruitful torment in the school instruction of the present time is the excessive use of exercises in foreign languages'.[2]

References

1. BENNETT, W. A. (1969) *Aspects of Language and Language Teaching*. Cambridge University Press.
2. PALMER, H. E. (1921) *The Oral Method of Teaching Languages*. Cambridge: Heffer.

DAVID SMITH

Leicestershire Education Department

Prose translation

Introduction

Translation into the language has been the basis of teaching modern languages ever since they made their appearance in school curricula. Since it had been the mainstay of the teaching of Greek and Latin, its continuance into modern language teaching was thought quite logical. In fact, of course, it was not, because modern languages, which develop and change, and which continuously renew their idiom and their literature, provide a patently different study from that of the dead languages.

Since about 1960 there has been an increasing ground-swell against the teaching of prose translation, and against its appearing in the O-level examination. At present (1974) it is possible to avoid the prose translation in the O-level examination of almost all the boards, and there is every indication that it will soon disappear from some A-level syllabuses. Several universities already exclude it from their first-year undergraduate course. The arguments against the prose are concerned less with the examination test as such than with its back-wash effect on teaching techniques. As a test, it provides a fairly objective means of assessment, in fact. As a teaching technique, continual translation into the foreign language is almost totally self-defeating.

The reasons for this are many and have been frequently rehearsed elsewhere.[1] The most important of them is that adequate translation into a language is very difficult unless the translator has such a corpus of accurate foreign language at his disposal that his fluent production of the accurate idiom of the language will not be hindered by the intrusion of the mother-tongue idiom. To give only one example, continual cross-reference between French and English is unlikely to produce *Il fallait le dire* as a translation of *You should have told me*.

This translation of the English is not 'difficult'. A person who has said the French often would not say anything else – the words would be ringing in his ears, and he would produce them as an accurate, ready-made phrase. He probably would **not** do so, however, if the phrase had merely been memorized from a list of 'useful' phrases.

The same is true of those more frequent uses of language which are involved in the making of 'novel and appropriate responses' – a student who has the linguistic set patterns of French firmly in his head will tend not to deform those sets by Anglicisms. No amount of translation practice will ever establish idiomatic forms such as *Eh bien, oui alors là tu vois.* The establishment of the foreign-language 'sets' is the major task of the foreign-language teacher, and other contributors describe ways in which the objective can be achieved. The use of translation does not figure amongst them.

In brief, it is increasingly accepted that the best way to prepare pupils for prose translation is **not** by means of teaching via translation from the first.

An increasing number of teachers do not require prose translation of their pupils until **after O level**, and they often claim a feeling of considerable liberation when the exercise is no longer required. However, some will continue to want to submit candidates for this particular test at O level. Even in the latter case, there is no reason to begin translation from English until the beginning of the O-level year. Otherwise the end of the first-year sixth is quite early enough to begin prose translation.

To leave the exercise so late may require some courage on the part of the teacher – he should console himself with the knowledge that every postponement of this exercise, and thus every postponement of the intrusion of English into his scarce lesson time, increases directly the amount of time he has available for the active use of the foreign language itself. This, ultimately, is bound to help in the accuracy of translations eventually attempted.

At whatever stage – post or pre O level – prose translation is begun, it involves the teaching of a new skill, and it can be taught only as a development of the work which has gone before. That is, it can logically involve only those items of language taught before, and can be approached only through imaginative modification of techniques previously acquired.

What are the problems in doing a prose?

These can be summarized under three headings.

1. The language and concepts of the passage to be translated must be understood. For what follows it must be assumed that this is the case.

2. The relevant lexical and non-lexical items (the vocabulary and grammar) of the foreign language must be known – that is, the pupil must be able to produce them for himself and not merely recognize them. He must also be aware of the various registers of language, so that he does not produce items of the foreign language which, although semantically fairly accurate, are stylistically inappropriate to the context – *gâcher* belongs to a different register from *abîmer*, for instance (see in passage C below).

3. The pupil must be aware of the 'framework' of the foreign language to the extent that he is able to see it in sense units which may bear no word for word equivalence to the mother-tongue. As crude examples of this he will need to remember such things as the position of adjectives in French, or of the past participle in German. At a more sophisticated level he needs to be prepared to reshape the mother-tongue original to fit the thought processes of speakers of the foreign language.

Compare, for instance, this English sentence and the translation which follows it.

> *Even if you knew the Charnwood Forest as well as I do, I should nevertheless have great difficulty in conveying to you the peculiar charm I find in the place.*

> *Vous auriez beau connaître la Forêt de Charnwood aussi bien que moi, je n'en aurais pas moins beaucoup de peine à vous faire comprendre ce que j'y trouve de délicieux.*

The French is the result of a quite different line of thought from that which produced the English. An alternative and quite acceptable translation would be this:

> *Même si tu connaissais la Forêt de Charnwood tout aussi bien que moi, je ne saurais tout de même pas t'expliquer ce qui m'y plaît tellement.*

This version is in a quite different register, and pupils need to realize that the two translations are not, therefore, equivalent. And even though the second translation is closer to the shape of the English original, it nevertheless differs from it enough to make word for word translation unthinkable.

Towards the prose

If prose translation is begun no earlier than the O-level year, the pupil will 'be able, within everyday contexts, to understand, in the spoken and written form, instructions and inquiries, accounts of past events and present activities, and statements about future plans and conditional possibilities. He should be able to answer, within these various contexts, questions which demand more than understanding: to express an appropriate "productive" response, for which the facts may be found in or concluded from the text; for which the question will provide a significant cue; but the construction of which will depend on a mastery of the patterns involved. He will be able to use the language, in speech and in writing, to give spontaneous, non-responsive accounts similar to, but less complex than, those he is expected to understand'.[2]

The following exercises might be expected to be familiar: oral and written questions and answers based on heard and seen stimuli; guided composition, from pictures and from a proposed topic; *Nacherzählung*; and these exercises can be built on for purposes of the prose.

The prose requires a mental adjustment on the part of the pupil, since the conveying of English thoughts directly into the target language (henceforth called 'French') may have been strenuously discouraged so far. The adjustment should be gradual.

1. As a first step, therefore, the following exercise might be practised.

A passage is given in French, with certain phrases underlined. Pupils are required to replace these phrases with alternatives which give as nearly as possible the same sense. The exercise can be begun and the proffered versions can be discussed in class, with the teacher asking prompting questions, and with the class rejecting unsuitable ideas offered by pupils. Discussion can be largely in French, and might lead in the lower sixth to elementary discussions of style and register. After adequate class discussion, pupils write out the complete passage – perhaps for homework – with the appropriate alternative phrases inserted.

This exercise Roy Dunning has called 'internal translation'.[3] Internal translation depends upon *the ability of the learner to produce alternatives* from within his body of acquired knowledge, and requiring pupils to do this is a vital part of the teaching process. It results from continually asking questions such as these: *Dites-moi, qu'est-ce que cela veut dire, 'Il a un frère dans l'automobile'? Cela veut dire que son frère travaille dans une usine où l'on fabrique des voitures.* Or more simply perhaps: *Dites, qu'est-ce que c'est qu'un tire-bouchon? – C'est une sorte de vis en métal qui sert à tirer le bouchon d'une bouteille.* Mr Dunning's own example makes clear how internal translation can be encouraged. (Remember that his example forms part of a specimen test paper, and that it would be adapted for class use.)

> ***En sortant** du Rex, Jeanne a découvert que sa caméra **neuve avait disparu de sa voiture qui se trouvait en stationnement non loin** du cinéma. Elle avait non seulement oublié **la présence de la caméra** dans la voiture, elle avait même **laissé la voiture ouverte,*** etc.

Internally translated, such a passage might become something like this:

> *Lorsqu'elle est sortie du Rex, Jeanne a découvert que la caméra qu'elle venait d'acheter n'était plus dans sa voiture, qu'elle avait laissée garée près du cinéma. Elle avait non seulement oublié que la caméra était dans la voiture, mais elle avait même quitté sa voiture sans la fermer à clef,* etc.

2. Paraphrase in the language is a good way into another form of internal translation, since it involves the production of an original text closely modelled on a well-absorbed original. Class work may lead to a skeleton framework of main points and main linguistic items to be included and the exercise can be written up for homework. All discussion should be, of course, in the foreign language. An excellent discussion of paraphrase as an exercise appears in M. J. C. Holland's contribution to the Schools Council Working Paper 28.[4]

3. This close absorption of an original model is the key to success

in the early stages of prose teaching. The work of the first four or five years will have involved intensive question and answer work orally and in writing, based on texts, with emphasis laid particularly on new patterns and idioms. After such work the texts or portions of them could be used as material for **translation into English**. If an agreed model English version is produced, based on pupils' work, this will provide the basis for a class retranslation into French – with the original French out of sight, of course. The final agreed version may be different in some respects from the original French text, with which it can sometimes be profitably compared. At first the texts for translation should be short – perhaps two brief paragraphs only. The translation into **English** may well be the pupils' first encounter with such an exercise. If so, they will not find it easy to search for the most accurate, idiomatic forms of English. This stage should not be rushed; it provides practice in linguistic selection and rejection of a similar order to that presented by the prose.

In the sixth form an added dimension is given to this exercise if the French *assistant* is invited to suggest variations to the French offered by pupils. It is sometimes an advantage if he has not seen the original French text. Again, such interventions can lead to varying degrees of discussion on style and register.

4. A development of the above exercise is to use the original French text for the usual range of exercises, and then to ask the pupils to translate into French a **ready prepared English version**, produced by the teacher and modelled on the original, but shorter than it. This exercise is marginally harder than exercise 3 above, since the English version will have a different range of constructions from the original, of which it is a modification. Such English versions should not be intentionally crammed with difficulties.

Since the late approach to prose translation postulated here involves the learning of a fairly complex new skill, it is essential to proceed by easy steps, and not to discourage pupils needlessly.

5. At sixth form level an exercise which can be interesting and useful is the **comparison of 'parallel texts'**. The careful examination of a French original and of an accurate English version of it helps with the building up of the pupil's appreciation of the 'framework' of the foreign language discussed earlier. Sources of such parallel texts include commercially available translations of French novels and short stories, the Penguin Parallel Texts series, and, at a very advanced level, works such as *Essays in Translation from French* (by

R. L. G. Ritchie and C. I. Simons, published by Cambridge University Press). Added interest accrues if two different translations are available for comparison: this is true, for instance, of certain Maigret stories.

6. An additional source of English texts for translation is the **language essays of pupils**. Generally the practice is for a class to write essays on one proposed theme. From these the teacher can produce a composite version, which he then puts into English; this becomes the passage to be translated. Again, the range of ideas and idiom is not new to pupils, and the exercise should move fairly smoothly. This is particularly the case if the essays have been prepared in class by means of close study of original texts treating similar themes.

7. Eventually the teacher will feel the need to move on to **translation** 'from cold', not based directly on other material. There is no logical reason to want to do so very quickly. Provided the proses produced as the result of exercises 2–6 above are accurate and idiomatic, adequate progress is being made – it is far more important at all stages of language learning and in all types of exercise for pupils to experience success and to make continuous progress than for them to be confronted continually with the 'real thing', which may be beyond their capacity.

The first translations based on totally fresh topics need to be fairly short and the language content needs to be familiar. New linguistic material is best encountered in reading or provoked in discussion by the teacher rather than in the course of a prose translation, for unknown material cannot be recalled from past language experience – **and it is on such recall that success in prose translation depends**.

Experienced teachers will realize the importance of including in the texts selected, from an early stage, examples of those 'tricks' which are in fact peculiar differences between the mother-tongue and the foreign language – inversion of the verb in German, and after speech in French, mute 'e' and 'es' in French, and so on. These will already have been encountered continually in texts, but the prose translation gives a chance to systematize possibly random observations. In the production of agreed class translations, it is useful to ask **pupils** to write the material offered on to the blackboard; this allows the teacher to spot mistakes early and to ask for correction from the pupils.

Summary

To approach foreign-language teaching predominantly through translation techniques is to misunderstand both the nature of language acquisition (see Belyayev[5] for a discussion of this point) and what is involved in translation into another language.

Translation into the language should be seen as only one aspect of the learning process, and prose translation as a formal exercise should be seen as intimately linked with several other types of exercise, which can directly enhance its interest and its accuracy. The problems created by teaching prose translation have sometimes led to excessively vehement reaction against it. It is, in fact, a skill which can be successfully taught provided it is seen in its right perspective.

What follows is a small practical example. It is a record of a piece of work conducted by this contributor, at Lutterworth Upper School, in December 1973, with a lower sixth form group. The group had previously **never** translated a continuous text into English (they had been asked occasionally 'What does that phrase (or sentence) mean?'), and had never done any translation into French apart from occasional isolated phrases. The **alternatives** produced in the final version C are important. They highlight the quite crucial role played in the pupils' teaching so far of the provision of **explanations in French** of other words and phrases encountered in texts – they are, in fact, examples of 'internal translations'.

Passage A is a portion of a chapter previously studied and used for a variety of exercises [6] Passage B is the 'agreed' English version worked out in class. Passage C represents the retranslation done communally.

PASSAGE A

Ils n'ont pas envie de se promener dans les rues de Bondy le soir, par exemple pour prendre un verre dans un café.

'Nous sommes allés voir les feux d'artifice un 14 juillet,' raconte Simone Doublot. Et elle ajoute, comme si elle évoquait un mauvais souvenir: 'Mais j'ai pris froid.' Un autre jour, ils sont allés assister à l'arrivée du Tour de France au Parc des Princes. Ils mentionnent l'événement.

Maintenant que Simone a cessé de travailler comme concierge dans leur HLM, les heures supplémentaires du samedi matin, payées à

50 pour cent de plus que le taux normal, ont pris une grande importance.
Mais ce sixième jour de travail détruit le week-end.

PASSAGE B

They have no wish to walk about the streets of Bondy in the even-
ings – to go for a drink in a bar for example. 'We once went to see a
firework display on the 14 July,' Simone Doublot tells. And she
adds, as if recalling an unpleasant experience, 'but I caught a cold'.
Another day, they went to see the finish of the Tour de France at the
Parc des Princes. They talk about this as though it were an exceptional
event.

Now that Simone has given up her job as caretaker in their block of
flats, the overtime that Pierre puts in on a Saturday morning, and
which is paid at time and a half, has assumed great importance. But
having to work an extra day ruins the weekend.

PASSAGE C

Ils ne veulent pas | n'ont pas envie de se promener dans les rues de
Bondy le soir pour boire | prendre un verre dans un bar | bistrot, par
exemple. 'Une fois, nous sommes allés voir les feux d'artifice le | un
quatorze juillet,' dit | raconte Simone Doublot. Et elle ajoute, comme
si elle évoquait | se souvenait d' | se rappelait une mauvaise expérience –
'Mais j'ai pris froid | attrapé un rhume | je me suis enrhumée'. Un autre
jour, ils sont allés assister à | voir la fin | l'arrivée du Tour de France au
Parc des Princes. Ils parlent de cela comme si c'était un événement
exceptionnel. | Ils mentionnent l'événement.

Maintenant que Simone a cessé | fini son travail | s'est arrêtée de
travailler comme concierge dans leur HLM, les heures supplémentaires
que Pierre travaille le samedi matin, et qui sont payées à 50 pour cent de
plus que le taux | tarif normal, ont pris une grande importance | sont
devenues très importantes. Mais ce sixième jour de travail | mais
travailler un sixième jour | mais ayant à travailler un sixième jour
détruit | abîme | gâte | gâche le week-end.

It will be seen that passage C is different in some respects from
passage A, to which, however, it bears a very strong resemblance. The
level of language accurately produced in this **first ever** set translation
seems to be at least as high as would have been expected under any
other teaching system during the first term of the lower sixth form
year.

Notes and references

1. For instance, in the pamphlet *Modern Language Courses in the Sixth Form*, issued by the Modern Language Association in 1968.
2. HILL, N. in RUSSELL, C. V. (ed.) (1970) *Post O-level Studies in Modern Languages*, pp. 27–8. Oxford: Pergamon. Mr Hill's chapter in this book gives interesting guide-lines for the transition from O level to Advanced studies.
3. DUNNING, R. in Appendix F of Schools Council Working Paper 28, *New Patterns in Sixth Form Modern Language Studies*, pp. 77–81. London: Evans/Methuen Educational, 1970.
4. HOLLAND, M. J. C., op. cit. in 3, pp. 63–73.
5. BELYAYEV, B. J. (1963) *The Psychology of Teaching Foreign Languages*. Oxford: Pergamon.
6. From BAVER, C., BARTON, M. D. and O'CONNOR, P. (1964) *Lire, parler et écrire,* p. 244. New York: Holt, Rinehart & Winston.

PART 10

Sixth form work

The chapters in this section contain a lot of suggestions which are necessarily tentative. It would be surprising if this were not so. There are so many differences of opinion about method and content – Which language do we use? What kind of language do we read? – that it is fair to say that there is no fixed concept of what sixth form language teaching is, but simply a lot of individual conceptions.

The danger in much sixth form work is that it is dominated by the study of literature *per se* and by preparation for A-level translation papers. In the first three chapters language teaching is not seen as preparation for translation but as a much more varied and sophisticated continuation of the kind of oral and written work which might legitimately have been done before the sixth form. There is no suggestion that the sixth-former is suddenly marvellously able to converse on a wide range of topics in the foreign language. The teacher is still the guide, offering models and even encouraging use of the mother-tongue when insistence on the foreign language would seriously inhibit discussion.

Helen Port and Michael Robinson both hope that reading a book will not be equated solely with the acquiring of accepted literary tenets. They want it to be an enriching language experience and a stimulation to personal thought. Reading a book in a foreign language should, they feel, contribute to sympathetic understanding both of the author and the people for whom he is writing. Neither underestimates the difficulty of this task either conceptually or linguistically.

The last two chapters touch on the vast area of non-A-level courses. They are concerned with the 'beginners' course' and the 'general studies course'. Neither writer is prepared to limit these courses to traditional translation and rule-learning activities; they describe here their personal attempts to vary the work and make it more appealing.

ALAN W. HORNSEY

University of London Institute of Education

The first lessons on a book

The following assumptions underlie these three lessons:

1. that the class has just entered the first-year sixth;
2. that the whole class has already reached O-level standard;
3. that some oral work has been done in the lower school;
4. that the linguistic and intellectual maturity of the class has not undergone a sudden metamorphosis in the few weeks since it was a fifth form;
5. that 'literature' and 'language' are not rigidly separated as though they were unconnected;
6. that the foreign language still deserves to have a leading role in the lesson, but that it is not necessarily the appropriate medium for personal discussion – of style or aesthetics, for example;
7. that these opening lessons will do a good deal of the spadework necessary if the class is to be able to progress to reading the book fluently.

The text is the first page of *Was dir nicht angehört,** a story by Manfred Hausmann, which has been popular with the examining boards as a prescribed text for A level. Each pupil will already be in possession of a text before the three lessons and they will have been asked to look through the first six sides – not to understand every detail but to get a rough idea of what the story is about.

Das Spiegelbild

Der Bus rauschte durch die Vororte, die sich, einer in den andern übergehend, nördlich von Bremen an der Unterweser entlangziehen: Vegesack, Aumund, Blumenthal, Rönnebeck. Von Zeit zu Zeit wirbelten novemberliche Böen durch die Straßen und trieben schräg ineinandergewehte Regenstreifen vor sich her. *Wenn sie auf den Bus trafen, klang es, als würde ein Eimer mit Erbsen gegen ihn geschüttet.*

* HAUSMANN, M. (1962) *Was dir nicht angehört*, p. 31. London: Harrap.

Da Meinert Nobis unmittelbar hinter dem Fahrer saß, konnte er durch die vordere Scheibe, die der hin und her schwingende Wischer von den strömenden und zuckenden Wassern frei hielt, beobachten, wie das Wetter den wenigen Menschen zusetzte, die sich auf die Straße gewagt hatten.* Er überlegte, auf welche Weise er die beiden Schallplatten, die er, wohlverpackt zwischen zwei Wellpappen, in seinen Händen hielt am sichersten von der Haltestelle durch den Regen nach Hause bringen könnte. Um die eine machte er sich nicht viel Gedanken, um diese Tanzplatte, die er für seine Mutter hatte besorgen müssen, seine Liebe galt vielmehr der anderen mit dem Allegro und dem Andante aus Johann Christian Bachs* Symphonie. Das beste würde sein, wenn er die Kapuze von seinem Anorak, den er vorige Woche zu seinem achtzehnten Geburtstag bekommen hatte, abknöpfte und das Paket hineinschöbe. Dann konnte der Regen den Platten nichts anhaben.* Jedesmal, wenn er daran dachte, daß er in einer Viertelstunde die langsam aus den Tiefen des Weltraums heraufhallende Schwermut der Oboen und die ziehende Süße* der Streicher hören sollte, fühlte er ein Kribbeln in seinen Zehen.

Notes

trieben schräg ineinandergewehte Regenstreifen vor sich her: 'drove ribbons of rain before them, blowing them obliquely across one another.'

die sich auf die Straße gewagt hatten: 'who had ventured abroad.'

Johann Christian Bach: the eleventh son of the famous composer, Johann Sebastian Bach, he was born in Leipzig in 1735 and died in London in 1782. He is generally known as 'the English Bach' because he spent the last quarter-century of his life in London as an opera and concert director; he was also music master to the family of George III. He wrote operas, symphonies and compositions for the harpsichord.

Dann konnte . . . anhaben: 'Then the rain could not harm the records'. The imperfect indicative (and not the imperfect subjunctive) is used to suggest that mentally this is already a *fait accompli*.

die ziehende Süße: 'the long drawn-out sweetness'. An inadequate rendering of *ziehend*, because the word is used here for the richness of its associations: (i) it describes the quality of the sound: *lang hinausgezogen*; (ii) it suggests movement: *ziehen* (page 41 of this text has 'die ziehende Wasserfläche'), attraction: *anziehen*, and pain: *ziehende Schmerzen*. Cf. the following examples from the author's works: '*die schmerzlich ziehende Süße eines Streich-quartetts*'; '*die ziehende schmerzliche Spannung . . . eines Rilkeschen Reimgefüges*': '*das ziehende Spiel des Lichts im grenzenlosen Himmelsraum*'.

(The question and answer exchanges in these lessons are obviously idealized, and teachers will recognize that there are points where more repetition will be necessary and where answers will have to be corrected: even sixth-formers make mistakes.)

First lesson

Teacher	Pupil
Wie heißt dieser Abschnitt des Buchs?	*Das Spiegelbild.*
Wo sieht man ein Spiegelbild?	*Im Spiegel.*
Wann benutzen Sie einen Spiegel?	*Wenn ich mir die Haare kämme / wenn ich mich schminke.*
Und Ihr Vater?	*Wenn er sich rasiert* (Jane).
Was benutzt Janes Vater, wenn er sich rasiert?	*Einen Spiegel.*
Nur einen Spiegel?	*Nein, ein Rasiermesser natürlich auch.*
Was sieht man eigentlich im Spiegel?	*Sich selbst.*
Ja, aber in meinem Wagen, z.B., habe ich einen Spiegel – einen Rückspiegel. Warum? Um mich selbst zu sehen?	*Nein, andere Wagen.*
Nur Wagen?	*Nein, Fahrräder auch.*
Ja, also den ganzen Verkehr. Hinter mir oder vor mir?	*Hinter Ihnen.*

This brief exchange serves the double purpose of emphasizing the role of the mirror, which is to be important later in the chapter, and of restricting the language so as not to discourage the new sixth-former.

Wo beginnt dieser Abschnitt des Buchs?	*In einem Bus.*
Wo ist der Bus?	*In Bremen.*
Tatsächlich! Oder in den Vororten?	*In den Vororten.*
Was ist ein Vorort?	(Silence)
Hier z.B. ist London (blackboard sketch) *und hier das Stadtzentrum und hier Wimbledon, Hampstead, Ilford usw. Sie sind alle Londoner Vororte.*	
Was ist Wimbledon?	*Ein (Londoner) Vorort.*
Und das? (pointing)	*Das Stadtzentrum.*

The teacher now produces a sketch of Bremen and district or, better still, photocopies of an actual map.

Was ist das?	*Bremen.*
Und das?	*Das Stadtzentrum.*
Und das ist Rönnebeck. Was ist das?	*Ein Vorort.*
Jawohl, ein Londoner oder ein Bremer?	*Ein Bremer.*
Und wo liegt Bremen? an welchem Fluß? im Norden oder im Süden?	

A short comparative weather table – sun, rain, temperature – can now be used to compare Bremen, Rome, London, Newcastle, Glasgow. The location of Bremen and the weather conditions prevailing there in November are all relevant to the rest of the story.

Beschreiben Sie den Anfang der Geschichte!	*Ein Bus fuhr durch Bremer Vororte. Es regnete.*
Und die Jahreszeit? Frühling?	*Nein, Herbst.*
Woher wissen Sie das?	*Aus dem Wort 'novemberliche'.*
Ja, also wann genau im Herbst?	*Im November.*
Wissen Sie, was eine Bö ist?	*Nein.*
Eine Bö ist ein leichter Windstoß. Wie war das Wetter?	*Es regnete.*
Und?	*Es war windig.*
Und deswegen fiel der Regen schräg.	

A blackboard sketch is called for:

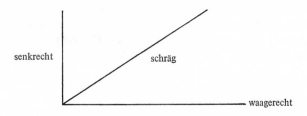

Wenn man unter dem Dach eines Gebäudes wohnt, dann hat das Zimmer oft schräge Wände:

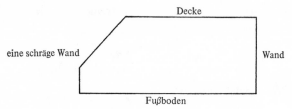

Warum fiel der Regen schräg?   *Weil es windig war.*
Oder wegen . . .?   *Wegen des Winds.*
Und warum waren die Straßen
  naß? Wegen?   *Wegen des Regens.*
Und warum ist es heute so kalt in   *Wegen des schlechten Wetters,*
  der Schule?   *wegen des Kohlenmangels,*
                      wegen der Energiekrise, usw.

The last part of the lesson is then conducted in English. A comparison could first be made between the bald facts of the story, *der Bus fuhr durch die Bremer Vororte, es war im November, es war windig, es regnete,* and the way a German, writing for Germans, has expressed these facts. Attention could be drawn, for instance, to *rauschen* as a much more 'watery' sounding word than the neutral *fahren* and to the way statements about date and weather are made obliquely: *novemberliche Böen, Regenstreifen.* The final sentence could be translated into English and the class could discuss their renderings and also the appropriateness and effectiveness of the simile.

Second lesson

One pupil could be asked to give a brief summary in German of the facts contained in the first eight lines and the teacher might then read aloud the next paragraph.

Wer ist Meinert Nobis?	*Ein Junge.*
Weiß ein Deutscher das, wenn er erst anfängt, das Buch zu lesen?	*Nein.*
Was weiß er?	*Nur daß er männlich ist.*
Wie?	*Aus dem Namen.*
Und?	*Aus dem Wort 'er'.*
Wo saß er?	*Im Bus.*
Hinten oder vorne?	*Ich weiß nicht.*
Doch. Er saß UNMITTELBAR hinter dem Fahrer – unmittelbar, das heißt 'direkt'. Und wo sitzt der Fahrer in einem Bus?	
Hinten?	*Nein, vorne.*
Ja, also wo saß Meinert?	*Vorne.*

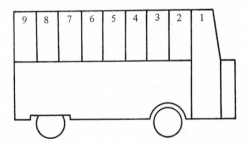

1. *Der Fahrer.**
2. *Meinert.**
3. *Das Mädchen.**
4. *Ein Soldat.*
5. *Die umfangreiche Dame mit einem Regenschirm.**
6. *Niemand.*
7. *Ein Blinder.*
7. *Der Baß.**
9. *Eine Krankenschwester.*

(An asterisk marks a character who actually appears in the book.)

Sketch useful for establishing: *die vordere Scheibe* (and *Scheibenwischer*), *vorne / hinten, die vordere Tür, rechts / links* and for practice of *vor* / *hinter* with nouns – people who get on or off the bus (*der Baß, das Mädchen, die umfangreiche Frau mit dem Regenschirm*) together with one or two added by the teacher (*ein Soldat, eine Krankenschwester, ein Blinder*).

Wie war das Wetter?	*Es regnete.*
Ja, und was hielt die vordere	
Scheibe vom Regen frei?	*Der Scheibenwischer.*

At which point would reasonably occur an introduction to *Duden*: *Bildwörterbuch* and teacher and class would together look at section 186 *Kraftwagen II*.

Was sah Meinert Nobis auf den	
Straßen?	*Menschen.*
Viele?	*Nein wenige.*
Warum?	*Weil es regnete.*
Oder wegen . . .?	*Wegen des Regens, des*
	schlechten Wetters.

This part of the second lesson has been aiming at two things: establishing relative positions in the bus because this is important for the story and encouraging the class to look at the text with sufficient attention to pick up the clues (*unmittelbar*).

Sprach Meinert mit jemand?	*Nein, er überlegte.*
Was ist ein anderes Wort für	
'*überlegen*'?	(Silence)
Nachdenken, sich Gedanken	
machen. Also, er dachte nach.	
Was hatte er mit?	*Zwei Schallplatten.*
In einer Tasche?	*Nein.*
Nein, in Wellpappe gewickelt.	

Here a wavy line on the board would draw attention to *Wellen* and there will probably be a cardboard box lying about which can be used to illustrate *Pappe* and *Pappkarton*. *Wellblech* might also usefully be taught at this point and also some work done on *in Papier, Pappe, ein Taschentuch, Plastik usw gewickelt*. This might lead usefully to:

Wenn Sie etwas durch den Regen tragen müssen, dann wickeln	
Sie es in Plastik ein (*as an*	
example). *Warum?*	(Silence)
Weil Plastik wasserditch ist.	

Ist Leder | Papier | ein Taschentuch |
Glas wasserdicht?

Asbest as *feuerfest* and a room as *schalldicht* might be usefully added.

Und ist Wellpappe wasserdicht?   *Nein.*

Und es regnete, und Meinert hatte
zwei neue Schallplatten in
Wellpappe, er saß in einem Bus,
er würde bald aussteigen müssen.
Wo?   *An einer Haltestelle.*

Ja, und dann zu Fuß wohin gehen?   *Nach Hause.*

Was war also sein Problem?   *Wie die Platten trocken nach*
                                          Hause bringen.

In other words, through a series of simple steps, the language environment of Meinert's thought has been covered – an essential early step
in an approach to reading literature in a foreign language.

Wieviele Platten hatte Meinert?   *Zwei.*

Zwei Tanzplatten?   *Nein, nur eine war eine*
                                          Tanzplatte.

War sie für Meinert selbst?   *Nein, für seine Mutter.*

Und die andere – Tanzmusik oder
klassische Musik?   *Klassische Musik.*

Von Mozart?   *Nein, von Bach.*

Auch für Meinerts Mutter?   *Nein, für sich selbst.*

Was für Musik scheint Meinert
gern zu hören?   *Klassische.*

Was wissen wir also von Meinerts
und Frau Nobis
Musikgeschmack?   *Sie haben nicht denselben. Er*
                                         hört klassische Musik gern,
                                         und sie Tanzmusik.

Fassen Sie kurz zusammen, was
Sie jetzt von Meinert wissen!   *Männlich; wohnt in Bremen;*
                                         hat eine Mutter, die
                                         Tanzmusik gern hört – hat
                                         selbst klassische Musik gern.

Wissen wir, wie alt er ist, wie er
aussieht?   *Nein, noch nicht.*

Ja, also passen Sie auf!

Was trug Meinert, so weit wir
wissen?   *Einen Anorak.*

Was ist ein Anorak?   *Ein Mantel.*

Wasserdicht?   *Gewöhnlich ja.*

Ein Regenmantel also?	*Nein. Kürzer.*

Teacher or one of class produces an anorak – to establish its characteristics: *Reißverschluß, Länge, wasserdicht, Futter.* Above all, *eine Kapuze, die man abtrennen kann | eine abtrennbare Kapuze.* Someone in the class might well have the kind of raincoat that has an '*abtrennbares Futter*'.

Warum wollte er die Platten in seine Kapuze hineinschieben?	*Weil sie wasserdicht war.*
Ja, um sie vor dem Regen zu schützen.	

Was trägt ein Mensch, um sich vor dem Regen zu schützen? is an obvious next question. This would lead to revision or introduction of objects like *Sicherheitsgurt, Asbestanzug, Handschuhe, Gummistiefel, Kittel, Schürze, Sonnenbrille* and other protective garments and then, in the definition of such garments, to a lot of practice of *schützen vor.* The last question might refer to the hood of an anorak, its normal use and Meinert's decision about it?

*Was scheint Meinert wichtiger zu sein,
seine Haare oder die Schallplatten?*

This involves the class in expression of opinion and personal likes:

Was hätten Sie getan?	The pupil possibly needs here the expression *es kommt darauf an.* If he/she does not know it, this seems to be the moment to teach it.
Worauf kommt es an?	Again, they will know what they want to say, but at this stage of the sixth form they will need further helpful suggestions from the teacher: *ob Sie gerade vom Frisör kommen*; *ob Sie gerade ins Kino gehen, und zwar mit Ihrem Freund	Ihrer Freundin.*

The teacher is helping the pupil towards expressing personal opinion. In other words, talk is not strictly restricted to the absolutely relevant and to the reformulation of content or of accepted literary views. After which, talk returns to the anorak:

Wie alt war der Anorak?	*Eine Woche.*
Warum hatte Meinert vor einer Woche einen neuen Anorak bekommen?	*Weil er Geburtstag hatte.*
Welchen?	*Seinen achtzehnten.*

*Was wissen wir jetzt Neues von
    Meinert?*   *Daß er achtzehn Jahre alt ist.*
*Ja, mit anderen Worten, ein
    bißchen älter als Sie.*

At this point reference could be made again in English to the narrative style of the author – the way he conveys information indirectly, and a note could be made of the various aspects of Meinert which we have been able to pick up from just the few lines read: age, dress, likes in music. A short, simple written exercise might be done to check what has been learnt:

1. *Was wissen wir von Bremen?*
2. *Was wissen wir von Meinert Nobis?*
3. *Wie heißt auf Englisch: rauschen, wasserdicht, feuerfest, wegen der novemberlichen Böen, unmittelbar, schräg?*

Homework

1. Pupil most interested in music to prepare a sheet for rest of class on basic music terms: *Duden, Bildwörterbuch, 299–300.*

2. Another to look at *Duden 301–3, 306* and draw class's attention to names of musical instruments which are different in German from English.

3. Another to look up J. C. Bach and J. S. Bach in *Brockhaus* and prepare a two-minute talk on them – who they were, relationship, what they did, where they lived, etc.

4. Another to do the same with Mozart (who appears later in the book, or, at least, his music does!)

If there are more than four in the class, they could be asked to do the work in small groups. It is, of course, assumed that schools do not expect pupils to do sixth form work in German without making sure that a small selection of the necessary reference books and dictionaries are available in the library. The intention of this homework is:

– to introduce the idea of using such monolingual German reference books, of researching and then sharing information;

– to give help as the pupils point out what difficulties arise in interpreting the data in such books – it is surprising, for example, which abbreviations the teacher takes for granted but which are like riddles to the pupil;

– to introduce the lexis of music – essential if reading is to be 'fluent' later in the book.

Third lesson

1. Class together looks at *Duden*, 299–303, 306.

2. German assistant (if available) gives a two-minute summary of *Brockhaus* information on, say, Beethoven. Pupils 3 and 4 (above) give their summaries. Teacher and assistant correct, ask questions, make suggestions, draw attention to words like *Klavierkonzert, Symphonie, Satz*.

3. Study the labels on one or two German recordings to find terms like *Tenor, Solist, Orchester, Chor, Kapelle, Dirigent*.

4. Listen to a snippet of Bach (borrowed if necessary from music department – J. C. Bach if possible) and teacher and assistant discuss the music and their reaction to it. This allows the new sixth-former to hear some of the ways a German talks about music.

All the above seems an essential preparation if the class is to cope easily with the rest of the book.

5. Translate into English the last five lines of the page – discussing various English equivalents, discussing the footnote on *ziehende Süße* and initiating comment on the image of itching toes.

6. Teacher answers any other questions which the pupils might have about the language on this page of text.

What is gained by embarking on a study of a book in this way?

– The work is still recognizable in terms of that which was done before the sixth form. There are pupils who opt to do German on the basis of their past experience and then discover too late that 'sixth form German' is an entirely different beast, made up largely of literary studies.

– Language work is being done at the same time as an introduction to literary aspects. Patterns like *schützen vor* are practised and translation work is put into a known context. If prose translation is required, it might be best at this stage to concentrate on re-translation of pieces of the book – using German which has been met in use rather than contrived or guessed at on the basis of dictionaries or grammars.

– The teacher, who knows the whole book, is able to guide the pupils towards those aspects which provide vital grounding for studying more freely the rest of the book – style, content and lexis.

– Oral work is not suddenly highly sophisticated discussion but is based on a steady progression from facts towards views and opinions.

– Culture (German geography and music, for example) have their part to play without needing to be identified with a separate and formal area called *Deutschlandkunde* or *Landeskunde*.

Finally may I stress that I have taken the first three lessons at this pace and only covered one page because I see this as essential preparation for the book as a whole. I am *not* suggesting that the whole book should be treated in this way. The teacher will make his own selection, and whole sections of the book will be read privately by the pupils with the teacher only interested in checking that the reading has been done and in giving help when clarification is asked for. I am not advocating that poetry, or even all prose, should be submitted to this kind of linguistic treatment, but I feel that the language of a book like *Was dir nicht angehört* is worth close study and that the content is accessible to sixth-formers' views and their own reflection. The foreign language and the mother-tongue both seem to have a part to play in this process. I am also suggesting that first literary judgements and evaluations should stem from the text itself, and that 'background' and the 'introduction' to the book could wait till later when the book itself has been experienced.

MARGARET MARY VARLEY

Lutterworth Grammar School, Leicestershire

Class work on a French text

There is a wealth of material for use in the sixth form (course-books, collections of passages for translation, articles taken from magazines and newspapers) and in each category there is something which really 'works' with a class. Perhaps the richest source is the daily newspaper because of the variety of style and content which it has to offer – news items, political and social problems, reviews, theatre, sport, fashion – and the immediacy of the current newspaper is an important factor for most of these topics.

In choosing a text for intensive study, great care is needed – to ensure that it is authentic French written for French readers, and also appropriate in language and content to the ability and interests of the learners. A too difficult passage undermines confidence. My heart bleeds for those pupils whose initial contact with authentic French is their first lesson in the lower sixth when they are presented with a set-book, Balzac perhaps or *La Peste*. What a daunting experience that must be! At sixth form level (and indeed at all levels) we are forever seeking ways of interesting our pupils, widening their awareness, enriching their vocabulary, stimulating talk, assisting their writing, increasing their knowledge of grammar and syntax, and attuning their ears to the sound of French.

It is rarely possible to find texts which afford opportunity for all this. One text may be particularly rich in examples of a certain syntactical point, such as the position of the subject after the verb in a relative clause beginning with *que*, whilst another text may be specially valuable for its ideas, its vocabulary, its humour. Whatever the virtue of the passage chosen, it must give opportunity for practising the basic language skills. It should not be so long that it drags on and stifles interest, but it should be long enough to allow some satisfying work to be completed in one teaching period (however much time is devoted to it subsequently), so that the class has a sense of achievement at the end of the lesson.

396

If the passage is appropriate to the group, even the least adventur-
ous and able will be capable of contributing or answering a question,
and with wise guidance and the co-operation of the French *assistant*
a good article will lead to further discussion of related themes. These
can in turn be supported by other suitable articles, where the likelihood of meeting some of the vocabulary first met in the original
article is great, thus contributing to the growth of the pupils' confidence. Again we must ensure that these further readings are not too
difficult either in lexical content or ideas.

The text suggested here is of manageable length, for it can be heard,
read and appreciated at a certain level in a single teaching period.
However, more than one period will have to be devoted to it if its
many possibilities are to be fully exploited. The less confident
members of the group will be able to answer straightforward questions on geography and thereby gain in confidence, whilst the more
able may be stimulated to discuss holidays in general and package
tours in particular. One might go on to study French ways of treating
questions like the *désaoûtisation* of holidays, the death-toll on the
roads, traffic congestion and pollution of the environment, and
colonies de vacances, about which articles appear regularly each
year and which also represent a particularly French holiday form.
The whole question of leisure in an industrialized society might be
broached, and in the hands of a willing and adequately briefed
French *assistant* could lead to consideration of job satisfaction, strikes,
boredom, and even such issues as the nature of an acquisitive society.
Whatever discussions occur, they can be supported by suitable
articles, and subsequent essay work along the lines of the discussions
is possible.

*J'ai vu Pochet à son dernier retour de croisière, il paraissait harassé.
Les temporaux saillants, la glotte instable, la paupière sautillante, il
offrait tous les signes de l'épuisement nerveux. On aurait pu penser qu'il
revenait d'une guerre.*

– Je reviens, me dit-il, de croisière . . .

*Il revenait, en vérité, de loin. C'était une croisière organisée de
Marseille à Marseille, 78 550 francs pourboires compris et qui, pour
ce prix forfaitaire, lui avait permis, en vingt jours, de tout faire – la
Sicile et la Grèce, Istanbul et le Caire.*

– Content? lui demandai-je.

– Inoubliable, me dit-il, mais un peu fatigant. Les escales . . . vous

comprenez . . . On n'a guère le temps de souffler . . . Bateau-car, car-bateau . . . On pourrait se reposer, parfois, mais on se laisse toujours tenter: vous êtes à Athènes . . . On vous parle de Delphes . . . C'est trop bête d'être là et de ne pas faire Delphes!

Alors il a fait Delphes. Il a fait Rhodes. Il a fait Chypre. Visiblement, il en avait trop fait. Était-ce le Parthénon? Ou bien les Propylées? Il y avait quelque chose qui n'avait pas passé. Quelque fût de colonne, sans doute, ou quelque stylobate, qui lui restait sur l'estomac.

Je suivrais volontiers Sonia dans ses idées de croisière, si c'était une petite croisière à moi.

Mais il y a deux choses qui me déplaisent dans les croisières organi-sées. D'abord, c'est qu'elles le soient. Il me suffit de lire dans le pro-gramme: 'Jeudi 27: matinée libre; 15 heures: déjeuner froid sur l'Acropole, suivi d'une conférence explicative par le professeur Regimbault', pour sentir mes orteils se recroqueviller dans leurs plus casanières pantoufles. S'il y a des 'matinées libres', c'est que, le reste du temps, on ne l'est pas vraiment. Avec les paniers-repas on vous remet sans doute, dans un petit paquet, la liste des émotions à éprouver, et la façon: 'Ici, monsieur, frémissez!'

Si j'ai peu de goût pour le tourisme organisé, c'est sans doute parce que j'ai été élevé dans un monde où, si l'on voulait aller à Rome, il fallait tout de même s'occuper du voyage. Comme le monde a changé! A notre époque – le prospectus que j'ai sous les yeux en fait foi – on vous recommande de ne vous occuper de rien. On est en train de créer le tourisme super-confort, avec direction assistée, faux frais assurés, relations avec la métropole garanties par transistor et remboursement prévu par la Sécurité sociale pour cheville foulée en escaladant l'Acropole. Le hasard, ce hasard qui faisait encore le charme des voyages de ma jeunesse, on ne lui laisse que de maigres 'matinées libres'.*

*Bauer, C., Barton, M. D. and O'Connor, P. (1964) *Lire, parler et écrire*, p. 234. New York: Holt, Rinehart & Winston.

Before the article is distributed to the class, it is read once by the *assistant* or the teacher, who then puts a number of questions designed to check minimum comprehension:

> *De quoi s'agit-il dans cet article?*
> *Quel genre de vacances?*
> *Expliquez ce que c'est qu'une croisière.*
> *Quelles villes a-t-il visitées?*
> *Dans quel état en est-il revenu?*
> *Pourquoi est-il si fatigué?*

Then, with copies of the article in front of them, individual pupils are asked to read a few lines. After each reading, systematic questioning in French is undertaken to ensure complete comprehension and oral participation, opportunity being given for every member of the group, whatever his ability, to answer something correctly. These might be some of the questions or requests:

> *De quel port est-il parti?*
> *Sur quelle côte se trouve ce port?*
> *Nommez d'autres ports français.*
> *Combien a-t-il payé?*
> *Combien de jours est-ce que la croisière a duré?*
> *Définition d'un pourboire.*
> *Quelle est la capitale de la Grèce?*
> *Où se trouve Le Caire?* (Opportunity exists here for practising Le Mans, Le Bourget and Le Havre preceded by *à* or *de*.)
> *Comment appelle-t-on le dieu dont le temple se trouve à Delphes?*
> *Donnez-moi un synonyme de 'souffler'.*
> *Quel est le contraire de 'se reposer'?*
> *Quand se repose-t-on?*
> *Donnez-moi le contraire d'une 'semaine reposante'.*
> *D'autres mots de la famille 'tenter'.*
> *Comment appelle-t-on celui qui assiste à une conférence?*
> *Et celle qui y assiste?*
> *Quel est le masculin de l'adjectif 'explicative'?*
> *Exprimez autrement la phrase 'il y a deux choses qui me déplaisent'.*
> *Quand porte-t-on des pantoufles?*
> *Quels autres articles porte-t-on aux pieds?*

Most of this sort of questioning will be revision, making active a vocabulary which for most pupils may still have been passive; and synonyms, opposites and alternatives will elucidate meaning where necessary.

Some words will not be known by anyone in the group, and these will be explained in French (e.g. *escale*), or by pointing (e.g. *cheville, temporaux*) or by translation into English (e.g. *faux frais, se recroqueviller, casanière, éprouver*). The architectural terms are best explained with the support of a sketch on the blackboard of a row of pillars: one points to the *fût*, adding that *cette partie-là entre la base et le chapiteau* (pointing to each part) *s'appelle le fût*; and a simple statement that *un stylobate est la base d'une rangée de colonnes,* made while pointing to the appropriate part of the sketch, will resolve that problem. Here is the opportunity for a brief, simple digression into the province of architecture, showing pictures of Doric, Ionic and Corinthian pillars, and examples of classical buildings in Provence – there is no reason why any sixth form work in any subject should be conceived as rigidly subject bound. The geographical content of the passage is considerable and the name *Istanbul* could even lead to a brief historical digression taking in *Constantinople* and *Byzance* on the way.

In the early stages of the sixth form course some pupils will probably not know about the complementary use of *le* to represent the adjective in the two sentences: *D'abord, c'est qu'elles le soient; on ne l'est pas vraiment.* This is the moment to explain it and to make a mental note to point out further examples when they occur in subsequent study. It will also be necessary to check the group's ability to account for the use of the subjunctive in the text, an area of verb usage with which they are probably not very familiar.

Revision exercises can profitably be compiled on two other points: the construction common to many verbs in *la croisière lui avait permis de tout faire,* and the tenses in 'if' clauses, beginning with *je suivrais Sonia dans ses idées de croisière, si c'était une petite croisière à moi.* In the first case pupils can supply some of the other verbs which require this construction, and in the second it may be a good moment to revise the usual sequence of tenses with 'if' clauses in the present, imperfect and pluperfect. Completion exercises, sometimes supplying the main clause, sometimes the subordinate, are appropriate.

The final two sentences are especially suitable for use as a quick dictation, for they force our attention on *assistée, assurée, garanties, prévu* and *foulée,* all of them past participles used adjectivally, and they remind us of the gender of words ending in *-ion, -ille* and *-ment*.

All the humour in the passage is not immediately apparent, and sentences like *il revenait, en vérité, de loin* need explanation. It is unlikely that the class will know that this means he was regaining consciousness. They might enjoy this kind of humour and this is the moment to suggest to them that they might like to look out for other works by Daninos in the library and to try out some of them for themselves.

FRANK WILLCOCKS

Bedfords Park School, Romford

Language work in the sixth form

Modern linguists in the sixth form fall into three main groups,
according to the Schools Council Working Paper 28[1]: those who
study a modern language to A level and beyond, those who follow
non A-level courses, and those who begin a language course in the
sixth form. This chapter will be based on my experience with the
first of these groups, though much of what I say is relevant to them
all. My illustrations will be from the study of French, but will no
doubt be largely applicable to other modern languages.

In considering the approach to language work in the sixth form,
I must first remember that my pupils may have opted for French for
many different reasons, varying from those who hope ultimately to
read a degree in modern languages to those who take the subject as a
necessary, or perhaps compulsory, adjunct to some other chosen
discipline. It would be idle to pretend that there can be anything so
absolute as an ideal syllabus for such diverse needs. But if we think of
language learning as a gradual and continuing process, of which the
sixth form is merely one stage, then we can attempt to arrive at a
modus operandi appropriate to the command of language so far
achieved and the stage of maturity reached by the pupils.

I must recognize that most of my pupils will cease to be specialist
linguists after the A-level examinations, that, indeed, for many of
them, the grade achieved, or even 'success' or 'failure' will be of only
marginal significance – or perhaps none at all. There may even be
some pupils who will never use the language again as a means of
communication. Can the work that we do be relevant for all these
pupils? I think it can, but we must first reject the idea that there is a
corpus of language which must be mastered, at all costs and in all its
most subtle nuances, by all pupils. We must not pay too high a price
for rigorous insistence on grammatical accuracy and for the acquisition of certain esoteric linguistic skills which may be largely irrelevant for a majority of students. There will be some for whom

ultimate mastery of all the structures of the language is essential; there will be others – usually more in my experience – for whom a too rigorously analytical approach will actually inhibit progress.

Some students will have a bent for what some linguists have called '*langue*', others will have a greater aptitude for '*parole*'. We must try to cater for all, taking the needs of our pupils as the starting-point. 'What is learned may be smaller in quantity and greater in relevance' (p. 36).[2]

I believe, moreover, that while language work must take the lion's share of sixth-form studies, it must be much more than the perfecting of a communication skill. It should be an experience, an adventure, a sowing of seeds which will bear fruit in places and at times often unsuspected alike by pupil and teacher. When I consider how the ramifications of a study of French which began some thirty-five years ago have enriched my life, I must strive to open the way to similar experiences for my pupils, without forgetting that such enrichment can be experienced via routes less academic than my own, but none the less valid for that.

It follows that the content of our work must be as diverse as possible and that the approach must be eclectic. Content will inevitably reflect some of my own predilections, but I must try to be as catholic as I can. And in my approach, while it may be appropriate on occasions to doff my cap here to the behaviourists, there to the mentalists, or to the structuralists or to the bilingualists or a score of other theorists, I must remember, as one writer on linguistics has it, that 'language teaching still depends very heavily on the intuitive interpretations that the teacher constantly has to make'[2] (p. 229).

Content, approach – context. It is a truism that the latter must be as meaningful as possible. Ideally every student should spend time in France, and one hears of more and more valuable initiatives in this direction, but it is important that they should be balanced against the needs of the students' other sixth form studies. However, it cannot be emphasized too much that education authorities have a responsibility to create conditions in which students can have first-hand experience of the country of their target language – and, in particular, to ensure that those who come from less privileged and less articulate backgrounds are not handicapped by financial and environmental considerations.

But for most of the two years of the average sixth-form course the teacher will have to provide the best possible substitutes for foreign travel. It is hardly necessary to dwell upon the more obvious aspects of this task – rendered quantitatively easier but selectively more difficult by the plethora of audio-visual material now available. It is true that such aids can be as valuable a stimulus in the sixth form as elsewhere – and the simplest and cheapest are often the best. A post-card which I brought back from my summer holiday in France, showing a car which had been 'surprised' by the tide on the causeway linking the mainland with the island of Noirmoutier, riveted the attention and provided conversational material for a whole lesson. It would have been too small a visual aid for a large class, but with a group of five, we were able to sit around my table in an agreeably relaxed atmosphere.

One of the best weapons in the teacher's armoury is a plentiful supply of reference books about France. Publishers are understand-ably keen to sell **sets** of books on a wide variety of topics. This can prove very expensive and often one copy, judiciously used by the teacher, will suffice. Particularly valuable are those books which contain statistical and other information in tabular or diagrammatic form. Extracts can be put on the blackboard and form the basis of much interesting language work, either structure based or of a more general character. These are visual aids which provide both an 'anchor' and a stimulus for the student.

What I have said earlier about content and context suggests that the approach will often be 'situational' in the early stages of a sixth-form course. Many students will already have a basic command of the language required for the most obvious situations, but that command will need to be consolidated and broadened to cope with more sophisticated requirements. This work is similar in character to that done for O level and need not be spelt out in detail. But one hopes that ultimately one's students' linguistic experience will go well beyond buying a ticket at a railway station or ordering a meal in a restaurant. One hopes that they will be able to sustain an inter-esting conversation with a native French speaker – and for this they will need awareness of France as well as some linguistic skill. I recorded recently with my Upper Sixth a conversation lesson de-signed to help meet such objectives. I should like now to examine that lesson in some detail. The original text is taken from an invalu-able publication called *Comment vivent les Français*.[3]

I quote here that part of the text which served as a basis for the lesson in question:

Mademoiselle F. a 76 ans. Elle a fait de nombreux métiers sans être jamais salariée. Elle a travaillé toute sa vie chez elle comme couturière, brodeuse ou repasseuse. Sa cousine G., qui a été chanteuse au Grand Théâtre de Lyon, puis professeur de chant, a 68 ans. Elles vivent toutes les deux ensemble dans un vieil appartement trois pièces qu'elles paient 70 francs par mois. Elles se chauffent en hiver avec un poêle à charbon et ont fait installer un chauffe-eau à gaz dans le cabinet de toilette.

Les allocations de Mademoiselle F. sont de 360F par mois, et celles de Mademoiselle G. de 300F. C'est Mademoiselle G. qui fait les courses, et c'est Mademoiselle F. qui fait la cuisine. Une cuisine peu compliquée. A midi un peu de viande ou de poisson, beaucoup de légumes et un fruit. Le soir, une soupe et un morceau de fromage ou du café au lait et une tartine de confiture.

Souvent un neveu ou une petite-nièce montent les voir et leur laissent un bébé à garder pour la journée. Des voisines leur demandent quelquefois de venir garder leurs enfants le soir; c'est pour elles l'occasion de regarder la télévision. Elles n'ont chez elles que la radio qu'elles écoutent d'ailleurs à longueur de journée. Elles se couchent 'comme les poules' entre 8 et 9 heures du soir, selon la saison, sauf les quelques soirs où elles doivent terminer un tricot.

In an earlier lesson I read to the class a longer extract, including the part quoted above. After two readings of the text, one rather slow and accompanied by a minimum of '*explication*', the other much quicker, the pupils were asked to write their own version in French and to try to fill in by personal research any gaps in their understanding of what they had heard. (They had been allowed to take notes in French during the readings.) I corrected their work carefully and discussed grammatical problems and common errors arising from it. The subject was then dropped for some weeks and on the eve of the recording the pupils were invited to revise their corrected copies and be ready to discuss the subject in French.

My first question elicited some information about *un emploi salarié*, which I supplemented with some facts about the widespread practice in France of monthly payment. I suppressed a desire to talk about *le SMIG* on the grounds, I think, that this was too great a digression at such an early stage in the lesson. I resisted another – linguistic this time – on the lines of *mensuel > hebdomadaire > quotidien*, etc. Was this a sound linguistic intuition or not? We proceeded to some straightforward definitions of *couturière* and *brodeuse*. For the latter, *une femme qui brode les vêtements*, I prompted, *Oui, qui fait quoi?* and got back *qui fait de la broderie*. The definition of *repasseuse* led to the question *avec quoi . . . ?* and an opportunity – not taken until I insisted – for a pronoun substitution: *elle les repasse avec . . . .* My next question, *Qu'est-ce qu'il faut faire avant de les repasser?* evoked an immediate response, *il faut les laver et les sécher,* but *Pourquoi faut-il les sécher?* drew a blank until I gave a supplementary question *Comment sont-ils . . . ?* and got the delightfully spontaneous and unexpected answer, *Ils sont inconfortables,* which provoked laughter and reduced much of the tension caused by the fact that this was a recorded session. We did go on to *mouillé,* cleared up a confusion in which one pupil thought he heard *muet* and incidentally elicited a definition of this latter word.

What I have described so far took only a very short time, but I suggest that the potential gains are already considerable:

1. We have as the basis for our discussion a meaningful French context, in which it is possible for us to identify with some of the problems of old age in France and perhaps compare them with what one knows of similar problems at home. We have also a springboard for a future discussion about *les salaires* in general and *le SMIG* in particular (especially as we have no equivalent in Britain). We shall be able to make interesting comparisons with other 'case histories' already studied from the book referred to above.

2. We have had practice in the useful linguistic technique of defining words, several of which are new to the group.

3. We have had practice in pronoun substitution, which most pupils do not make as readily in a foreign as in their native language, and in the *il faut* construction.

4. We have had the sort of spontaneous answer which encourages the relaxed atmosphere so essential for this kind of work.

Let us now consider some of the more significant points in the rest of the lesson. (I shall not examine the avenues explored less successfully, but I do acknowledge that there were some – as in most lessons.)

1. A question about the flat required an expression of opinion – since the information was not in the text – and evoked in the answer the expression *se composer de . . .* – imperfectly remembered from a previous discussion, but not, at least, completely forgotten. The

opportunity was taken to reinforce its use and to revise the names of rooms in the house and the distinction between *salle* and *pièce*. (It is dangerous to assume the simplest knowledge, even in sixth-formers!) When I demurred at a definition of *cuisine* which began *la cuisine est une chambre . . .*, although the rest was good, another pupil offered immediately *on dirait . . .*, which I reinforced with *on dirait plutôt . . . .* I reminded myself that the boy who then offered *une salle de séjour est une pièce où l'on regarde la télévision, où l'on mange si on n'a pas 2 pièces* had only recently passed O level at the third attempt.

2. Mention of the *chauffe-eau à gaz* gave us the opportunity to draw the distinction between *installer* and *faire installer*, linked with some further pronoun substitution. When we arrived at *elles l'ont fait installer dans le cabinet de toilette*, the question *pourquoi pas dans la salle de bains?* produced first *parce qu'il n'y a pas de salle de bains* and then *parce qu'il n'y en a pas.*

3. Having established the facts of the *allocations* received by the old ladies, I took the opportunity to talk of the pupils' own earnings. Four out of five do Saturday jobs. We were able to make good use of *toucher* and *gagner* and to make comparisons – *mieux payé que*, etc. One girl offered *je touche le même que J.*, one boy *je touche à peu près £4*. It was much more than the rest – my spontaneous reaction was *c'est un aristo*! [sic], which was understood and provoked laughter. I wonder if it would have been understood out of context! G. does not have a Saturday job – we all know why – so her answer – *je ne touche rien* – was almost lost in laughter. To make sure the point is not lost, I asked someone else to explain – *elle ne touche rien.*

4. We corrected an inaccurate use of the *demander* construction and a misleading absence of liaison ($|\varepsilon l|$ for $|\varepsilon lz|$ in *elles écoutent*) without interrupting too much the flow of conversation. *Elles écoutent la radio à longueur de journée* provided the cue for another switch – this time to the pupils' own leisure activities and to use *passer le temps à. . . .* A question about Sunday brought out *faire la grasse matinée*. Three out of five did not know it, the fourth offered by way of explanation, *elle est paresseuse, elle reste au lit*. (A few moments before I had offered to G. the jocular explanation *vous êtes une paresseuse* for her not earning on Saturdays.)

5. The lesson ended on musical instruments. G. is a serious student of the violin. Hence *elle passe le samedi à jouer du violon*. With the aid of some mime, we moved on to *jouer de la trompette, du piano, de la guitare* – not without some confusion in genders!

It is not often that I take time to analyse a lesson so closely or to hear it again on tape. Having done both those things, the following additional comments seem relevant and pertinent.

1. The text is not a difficult one. Obviously a second-year sixth form group should be able to understand a much more sophisticated passage. But it has been chosen as a vehicle for conversation and aided composition – the concepts and the syntax must be of a kind that can be handled with confidence. The passage has other virtues, too. I have already suggested that it is a meaningful French context. It also lends itself, as I have shown, to extension into the pupil's own lives, and it contains much useful vocabulary – mostly of a 'domestic' kind, arguably one of the most frequently needed.

2. I am struck again by the importance of establishing something which approximates to a natural conversation. Confidence and relaxation are clearly vital elements in improving one's command of a foreign language.

3. The text and the conversation which ensued will, as I have suggested, provide us with material for other lessons – if we can find the time! Since there is no absolute end product to language learning, the selection of material will always be somewhat arbitrary, but it should meet the basic criteria of increasing our linguistic and cultural awareness. We have already come across, in another 'case history', *la salle d'eau*, *le lavabo* and *la baignoire-sabot*. There, surely, is material for an interesting discussion about French sanitary arrangements – one which might well be conducted in English, as the general tone may be one of gentle irony – a difficult art to practise in a foreign language!

4. Leaving aside the more obvious ploys (e.g. the graded series of questions, or the incomplete sentence with an interrogative intonation before pausing for the student to supply the missing word or phrase) which teacher techniques seem to be the most profitable in a lesson of this kind?

(a) Frequent requests for definitions give valuable opportunities for creative language within a relatively limited framework (*une personne qui . . ., une pièce où l'on . . ., il sert à . . .*). This is particularly appreciated by the less gifted linguist. They also provide new vocabulary for some and revision for others.

(b) I tended to repeat those questions for which I was not too confident of an immediate response and to repeat the answer when it was satisfactory and likely not to have been produced by some of the other pupils. In this way the essence of a construction was often said three or four times by me, and the same number of times by the combined efforts of the pupils without, I think, any tedium. The risk of monotony can be much reduced by vocal variety from the teacher, by the addition to statements of appendages like *n'est-ce pas?*, which helps to challenge the attention of the pupils, and by frequent switches from first person to third person answers. I tried also not to provide answers until I was satisfied that no amount of prompting would elicit an answer from the pupils. But too many silences will spoil the atmosphere. The interpolation of mock-surprise exclamations like, *personne ne sait!* are often helpful in these circumstances.

(c) Not letting pupils 'off the hook' seems to me as important in the sixth form as in the lower school, although it is a temptation in a very relaxed atmosphere not to be too insistent. Within reason, one must be satisfied that ultimately all the pupils can answer all the questions put to them. I don't think chorus work is appropriate in this atmosphere, but repetition of correct answers – perhaps in a slightly modified form – can be obtained with the interpolation of such questions as *c'est vrai?* and *qu'a-t-il dit?* – the shorter the better – they help the flow of conversation.

(d) Adding *pensez-vous?, à votre avis?*, etc., to a question often gives the opportunity for a creative reply, as the information required may be only implicit in the text.

(e) The Giscardian stance, *Oui, mais . . .* is a useful teacher response to an answer which contains a partially accurate linguistic element or which does not tell you all you want to know. In fact, gentle prompting and encouragement is very much *de rigueur*. The horror that one may feel at some dreadful solecism – *ahurissant* is my favourite epithet in this context! – must be suppressed. I have found it useful – and therapeutic for me! – to substitute for such feelings a rather histrionic mock horror which, I hope, makes its impact without destroying the pupils' confidence. Some errors can be safely ignored in the interests of the flow of conversation – but not ignored too often.

(f) My final impression of this lesson is that we have been largely unaware of differences in linguistic achievement and aptitude – although they are considerable. Each has been able to contribute according to his own standards. Each has had, I believe, a fulfilling and enjoyable experience and each has progressed in linguistic command and confidence.

This lesson did not, of course, exhaust the teaching techniques relevant to this sphere. For example, on this occasion I asked all the questions, but it is equally important that the pupils should be able to ask questions as well as answer them. Sometimes, therefore, we take a similar text, and, having established an understanding of it, the pupils are encouraged to ask each other a wide range of questions about it.

Nor can an account of one lesson convey the breadth of material or the diversity of approach needed in a sixth-form language course. We must now examine, in more summary form, some of our other activities. In calling to mind those lessons that I remember with most satisfaction and affection – the best criteria? – I find that most of them have in common an element of spontaneity, of immediacy and of relevance. Not surprisingly these are also the lessons in which the pupils feel the greatest sense of involvement. For example, the starting-point of one conversation lesson was two facts known to us all: (a) that G. is a student of the violin and (b) that J. had passed his driving test the day before. Building around these facts, we concentrated on a limited number of expressions: *être reçu, échouer, apprendre(à)*, the use of *depuis* and the sequence of tenses with *si*. We proceeded gradually to such offerings as:

Si j'avais été reçu la première fois, je n'aurais pas dû repasser l'examen.

Si j'avais appris plus jeune à conduire, j'aurais pu participer aux 24 heures du Mans.

G. apprend à jouer du violon depuis de longues années.

Quand J. a été reçu à son permis de conduire, il apprenait depuis 3 mois.

As we built sentences, we copied them down for future reference. It was a less spontaneous lesson than the one previously described, but it was more concentrated in its linguistic aims and still had the important elements of immediacy and involvement.

The approach, I have suggested, should be eclectic. Let me take, then, a very different example. A set of words and expressions, culled almost at random from the *Dictionnaire du français contemporain*[4] was the *point de départ*. (I find dictionaries endlessly fascinating and I hope I have passed on to my pupils what an enjoyable exercise in self-help is the odd half-hour with one.) On the left-hand side of the blackboard a set of incomplete sentences, on the right-hand side the dictionary pickings in the wrong order. The two columns must be 'married' and the dictionary expressions adapted as the context requires. There will be mistakes, of course, hilarious ones sometimes, but we arrive at the right answers in the end, via a process which has been relaxing and enjoyable and which has, I hope, increased the pupils' awareness and love of language for its own sake.

Recently I heard the Head of Languages of a famous school say that all the members of his department work seventy hours a week. I think that was the figure. Certainly it was much too long! I resent very greatly spending too much of my leisure on the preparation which is held to be so essential for successful language teaching. I need my leisure, so that I can be a person first and a teacher second. That is one reason why I am addicted to French radio for source material, because I can listen to programmes like '*Inter-actualités*' while I am shaving or eating or washing dishes, and what I hear will often form the basis of a lesson the next day. Thus, recently, a programme about *la Ceinture de Sécurité* provided us with much valuable information and linked up neatly with J.'s new status as a driver.

The admirable Jacques Chancel's programme '*Radioscopie*' is also a rich source of material. Alas, I have all too few opportunities to listen to it, but I recall one programme in which his subject – whose name I don't remember – had lost his sight and his hands during the war. It was a moving witness of one man's struggles to overcome appalling hardships. I talked about it to my group – mostly in English, at first – but I took as my 'text' one sentence I remembered vividly: '*les infirmes ça se recrute chez les valides*'. We did not neglect the considerable linguistic interest of that one sentence (*contraire d'infirme? synonyme de valide?*, the colloquial use of *ça*, the implication of *chez* in this context), but on this occasion we concentrated on the wider implication of the statement. I confessed also to being much impressed by the subject's assertion that the loss of his hands was a greater handicap than the loss of his sight. At the end of that lesson I think we all had a greater awareness of the miracle of a pair of hands.

Records and tape-recordings of many kinds have great potential value in the sixth form – and the best are not necessarily those which have been specially prepared for the classroom. Recently we spent several lessons with a long-playing record by Jacques Brel and, in particular, the songs '*Les Timides*' and '*Les Vieux*', the one a little gem of alliteration and assonance, the other a moving poem of *le troisième âge*, already tackled in a different context and with a very different approach. We began with an hilarious session of trying to write down some of the many nouns and verbs which made up the *jeu de mots* of the first song. We compiled a formidable list which included such verbal delights as *se tortiller, sautiller, se recroqueviller* and *se mettre en vrille*. We paused to explain the references to *St Lazare* and *Elvire* (shades of Lamartine!), we reminded ourselves of the verbs of colour and we commented upon the different tone of one verse in which *Les Timides* have a brief access of *audace* – a reminder of the importance and subtlety of vocal variations in the act of speech. Later, of course, we tried to incorporate some of this into our permanent linguistic armoury.

Those who teach in or near London would be foolish to neglect its great potential for stimulating the learning of languages (to say nothing of the advantages of getting out of the classroom sometimes). Thus, recently, we had a 'French day' in London – a visit to the Cézanne exhibition at the Hayward Gallery in the morning (a first time on the South Bank for some of them) and a French film *La Nuit américaine* in the afternoon. We have had several follow-up lessons and not yet exhausted the linguistic and cultural interest of our day out. We looked, for example, at reproductions of some of Cézanne's oil paintings (the exhibition was confined to pencil drawings and water-colours), I gave a résumé in French of some aspects of his works and we noted some of the basic 'technical' vocabulary. As to the Truffaut film, we linked some of its more technical aspects with a topic we had discussed earlier, *Les métiers de la télévision*, the latter illustrated by some visual ORTF publicity material I had obtained at the *Salon de l'Enfance* when I was in Paris during the half-term holiday. I introduced the group to *La Nouvelle Vague* in the French cinema and the concept of *un film d'auteur*. Mention of Truffaut's film *Les 400 coups* led us to look at certain aspects of French education – with the aid of some statistics published by *L'Institut Français d'Opinion Publique*. We are already planning another 'French day', when our theme will be *à la recherche de la France et des Français à Londres*.

Obviously much of the language work we do can be linked to the books and topics we study. We follow the AEB A-level syllabus, we choose mostly modern texts – including such authors as Anouilh, Camus, Sartre, Chamson, Pagnol and soon, I hope, the fascinating *Les Saints vont en enfer* by Cesbron – and we deal with such topics as 'France as a European power', 'France under the Occupation' and the 'working-class movement in France in the twentieth century' Most of this work is conducted in English, but there are frequent opportunities to kill two birds with one stone. Last year, for example, my *assistante* took a series of lessons in French on *La Résistance* and I did some follow-up lessons in English to ensure that the material was thoroughly absorbed and understood.

And what of the role of the *assistant?* He can be a great asset, but his timetable must be flexible, especially at the beginning of the year, for much depends upon his personality, the more so since he usually has no experience of methodology. One needs time to get to know the *assistant* and find out how best he can contribute. I try to give each sixth form student two lessons a week with the *assistant*, normally in a group of two or three. Sometimes the *assistant* joins my lessons and we lead a discussion – perhaps taking opposite points of view. Sometimes the *assistant* gives a talk – into which I make some interpolation when I think something has not been understood or when the pace is getting too hot. Sometimes I round off such a talk with an extempore résumé in French to try to reinforce the main points made and perhaps to highlight some of the constructions and expressions used. Last year my *assistante* was an accomplished musician, from whom we all learnt something about the instruments of the orchestra. On one occasion she gave us a memorable account of a New Year's Eve Party at the home of a distinguished Belgian musician. All the guests had to make a musical contribution to a marathon, which began on the afternoon of 31 December and went on until the early hours of New Year's Day.

I have made little reference so far to what might be called the traditional language work of the sixth form – in particular the trinity of prose composition, free composition and translation. The first is to me a fascinating exercise and, no doubt, an intellectual discipline for which the highest claims can very properly be made. But when I reflect upon my own inadequacy in this most exacting work, I am bound to conclude that for most of my pupils it is a depressing and futile undertaking, for their limited linguistic experience does not equip them to approach the task with confidence – a fact which is all too often confirmed in the dismal end-product. I have no quarrel with those whose pupils are intellectually equipped to do this kind of work, but most of my students are not. But as long as prose composition forms part of the A-level syllabus, my approach is to confine ourselves to passages which are – if not re-translation exercises – at least very closely based on French models we have read or subjects we have discussed. The same criteria, I think, should apply to free composition work. There is, as far as I am aware, no evidence to suggest that regular practice in unseen prose texts or in unseen essay titles produces any better results than the method I have outlined above. Translation from French is open to some of the same objections as the other exercises, but here, I think, the balance is in favour of such work. The need to translate usually leads to a deeper understanding than the act of reading a text. It is, like prose composition, an absorbing exercise in comparative linguistics, but here the pupil usually handles his own language with more confidence. I think of 'version' as a very civilized activity, capable at best of increasing enormously one's sensitivity to language. Can one speak of method in this context? I think not, but the teacher who has read widely in both languages, without, however, living too vicariously on the printed word, is almost certainly the one who will have the most to offer his pupils in this area. A more recent exercise is the English prose summary of a long French extract. Of this I have only very limited experience, but I welcome it as an opportunity to practise an additional skill, for the ability to grasp the essentials of a narrative is one that has wide implications.

I have said nothing of language laboratories because I have no substantial experience of them; I have said little of textbooks for a different reason. In my view a 'course-book' is not essential at any stage in language learning and certainly not in the sixth form, but it can be turned to advantage when used selectively and not followed slavishly. We dip into the excellent *Actualités françaises*,[5] but the best of books date rapidly and they all lack the spontaneity that an alert teacher can bring to his work. He is the person best qualified to select material for his pupils, and he will often find better subject-matter in one copy of *France Soir* than in several chapters of a course-book. Textbooks for a specific task like translation from French are, of course, invaluable – provided the choice of passages is sound and catholic – for then they are a valuable time-saver for the teacher.

I cannot claim that this has been an exhaustive or even a representative account of language work in the sixth form, but I hope it has provided some useful talking points. The frequent parenthetical 'I think' is proof enough that after more than twenty years of teaching my approach remains essentially tentative and empirical.

I should like in conclusion to make three pleas.

1. We should try to avoid being too earnestly parochial in our approach. In common with our colleagues in other disciplines, we should work, through our chosen medium, to extend the empires of the mind and the heart and the imagination.

2. Although much of what I have written has been necessarily concerned with how to teach, we should avoid being too pre-occupied with method, especially that which is too firmly wedded to a particular theory of language learning. Most linguists accept that the role of linguistic science can only be advisory. Teaching a language creates human situations in which there are so many variables that it seems unlikely that science will ever provide us with anything like ideal solutions. Intuitions, impressions, judgements, even whims – based on experience – will very properly continue to play a major part. Christophersen[6] warns against an obsession with theory rather than practice: 'It is as if the proof of the pudding were no longer in the eating, nor in the recipe or the skill of the cook, but in the underlying nutritional or gustatory theory.'

3. We must avoid being over-ambitious. If we set our sights unrealistically high, we shall suffer proportionate disappointments and frustrations. One linguist[7] has calculated that, at best, the classroom environment is fifty times less effective than the natural environment. Another [2] (p. 133) reminds us that the structure of a language is so complex that 'it can be acquired only through wide exposure . . .'.

If we add to this the problems created by the varying ambitions and aptitudes of our pupils, the necessity for realistic aims is apparent. Wilkins [2] (p. 184) draws a distinction between 'integrative' learners – for whom 'the language and all it brings by way of culture is an end in itself' – and 'instrumental' learners – those who require a language 'as a means to some other end'. If we can be realistic and flexible, eclectic and imaginative, we may hope to help and stimulate the 'integrative' learners and even convert some of the 'instrumental' learners.

References

1. SCHOOLS COUNCIL (1970) *New Patterns of Sixth Form Modern Language Studies*, p. 1. Working Paper 28. London: Evans/Methuen Educational.
2. WILKINS, D. A. (1972) *Linguistics in Language Teaching*. London: Edward Arnold.

3. GIROD, G.-C. (1968) *Comment vivent les Français*, pp. 91–2. Hachette.
4. *Dictionnaire du français contemporain*. Larousse.
5. NOTT, D. O. and TRICKEY, J. (1970) *Actualités françaises*. London: English Universities Press.
6. CHRISTOPHERSEN, P. (1973) *Second-language Learning*, p. 20. Penguin Modern Linguistic Texts. Harmondsworth, Middx: Penguin.
7. DODSON, C. J. (1967) *Language Teaching and the Bilingual Method*, p. 50. London: Pitman.

H. M. PORT

Sydenham High School

Reading a French book

Any arts graduate will naturally begin his teaching of a foreign literature by making certain assumptions – that no word of English should be spoken, that every sixth-former studying a French set text can be counted on to prepare in advance and enthusiastically a certain scene in a play or chapter of a novel, and that everyone will, on entrance to the sixth form, even if they are not taking English Literature in an Advanced-level examination, have acquired some elements of literary appreciation of English writers and understand the meaning of literary terms. However, gradually one realizes, as I did, that this rigidity of approach needs to be modified and that flexibility is essential. I find that I have to vary my methods according to the text chosen and to the ability of the class – and A-level classes at present contain a very wide spread of ability.

The choice of a set text to suit the ability and progress of a group during its two-year A-level course is naturally very important; for example, a Racine play would be more usefully studied towards the end of the course. Such authors as Anouilh, Pagnol and Maupassant may be successfully studied in the first year. I think, too, that the choice of edition is important; one needs to find one which does not contain too many ready-made opinions in the editorial notes. Weak pupils will, when writing essays, tend to copy them without thought. I look for an edition with clear biographical notes, a synopsis of the other works of the author and also notes on the most important textual difficulties, for example, in the case of Marcel Pagnol, some Provençal words.

One's personal relation with the class is also very important. A humility in one's own approach to the text enables one to appreciate pupils' difficulties of comprehension, and helps to establish the relaxed atmosphere in which a ready response can be elicited and discussion of literary points profitably pursued.

What, then, in more detail are my aims in reading a French book

417

in the sixth form, and what do I hope that the student will 'get out of it'? I will take as an example *Le Château de ma mère*, by Pagnol, which we have on several occasions studied in the second half of the Lower Sixth year. Having regard to the wide span of ability, I hope that everyone, apart from the linguistic benefit and the mere enlargement of vocabulary – a very limited aim – will be able to extend his or her imaginative experience through an understanding of what Pagnol is describing, and take an interest in the people in the story, and in life in Provence during the early years of this century. I hope that some students will see the book as an historical document, as a reflection of the social world in which Pagnol lived. I would like to think that the more perceptive and sensitive student will be able to appreciate the intrinsic charm and subtlety of the author, and to assess his contribution to French literature in conjunction with the other authors studied during the course.

How, then, does one attempt to fulfil these aims, and how does one introduce the book? I have found it profitable, before beginning the detailed study, to attempt to place the set text in the general context of the author's work; in the case of Pagnol we have read *La Gloire de mon père*, the volume which precedes *Le Château de ma mère* in the trilogy *Souvenirs d'enfance*. Allocation of time can sometimes be a difficulty here. Ideally it would be a help if the pupils had been encouraged to read this for themselves during the previous holiday. (One cannot stress too much the importance of independent reading during the sixth form course; in fact, one would hope that private reading has been encouraged from the middle school upwards, and particularly in the fifth year.)

In two or three introductory lessons on the text, I would discuss the social and historical background of the author and give some biographical data. In the case of Pagnol, I would ask the class to find pictures of the landscape of Provence and to describe it, as it plays such an important part in his life. It is useful here to point out to the class that, as we begin to study the book, which describes the childhood of the author, they should note points of difference from, and also similarity to, their own childhood. Relating a text to their own experience, and also to permanent human values, will often enable members of a class to take part freely in discussion – something which many find difficulty in doing, particularly at the beginning of a sixth form course. One might ask what other autobiographies of childhood they have read in their own language. This might provide a useful starting-point.

In planning the lessons for detailed study, I am assuming that I am allotted for a term two lessons a week and about two hours' home-work time. I tell the class what we shall need to cover each week and give them a certain number of pages to prepare before each lesson. I tell them that we shall certainly not be reading the whole text in class.

At the beginning of the next lesson, I ask them if they have any textual difficulties. One can often, at this point, discover if anyone has not done the preliminary reading by asking questions about meanings of words and phrases. Next I ask for an oral summary, in French, of what they have read. This also helps to ensure that individual preparation gets done. For some pupils who have not found oral fluency easy to achieve at Ordinary level, talking in French about a work of literature is difficult, but a start may be made by asking easy questions in the language, which require only factual answers. However, when, in the next part of the lesson, we begin to discuss, for example, analysis of characters, points of comparison, humour, I think it is more sensible to use English. I have found that trying to discuss analytical subjects in French, particularly in the first year of the course, is too difficult and off-putting for all except very able pupils. One wants as many of them as possible to contribute to discussion and to encourage them to have inquiring minds, and sometimes those who find it difficult to express themselves in French have more ideas to offer than those who are fluent in the language.

It is obviously not possible to comment in detail on every line in the text. In the second of the two weekly lessons, I would select one of the most interesting passages in the pages we have already dis-cussed and myself give a detailed commentary the first time. The choice of a suitable passage which best illustrates the main qualities of subject-matter and style we have already noted in the first of the two weekly lessons should help pupils to aim at precision and clarity in expressing themselves. Many pupils find this exercise difficult and they need to be shown how to tackle it, without giving a mere summary of the passage and its context. In the following weeks, and beginning with the more able, I ask each member of the class to give her commentary, and call upon the rest to discuss and criticize it with her. This is more profitably done in English in the first year of the course. In the case of a difficult, philosophical text, such as Camus' *L'Etranger*, or a Racine play, I might leave the detailed commentaries until we have finished studying the whole text.

While we are studying the text, I do not set analytical essay subjects. I ask the class to write, in English, simple character studies and to keep, in French, a summary of events, as we proceed with the text. When one first begins to set analytical subjects for essays, it is a help to the majority of the class to discuss orally beforehand the subject involved and the planning of the essay. Later on, of course, they must have practice in writing essays without help. Only at the end of the study of the text would I suggest works of criticism on the author and then only to the more able pupils.

I have to admit that I often do not achieve what I have set out to do. Sometimes, irrespective of ability, certain classes respond to different texts in different ways. The study of literature is a very personal one. I hope that, even if not at the time, but perhaps when they have left school, sixth form pupils will have gained some appreciation of the culture of the French people and will wish to read French for pleasure.

MICHAEL ROBINSON

Huish's Grammar School, Taunton

Reading a German book

The major problem to be faced in the early stages of reading German in the sixth form is that of linguistic difficulty. This makes the choice of books for study a difficult one. I have found that good starting-points for sixth form reading, which at this stage would include both literary and non-literary texts, are the final parts of a number of modern language courses. These often contain a good selection of short extracts from German newspapers, books and magazines, and allow the learner to read authentic German without the daunting prospect of a full-length book ahead. When he then does reach the stage at which it is felt that a book can be tackled, he already has some experience of the way in which a German author, writing for fellow Germans, expresses his ideas.

I think that one has to admit that, whatever text one chooses, there will be problems of vocabulary on a fairly large scale, even for pupils with good O-level passes, and, perhaps even more seriously, problems created by the characteristic structure of written German. Both difficulties can really only be solved by wider reading – a solution which clearly creates its own vicious circle. In the absence of this wider reading, one humdrum but effective way of dealing with problems of vocabulary and complicated structure is paraphrase. It is, of course, possible to get at the meaning of a word by defining it in German, and with nouns this is often a good approach, but this can be a deadening and monotonous process if it is in fact the teacher who is doing most of the defining. If pupils are asked to express a sentence or a phrase in a different way, then they are involved, and further use of the structure can be practised: *es war für Heinz ein nie zu vergessendes Erlebnis* in the text could lead to *es war ein Erlebnis, das Heinz nie vergessen würde.* Further examples of the first kind of sentence could be given to the pupils and they could re-phrase them on the model of the second sentence – practising relative clauses and also learning something about the differences between spoken and written German. Pupils soon become familiar with such techniques and lessons become increasingly more productive.

There will come a point, however, when one is defining in German or paraphrasing words or structures and the meaning refuses to become clear to the learner. There seems to be no point in prolonging definition and redefinition in such circumstances, especially if a reasonably accurate English equivalent is available. It must not be imagined, however, that a translation of a full sentence of German necessarily solves the whole problem of comprehension. It will do so in the case of a sentence like *mein Vater ist nicht hier,* but it certainly does not with '*wenn was dran wäre an diesen Entdeckungen, würden das doch die geistlichen Herren am ehesten wissen*' (Brecht, *Galileo*). Even the latter is a relatively simple example of a German sentence, yet the teacher will need to illustrate the use of *daran / dran* in other contexts, and even possibly *doch* and *am ehesten,* before the full flavour of the German sentence can be apprehended. If, then, a final check on comprehension is needed, a question like 'how could this be expressed in English?' is more revealing than 'translate this sentence'. It is probably only through painstaking and laborious confrontation with the German text, as in the earlier chapter on *Was dir nicht angehört,* rather than the easier activity of translation that the learner will make real progress in genuine reading.

Before leaving linguistic matters and moving on to literary and other work on books, I should like to mention a kind of language work based on the reading of full-length texts which can be done once some reading fluency has been established. If a book is to be studied as a whole and is to be read straight through, it will probably not be desirable to use it as material for intensive linguistic exploitation. There are, however, useful ways in which language work can be done in such a context. If one is reading Borchert's *Draußen vor der Tür,* it is useful, for example, to consider at the same time passages from Hildegard Knef's *Der geschenkte Gaul,* from Böll's *Das Brot der frühen Jahre* and from Albert Speer's *Erinnerungen.* (Examples which I have found to work in practice and which provide four strongly contrasted views of the war. All are 'literary' texts, but factual ones could also be used.) The length of passages chosen will vary according to the style of the book and the ability of the learners. Speer's style is not easy to cope with and 300 words from him are ample in this context. Substantially more could be taken from *Der geschenkte Gaul*, as the pace and tone of the book are more appealing to sixth-formers. A short passage from the Böll is sufficient to characterize his outlook (or, of course, a short story like *Damals in Odessa* could be used). The passages are then read at home by the pupils. They will find that there is a considerable community of vocabulary, even among such widely differing authors, and that, as they read through the four texts, their rate of comprehension begins to increase rapidly. Their own essay writing also benefits from seeing how different authors use different means to portray similar situations. To make the task rather more controlled, I have found it useful to ask for the preparation of groups of words and phrases, presented in context, which can then be used as a basis for discussion or the writing of an essay or a piece of narrative.

To give a more concrete example of these ideas, and also to suggest other linked texts away from the theme of war, let us look at work which could be done together with Brecht's *Galileo*. If one wants to focus on the side of the scientist's responsibility to the community, quite brief parallel texts could be taken from Dürrenmatt's *Die Physiker* and Kipphardt's *In der Sache J. Robert Oppenheimer*. Material can then be gathered under the headings of (a) the issues involved; (b) the personal views of these issues taken by the characters; (c) their views of the attitudes of the public and fellow scientists to these problems; (d) the solutions, if any, which are suggested. This material then provides an excellent basis for the classroom discussion in German of the scientist's place in society, and this could lead to the writing of an essay on the subject. Such collection of material from texts is not only seminal in terms of language work, but also provides a good basis for literary discussion, as it encourages pupils to look for the ideas in a text rather than just following the plot, and it also gives them a set of new perspectives on the book which they are studying. To be practical, it is worth pointing out that great expenditure on texts is not necessarily involved. With a small group, one copy of each text (except of course, the one being studied in full) is all that is needed, as pupils can swap them around among themselves. With a larger group, shorter texts could be duplicated, but this is less satisfactory than buying two or three copies of each book. They then serve the additional purpose of being available as library books. A further advantage of this procedure is that it not only broadens the range of the pupils' vocabulary and ideas, but also gives a foothold on books other than those read in class, and it is much easier to encourage wide reading in the language if one can point out that part of the book being recommended is known, was found interesting, and, possibly most important of all in the early stages, is known to be comprehensible linguistically.

Full-length texts being studied in the sixth form will probably fall into two categories: they will either be literary or will be of the kind now beginning to be set in newer A-level syllabuses, often having a geographical, historical or sociological bias. The latter, even when not 'set', can provide invaluable background to literary studies, and their more factual content can lend itself more easily to discussion – at the level of specific paragraphs or chapters or even on the whole book – in the foreign language than texts where the content is less 'tangible'. Books containing documentary data or reporting facts can easily be seen in terms of the kind of oral work discussed earlier in this book in the chapter by Norman Hill.

When a literary text is being studied, I feel that there is a strong case for discussion of literary aspects to be carried on in English. I have two main reasons for thinking this: one is that the pupils will not be in possession of the range of German necessary and the other is that they need their mother-tongue and its resources to help to grasp and formulate the essentially German qualities of a German book. This may sound too lofty to be of general relevance, but one example will serve to indicate what I mean. Walter Fendrich in Böll's *Das Brot der frühen Jahre*, in describing his late adolescence, manages to convey a sense of hunger and privation unknown to English adolescents in recent years. Fendrich's situation is peculiarly German and belongs to a particular period. Arriving at a critical view of how Böll manages to bring this situation to life again would be inhibited if all discussions were reduced to the level of a sixth-former's German.

Finally in the matter of literary discussion, I feel that it is important, as in everything else, that the group is fully involved in the talk that is going on and is arriving at conclusions by thinking through to them. The teacher is there to guide, not to provide predigested solutions. He will formulate questions which will lead the pupil to consider the issues for himself. It is more valuable to ask a question like 'Why does he react like this?' than to say 'What tells us that he is feeling rejected at this point?' The first kind of question can lead to the involvement and broadening of the imaginative sympathies which should be the result of literary study; the second, by providing the key to the situation and merely requiring a mechanical recognition of the point at which it occurs, is likely to lead to a much more superficial view of the text.

TERENCE BEST

Brentwood School

The short course in Italian: the imperative

My situation in the teaching of Italian is probably typical: it is offered as an optional subsidiary subject in the sixth form at the rate of three periods a week for two years. Usually between a half and two-thirds of the set take O level at the end of the course, while the rest do it for love.

This situation has both problems and advantages: the problems are lack of time and the awkward age of the pupils – 15 plus to 16 plus does not seem to be a good age at which to begin the study of a new language because, being sophisticated sixth-formers, they are often less willing to work at mastering basic grammatical forms than they were at 11 or 12; the advantage is that, having all done French to at least O level, and most of them having done Latin, they are on familiar ground with many of the structures of Italian, although this can lead to tiresome *francesismi*, which are sometimes difficult to eradicate: *Vado vedere gli amici* instead of *Vado a vedere gli amici*.

My approach is basically oral, but I find that at this age, with very or quite able pupils, a good deal of straight grammar is the quickest aid to learning the structures. My approach to the imperative is an example of what I mean.

The imperative has its own special problems, and the complexity of Italian forms of address means that the parallel with French, so valuable in other areas, is of little use. The systematic study of the imperative, as opposed to the acquisition of *mi mostri* and similar phrases in context at an early stage, is delayed until fairly late in the course; it comes immediately after the learning of the present subjunctive, which is a prerequisite. The basic indicative forms are, of course, already thoroughly learnt. Five stages can be identified:

1. A fundamental point is the distinction between the third person polite form and the other parts of the imperative (I ignore the third

426

plural, except in passing, as it is rare in modern Italian usage); the third singular is the most important form, and easy to learn once the present subjunctive is known, since it is identical with that tense at all times. Having established in the pupil's mind that the easiest way to arrive at the present subjunctive, should the habits inculcated by drills fail, is to start from the 1st person singular of the present indicative: *vengo→venga*, it seems sensible to drill the imperative in the following way: 'I shall ask you whether I ought to do something, and you are to give me a clear instruction to do it'. Thus *Vengo subito?* should elicit the reply *Sì, venga subito*, and *lo faccio per gli amici?* gives *sì, lo faccia per gli amici*, etc. By incorporating the object pronoun as in the second example, I make the important point about its position before the verb, a vital difference from the other imperative forms. For the negative the instruction could be: 'I am doing certain things which I should not – tell me not to'. Thus *lo mostro→non lo mostri,* etc. At this point it is worth while emphasizing the 'odd-man-out' position of the *-are* verbs, namely that the subjunctive, and therefore the third person imperative, ends in *-i* and not in *-a*. This is vital later on and, if not clearly taught, can be a source of great confusion.

The above material can then be further exercised by indicating to the learners the indirect commands of a man to his secretary and asking them to give the man's actual words:

Il Signor Carloni ha detto alla sua segretaria di scrivere una lettera. Quali sono state le sue parole?
    Scriva una lettera.
poi, le ha detto di telefonare a Londra.
    Telefoni a Londra.
poi, le ha detto di far aspettare un cliente.
    Lo faccia aspettare.
poi, le ha detto di essere cortese.
    Sia cortese.

2. We now move on to the *noi* form. Being identical with the present indicative, there are no conjugation problems, but it is necessary to practise the differences of intonation which alone indicate whether *mangiamo adesso* means 'we are eating', 'shall we eat?' or 'let us eat'.

3. Next comes the *voi* form, which I teach as being the plural of both *tu* and *Lei* – I know that this is an oversimplification and that

Italians themselves disagree about it, but I believe it is a reasonable generalization about current trends of usage. Being based on the indicative forms (except for *avere, essere* and *sapere*), there are again no problems, except to emphasize the postposition of the object pronoun – *mangiatelo* – as distinct from both the indicative (*lo mangiate*) and the *Lei* form of the imperative (*lo mangi*).

4. It is when we come to the *tu* form that we have difficulties: it is essential, given the short time available, to think analytically here and to make the learners distinguish between the *-are* verbs and the rest. Dealing with 'the rest' first, I practise extensively the basically simple fact that the imperative is, like the *voi* form, the same as the present indicative (*vendi la casa*), but remembering the different position of the object pronoun (*vendila, finiscilo*). Only when this is firmly established do I dare to attack the problem of the *-are* verbs, with their form in *-a* instead of *-i*, explaining a possible reason for it (avoiding confusion with the third person). And so we practise at length such things as *Maria canta? – Oh Maria, canta meglio!* Using people whose relationship is appropriate to the use of *tu*, one can also use a drill like the one about Signor Carloni above.

It is now safe to deal with the negative of the second person singular – *canta→non cantare, vendi→non vendere* – by inviting pupils to complete sentences thus:

> *Maria, mangia questo dolce, ma* . . . (reply: *non mangiare quello*).
> *Carlo, leggi questa lettera, ma* . . .   (reply: *non leggere quella*).

I delay until the end of this section, because there is so much to learn and practise, the few irregular second person singulars – *avere, essere, sapere, dare, fare, stare, andare, dire*. They are not difficult to acquire, though the compounding of *di, fa,* etc., with the object pronouns needs practice, both in speech and in writing: *dimmi, fallo*.

5. This is the consolidation stage. So far each topic has been presented separately, and the pupils have found it reasonably straightforward. There can be no doubt that the greatest difficulty in learning the Italian imperative is to arrive at a mastery of the confusing situation in the second and third persons singular:

	-are verbs	others
2	*canta*	*vendi*
3	*canti*	*venda*

Which person is the form which ends in *-a?* Three steps are taken:

(a) I now present a consolidation exercise: 'Repeat in the imperative as indicated the phrase *mangiare la mela.*'

 i. *per favore, Maria* . . . (it is established that Maria is everyone's girl-friend, and therefore familiar) reply: *mangi la mela.*
 ii. *per favore, signora* . . .   *mangia la mela.*
 iii. *per favore, signori* . . .   *mangiate la mela.*

Similarly with other conjugations and irregular verbs:

vendere il libro
 i. *per favore, Maria* . . .   *vendi il libro.*
 ii. *per favore, signora* . . .   *venda il libro.*
 iii. *per favore, signori* . . .   *vendete il libro.*
leggere la lettera
 i. *per favore, Maria* . . .   *leggi la lettera.*
 ii. *per favore, signora* . . .   *legga la lettera.*
 iii. *per favore, signori* . . .   *leggete la lettera.*

(Attention here to soft and hard *g*s)

What the pupils have to do here is to decide rapidly which rule applies to which conjugation and apply it instantaneously. I cannot see how one can make them **feel** at this stage that if you say *mangi*, you are being polite and formal, but if you say *vendi*, you are being familiar; this can only come with practice and experience, and I am convinced that grammatical analysis is called for at this stage with sixth-formers and with limited time available. It is surprising how good they can be at this exercise after only a little practice. The exercise is followed with a comprehension test in which I give examples with the conjugations mixed: *vendi la macchina, mangi questo pane, finisca la lezione*, etc., and my pupils have to tell me whether I am addressing Maria or the headmaster.

(b) Object pronouns are now introduced into the exercise. For *mangiare la mela* a double modification is required, e.g. *mangiala* (second person) or *la mangi* (third person). This exercise usually causes heavy casualties at first and it is a very good exercise for encouraging quick thinking. It drills one vital structural distinction between the second and third person forms, namely that the mere shift from a familiar form of address to the polite form effects a basic change in word order: *vendila→la venda*. Again the comprehension exercise is useful; a good variant is to give a phrase with a noun object and require a pronoun in response: given *vendi la casa*, they must recognize that it is second person before being able to respond correctly with *vendila*, while *venda la casa* requires *la venda*.

(c) When the object pronoun system has been learnt in its more complex patterns (*me lo dà, glielo diamo*), the time is ripe for the ultimate stage in the control of the imperative, namely its combination with the pronouns, as in *dimmelo, scrivetegliela, non parlarmene*, etc. Thus:

te lo dico?	*sì, dimmelo.*
diamo questa lettera al padre?	*sì, dategliela.*
ti parlo di queste cose?	*no, non parlarmene.*

The drills already given as examples are, of course, ideal material for language laboratory work; in the absence of a laboratory, I find that it is useful to record them on tape, with timed spaces for the responses (4 to 8 seconds according to difficulty), and play the tape to the class, making them reply in the limited time available. One could, of course, recite the drills oneself without the tape, but the mechanical nature of the timed gap prevents a too sympathetic letting up for the pupil who answers too slowly.

The foregoing is an account of a method used in a particular situation with a particular type of pupil. Like all teaching methods it has to be adapted to changing circumstances and to different classes: sometimes one has a gifted group, all heading for A1 grades in A- and S-level French and German, and these, of course, master the material without difficulty; but in the very nature of sixth form subsidiaries one has – and, indeed, hopes to have – generally a wide range of talent, with pupils doing a wide range of main subjects. I find that even those with little linguistic flair can learn a reasonable amount of Italian, provided that the drilling is intense, that the work is predominantly oral and that one takes every opportunity to make the lessons amusing and lively.

G. H. BARTON

Thomas Rotherham College, Rotherham

French as a non-examinable option

This chapter is written on the assumption that such courses are most likely to appear on the timetable as part of the General Studies provision, though it is hoped that some of the points might also have some value if examinations such as C E E become more widespread.

Certain factors need to be borne in mind in devising such a course.

1. The students will almost certainly range in ability from those whose knowledge of French is sketchy to those who could well have studied it to A level.

2. The course tends to lack status in the eyes of some students, since it is not one of their main A-level subjects and may well be time-tabled for only one period per week.

3. One has, however, the advantage of not being tied to a particular examination syllabus and of being free to experiment. If we consider the course from the point of view of examination requirements at all, the most likely aim will be to enable students to answer a compre-hension question on an A-level General Studies paper.

This gives a basis for the course, but one must think in terms of providing more than a succession of written comprehension exer-cises. One should also try to improve the students' understanding of the spoken language (not only ordinary everyday speech, but also language used to express facts in speech, e.g. the lecture or broadcast talk) and their ability to express themselves in the language.

Since the course will depend on so many factors – availability of staff, timetable problems, numbers of students and their levels of previous attainment, etc. – all that I can hope to do in a short chapter is to offer a few ideas and hope that they may be of some value.

As far as organizing the course and choosing materials is concerned, I would make the following points:

– one should try to ensure, as far as possible, that the students in a given group have very much the same level of previous attainment;

– materials should be suited to the abilities of the students. They should also be suited to their interests. The majority will want to read factual material rather than passages chosen for their aesthetic, literary or linguistic merit. What one might call 'popular scientific' and 'current event' topics, in the broadest sense, tend to be well received;

– variety is the essence of such a course, and the wider the range of experiences of French that one can present to the students the better. In any case, it is difficult to maintain their interest in one theme or topic if there is a gap of, say, a week between lessons. Therefore, it is important that, if possible, each piece of work should be short enough to be dealt with in one lesson.

Let us first turn our attention to the selection of material for straightforward comprehension work in the classroom.

Bearing in mind the criteria just mentioned, where does one find such material? The obvious move is to look for published collections of suitable passages. Harrap,[1] John Murray[2] and Pergamon Press[3] each publish books specifically designed for this type of work. They contain passages of a variety of types and questions to test comprehension.

If one wishes to produce one's own material, newspapers and magazines such as *Paris Match* are a fruitful source. The French is up to date and it is not difficult to find extracts that will interest the students. The passages should be chosen because they lend themselves to comprehension work by having plenty of factual content or an easily recognizable argument. A good translation passage is not necessarily a good comprehension passage. The fact that students would find a passage rather difficult to translate does not mean that they will be unable to answer questions on it. Laborious 'word for word' translation should be discouraged, since it will inhibit intelligent reading to get the gist of the passage, the latter being a much more desirable and relevant activity for these students.

The type of question to be put can often be a problem. I am convinced that the best way of testing whether a student has really understood a passage and of making him confident to read without necessarily translating every word is to put questions in English to be answered in English. If, however, the A-level General Studies paper (such as that of the JMB) which many of these students will eventually sit presents multiple-choice questions, then it is only fair to the students that they should be given practice in this type of question from time to time. Indeed, with a second-year sixth group such work may need to occupy a considerable proportion of the time available. The finding of suitable passages for multiple-choice questions and the setting of the questions can present many difficulties. There are books on the market published by Edward Arnold,[4] Harrap[5] and Heinemann[6] containing French multiple-choice questions that are intended for preparing students for examinations such as the JMB O-level alternative syllabus. I am afraid I know of no book of passages with English multiple-choice questions of the standard and type set by, for instance, the JMB in A-level General Studies.

On the point of oral or written answers, I generally favour written answers, since (a) all students are doing the same amount of work and (b) the fact that written answers are required engenders a more serious approach on the part of the students.

As for marking, I believe in checking answers orally with a group as soon as the exercise is finished. This allows immediate discussion of any difficulties and ensures the completion of the piece of work, leaving no loose ends to be tied up perhaps a week later, by which time the students will have forgotten why they wrote what they wrote.

Variety can be introduced into reading comprehension work by giving each member of the group a newspaper or magazine such as *Paris Match* or *Elle* and letting them see what they can make of it. They will often need a great deal of help but thoroughly enjoy it, simply because they are handling the real thing. At first they will tend to read only the advertisements and photograph captions, but what does this matter? If one feels that one must test what they have done, one can get them to write, in English, a précis of what they have read, perhaps asking them to read it to the group, or by simply circulating and asking them about it there and then. For such lessons it will be found useful to have a few copies of a dictionary such as Harrap's *Concise Dictionary* available in the room for reference.

There is no reason why one should not turn to French literature for material. In this respect Maupassant's short stories are an obvious choice. They appeal to students and many are short enough to be dealt with in one or two lessons. This may seem to contradict what I said previously about choosing material to last for one lesson, but with a little manipulation the story can be left at such a point as to ensure that the students are eager to continue the next time they meet.

Laborious translation should be avoided. The group can be asked to read a section to themselves and then be tested to see that they have the gist of the story. Another approach is to give the group a summary of certain parts of the story and then ask them to translate orally (and fairly freely) the more important and/or interesting sections: e.g. in *La Parure*, Mme Loisel's reaction to the invitation, the loss of the necklace, the cost of replacement and the dénouement. I have always found that groups enjoy stories read in this way and are ready to discuss them intelligently afterwards.

Turning from reading work in the classroom, good use can often be made of the M. Carré series of film-loops published by Macmillan. The difficulty of the questions can be varied to suit the ability of the group and with a small, able group one can even ask them to take it in turns to provide a commentary for twenty to thirty seconds.

What use can be made of the language laboratory in such courses? It is in the language laboratory that one can most easily achieve the other aims of the course, i.e. to improve the students' understanding of spoken French and their use of it. Normal exploded reading passages can be used, preferably with comprehension questions in French, to be answered in French, at the end, but rather more interesting exercises can be produced by slightly adapting commercial material.

Harrap publish *Valentine voyage: a French course for tourists*.[7] I have adapted it as follows:

1. Students hear original scene.
2. Students practise exploded version.
3. Questions of my own devising based on the scene, e.g. on *Leçon 4, A la banque*:

Answer in French

   (a) *Combien de francs Valentine veut-elle obtenir?*
   (b) *Que faut-il faire pour encaisser un chèque?*

Translate into French:

   (a) I have some English pounds to change.
   (b) What is the rate of exchange of the English pound?
   (c) Can I change a traveller's cheque?

Another commercial course which lends itself to adaptation and is particularly suitable for those students with little knowledge of

French is the Linguaphone course. In this course alternate chapters contain material on a subject and a conversation using that material. I use it as below, taking *Leçon 3, Notre maison* and *Leçon 4, Conversation* as examples:

1. Students hear *Leçon 3*.
2. Exploded version of *Leçon 3*. Students practise.
3. Students hear *Leçon 4*.
4. Exploded version of *Leçon 4*. Students practise.
5. This section is an exploded version of *Leçon 4*, but has all the responses omitted. The students, with their books shut, try to answer as many of the questions as possible. The pauses are made longer than on the original exploded version.

Aural comprehension exercises are also very useful. One method of presentation is to play the whole passage through, then play it again in sections. Each section is preceded by the questions that will be asked on it and followed by the questions with pauses for answers and, of course, the correct answers.

An exercise with which I have been experimenting recently and which has been well received is to require the students to take part in a conversation in French on tape. The system operates as follows: the students have in front of them a sheet with blanks where they will hear French on the tape and replies in English for them to make. These may be in the form of specific words to translate or a general instruction. I can best illustrate this by quoting the instructions the students hear at the beginning of a tape, part of a script and the instructions preceding the correct version they hear:

Instructions: 'In this exercise you are required to take part in a conversation in French. Half of the conversation is given on the tape. On the sheet in front of you are the replies for you to make. Where a time is given, this indicates the length of the pause that has been left.'

Extract from script. The sections within brackets (-) appear as blanks on the students' sheets.

Reporter. (*Pardon, monsieur, nous interviewons des touristes. Auriez-vous l'amabilité de nous dire quelques mots?*)
You. Certainly, what do you want to know?
Reporter. (*D'abord, qui êtes-vous et d'où venez-vous?*)
You. Tell him! 10 seconds.

Reporter. (*Merci. Voudriez-vous me dire quelques mots au sujet de Rotherham?*)

You. Tell him! 30 seconds.

Instructions before correct version: 'There now follows a correct version. The original French remarks that you heard will be repeated, followed by a suggested translation of the English remarks that you were given. Each translation will be followed by a pause for you to repeat it. Where you were given a time limit we have suggested one or two of the sort of things which could have been said. Repeat each of these in the pauses.'

This is, of course, quite difficult and was originally intended for use by first-year A-level groups, but there is no reason why an able group following a course such as we are discussing should not cope with it. For the less able groups there are always simpler situations such as buying a few things in a grocer's, ordering a meal, giving directions in the street. I would stress that these are still experimental as far as I am concerned and are obviously open to criticism and development. It has recently been suggested to me that *Vigeois* by G. J. P. Courtney[8] would be useful reading to accompany such work, but I must admit that I have not yet been able to try it.

Finally I would suggest the use of French pop and folk songs. Naturally one has to choose the singers carefully, but I would comment that most of the French singers I have heard seem to enunciate rather more clearly than their English counterparts. One singer who is particularly good from this point of view is Richard Anthony and in addition many of his songs are French versions of songs with which the students are probably already familiar in English, e.g. '*Ecoute dans le Vent*' – 'Blowing in the Wind'. Guy Béart's record of old French songs '*Vive la Rose*' always proves very popular, as do songs by Graeme Allwright. The amount of help needed by students will obviously vary considerably. Some will cope quite well, needing only to be helped with the meaning of a few words or phrases after a first hearing. With others it may be better to let them see the words, translate them as a group and then listen to the songs.

There are topics that I have not been able to touch upon, but what I have tried to do is to put forward a few ideas that might form the basis for a rewarding course. What to use and how to use it depends, as always, on the teacher's judgement. Only the teacher of a particular group knows what they are capable of and what will appeal to them.

References

1. OWEN, G. B. (1966) *General Exercises in French Comprehension from Contemporary Texts.* London: Harrap.
2. BARTON, G. H. (1967) *Recueil.* London: John Murray.
3. LIGHT, E. and HOWITT, J. B. (1966) *General Studies French: a guide for sixth forms.* Oxford: Pergamon.
4. SHAW, L. and WALL, J. Elton- (1972) *Réalités.* London: Edward Arnold.
5. MACKERETH, J. D. and DERHAM, L. M. (1969) *Choisissons bien!* London: Harrap.
6. MOUNTJOY, M. E. (1973) *Ecoutez d'abord.* London: Heinemann Educational.
7. GUENOT, J. (1964) *Valentine voyage: French for tourists.* London: Harrap.
8. COURTNEY, G. J. P. (1969) *Vigeois.* London: Longman.

Bibliography

The following bibliography is divided into a *General* section – including books likely to be of interest to all modern language teachers, a selection of periodicals and bibliographies – and *specialized* sections, relating to the numbered sections of the book in which they are referred to.

Teachers who require up-to-date bibliographical information should refer to the Centre for Information on Language Teaching and Research (CILT), 20 Carlton House Terrace, London SW1Y 5AP, which regularly publishes lists of teaching materials, specialized reading lists and periodical reports on particular aspects of language teaching. At the same address the Language Teaching Library (jointly maintained by CILT and the English-Teaching Information Centre) contains a comprehensive reference collection of books, periodicals and teaching materials, open to the public Mondays–Fridays.

1. General

ALLEN, J. P. B., and CORDER, S. P., *editors* (1973–4) *The Edinburgh course in applied linguistics* Vol. 1: Readings for applied linguistics; Vol. 3: Techniques in applied linguistics. Oxford University Press.

BELYAYEV, B. V. (1963) *The psychology of teaching foreign languages*. Pergamon.

BENNETT, W. A. (1968) *Aspects of language and language teaching*. Cambridge University Press.

BILLOWS, F. L. (1961) *The techniques of language teaching*. Longman.

BROOKS, N. (1964) *Language and language learning* (2nd edn). New York: Harcourt Brace.

BROWN, R. (1959) *Words and things*. Glencoe, Il.: Free Press.

BURSTALL, C. (1970) *French in the primary school: attitudes and achievement*. National Foundation for Educational Research in England and Wales.

CALVERT, F. I. (1965) *French by modern methods in primary and secondary schools*. Huddersfield: Schofield and Sims.

CENTRE FOR INFORMATION ON LANGUAGE TEACHING AND

RESEARCH (1972) *Teaching modern languages across the ability range.* CILT.

CENTRE FOR INFORMATION ON LANGUAGE TEACHING AND RESEARCH (1973) *Language and language teaching: current research in Britain 1971–72.* Longman.

CENTRE FOR INFORMATION ON LANGUAGE TEACHING AND RESEARCH (1973) *Modern languages and European studies.* CILT.

CENTRE FOR INFORMATION ON LANGUAGE TEACHING AND RESARCH (1974) *The space between . . . English and foreign languages in school.* CILT.

CHRISTOPHERSEN, P. (1973) *Second language learning: myth and reality.* Penguin.

COLE, L. R. (1969) *Teaching French to juniors* (2nd edn). University of London Press.

CRYSTAL, D. (1971) *Linguistics.* Penguin.

DAVIES, A., editor (1968) *Language testing symposium: a psycholinguistic approach.* Oxford University Press.

DODSON, C. J. (1967) *Language teaching and the bilingual method.* Pitman.

DUNKEL, H. B. (1948) *Second language learning.* Boston, USA: Ginn.

DUTTON, B., editor (1965) *A guide to modern language teaching methods.* Cassell.

FINOCCHIARO, M. (1964) *Teaching children foreign languages.* New York: McGraw-Hill.

HALLIDAY, M. A. K., MCINTOSH, A. and STREVENS, P. (1964) *The linguistic sciences and language teaching.* Longman.

HARDING, D. H. (1967) *The new pattern of language teaching.* Longman.

HODGSON, F. M. (1955) *Learning modern languages.* Routledge and Kegan Paul.

HUEBENER, T. (1967) *Audio visual techniques in teaching foreign languages* (rev. edn). University of London Press.

JAKOBOVITS, L. A. (1970) *Foreign language learning: a psycholinguistic analysis of the issues.* Rowley, Mass. USA: Newbury House.

JAMES, C. V., editor (1963) *On teaching Russian (a symposium).* Pergamon.

JAMES, C. V., and ROUVE, S. (1973) *Survey of curricula and performance in modern languages 1971–72.* Centre for Educational Technology, University of Sussex and Centre for Information on Language Teaching and Research.

JESPERSEN, O. (1956) *How to teach a foreign language.* Allen and Unwin. (First published 1904.)

LADO, R. (1964) *Language teaching: a scientific approach.* New York: McGraw-Hill.

LIBBISH, B., editor (1964) *Advances in the teaching of modern languages. Vol. 1.* Pergamon.

MACKEY, W. F. (1965) *Language teaching analysis.* Longman.

MATHIEU, G., editor (1966) *Advances in the teaching of modern languages. Vol. 2.* Pergamon.

OLDFIELD, R. C., and MARSHALL, J. C. editors (1968) *Language: selected readings.* Penguin.

PALMER, H. E. (1943) *The oral method of teaching languages.* Heffer. (First published 1921.)

PALMER, H. E. (1968) *The scientific study and teaching of languages.* Oxford University Press. (First published 1917.)

POLITZER, R. L. (1965) *Teaching French: an introduction to applied linguistics* (2nd edn). Blaisdell.

POLITZER, R. L. (1968) *Teaching German: a linguistic orientation.* Blaisdell.

RIVERS, W. M. (1964) *The psychologist and the foreign language teacher.* University of Chicago Press.

RIVERS, W. M. (1968) *Teaching foreign language skills.* University of Chicago Press.

RICHARDSON, G., editor (1967) *Aspects of education no. 6: a new look at modern language teaching.* University of Hull, Institute of Education.

ROWLANDS, D., editor (1972) *Group-work in modern languages.* University of York.

SCOTTISH EDUCATION DEPARTMENT (1970) *Modern languages and the less able pupil.* Edinburgh: HMSO.

STERN, H. H., editor (1969) *Languages and the young school child.* Oxford University Press.

VALDMAN, A., editor (1966) *Trends in language teaching.* New York: McGraw-Hill.

VALETTE, R. M. (1967) *Modern language testing: a handbook.* New York: Harcourt Brace and World.

WALLWORK, J. F. (1969) *Language and linguistics: an introduction to the study of language.* Heinemann.

WILKINS, D. A. (1972) *Linguistics in language teaching*. Edward Arnold.

WILKINS, D. A. (1974) *Second-language learning and teaching*. Edward Arnold.

Periodicals

Audio-visual language journal: journal of applied linguistics and language teaching technology. Audio-visual Language Association.

Foreign language annals. American Council on the Teaching of Foreign Languages, New York.

Le français dans le monde: revue de l'enseignement du français. Paris.

IRAL: International review of applied linguistics in language teaching. Julius Groos Verlag, Heidelberg, West Germany.

Journal of the Association of Teachers of Italian.

Journal of Russian studies. Association of Teachers of Russian.

Language teaching and linguistics: abstracts (formerly *Language-Teaching Abstracts*). Cambridge University Press.

Modern language journal. National Federation of Modern Language Teachers, St Louis, Mo.

Modern languages. Modern Language Association, London.

Modern languages in Scotland. Scottish Centre for Modern Languages, Aberdeen.

Treffpunkt: journal of the Association of Teachers of German.

Vida Hispanica: journal of the Association of Teachers of Spanish and Portuguese.

Bibliographies

CENTRE FOR INFORMATION ON LANGUAGE TEACHING AND RESEARCH: *Teaching materials* – comprehensive sectionalized lists of currently available language courses and materials for class use. *Selected reading lists* – annotated introductory bibliographies. *CILT Reports and Papers* – collections of papers and discussions of outstanding problems in language teaching and research with select bibliographies). (Details available in current publications list free on request from CILT.)

CENTRE FOR INFORMATION ON LANGUAGE TEACHING *and*

ENGLISH-TEACHING INFORMATION CENTRE (1972) *A language-teaching bibliography* (2nd edn). Cambridge University Press.

NOSTRAND, H. L., and others (1965) *Research on language teaching: an annotated international bibliography 1945–64* (2nd edn). Seattle: University of Washington Press.

ROBINSON, JANET O. (1969) *An annotated bibliography of modern language teaching: books and articles 1946–1967*. Oxford University Press.

2. Specialized

Section 2. Grammar

DUBOIS, J. (1967) *Grammaire structurale du français: le verbe*. Paris: Larousse.

GILBERT, M. (1961) 'Some problems of language teaching.' *Modern Languages* 42–2.

MARTINET, A. (1958) 'De l'économie des formes du verbe en français parlé' *in Studia philologica et litteraria in honorem L. Spitzer*. Bern: Francke.

SHANE, S. A. (1968) *French phonology and morphology*. Cambridge, Mass.: MIT Press.

STEVENSON, J. (1964) *Ich kann's: an illustrated German course*. Bell.

Section 4. Exploiting a text

CLARKE, J. (1969) 'Competence and performance: the missing links.' *Audio-visual Language Journal* 7–1.

COLE, L. R. (1969) 'The structured dialogue: an attempt to integrate structural and situational approaches to language teaching.' *IRAL* 7–2.

COOK, V. J. (1970) 'The creative use of language.' *Audio-visual Language Journal* 8–1.

HILL, N. (1968) *Faits Divers*. Harrap.

HORNSEY, A. W. (1972) 'Mr Best's ladder: question-and-answer work in foreign-language teaching.' *English Language Teaching* 24–2.

HORNSEY, A. W. (1973) 'A foreign language for all: the questions to be answered.' *Modern Languages in Scotland*. No. 1. 1973.

MAHLER, G. and SCHMITT, R. (1967–8) *Wir lernen deutsch*. Frankfurt: Diesterweg.

MCNAIR, J. M. 'Putting the question.' *Modern Languages* 54–1.

RUSSELL, C. V. and WILLIG, P. L. (1965) *German tests without translation*. Pergamon.

WILLIG, P. L. (1966) *Teacher's handbook to 'German tests without translation'*. Pergamon.

Section 6. *Visuals*

ALLENDORF, O. and WIESE, J. G. (1972) *Taschenbuch der overhead projektion*. Cologne: Interorga.

COLE, L. R. (1968) 'The psychology of language-learning and audio-visual techniques.' *Modern Languages* 49–4.

CORDER, S. P. (1966) *The visual element in language teaching*. Longman.

CREDIF (1961) *Recherche sur la compréhension du film fixe*. Paris: Ministère de l'éducation nationale.

GUBERINA, P. (1964) 'The audio-visual global and structural method' *in* Libbish *editor Advances in the teaching of modern languages vol. 1.* Pergamon.

GUENOT, J. (1964) *Pédagogie audio-visuelle des débuts de l'anglais*. Paris: SABRI.

GUENOT, J. and others (1962) 'Etudes sur l'évolution de l'aptitude des sujets à lire les vues fixes et introduction à une étude sur la lisibilité des vues fixes' *in Études de linguistique appliquée, No. 1.* Université de Besançon. Paris: Didier.

JERMAN, J. A. (1965) 'Audio-visual methods in modern language teaching' *in* Dutton B. *editor. Guide to modern language teaching methods.* Cassell.

KAMENEV, V. (1962) *Cours audio-visuelle de français* (*préliminaire*) *Première série. Livre du professeur.* Tavor Aids, EFVA.

MALANDAIN, C. (1962) 'Etude de la reconstitution d'un récit chez l'enfant à partir d'un film fixe.' *Enfance* 15, Paris.

MALANDAIN, C. (1966) *Utilisation des films fixes pour l'enseignement des langues vivantes aux enfants*. Paris: Didier.

MARROW, G. D. (1970) 'Teaching with *Voix et images de France*.' *Audio-visual Language Journal* 8–2.

MIALARET, G. (1961) 'Les aspects psychologiques: l'enfant et les aides audio-visuelles.' *Cahier de pédagogique moderne sur les techniques audio-visuelles au service de l'enseignement.* Paris.

MIALARET, G. and MALANDAIN, C. (1962) 'La perception du film fixe chez l'enfant.' *Etudes de linguistique appliquée*. No. 1. University of Besançon. Paris: Didier.

MIALARET, G. (1966) *The psychology of the use of audio-visual aids in primary school education*. Paris: UNESCO.

MILAN, W. (1972) *Arbeiten mit dem Tageslichtprojektor*. Munich: Bayerischer Schulbuch Verlag.

RICHARDSON, G. (1964) 'The use of visual aids in the teaching of modern languages' *in* Libbish *editor Advances in the teaching of modern languages* vol. 1. Pergamon.

RICHARDSON, G. (1957) 'Visual aids and language teaching.' *Modern Languages* 3.

RICHARDSON, G. and FLETCHER, W. (1968) *Histoires illustrées: free composition in French*. (First published 1951.) Edward Arnold.

SCHULZ, M. J. (1965) *The teacher and overhead projection*. Prentice Hall.

SLADE, D. (1970) 'Teaching with TAVOR.' *Audio-visual Language Journal* 8–2.

SUMNER, W. L. (1950) *Visual methods in education*. Oxford University Press.

TOPPING, A. (1968–9) *Les Duval, premier livre de français*. Books 1–3. Edward Arnold.

VERNON, M. D. (1962) *The psychology of perception*. Penguin.

VERNON, P. (1972) 'It's all a question . . . of pens and scrolls.' *Times Educational Supplement*. 1 September 1972 and 15 September 1972.

VINCENT, A. (1970) *The overhead projector*. National Committee for Audio-visual Aids in Education.

Section 7. Pronunciation

AGARD, F. and DI PIETRO, R. (1965) *The sounds of English and Italian*. University of Chicago Press.

ARMSTRONG, L. (1955) *The phonetics of French*. (First published 1932.) Bell.

AVANESOV, R. I. (1972) *Russkoi Literaturnoe proiznoshenie* (5th edn). Moscow: Proveschenie. (Available from Collets Bookshop.)

JONES, D. and WARD, D. (1969) *The phonetics of Russian*. Cambridge University Press.

KUHLMANN, W. (1955) *Deutsche Aussprache*. Freiburg: Bielefelds.

LEON, P. R. (1969) *Pronunciation du français standard: aide mémoire d'orthoépie à l'usage des étudiants étrangers* (rev. edn). Paris: Didier.

MALMBERG, B. (1969) *Phonétique française*. Malmö: Hermods.

MOULTON, W. G. (1962) *The sounds of English and German*. University of Chicago Press.

NAVARRO, T. T. (1967) *Manual du pronunciación española* (13th edn). Madrid: Cousejo Superior de Investigaciones Científicas. Instituto 'Miguel de Cervantes'.

REMAGNOLI, A. (1968) *Manuale di pronuncia dizione articolazione*. Milan: Mursia.

STOCKWELL, R. P. and BOWEN, J. D. (1965) *The sounds of English and Spanish*. University of Chicago Press.

WARDALE, W. L. (1955) *German pronunciation*. Edinburgh University Press.

WARMANT, L. (1968) *Dictionaire de la prononciation française* (3rd edn). Gembloux: Hatier-Ducolot.

Section 8. Reading

ALDERSON, C. (1967) *Magazines teenagers read*. Pergamon.

AUSTIN, M. C. and MORRISON, C. (1963) *The first R: the Harvard report on reading in elementary schools*. Collier-Macmillan.

BEATTIE, N. M. (1970) 'What constitutes a good reader?' *Modern Languages* 51–3.

BEATTIE, N. M. (1971) 'Reading as a preparation for sixth-form work.' *Audio-visual Language Journal* 8–3.

BEATTIE, N. M. (1973) 'Teaching dictionary use.' *Modern Languages* 54–4.

BEATTIE, N. M. (1973a) 'Reading aloud.' *Audio-visual Language Journal* 11–3.

BRITTON, J. (1971) *in Language, the learner and school: a research report by Douglas Barnes with a contribution by James Britton . . .* (rev. edn). Penguin.

CARSLEY, J. D. (1957) 'The interest of children aged 10–11 years in books.' *British Journal of Educational Psychology* 27.

CENTRE FOR INFORMATION ON LANGUAGE TEACHING AND RESEARCH (1974–) *Teaching materials* – current lists covering readers, etc. in French, Italian, German and Spanish.

CLARKE, J. (1968) 'French in the primary school.' *Audio-visual Language Journal* 6–2/3.

MODERN LANGUAGE ASSOCIATION (1970) 'Reading in a foreign language.' *Modern Languages* 51–2.

MORRIS, R. (1973) *Success and failure in learning to read* (2nd edn). Penguin.

NATIONAL ASSOCIATION FOR THE TEACHING OF ENGLISH. WARWICKSHIRE BRANCH (1968) *A survey of children's reading.*

NIDA, E. A. (1964) *Toward a science of translating.* Leiden: Brill.

NUFFIELD FOUNDATION (1967–70) *En avant* (stages 2, 3 & 4A). E. J. Arnold.

NUFFIELD FOUNDATION (1970) *A study of and concordance to five high frequency topics occurring in a selection of French magazines and newspapers* (mimeo).

PICKARD, P. M. (1961) *I could a tale unfold: violence, horror and sensationalism in stories for children.* Tavistock Publications.

SCHOOLS COUNCIL (1972–4) *A votre avis* (stages 5, 6, 7 & 8). E. J. Arnold.

THORNDIKE, E. L. (1917) 'Reading as reasoning: a study of mistakes in paragraph reading.' *Journal of Educational Psychology* 8. Washington.

THORNDIKE, E. L. (1934) 'Improving the ability to read.' *Teacher's College Record* 36. New York: Columbia University.

WALL, W. D. (1968) *Adolescents in school and society.* National Foundation for Educational Research in England and Wales.

WEST, M. (1955) *Learning to read a foreign language.* (First published 1926.) Longman.

WILLIAMS, A. R. (1951) 'The magazine reading of secondary school children.' *British Journal of Educational Psychology* 21.

WOOD, E. (1962) *Reading dynamics: notes on study reading, passing tests and 'hard reading'.* Reading Dynamics of New York.

Section 9. Writing

CAVE, G. N. (1972) 'From controlled to free composition.' *English Language Teaching* 24–3.

DODSON, C. J. and PRICE, J. E. (1966) 'The role of the printed word in foreign language teaching.' *Modern Languages* 47–2.

GELMAN, M. (1967) Dictation for testing and teaching. *Babel.* Melbourne 3–1.

GILBERT, M. (1972) *Cours illustré de français* (2nd edn). University of London Press.

RUSHWORTH, F. D. (1960). 'Free composition in the classroom.' *Modern Languages* 41–2.

TITONE, R. (1973) 'Some factors underlying second language learning.' *English Language Teaching* 27–2.

Section 10. Drills and exercises

BEILE, W. and A. (1971) 'Assessing specific language laboratory drills.' *Modern Languages* 52–2 and 3.

BREWER, R. A. (1966) *On translation.* Harvard University Press.

BUCKBY, M. (1970) 'Another look at drills.' *Audio-visual Language Journal* 8–3.

BUCKBY, M. (1967) 'Contextualization of language drills.' *Modern Languages* 48–4.

DAKIN, J. (1973) *The language laboratory and language learning.* Longman.

DELATTRE, P. (1971) *Les exercices structuraux pour quoi faire?* Paris: Hachette.

EDENER, W. (1972) 'The development of oral and written drills by free expression.' *Modern Languages* 53–1.

ETMEKJIAN, J. (1966) *Pattern drills in language teaching.* University of London Press.

HIGGINS, J. J. (1969) *A guide to language laboratory material writing.* Oslo: Universitetforlaget.

HILL, N. (1969) 'Exercices sur l'imparfait et le passé composé.' *Le français dans le monde* 66. Paris.

HILTON, J. B. (1966) *The language laboratory in school.* Methuen.

MALE, D. L. (1969) *Ça y est: twenty audio-lingual lessons.* Harrap.

MARTY, F. L. (1960) *Language laboratory learning.* Wellesley, Mass: Audio-visual Publications.

NEWMARK, L. and RIEBEL, D. A. (1968) 'Necessity and sufficiency in language learning.' *IRAL* 4–2.

OLLER, J. W. and OBRECHT, D. H. (1968) 'Pattern-drill and communicative activity: a psycholinguistic experiment.' *IRAL* 5–2.

REQUEDAT, F. (1966) *Les exercices structuraux.* Paris: Hachette.

ROSS, L. (1970) 'Improving the effectiveness of language laboratory work.' *Audio-visual Language Journal* 8–1.

SAGER, J. C. (1969) 'The language laboratory and contextual teach
ing methods.' *IRAL* 7–3.

SCARBOROUGH, D. R. (1968) 'The contextualized drill fallacy.'
Audio-visual Language Journal 6–2/3.

SCHNEIDER, B. (1968) 'Sprachlaborübungen für die gymnasiale
Oberstufe (Französisch)' *Praxis*. Dortmund.

SMITH, D. G. (1969) 'Contextualization: towards a more precise
definition.' *Audio-visual Language Journal* 7–3.

STACK, E. M. (1971) *The language laboratory and modern language
teaching* (3rd edn). Oxford University Press.

Section 11. Sixth form work

BAVER, C. and BARTON, M. and O'CONNOR, (1971) *Lire, parler et
ecrire* (rev edn.). New York: Holt, Rinehart and Winston.

DUNNING, R. and SUDRE, A. (1972) *La prise de la parole*. Heinemann.

GIROD, R. and GRAND-CLEMENT, F. (1969) *Comment vivent les
français*. Paris: Hachette.

GRAUBERG, W. (1968) 'The future pattern in sixth form modern
language teaching.' *Modern Languages* 49–1.

GRAUBERG, W. (1970) 'Set books in the sixth form course.' *Modern
Languages* 51–4.

HELLSTRÖM, S. G. and JOHANSSON, S. G. (1973) *Choisi pour vous*.
Heinemann.

HORNSEY, A. W. (1970) 'Set books and sixth-form studies.' *Modern
Languages* 51–4.

MODERN LANGUAGE ASSOCIATION (1968) *Modern language courses
in the sixth form*. MLA.

NOTT, D. O. and TRICKEY, J. E. (1971) *Actualités françaises*. English
Universities Press.

RUSSELL, C. V., *editor* (1971) *Post 'O' level studies in modern languages*. Pergamon.

SCHOOLS COUNCIL (1970) *New patterns in sixth form modern language studies*. Working paper no. 28. Evans/Methuen.

SWALLOW, T. (1971) 'Why drills?' *Audio-visual Language Journal*
9–2.

TURNER, J. D. (1965) *Introduction to the language laboratory*.
University of London Press.

Acknowledgements

Permission to reproduce the following is gratefully acknowledged to:
George G. Harrap and Co. Ltd. for the extract from *Faits Divers*
by Norman Hill on pp. 99 and 100; Cartes Tarides for the map on
pp. 104 and 105; Librairie Hachette for the extract from *Life in a
London Suburb* by Norman Hill on p. 146; *The Daily Express* for the
cartoon on p. 150; The Common Entrance Board for the illustration
on p. 203; Mark Boxer for the cartoon on p. 211, which appeared in
the *New Statesman* on 17th March 1972; Harper and Row (New
York) for the extract and illustration from *L'Art de la conversation*
by Yvonne Lenard and Ralph Lester on p. 212; *Credif* and Librairie
Marcel Didier for the illustration and extract from *Bonjour Line* on
p. 224; The Nuffield Foundation and E. J. Arnold and Sons for the
illustrations from *En Avant* stage 2, unit 6, on pp. 257 and 258, for
the illustrations from *Neron et Brigitte* stage 2, reader 2, on p. 259,
and for the illustration from *En Avant* stage 4A on p. 266; George
G. Harrap and Co. Ltd. for the extract from *Was dir nicht angehört*
by M. Hausmann on p. 384; Holt, Rinehart and Winston (New
York) for the illustration from *Lire, parler et écrire* by Bauer,
Barton and O'Connor, on p. 398.